KT-379-219

Essentials of Cooking

Published in 1999 by Artisan
A Division of Workman
Publishing Company, Inc.
708 Broadway
New York, New York 10003

Designed by Jim Wageman
Layouts produced by
Pamlyn Smith Design, Inc.,
and Lisa Sloane

Production: Ursula Schümer
Printing and Binding:
Neue Stalling, Oldenburg

Printed in Germany

ISBN 3-8290-6081-5
10 9 8 7 6 5 4 3 2 1

To my mother and my aunt Jane
for giving me my dreams

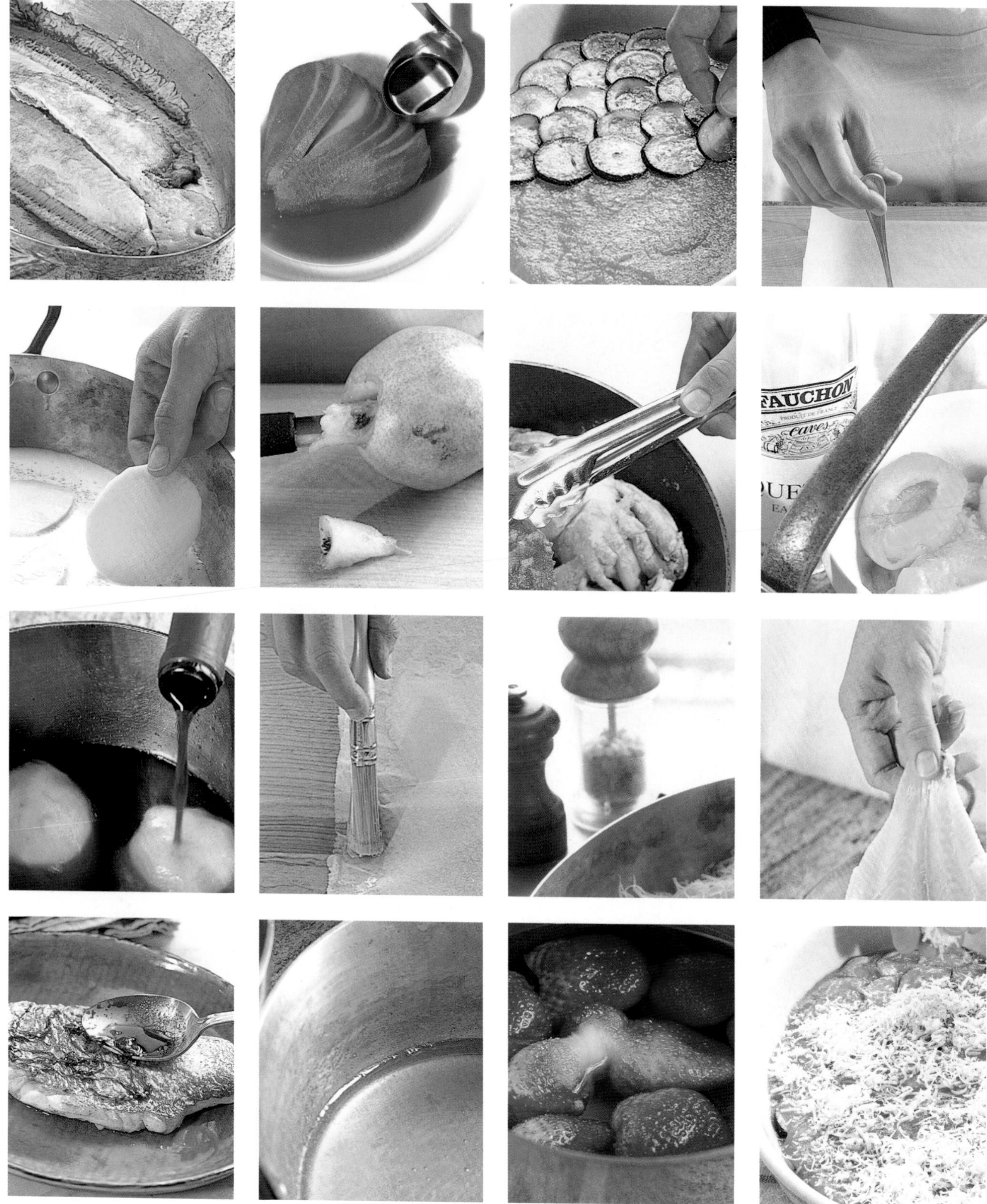
FAUCHON

Acknowledgments

So many people played such a vital role in the creation of this book that I must ask forgiveness from anybody I leave out here. I would first like to thank you, Ann Bramson, editor and the publisher of Artisan, who has now been with me for many years, for your work, not just on this book but on projects past, including *Vegetables* and *Fish & Shellfish,* and for your confidence in allowing me to undertake this (at times daunting) project. And thank you, Peter Workman, for your confidence and for signing the checks that made this possible. I must also express my appreciation to those people at Artisan who spent months poring over manuscript, galleys, and pages, doing their best to make this book sound and look its best. Thanks to Deborah Weiss Geline, Judith Sutton, and Dania Davey for your careful attention to detail and your, what to me seems magical, ability to imagine text and photographs in various combinations and to come out with something so beautiful. To Jim Wageman, thank you for your talents as a designer and for the restraint and good taste that seems to me now evident throughout the book. And to Vicki Semproni, Pam Smith, and Lisa Sloane, who produced the layouts. To Tricia Boczkowski, thanks for your patience with my endless phone calls, including that last-minute request for a table at the French Laundry.

And limitless gratitude to Stephanie Lyness. Without your extensive help with reorganization and hard work putting the manuscript into its final form, this book would not be as logical and approachable as it is.

Very special thanks must go to Debré De Mers, not only for your hands, which are in practically every photograph, and for your lips, which are in one, but for your friendship, enthusiasm, critical photographic eye, and for sharing with me all that food after we photographed it. And thank you for using your infallible good taste for selecting the props for the photographs. Thank you, Geraldine Cresci, for your help in styling the chapter opening photographs and for so many other things.

And I must always acknowledge my agents, Arnold and Elise Goodman, who stand behind me, rock-solid determined, and who, after so many years, I've grown to love and respect in ways that still take me by surprise.

Finally, thanks to the man with whom I share my life, Zelik Mintz, who sometimes seems to care more about the rewards and pitfalls of my life as a cookbook writer than even I do.

Contents

Introduction x

Basics 1

HOW TO:

Peel Vegetables 2
Shuck, Stem, Trim, and Seed Vegetables 7
Cut Up Vegetables and Herbs 10
Prepare Fruits 23
Take the Meat out of a Coconut 29
Make a Chicken Broth 30
Make a Fish Broth 32
Make a Crustacean Broth 34
Make a Green Salad 35
Make a Vinaigrette 37
Make Infused Oils 39
Make a Mayonnaise 41
Make a Hollandaise Sauce 44
Clarify Butter 46
Make a Flavored Butter 47
Make a Beurre Blanc 48
Make a Tomato Sauce 50
Make Fresh Egg Pasta Dough 51
Roll and Cut Fresh Pasta Dough 54
Make Stuffed Pasta Shapes 57
Make Gnocchi 60
Make Blini and Crêpes 61
Cook Risotto, Pilaf, Fluffy Rice, and Paella 63
Determine Doneness of Foods 66

Vegetables and Fruits 69

HOW TO:

Roast Vegetables 70
Make a Vegetable Gratin 73
Slow-Cook (Braise) Green Vegetables 75
Glaze Root Vegetables 76
Deep-fry Vegetables 77
Make Potato Chips and French Fries 80
Grill Vegetables 83
Steam and Boil Vegetables 86
Sautê Vegetables 89
Cook Artichokes 92
Make Mashed Potatoes and Other Vegetable and Fruit Purêes 94
Make a Vegetable Flan 97
Make a Chunky Vegetable Soup 98
Make a Creamy Vegetable Soup 100
Roast Fruit 101
Poach Fruit 104

Fish and Shellfish 107

HOW TO:

Poach a Big Fish 108
Poach a Small Fish 110
Poach Fish Steaks and Fillets, Small Whole Fish, and Shellfish 112
Cook Fish Fillets en Papillote 114
Bake Fish and Make a Sauce at the Same Time (Braise) 116
Roast a Whole Fish 118
Deep-fry Seafood 121
Grill Seafood 123
Sautê Seafood for a Crisp Crust 125
Cook Squid (and Other Tentacled Creatures) 128
Stir-fry in a Wok 130
Steam Shellfish 132
Shuck Oysters 134
Prepare Lobster 135
Prepare Soft-shell Crabs 138
Cook Crayfish 139
Use Salted Anchovies 142
Make Miso Soup 143

Contents

Poultry and Eggs 145

HOW TO:

Roast a Chicken 146
Poach Chicken in a Pot 150
Cut Up a Chicken 151
Make a Chicken Stew 154
Make a Chicken Sautê 157
Make Fried Chicken 160
Grill Chicken 161
Sautê Breaded Chicken Breasts 162
Make a Chicken Liver Mousse 165
Roast a Turkey and Make Giblet Gravy 166
Cut Up a Duck 170
Boil Eggs 172
Poach Eggs 174
Bake Eggs 175
Make an Omelet 176
Make a Soufflê 177

Meat 183

HOW TO:

Roast a Leg of Lamb 184
Roast a Rack of Lamb and Make a Jus 187
Roast a Rack of Pork 189
Roast a Prime Rib of Beef 191
Grill (or Broil) Chops and Steaks 193
Sautê Steaks, Chops, Noisettes, and Medallions (and Make a Pan Sauce) 195
Sautê a Small Whole Loin of Pork, Veal, or Venison 199
Make Pot-au-Feu and Other Boiled Dinners 200
Poach a Tender Cut of Meat 202
Make a Pot Roast 203
Make a Stew 206
Cook Veal, Beef, and Lamb Shanks 209
Make a Stew Without Browning 210
Make a Veal Stew 212
Prepare Sweetbreads 214

Working from Scratch 219

HOW TO:

Prepare a Whole Round Fish 220
Fillet a Salmon 224
Bone a Whole Round Fish 226
Prepare a Whole Flatfish 230
Scale, Clean, and Bone Whole Small Fish 236
Hot-Smoke Fish Fillets 237
Cold-Smoke Fish Fillets 238
Cure Seafood (Brining and Salting) 239
Trim and Cut Up a Breast of Veal for Stew 241
Trim and Partially Bone a Leg of Lamb 242
Butcher a Double Rack of Lamb 244
Trim and French a Rack of Lamb 246
Trim and Roast a Saddle of Lamb 250
Cut Up a Rabbit 254
Prepare and Braise a Large Rabbit 257

Glossary 261

Glossary 261

Index 289

Introduction

Sometimes, when I'm flipping through the cookbooks in bookstores, I'm left with a gnawing feeling that there are certain things about cooking that I need to express—a sense of something missing, something left unexplained, like the frustration of being in a discussion at a dinner party and feeling unable to get an important point across. It was this frustration that spurred me to write this book.

I decided that I wanted to create a kind of guidebook or reference of techniques for people who may be used to cooking from recipes but who want more confidence and a sense of freedom in the kitchen. Recipes are tyrannical, often intimidating, and even though I've written thousands of them, I question their effectiveness in teaching people how to cook. Techniques, on the other hand, teach us how to get the most out of an ingredient and challenge us to use our intuition and follow our palates.

I divide techniques into two categories. There are the minor ones, which make life in the kitchen smoother and more efficient: tips for quick peeling, stemming, and chopping. And there are the big ones that turn you into a cook. Of these, there are surprisingly few. Once you've gotten a handle on roasting, poaching, grilling, frying, steaming, sautéing, and braising, you'll know how to cook most foods, and if you understand the logic of how these techniques work, you'll be able to improvise intuitively and give your own special style and identity to your cooking.

Some techniques, however, are almost impossible to get across in words and require some kind of visual cue. Because I've wrecked entire afternoons screwing together my own garden furniture and bookcases, it's easy for me to imagine one of my poor readers, string in hand, trying to truss a chicken and after ten minutes, forgetting trussing and moving on to strangling. So I decided to illustrate certain techniques with an almost obsessive number of color photographs. I've tried to make the photographs cheery (see how easy this is!) and life-like—they were shot under real-life conditions in my cramped Brooklyn apartment—so that if the going gets rough, things won't seem utterly hopeless.

Organizing this book was a bear. With the help and encouragement of my editors, we decided to divide the book into six chapters that include the fundamental "how-to" techniques that show and tell you right off the bat *what* to do. We put definitions and some of the whys in a Glossary, but at the end of each how-to technique, we tell you where in the Glossary to go to find this information. Not only are you directed to the related Glossary entries, but you are also directed to other techniques in the text. These appear under the See Also heading. By following the cues, the elements of technique end up tied together in a logical way.

At the end of How to Roast Vegetables, for example, the See Also heading tells you where to look for instruction on how to turn vegetables for roasting, how to make fresh bread crumbs to top roasted vegetables, and how to make chicken stock to glaze vegetables while they roast. Or, because vegetables taste particularly good when they're roasted alongside a chicken or leg of lamb, you see where to go to learn how to roast poultry and meats. And because you may end up with a bunch of beet greens if you're roasting beets, there is a listing for how to cook greens. The result of all this is that you can use the book as a quick reference or you can peruse at your leisure, flipping back and forth, and discover the lovely systematic logic inherent in the most basic and essential ways to cook.

However, some techniques are like Chinese boxes, containing techniques within techniques. I also wanted to make sure that no element got passed over as you worked through the sequence of photographs and step-by-step explanations. Roasting a chicken, for example, is inherently a very simple thing to do, but there are smaller techniques, like trussing, skimming fat off the roasting juices, perhaps thickening the roasting juices with flour or garlic purée, that are performed to show off the roast chicken at its best. But all of these "sub-techniques" can be used in other recipes or preparations as well and I didn't want them to get lost under the roast chicken heading. Therefore, we have also illustrated "smaller" techniques like degreasing, thickening vegetable purées, and making a roux.

Although recipes aren't always given in traditional form with specific amounts of ingredients and cooking times, enough information for you to cook nearly 150 dishes is provided. We show you how to cook by teaching you basic preparations, opting for ways of looking, tasting, touching, smelling—even listening as you cook. In How to Make a Vegetable Gratin, first you get the basic technique: Vegetables are layered in a low-sided casserole and baked under a crisp topping. Then you see how to vary the technique when you use different vegetables. There isn't a measurement for liquid because the quantity is determined by the size of the dish and the amount of vegetable; instead you are given guidelines for judging the correct amount. Oven temperatures are also guides because oven thermostats are often wrong, but you also learn what the gratin should look like as it cooks so that you can raise or lower the temperature as needed.

Kitchen Notes and Tips, which appear throughout the book, offer overviews, guidance, tips, cooking times, oven temperatures, proportions, measurements, occasional equipment notes, and suggestions for how to use the technique to make other dishes.

The chapter called Working from Scratch includes more complicated techniques that might be intimidating for beginners. You can have some of these techniques—filleting a fish, trimming a rack of lamb—done at the fish store or by the butcher, but anyone cooking professionally needs to know how to do them. And whether you're a professional or not, if you cook a lot, you may start to get picky and do things yourself. (My fish guy never gets all the scales off the fish and the butcher makes a face if I ask him to French a rack of pork.)

Carving is another matter. It used to be de rigueur, at least for men, to know how to carve. It was a status symbol, like knowing how to ride or play tennis. Most of us don't worry about such things anymore (or at least won't admit it), and while this may be for the best, I think one of life's lovely rituals has been lost. Even the holiday turkey is carved, almost surreptitiously, in the kitchen, and the homey American gothic majesty of that giant golden bird is all but forgotten. My mission is to bring carving back to day-to-day life, so you'll find all kinds of things to carve—including whole fish, flat and round—enabling you to turn the simplest roast or sautéed piece of fish or meat into an elegant, but not overly formal, meal.

Essentials of Cooking is a kind of kitchen companion, one I hope will make you want to cook, will help you out of the occasional jam, and will help you cook with confidence, maybe even with a little cockiness, because out of assurance comes creativity, and that's when the real fun begins. You may want to use *Essentials of Cooking* with other cookbooks, like a writer might use a dictionary or thesaurus, to make sure you're on the right track or to understand why (or why not) to use a particular method. But my biggest hope is that over time you who use this book will free yourself from the numbing exactitude of recipes and head boldly into market or kitchen with confidence and joy.

Basics

HOW TO
Peel Vegetables

You may be most comfortable with a specific type of peeler and use it for all vegetables. But the trick to peeling quickly and with the minimum of waste is to use a variety of tools, depending on the fruit or vegetable you're peeling. A swivel-type vegetable peeler is best for vegetables with thin, delicate skins, such as asparagus and carrots. A peeler with a fixed blade is better for vegetables with thick skins that require deeper peeling, such as turnips and eggplant. For very thick skinned vegetables, such as celeriac, a paring knife works best, because it allows you to reach into the nooks and crannies below the surface of the peel.

Some vegetables, such as onions, tomatoes, bell peppers, and chestnuts, require special peeling methods.

To Peel Asparagus with a Swivel-Type Peeler

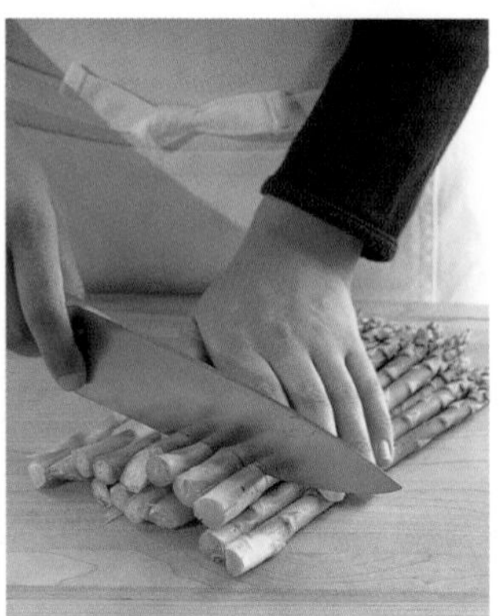

Peeling asparagus helps it cook evenly and makes it easy to eat nearly the entire stalk.

1. Cut off the woody ends, usually about an inch or two.
2. Peel the asparagus up to the base of the tips by moving rapidly back and forth along the length of the stalk with a swivel peeler. Keep the stalks flat on the cutting board so they don't break. Very thick asparagus can be peeled with a nonswivel peeler or a paring knife.

Kitchen Notes and Tips

- Each type of peeler is most effective used a specific way. A swivel-type peels with a back-and-forth movement, or by moving it away from you. Use nonswivel peelers by peeling toward yourself, as if you were using a knife.
- Peel thin-skinned vegetables such as carrots and asparagus with a swivel-type peeler.
- Peel thicker-skinned vegetables such as eggplant, turnips, and potatoes with a nonswivel peeler.
- String fennel and celery with either a peeler or a knife.
- Peel very thick skinned vegetables such as celery root and winter squash with a knife.
- A short plunge into boiling water will loosen the peels of onions and tomatoes and the inner peels of peeled chestnuts. This trick is especially handy for peeling pearl onions.
- Many people don't think peeling asparagus is worth the bother, but peeled asparagus is easier to cook because the stalks cook in the same time as the florets—and you can eat the whole stalk if it's been peeled.

To Peel Eggplant with a Nonswivel Peeler

1. Cut the ends off the eggplants.
2. Peel the eggplant by peeling toward you.

To Peel Celeriac with a Knife

1. If the celeriac still has the greens attached, cut them off where they join the bulb.
2. Peel the celeriac by rotating the bulb against the paring knife.

To Peel Turnips with a Nonswivel Peeler

If the turnip still has its greens, cut the greens off where they join the bulb. Otherwise, just cut off the hard end where the greens once were. Peel the turnip by rotating it against the blade of the peeler. (You can also use a paring knife.)

To Peel Chestnuts

Chestnuts actually have 2 peels—a thick outer peel and a thin inner peel that clings to the meat of the chestnut.

1. Make a large X on the flat side of the chestnut. Be sure to cut completely through the peel, but not into the meat. Soak the chestnuts in warm water for 15 minutes; drain. Roast the chestnuts in a 350°F oven for 15 minutes, or until the outer skin curls away from the X.
2. Peel the chestnuts while they're still hot. (You may need to use a kitchen towel.) If they cool and become difficult to peel, put them back in the oven for 5 minutes. To remove the inner peels, plunge the peeled chestnuts into boiling water for about 2 minutes. Drain and immediately rub them in a kitchen towel. Most of the peels will come off.

To Peel Fava Beans

Unless they are very small and immature, after fava beans are shelled, each bean must be peeled to remove the bitter outer skin.

1. Slide your thumb along the seam running down the side of the bean, separating the 2 halves of the pod as you go.
2. Peel each bean using your thumbnail or a small paring knife. If you have a large number of beans to peel, plunge the shucked beans in boiling water for about 30 seconds, drain, and rinse with cold water to make the peeling easier.

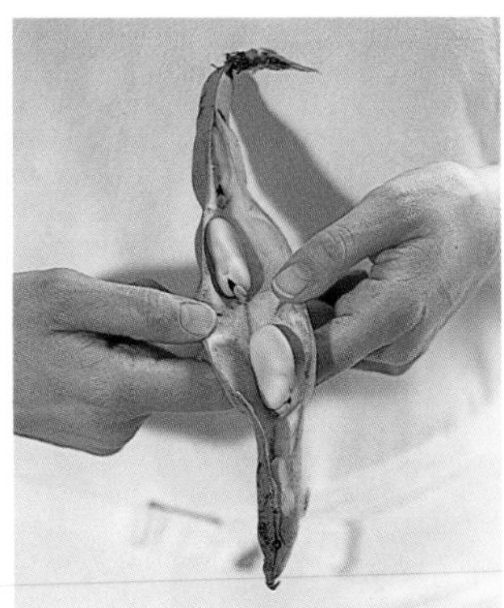

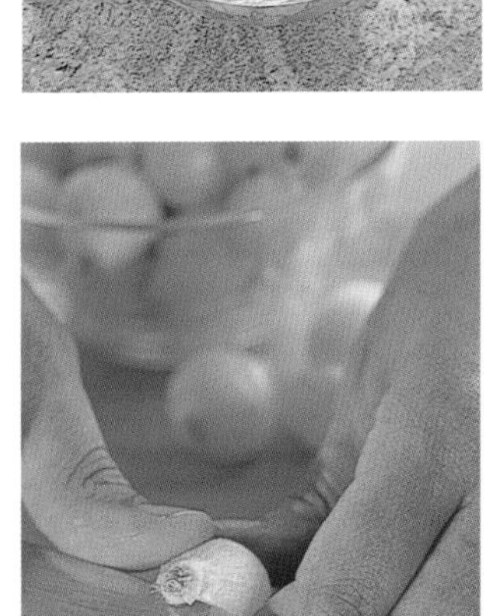

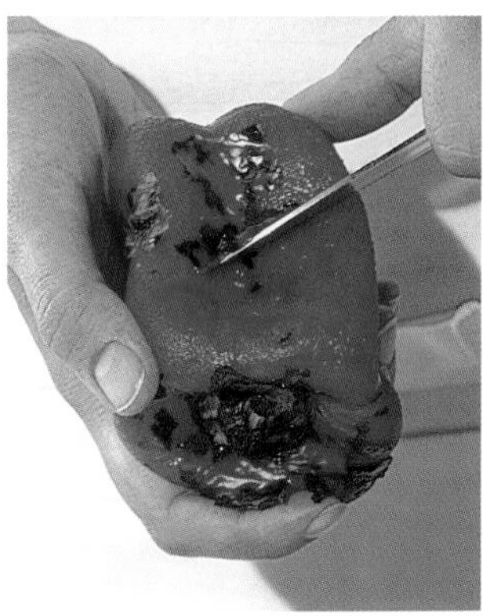

To Peel Fennel

1. Cut off the fennel stalks where they join the bulb. (These can be saved and added to broths. The small leafy fronds can be lightly chopped and used as an herb or as decoration.)
2. To eliminate the stringy filaments and any brown sections, peel the fennel bulb with a swivel or nonswivel peeler or paring knife. Hold the fennel with your thumb pressed against the bottom and work the peeler toward you.

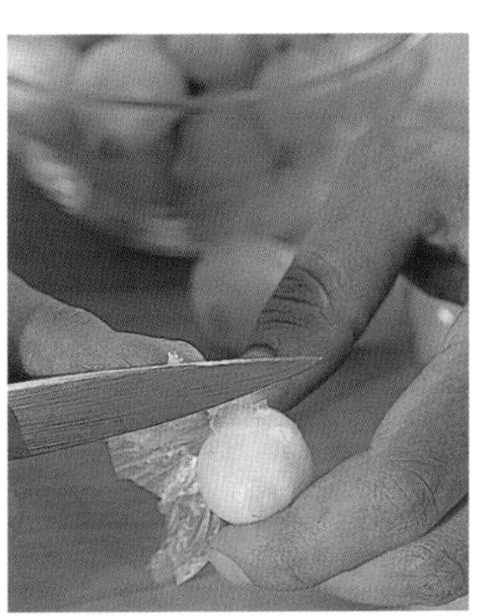

To Peel Pearl Onions

1. Pour boiling water over the onions and let sit for 1 minute. Drain in a colander and rinse with cold water.
2. Cut off the tiny root ends of the onions.
3. Peel off the thin outermost peel with a paring knife.

To Roast and Peel Bell Peppers

When roasted and peeled, bell peppers (and certain hot chiles) become more flavorful and tender.

1. Place the peppers directly over a gas burner, on a grill, or under a broiler. (Or, for an electric stove, bend down the 2 ends of a coat hanger and place on the hot electric coil. Place the pepper on the hanger.) Char the peppers, turning occasionally, until completely blackened.
2. Pull off as much of the blackened peel as you can with your fingers. Remove stubborn patches with a paring knife.

To Peel Tomatoes

Most of the time, it isn't necessary to peel tomatoes. When you're making a tomato salad, for instance, peeling is optional. But when using tomatoes that are somewhat out of season, peeling will improve their texture. It's also essential to peel tomatoes for tomato concassée; otherwise, the peels end up as little coils floating around in the sauce.

1. Use a paring knife to cut the stem end out of the tomatoes. Plunge the tomatoes into boiling water for 15 seconds if they are ripe, 30 seconds if underripe.
2. Drain the tomatoes in a colander and rinse them immediately under cold water, or plunge them into ice water.
3. Peel back the skin in strips by pinching it between your thumb and a paring knife or just slide it off with your fingers.

See Also

To make a tomato concassée, page 50
To seed tomatoes, page 36

Related Glossary Entries

Blanch
Concassée
Coulis

HOW TO

Shuck, Stem, Trim, and Seed Vegetables

To Shuck Corn and Remove the Kernels

Use corn kernels in soups, creamed corn, and salsas.

1. Peel off the green husks and the thin silk that runs along the kernels. If the silk is hard to remove, rinse the corn under cold running water while brushing with a stiff nylon brush.
2. Remove the kernels by cutting down the sides of the corn with a sharp chef's knife.

To Trim Brussels Sprouts

1. If you have a whole stalk of Brussels sprouts, cut the individual sprouts off where they join the stalk. If you've bought loose Brussels sprouts, cut off the base, which may have darkened and dried out slightly.
2. If the Brussels sprouts are large, cut them in half or into quarters.
3. Brussels sprouts can also be "deconstructed" by cutting the leaves away one by one. Brussels sprout leaves can be sautéed or steamed in the same way as other leafy green vegetables.

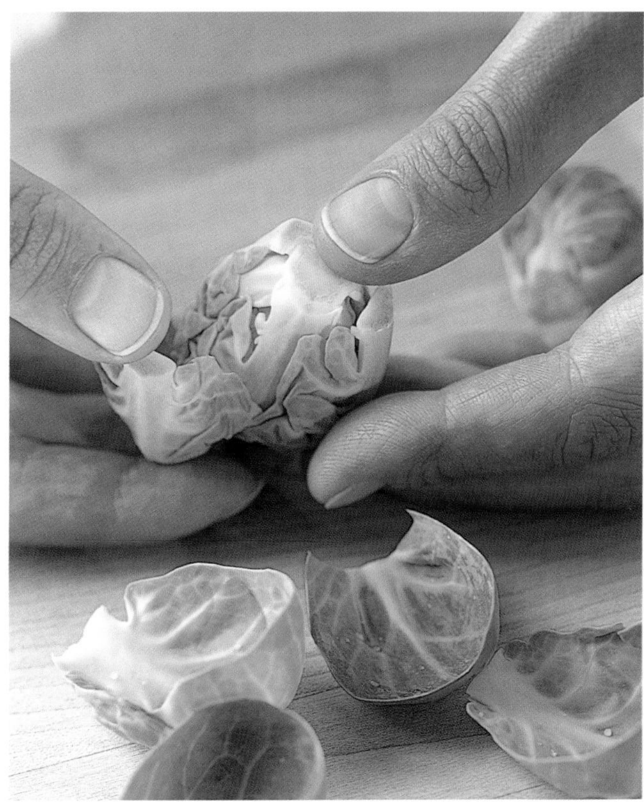

To Trim Cauliflower

1. Tear the green leaves and stems off the base of the cauliflower. Cut around the underside of the cauliflower with a paring knife, removing any green stems.
2. Cut around the inside of the cauliflower, removing most of the core.
3. Detach the florets where they join at the center core.
4. Cut through the base of the florets to separate them into smaller florets.

Stemming Greens

For most leafy greens, remove the tough stems before cooking. Greens with tender leaves that tear easily, such as spinach and sorrel, can be stemmed by hand. Greens with bigger, tougher leaves, such as Swiss chard, are best stemmed with a knife.

To Stem Spinach

Hold the spinach leaf between your thumb and forefinger and pull back the stem so even the strip of stem attached to the back of the leaf comes away.

To Seed Cucumbers

1. Cut the cucumber lengthwise in half.
2. Scrape out the seeds with a spoon.

To Stem Swiss Chard

Fold the leaf in half so the stem runs along one side. Cut between the stem and the leaf.

To Trim and Wash Leeks

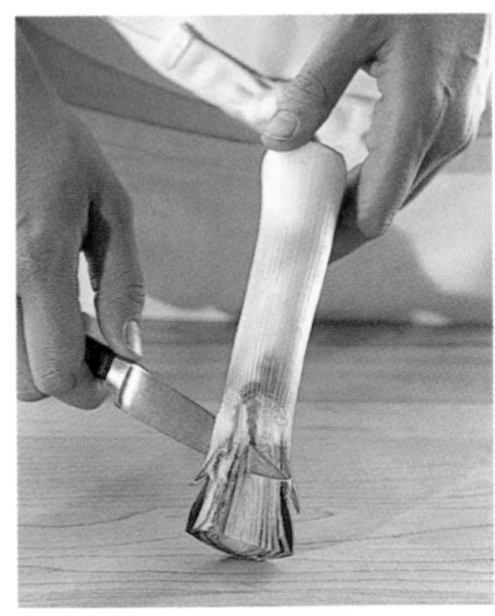

1. Cut the root off the leek where it joins the base. (Don't cut too far up along the white of the leek, or the leek will fall apart.)
2. Cut the greens off an inch or two above the first hint of green on the white.
3. Whittle off the outermost dark green leaves from the leek white.
4. Cut the leek lengthwise in half.
5. Hold the leek half, upside down (so dirt doesn't lodge deeper into the leek), under cold running water. Rub each leaf between your thumb and forefinger to loosen any dirt.

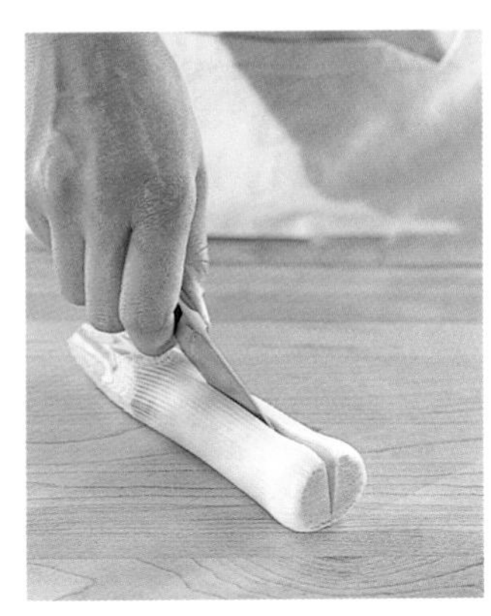

To Core and Seed Roasted Bell Peppers

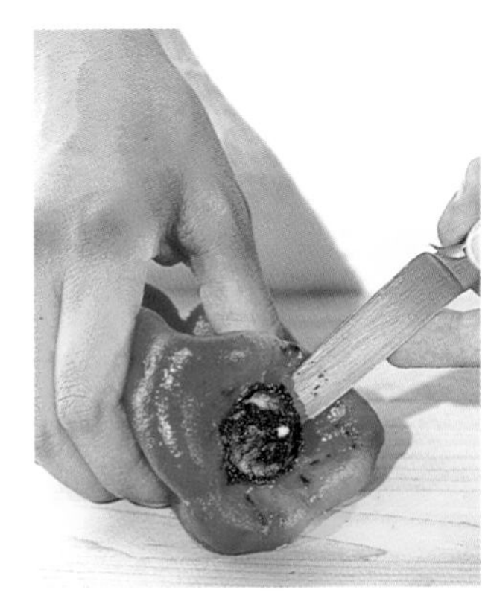

1. Cut completely around the core of the peeled pepper with a paring knife.
2. Pull the core out with your fingers.
3. Cut down through one side of the pepper and spread the pepper open.
4. Cut away and discard the strips of white pulp on the inside of the pepper. Push away the seeds with the knife or your fingers. (You can also quickly rinse them out under running water.)

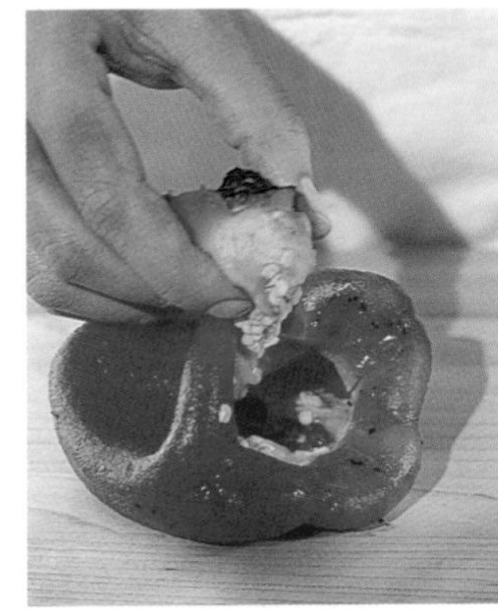

See Also

To roast and peel bell peppers, page 5

HOW TO

Cut Up Vegetables and Herbs

The best way to cut up vegetables depends on their size and shape and how you're going to use them. Usually, they are chopped, diced, minced, or sliced; occasionally, they are shredded or julienned. How do you decide whether to chop, slice, or julienne?

Chopping usually means to cut foods into smaller pieces of no particular shape and no particular size. Chop vegetables and herbs when appearance isn't important, or when the vegetables will be strained out of a sauce or broth and not served. Generally, vegetables are chopped larger for longer-cooking dishes and smaller for shorter-cooking dishes. Mincing simply means to finely chop, and it is used for dishes that cook very quickly, or when you want to leave the minced food in the dish, as in a pan sauce.

Dicing means exactly what it sounds like, cutting the food into cubes, like dice. Dice when appearance *is* important. The French give different names, such as *brunoise* and *macedoine*, to refer to different-sized dice.

Shred, julienne, and *chiffonade* all mean to cut into thin strips. Leafy vegetables such as cabbage are shredded; leafy herbs and greens such as basil and spinach are cut into chiffonade. And other vegetables, such as root vegetables, are cut into julienne. Julienning is the first step in cutting a vegetable into the tiny dice called brunoise.

Vegetables may also be cut into larger shapes to be used as garniture for braises, roasts, and stews or for serving on their own. Vegetables such as turnips and fennel are often cut into wedges. Vegetables can also be "turned," which means to trim the vegetable into an attractive oval shape with rounded sides (see page 21).

Chopping and Mincing

To Chop and Mince Onions

Onions, shallots, and garlic are chopped in the same way.

1. Place a peeled onion half, root end away from you, on the cutting board. Cut it lengthwise into thin or thick slices, depending on how finely or coarsely you want it chopped, leaving the slices attached at the root end.
2. Slice horizontally through the slices, again being careful not to cut through the root end.
3. Slice the onion crosswise. For minced onions, continue to chop until very fine.

To Mince Garlic and Make Garlic Paste

Garlic paste has an even finer texture than minced garlic. Use garlic paste when you want a very smooth texture, as in a mayonnaise or in a soup or for making pesto without using a mortar with a pestle.

1. Place the side of a chef's knife on the garlic clove and give the knife a quick whack with the heel of your hand. Pull off the skin. Trim the tiny root end off the peeled garlic clove. Place the garlic flat side down on the cutting board. If the clove is large or doesn't have a flat side, cut it in half through the root end and place the cut side down.
2. Slice the garlic lengthwise with a very sharp paring knife, leaving the slices attached at the root end.
3. Make three horizontal slices through the garlic.
4. Finely slice the garlic crosswise.
5. To crush minced garlic to a paste, place it near the edge of the cutting board and crush it, a tiny bit at a time, with the side of the chef's knife. Lean firmly on the knife with the heel of your hand.

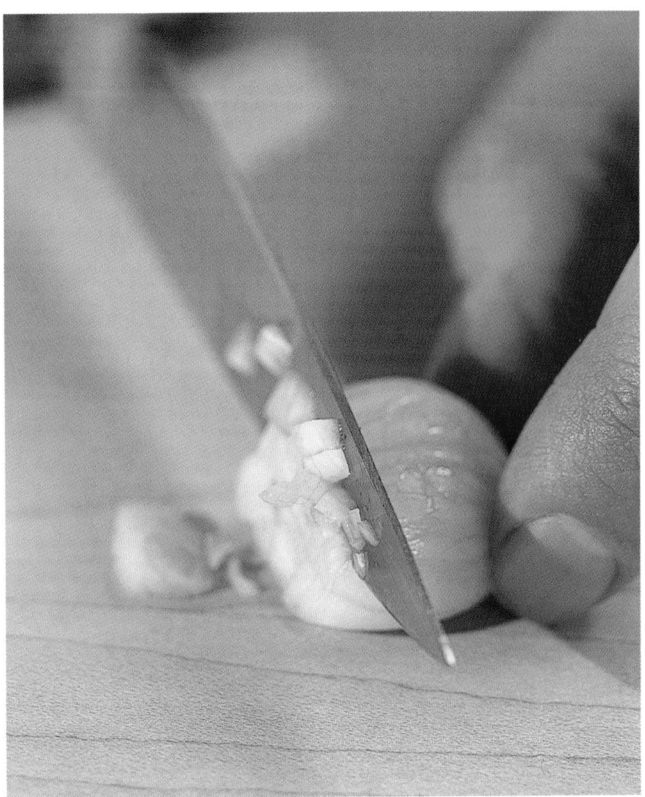

Kitchen Notes and Tips

HOW TO CHOP AND MINCE

Vegetables can be chopped or minced by rapidly moving a chef's knife up and down over the vegetable. This is simple to do, but there are a few tricks that make the process more efficient.

- Chop a fairly large amount at once so you're using the entire knife blade. (Unless you only have a very small amount of something to chop, it doesn't make sense to have only a small section of the blade doing the chopping.)
- Keep whatever it is you're chopping in an elongated pile parallel with the knife blade—again, so that the whole knife blade is in use.
- You'll have the most control if you grip the knife as close to the blade as possible. In fact, your thumb and forefinger should pinch the sides of the knife blade, while the rest of your hand wraps around the handle.
- Keep the tip of the knife blade firmly pressed against the cutting board while you chop to steady the knife and make it easier to control. (Many cooks press on the back of the knife with their free hand to steady it, but if you keep the tip of the knife firmly planted on the cutting board, this won't be necessary, and you can then use your free hand to keep sliding whatever it is you're chopping under the blade.)
- For some chopping, especially of very soft foods and herbs, you may find it easier to

use the knife in the same way as when slicing: Instead of holding the knife tip against the cutting board, move the whole blade up and down. If your hands get tired, you can switch to a third method: Hold the knife blade with both hands, one hand near the tip and one near the handle, and move the whole knife rapidly up and down.

HOW TO SLICE

- Slice vegetables by hand or with a vegetable slicer. A vegetable slicer is the easiest way to make very thin, even slices.
- When slicing by hand, hold the vegetable with one hand, with your fingers curled under so they don't get in the way of the knife. By keeping the side of the

knife blade right up against the knuckles of your hand, you can control the thickness of the slices by slowly moving your hand back along the length of the vegetable as you slice. This frees your cutting hand to move the knife very quickly. You can usually lift the knife completely off the cutting board when slicing, but if the vegetable is very hard, you may need to keep the knife tip pressed firmly against the cutting board to stabilize the knife and allow you to use more force.
- It's always easier to slice into half-rounds than rounds because, with half-rounds, you're working with a vegetable that has one flat surface to keep it steady.

HOW TO DICE

- Dicing is more methodical than chopping because dice should be regular and all the same size. Depending on how precise the dice need to be, a vegetable is usually first cut into even strips or julienne and then the strips or julienne are sliced.
- Very fine dice (slightly smaller than ⅛ inch) are called brunoise; slightly larger dice (a little smaller than ¼ inch) are called macedoine.
- It's rarely necessary for home cooks to cut vegetables into perfect dice. Irregular dice are usually okay, as long as the pieces are about the same size. It's much easier to cut carrots and other cylindrical vegetables (such as parsnips) into small triangular pieces than into perfect cubes.
- To cut a round vegetable into perfect dice, cut off the sides so you start out with one large cube as on page 17. If you want to save the trimmings (they freeze well and can be used for soups or purées), peel the vegetable first; otherwise, don't bother.

HOW TO SHRED, JULIENNE, AND CHIFFONADE

- You can shred cabbage by hand or with a vegetable slicer.
- To cut vegetables into julienne, thinly slice the vegetables, stack the slices, and slice them again. The size and thickness of the julienne is determined by how thick you make the slices.
- Plastic vegetable slicers and mandolines have julienne attachments, but most only offer one or two sizes (which never seem to be the right one) and it can be very difficult to force a vegetable through the many tiny blades. It's generally better to slice the vegetable on the slicer and then julienne the slices by hand.
- To cut herbs or leafy vegetables into chiffonade, stack the leaves, a few at a time, roll into tight little cylinders, and finely slice them. Because some leafy herbs, such as basil, turn dark when sliced, toss them with a few drops of olive oil to protect them from the air and to slow the darkening.

HOW TO TURN VEGETABLES

- "Turned" vegetables are cut and trimmed into elongated oval shapes that look a little like miniature footballs. To turn a vegetable, you usually first cut it into sections or wedges, then round off the sides with a small paring knife. To determine how to cut up a vegetable before turning, look at it to see how you can get the most out of it and minimize waste. It's usually best to cut cylindrical vegetables first into sections and round vegetables into wedges or rectangles.
- Trimmings from turned vegetables can be saved for soups or purées.

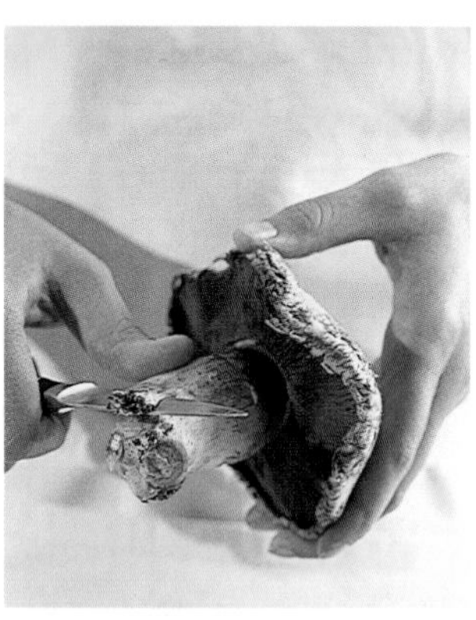

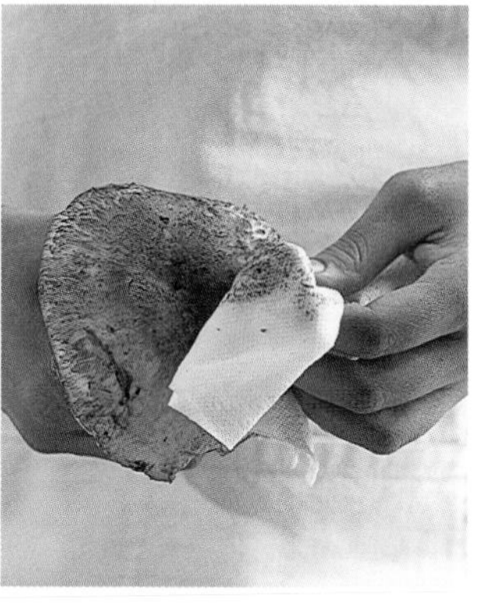

To Chop Mushroom Caps and Stems

For large mushrooms, slice the stems and caps separately.

1. If the mushroom stems are dark or very dirty, trim them with a paring knife.
2. Rinse mushrooms quickly under running water in a colander or wipe them with a moist paper towel.
3. Snap off the stems and slice the caps.
4. Hold the slices together and cut across the slices.
5. Slice the stems.
6. Chop the stems and diced cap as you would other vegetables. For small mushrooms, slice the cap and stem together and then chop.

To Chop Parsley

This method can be used for most herbs and leafy vegetables. When chopping herbs, make sure the herbs are perfectly dry, or they'll form wet clumps once chopped.

1. Cut off parsley stems while still tied (save for broth or a bouquet garni, or discard). Mound the leaves in a pile so you're chopping a lot at once.
2. With your free hand, push the leaves under the knife while rapidly moving the blade up and down. Press the tip of the knife against the cutting board to stabilize the knife. If your hands get tired, hold the blade with both hands and chop quickly.

To Chop Carrots into Triangular Pieces

This method can be used for other cylindrical vegetables such as parsnips, zucchini, or cucumbers, and for stalks such as celery. For celery, cut the stalks lengthwise into strips and then slice.

1. Cut peeled carrots lengthwise in half. If the carrots are long, cut them crosswise in half. Cut each piece into 3 long wedges.
2. Slice the carrots into miniature triangles (irregular dice).

Slicing

To Slice Carrots into Rounds

When appearance isn't important, slice carrots and other cylindrical vegetables lengthwise in half first so they stay steady on the cutting board while you're slicing. But for some dishes, it's important to cut the vegetables into rounds because they look better; in that case, leave the vegetables whole.

To Slice Carrots into Half-Rounds

Cut carrots lengthwise in half. Place halves flat side down on the cutting board. Slice while holding the tip of the knife firmly planted against the cutting board and slowly inching back with your other hand as you work down the carrot.

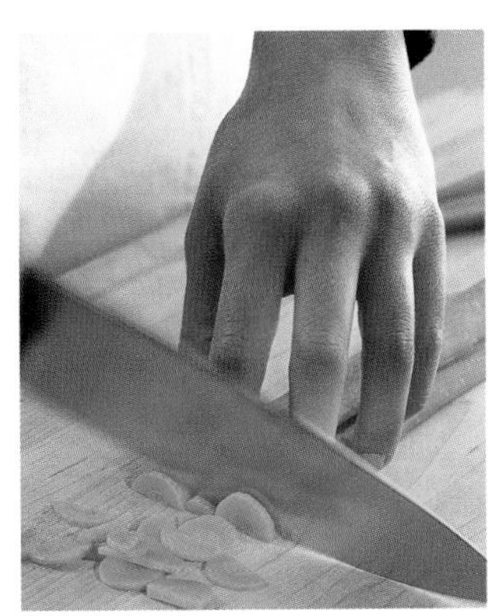

To Slice Zucchini into Rounds

Zucchini and other soft cylindrical vegetables such as cucumbers can be sliced very quickly and accurately by holding the vegetable with one hand and slowly inching back with your other hand as you slice.

To slice zucchini, cut off the stem end. Hold the zucchini with one hand with your forefinger folded under so that the blade slides up and down against the knuckle and your finger stays out of the way of the knife. Slice quickly up and down with your other hand.

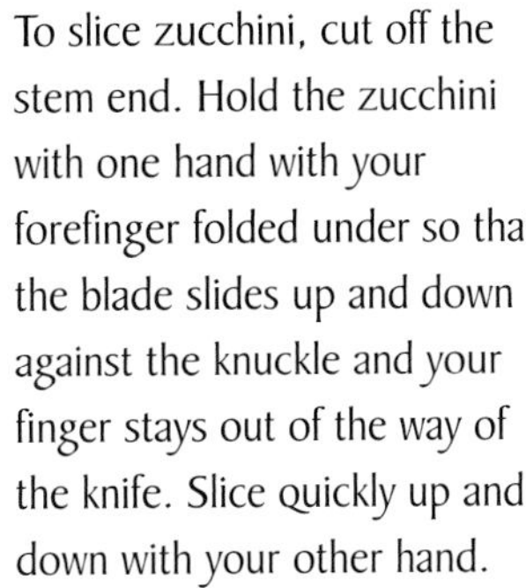

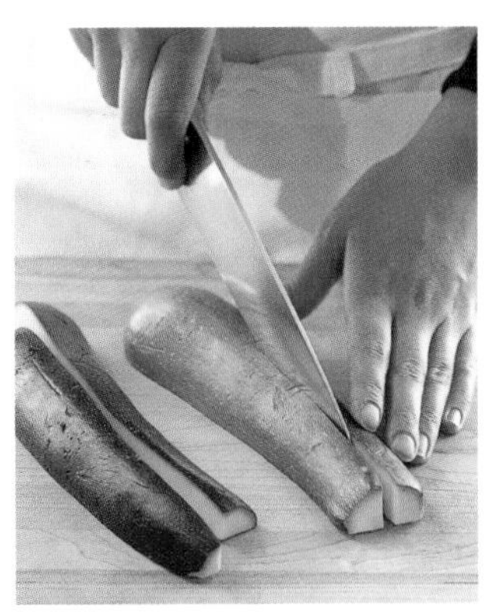

To Cut Zucchini into Triangular Pieces

For some dishes, such as soups or pasta dishes, whole rounds are too large. In these cases, the zucchini can be cut lengthwise in half or into quarters and then sliced. Slicing into triangular pieces is easier than slicing into rounds as one side lies flat against the cutting board.

1. Cut the stem end off the zucchini and cut the zucchini lengthwise into 4 or more wedges.
2. Slice 2 or more of the wedges at once.

To Shave Fennel with a Plastic Vegetable Slicer

A plastic vegetable slicer, set on the thinnest setting, will slice foods paper-thin.

Slide the fennel back and forth over the blade. Keep your fingers spread out to keep them out of the way of the blade. When you get closer to the blade, use the hand guard.

To Slice Cucumbers More Efficiently

Long vegetables and strips of vegetables can be stacked so that you are slicing more than one at a time.

1. Cut the cucumber in half lengthwise. Scoop the seeds out of each cucumber half with a spoon.
2. Place halves on top of each other, and slice them together. Use the fingers of your free hand to hold the halves together as you slice.

To Slice Truffles

Though truffles are easy to slice by hand or with a plastic vegetable slicer, a truffle slicer is convenient and attractive if slicing truffles at the table.

Adjust the slicing thickness with the small nut set to one side of the blade. Move the truffle quickly back and forth against the blade.

Related Glossary Entry

Slicer (also for a photograph of a hand guard)

Dicing

To Dice Turnips

Round vegetables can all be diced in this way.

1. Slice off the sides of the peeled turnip so you end up with a perfect cube.
2. Slice the cube. The number of slices depends on the size of the dice; be sure the slices are all the same thickness.
3. Holding the slices together with your fingers, slice them so you end up with sticks.
4. Holding the sticks—sometimes called *bâtonnets* (from the French for "rod")—together, cut them into dice.

Related Glossary Entries

Brunoise
Macedoine

Shredding, Julienning, and Cutting into Chiffonade

To Core and Shred Cabbage

1. Cut the cabbage into quarters through the center core.
2. Cut the core out of each quarter.
3. Slice each quarter very thin with a vegetable slicer or chef's knife.

To Cut Beets into Julienne or Bâtonnets

Round vegetables such as turnips or celeriac can also be cut in this way.

Slice peeled boiled or roasted beets. Stack the slices and slice into fine strips called julienne or into thicker sticks called bâtonnets, as shown here.

See Also
To roast and peel beets, page 71

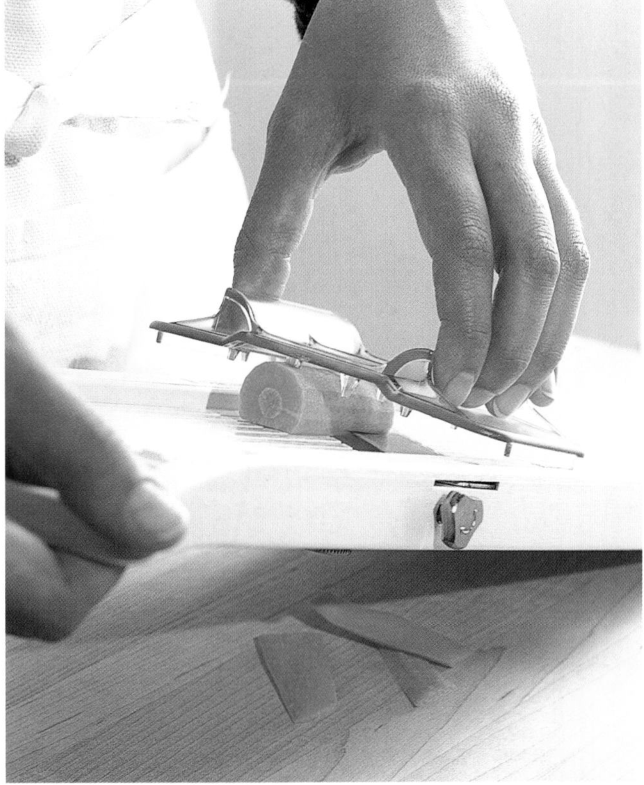

To Julienne Carrots

Parsnips and other cylindrical vegetables can be julienned exactly as shown here. Round vegetables such as turnips are best sliced and the slices stacked and thinly sliced into julienne.

1. Cut peeled carrots into sections the length of the desired julienne.
2. Cut lengthwise slices off 4 sides of each carrot section until you get down to the yellowish core. Discard the core.
3. Or, use a vegetable slicer to shave slices off the 4 sides of the carrot sections.
4. Stack the slices—don't try to slice more than 2 or 3 at a time—and hold them in place with the fingers of one hand.
5. Cut the slices into strips as wide as they are thick.

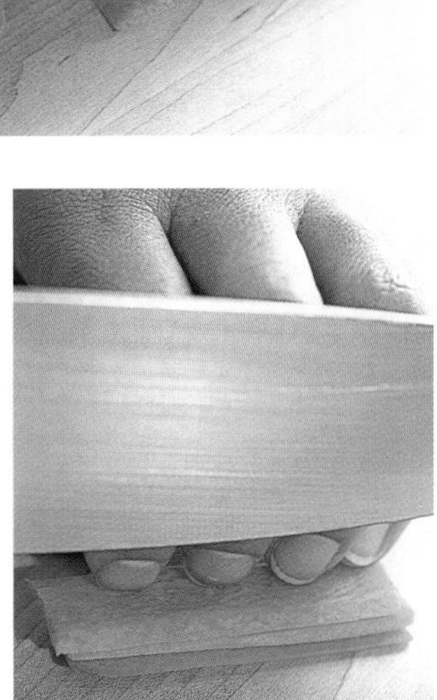

To Julienne Roasted Bell Peppers

After removing the seeds and white pulp from the inside of a bell pepper, spread it flat on the cutting board and slice into fine strips.

See Also

To roast and peel bell peppers, page 5
To core and seed roasted bell peppers, page 9

Related Glossary Entry

Slicer

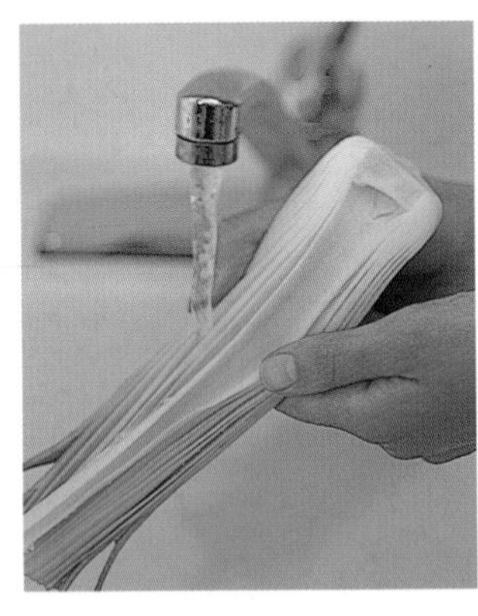

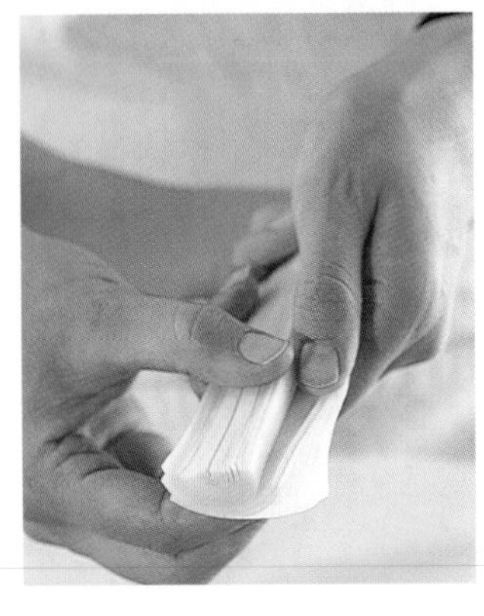

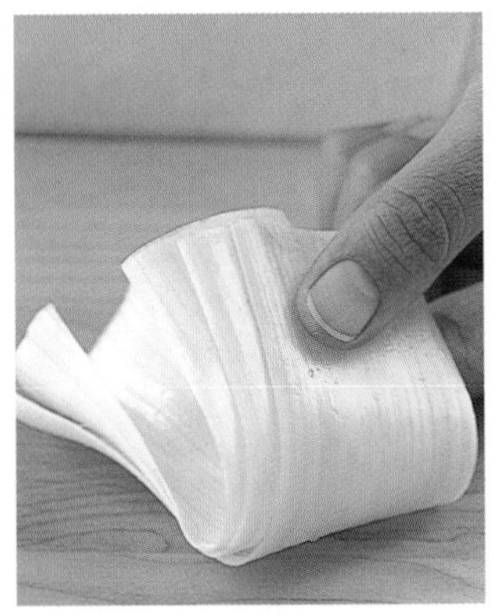

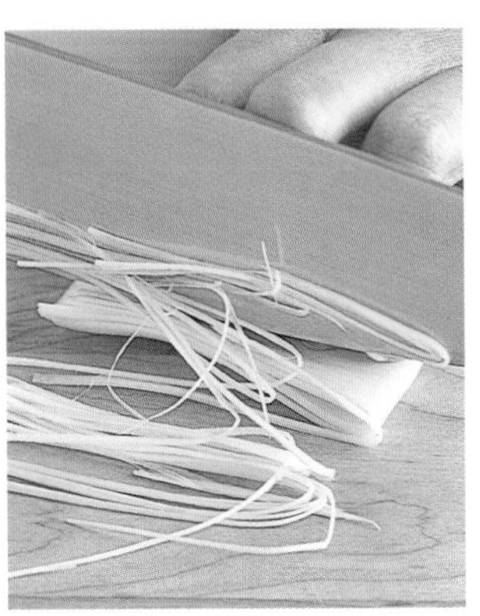

To Julienne Leeks

Leeks must be julienned entirely by hand.

1. Remove the greens, halve the leek, and wash under running water.
2. Cut about ¼ inch off the root ends to make it easier to separate the individual white leaves.
3. Peel back and remove 3 of the leaves at a time.
4. If the leaves are more than about 3 inches long, fold them in half. (If they are very long, cut them in half.)
5. Hold the leeks firmly in place with one hand and slice with a chef's knife.

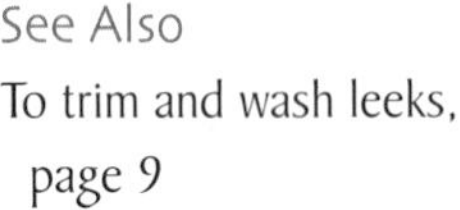

See Also
To trim and wash leeks, page 9

To Cut Basil into Chiffonade

This method can be used for any leafy green. For most greens such as spinach and chard, which don't turn black when cut, sprinkling with olive oil is unnecessary.

1. To keep them from turning black, sprinkle basil leaves with a few drops of olive oil. Rub the leaves so they're all thinly coated with oil.
2. Stack the leaves, 2 or 3 at a time, and roll into tight cylinders.
3. Slice the leaves into thin strips.

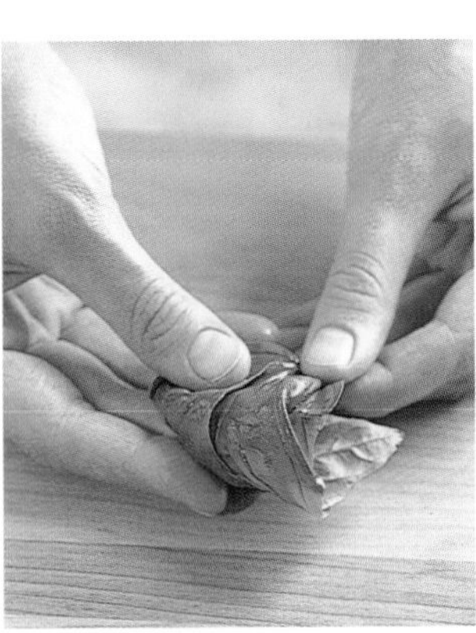

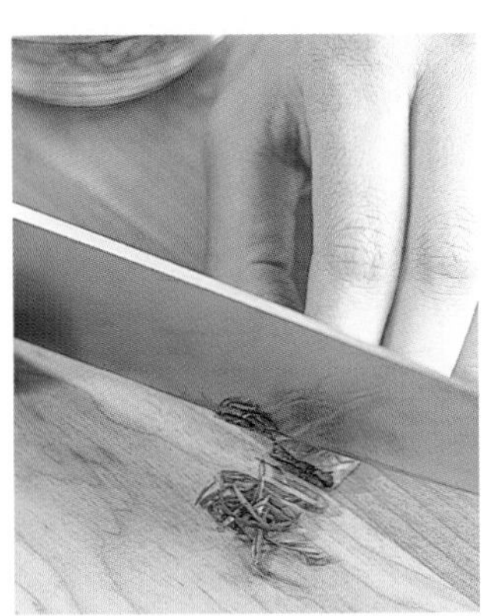

Shaping Vegetables: Turning and Cutting Wedges

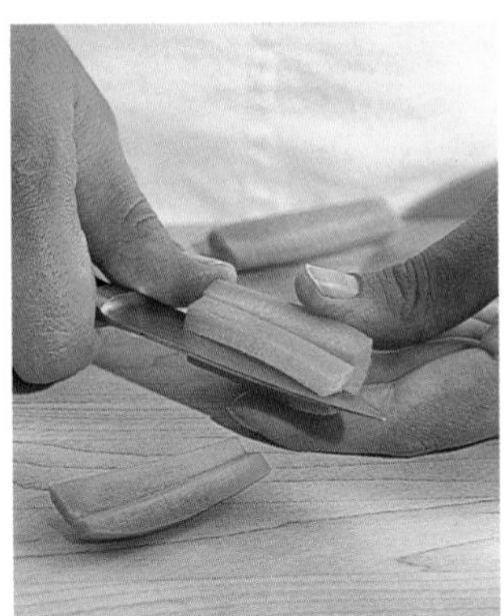

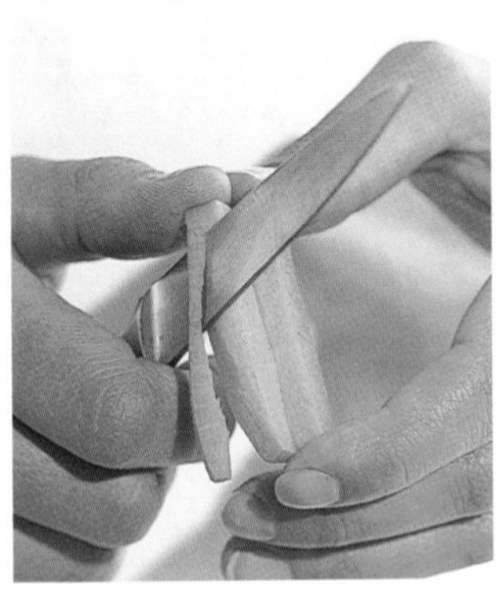

To Turn Carrots

This method also works for cylindrical vegetables such as parsnips and zucchini. You can cut carrots into sections and then turn each whole section, but this method leaves much of the best part of the carrot—the orange outer part—on the cutting board. It's better to remove the core from the carrot sections first and then trim the sides of the sections to give them an attractive rounded appearance.

1. Cut peeled carrot sections into wedges. Keep the wedges the same size by cutting as many as 5 wedges out of very thick sections and as few as 2 out of thinner sections.
2. Slide a paring knife along each side of the yellowish core and snap out the core.
3. Rotate the sides of the carrot sections against the blade of a sharp paring knife.

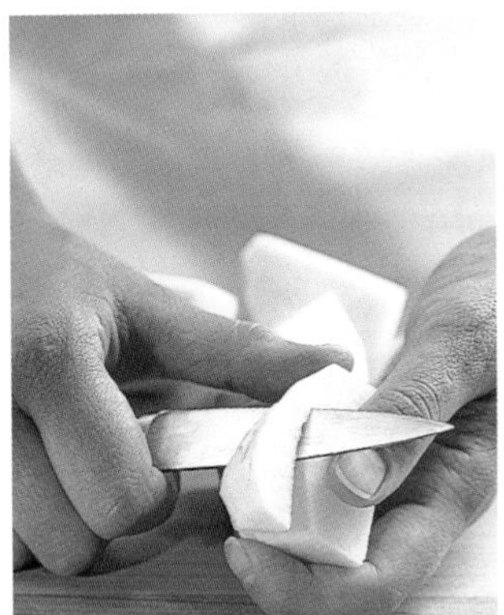

To Turn Turnips

This method works for all firm round vegetables. It's most convenient to cut turnips into wedges *before* rounding off their edges by turning. The number of wedges depends on the size of the turnip and the desired size after turning. Small turnips can be halved and halved again to produce 4 wedges, as shown here, while larger turnips and other round vegetables can be cut into 6 or even 8 wedges before turning. If you're confronted with very large round vegetables and want relatively small turned pieces, halve the vegetable crosswise through its "equator" and then cut each of these halves into wedges.

1. Cut the turnip into quarters (or more wedges).
2. Trim the sides of the wedges by rotating the wedges against the knife blade. Try to trim the whole length of a side in one single motion so you end up with a continuous arc. If you stop in the middle, the side will be faceted instead of evenly rounded.

To Cut Fennel into Wedges

1. Trim fennel branches.
2. Peel fennel with a vegetable peeler.
3. Cut the bulb in half. Be sure to cut through the middle of the core—visible on the bottom—so that some of the core stays attached to each wedge and holds it together.
4. Cut each half into 3 to 6 wedges, depending on the size of the fennel, always starting in the center of the core.

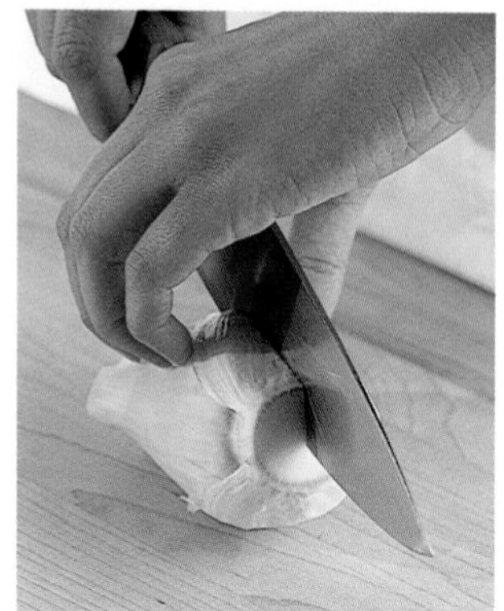

To Cut Turnips into Wedges

Cut peeled turnips lengthwise in half. Cut each half into as many wedges as you like.

HOW TO

Prepare Fruits

Fruits differ so much in shape, size, and structure that they demand a variety of different techniques to peel, seed, stem, zest, and/or slice them.

Preparing Apples

To Peel Apples

1. Cut the stem end out of the apple by inserting a peeler into the apple and rotating.
2. Peel the apple by rotating it against the peeler blade. A nonswivel peeler is best.
3. Immediately rub the peeled apple with a lemon half to keep it from turning dark.

To Section and Slice Apples

1. Cut peeled apples in half from top to bottom.
2. Cut each half into two or more wedges. Cut the core out of the center of each wedge.
3. To slice, slice the halves or wedges across. (Apple slices can be tossed with lemon juice to keep them from darkening. But never soak apples in lemon water—as you would for artichokes—it will leach out all their sweetness and make them taste almost like cucumbers.)

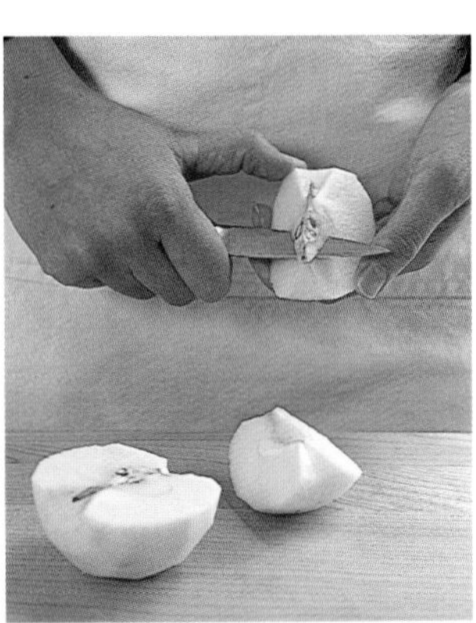

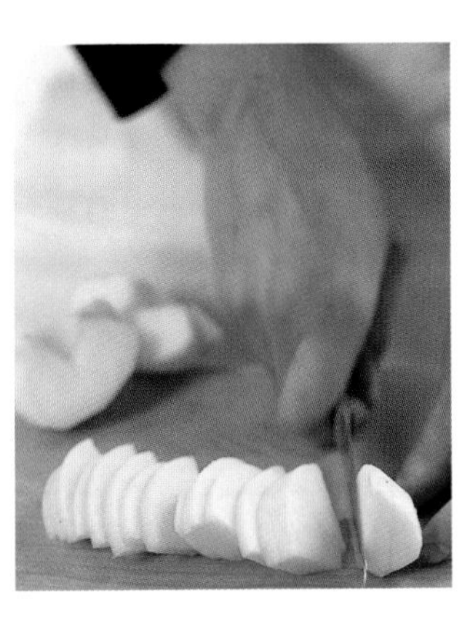

Preparing Citrus Fruits

An orange and a lemon are shown here, but these techniques work for all citrus fruits.

To Peel Oranges Without Leaving Any Membrane

1. Cut the ends off a seedless orange just far enough to expose the flesh.
2. Place the orange on a cutting board and carefully cut away the peel with a paring knife. Remove as little flesh with the peel as possible by following the orange's shape.

To Slice Peeled Oranges

Slice the peeled orange into rounds.

To Cut Peeled Oranges into Sections

1. Use a paring knife to cut along the inside of the membranes that separate the wedges. Slice only down to the center of the orange.
2. Continue cutting along both sides of each membrane, working over a bowl to catch the juices and letting the sections fall into the bowl.
3. Squeeze the membranes to extract all the juice.

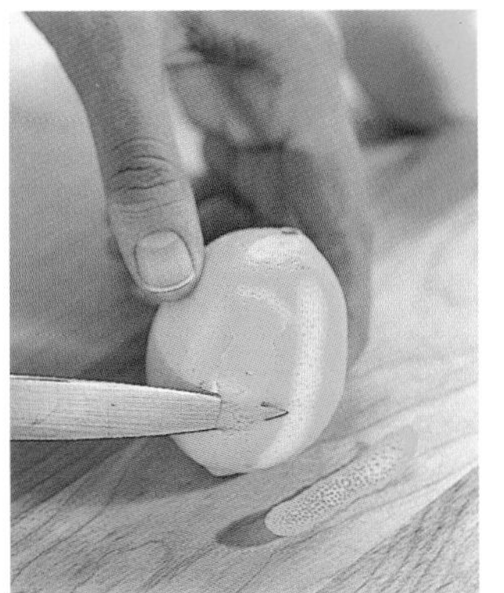

To Julienne Lemon Zest

1. The easiest way to julienne lemon zest is with a zester, which removes the zest in tiny strips.
2. If you don't have a zester, carefully slice the zest off in strips with a paring knife or a peeler. If some white pith is left on the inside of the zests, trim it off.
3. Cut the strips of zest into very fine julienne.

Preparing Stone Fruits

To Pit Cherries

Most cooks have a favorite method for pitting cherries. Instead of using a cherry pitter, which takes a lot of the cherry flesh with it, push the pit out with a chopstick.

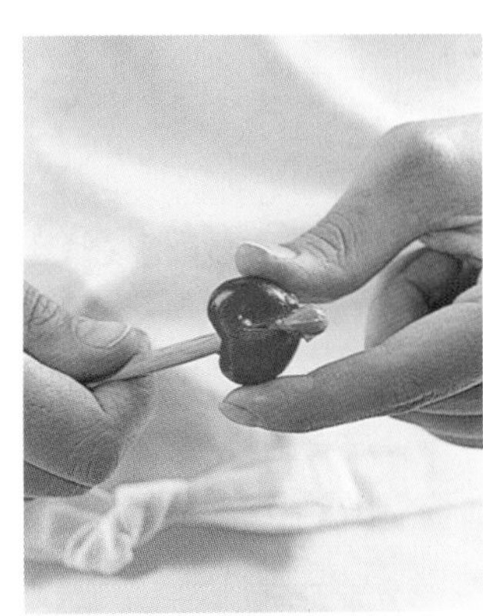

To Pit Apricots

1. Cut all the way around the apricot, going down to the pit, with a small paring knife.
2. Pull the 2 halves apart with your fingers and remove the pit.

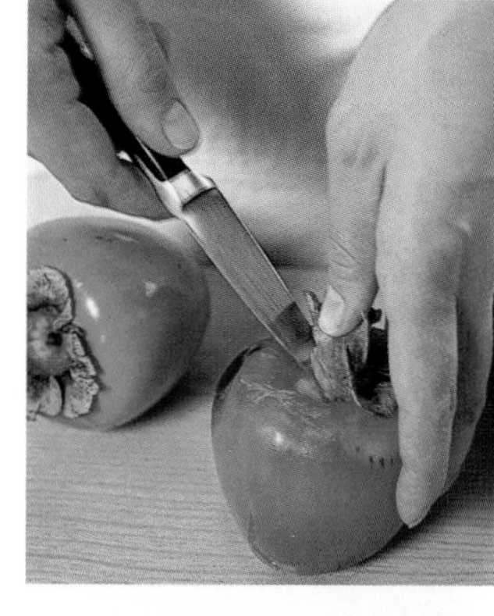

Preparing Exotic Fruits

To protect their soft flesh, kiwis and persimmons are peeled using a spoon.

To Peel and Slice Kiwis

1. Cut the ends off the kiwi with a sharp paring knife.
2. Slide a soupspoon just under the skin and twist it around, scraping against the inside of the peel while not cutting into the flesh. Slide the spoon all the way through to the other end of the kiwi, completely detaching it from the skin.
3. Slide the kiwi out of the skin.
4. Slice peeled kiwis into rounds.
5. Or cut lengthwise into wedges. If the center core of the fruit is hard, trim it out of each wedge.

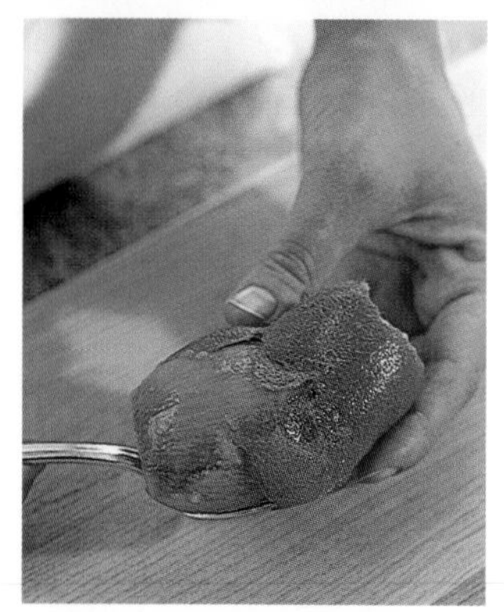

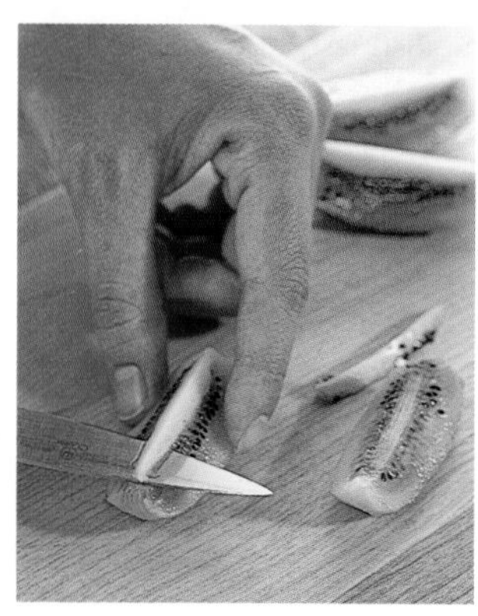

To Prepare Persimmons

The persimmons should have the texture of overripe tomatoes.

1. Cut the stem end out of the persimmons.
2. Cut the persimmons in half.
3. Scoop out the flesh with a spoon.

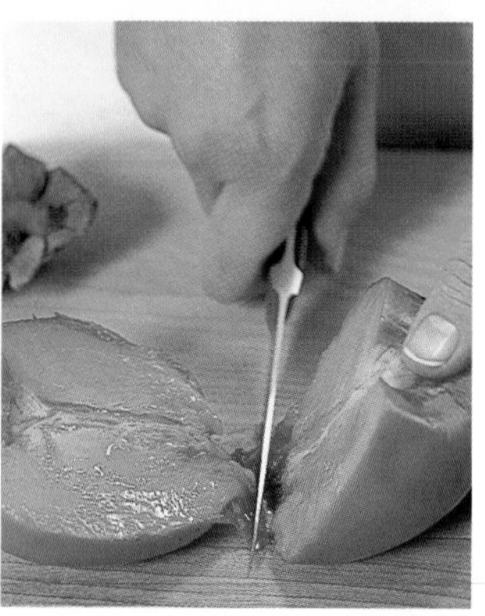

To Peel and Section Pineapple

1. Twist off the leafy top and discard.
2. Cut off both ends, exposing the flesh. Stand the pineapple on a cutting board. (Make sure the cutting board is very clean—pineapples like to absorb other flavors.)
3. Slice all around, cutting deep enough to eliminate the small brown pits. (Or don't slice as deep, and then cut the pits out one by one with a paring knife. This saves pineapple but takes time.)
4. Cut the pineapple lengthwise into quarters or sixths, cutting through the center core.
5. Cut the core off each quarter or sixth and discard.
6. Slice the pineapple into wedges.

To Pit and Peel Mangoes

1. Cut the mango in half, starting from one of the more pointed sides of the mango. (Mangoes have a large flat pit, which you want to approach from the side.) With the knife, skirt along the pit, slicing around it and halving the mango.
2. Slide the knife under the pit and cut it away from the mango.
3. Make a series of slices lengthwise and then crosswise in the mango flesh to form a crosshatch pattern. Be careful not to cut through the skin—the mango will not only be harder to peel, but you might cut your hand.
4. Turn each mango half inside out and spoon out the cubes of mango flesh.

To Trim Strawberries

Don't just cut the stems off—you'll waste strawberry. Instead, cut the stems out by rotating a paring knife around the top of the strawberry, leaving a small cone-shaped indentation. (Always rinse strawberries before hulling, not afterward, or they'll get waterlogged.)

HOW TO

Take the Meat out of a Coconut

When buying a coconut, hold it up to your ear and give it a shake. You should hear liquid sloshing around inside.

To Take Out the Meat

1. Twist a Phillips head screwdriver into 2 of the indentations (the eyes) at one end of the coconut. If you have difficulty, pound the screwdriver into the holes with a hammer. Drain off the coconut juice. It makes a delightful sweet drink but is not the same as coconut milk.
2. Bake the coconut in a 350°F oven for 20 minutes to make the flesh pull away from the shell. Wrap the coconut in a towel, place it on a hard surface, and crack open with a hammer.
3. Pull the coconut apart. Use a regular screwdriver to snap the white interior away from the hard outer shell.
4. Peel off the brown skin with a vegetable peeler.

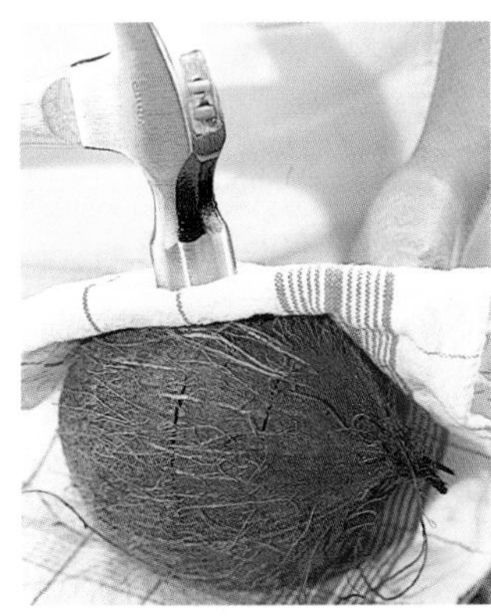

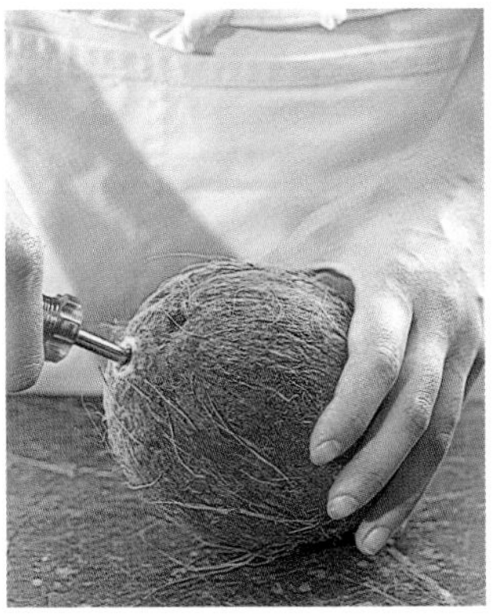

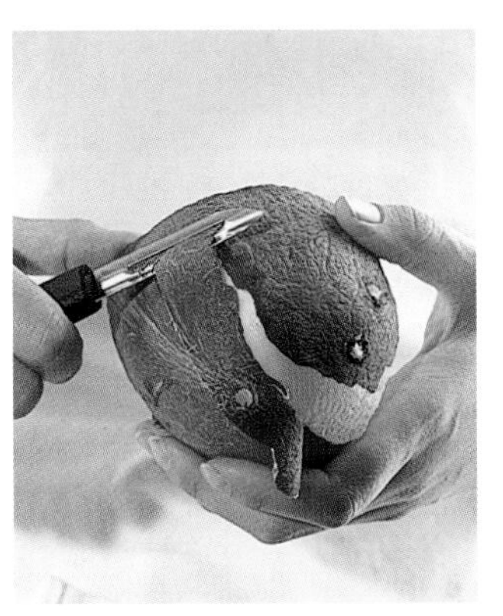

To Grate Coconut and Make Coconut Milk

Many cooks confuse coconut milk with the liquid found inside a coconut. Coconut milk is made by infusing grated coconut with boiling water and then straining the mixture.

1. Grate the peeled coconut meat by hand or in a food processor and place it in a bowl.
2. Pour over enough boiling water to barely cover the grated coconut.
3. Let the coconut milk sit for 15 minutes, then strain through a fine-mesh strainer, pressing down on the coconut with a ladle to extract as much of the coconut milk as possible. Then pour more boiling water over the used coconut and repeat the process, to get a second pressing from the coconut.

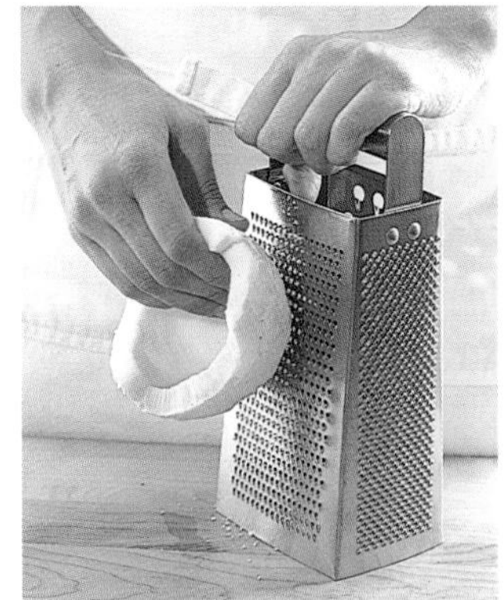

HOW TO

Make a Chicken Broth

Broths, also called stocks, are essential to many dishes. A great number of soups and sauces are based on broths. Stews, sautés, and daubes are moistened with broth. Traditional French restaurant kitchens have veal, chicken, and beef broths on hand, but I simplify things by using white chicken stock for light-colored and delicately flavored preparations, and brown chicken stock for darker, more robust dishes.

White chicken broth is made with raw vegetables and chicken and has a light color and flavor. It's used in pale soups and other light-colored or delicate-tasting dishes, such as white chicken fricassée and veal blanquette. Brown chicken broth is made with bones and vegetables that are browned in a roasting pan in the oven before the water is added. Because of this preliminary caramelization, brown broth has a richer flavor and darker color than white broth. Brown chicken broth is used in brown chicken fricassées, such as coq au vin, and in daubes, stews, and pot roasts.

White Chicken Broth

1. Combine chicken parts with aromatic vegetables and a bouquet garni. Add cold water to cover.
2. Bring to a gentle simmer for 3 to 4 hours, skimming off fat and scum from time to time.
3. Strain, allow to cool, and refrigerate.

Brown Chicken Broth

1. Spread chicken carcasses or parts and aromatic vegetables in a sturdy roasting pan.
2. Roast at 400°F until the parts are well browned, the juices caramelize on the bottom of the pan, and the fat is clear and floats. Transfer the chicken to a pot. Spoon off and discard fat.
3. Set the roasting pan on the stove, pour in water or broth, and deglaze the caramelized juices by scraping the bottom of the pan with a wooden spoon until all the juices have dissolved.
4. Pour the deglazed juices over the chicken parts. Add additional broth or water to cover. Simmer gently and skim off any froth or fat that floats to the top. Make a bouquet garni and nestle it in the broth.
5. Simmer for 3 to 4 hours, skimming off fat and scum every 30 minutes. Strain the broth and cool. Chill the broth overnight in the refrigerator. Scrape any congealed fat off the top of the broth with a large spoon.

Kitchen Notes and Tips

- Use chicken carcasses or cut-up whole chickens for broth, or, if easier to find (or less expensive), chicken wings and drumsticks.
- Count on about 2 cups of water per pound of solids. The water should barely cover the meat or bones—too much liquid makes the broth weak.
- Flavor broths with carrots, onion, celery, and, if you like, fennel branches, roughly cut into large chunks.
- Broths are degreased by skimming with a ladle while they simmer and then again, once they are chilled, by scraping off the fat that congeals on the top of the broth.
- A duck broth is prepared just like a brown chicken broth; for a particularly flavorful duck stock, moisten the bones with white or brown chicken broth.
- Don't ever put hot broth in the refrigerator or freezer: The heat of the broth will raise the temperature of the unit and compromise the other foods in it. Let broths cool at room temperature for an hour or two before refrigerating. If you're freezing the broth, chill in the refrigerator for several hours before moving it to the freezer.
- If you're preparing more than a couple of gallons of broth at once (more common in a restaurant than a home kitchen) or if your kitchen is especially hot, chill the finished stock in its container in a bowl of ice water to cool it quickly before refrigerating. If you're dealing with a very large pot of stock, it's often easier to float a container of ice in the broth to cool it. Just make sure the outside of the container of ice is perfectly clean.
- Broths can be stored for up to 5 days in the refrigerator and almost indefinitely in the freezer.
- If your broth has been in the refrigerator for 5 days, bring it back to the boil and then let it cool as described above. It will keep in the refrigerator for another 5 days. You can repeat this indefinitely.

To Make a Bouquet Garni

A bouquet garni is a bundle or packet of herbs that is added to broths, stews, and soups to give them a subtle herbal flavor and aroma. A classic French bouquet garni contains parsley (it's more economical to use just stems if you can use the leaves for something else), thyme, and bay leaves, but in different regions—and in different countries—other herbs are sometimes used. In the south of France, for example, flavorful ingredients such as dried orange peel are sometimes included. Most American cookbooks suggest tying the herbs in a packet of cheesecloth. This is useful when you're using dried herbs off the stem, but if your herbs—dried or fresh—are still on the stem, it's far easier just to tie the herbs together with string. Remember, also, that the size of a bouquet garni is determined by the amount of liquid it will be simmered in—from a bunch the thickness of your thumb for a small amount of sauce to a bunch the size of your forearm for a large stockpot full of broth. The bunch shown here is appropriate for a small pot.

See Also

To make a creamy veal stew, page 212

To make a stew without browning, page 210

Related Glossary Entries

Aromatic Vegetables
Broth
Caramelize
Deglaze
Degrease
Emulsion
Fricassée
Roast

HOW TO

Make a Fish Broth

A classic fish broth is made by gently simmering fish heads and bones in white wine and water with onions and a bouquet garni. Like other broths, fish broths can be made with uncooked bones for a light-colored and -flavored effect, or with bones that are first browned for a richer flavor. Lean nonoily fish such as flatfish, sea bass, striped bass, and snapper make good all-purpose white fish broths for use in sauces, braised fish dishes, and paellas. For a full-bodied brown fish broth such as the one used for bouillabaisse, brown the bones and vegetables before adding water so that their juices caramelize to give the broth a deep, rich flavor.

A red-wine fish broth such as the one used to make Snapper Baked with a Red-Wine Fish Broth is made with the browned bones of an oilier fish, salmon, which has too strong a flavor for a classic broth. This broth is made with red wine instead of water and white wine. Carrots add flavor and sweetness to red-wine fish broth but are rarely used in a classic white fish broth.

Kitchen Notes and Tips

- Count on about 2 cups of water per pound of bones. The water should just barely cover the bones—too much liquid will make the broth weak. When making a brown fish stock, you'll need slightly less liquid, because the bones will have fallen apart and will take up less room.
- Soak fish bones in cold water to get rid of any traces of blood, which would discolor the stock. Cut out the gills for the same reason.
- Snap the backbones in one or two places to break them up before cooking. This releases the gelatin in the bones (gelatin gives the broth body) and makes the bones more compact so that you can use less water. Leave heads whole; it's almost impossible to break them up, and they'll fall apart as they cook.
- Because fish broth cooks for less time than chicken broth, the onions must be cut smaller so they release their flavor; chop or slice them.
- Fish broth cooks for much less time than poultry or meat broths—20 to 30 minutes is sufficient—because the bones break down and release their gelatin quickly. Don't cook longer than necessary, or the broth will taste fishy.

Fish Broth

A classic fish broth is made by simmering the bones and heads—called "frames" by professionals—from filleted fish with sliced onions, a bouquet garni, a little white wine, and water. Fish broth should not be simmered for more than 30 minutes, or it will develop too strong a flavor.

1. Remove any guts from the fish's rib cage. (Some cooks gut fish before filleting, in which case the frames will not contain any, but it's easier to fillet the fish before gutting and then remove the guts from the frames, as shown here.)
2. Remove the gills.
3. Snap the fish's spine in a couple of places by bending it. Soak the fish bones and heads in cold water for a couple of hours. Leave the bowl in the refrigerator—or add ice— and change the water every 30 minutes.
4. Combine the drained fish heads and bones in a pot with a bouquet garni, sliced onion, and enough water to barely cover. Pour in a small amount of wine. Simmer for 20 to 30 minutes. Strain.

Concentrated Red-Wine Fish Broth

This broth is cooked down—reduced—almost to the consistency of a glaze and is used as a cooking liquid for braised fish and as a base for red-wine fish sauces. Add chopped parsley and whisk butter into concentrated red-wine fish broth to make an excellent sauce for salmon and other full-flavored fish.

1. Cut the gills out of the salmon head with heavy shears and discard.
2. Sweat onions and carrots in a heavy-bottomed pot.
3. Add the salmon head and bones and cook over medium heat, stirring occasionally, until the bones and head fall apart, about 15 minutes.
4. Continue cooking until a layer of caramelized juices forms on the bottom of the pot and the fat renders and separates. (The rendered fat can be poured off at this point, or it can be skimmed off later, after the wine has been added.)
5. Add a bouquet garni and enough full-bodied red wine to completely cover the head and bones.
6. Simmer gently for about 30 minutes. Skim off and discard any fat and scum on top.
7. Strain the broth into a saucepan and slowly reduce, skimming off any fat and scum, until lightly syrupy.

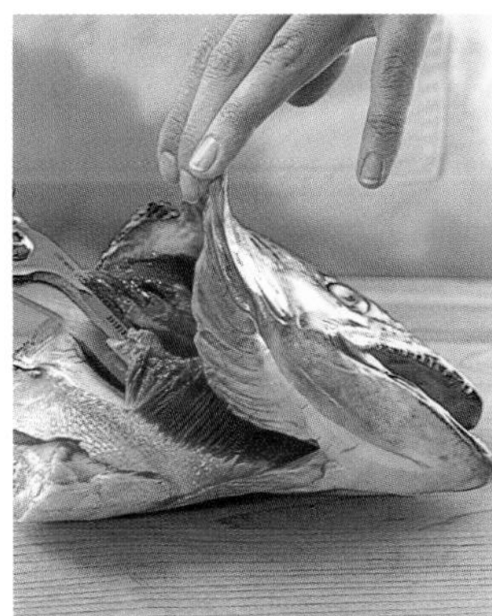

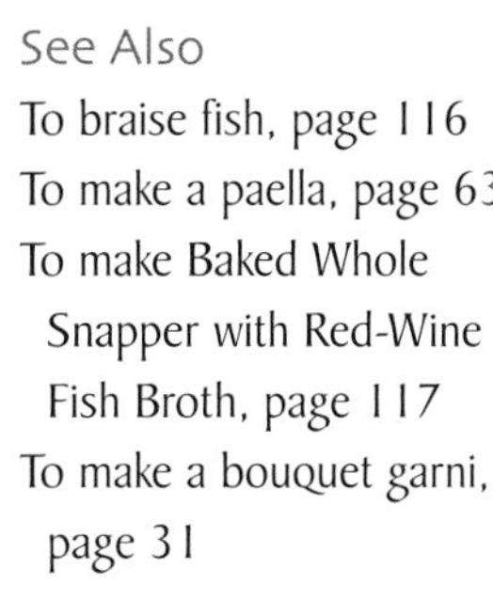

See Also
To braise fish, page 116
To make a paella, page 63
To make Baked Whole Snapper with Red-Wine Fish Broth, page 117
To make a bouquet garni, page 31
To make a chicken broth, page 30 (see also for general chilling and storage instructions for broths)
To make dashi, page 143

Related Glossary Entries
Broth
Monter au Beurre
Sweat

HOW TO

Make a Crustacean Broth

The shells and heads from crustaceans such as crab, lobster, crayfish, and shrimp can be used to make a flavorful crustacean broth. Crustacean broth is useful as a base for soups and sauces (see Box, page 139) and for cooking rice dishes such as risotto and paella. Usually crustacean broths are made with tomatoes because the tomatoes enhance the color of the broth and their flavor is a natural match. Herbs, usually in the form of a bouquet garni, are also added to crustacean broths, but tarragon—either chopped and added at the end or included in the bouquet garni—is especially delicious. If you're using crayfish or shrimp heads or lobster or crab shells, grind up the heads in a food processor—or crush them with the end of a European-style rolling pin, as shown here—so that all their flavor goes into the surrounding liquid. Don't put claw shells or thick crab shells into a food processor or you'll damage the blade. Since most shrimp come with their heads already removed, you may have to use just the shells from the tails. Freeze the shells in a plastic bag until you have enough for at least a small pot of broth.

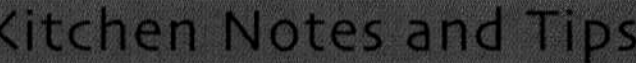

Kitchen Notes and Tips

- Crustacean shells and heads must be well broken up so the surrounding liquid extracts their flavor. They can be broken up with the end of a European-style rolling pin (the kind without handles), the end of a cleaver held up on end, or in a food processor. Hard shells, such as lobster crab, and crayfish claws, however, will damage the food processor blade and should be broken up by hand. Thin delicate shells, such as shrimp tail peelings, require no breaking up, but the shrimp heads, if you have them, do.
- Crustacean shells can be saved for up to 2 months, tightly wrapped in plastic wrap in the freezer, to accumulate enough to make a batch of broth.
- For rich soups or sauces, cream and butter can be used to extract flavor and color from crustacean shells (see Box, page 139).
- Crustacean broth has an affinity for tarragon, tomatoes, saffron, and cognac, all of which can be used to flavor sauces, soups, and rice dishes.

Shrimp Broth

Shells and heads from crustaceans such as crabs, shrimp, crayfish, and lobster make full-flavored broths that can be used in paella (the shelled shrimp are then cooked in the paella) or soup (a bisque is shellfish broth thickened with rice) or reduced for sauces.

1. Put shrimp shells and heads in a heavy-bottomed saucepan with chopped aromatic vegetables.
2. Crush shrimp heads and shells with the end of a European-style (the kind with no handles) rolling pin or the end of a cleaver held up on one end.
3. Add coarsely chopped tomatoes, a bouquet garni, and enough water to cover and simmer for about 45 minutes. Strain.

See Also

To make a bouquet garni, page 31

To make risotto and paella, pages 63 and 65

To make a crayfish sauce, page 141

Related Glossary Entries

Aromatic Vegetables

Broth

HOW TO

Make a Green Salad

When choosing greens for salads, you can't go wrong by combining lettuces within three basic categories: Mild-flavored greens such as Boston, romaine, red lettuce, Bibb, and oak leaf taste good together in simple, all-purpose salads, and the flavor of no one lettuce overpowers the others. Bitter, more assertive tasting winter lettuces such as endive, curly endive (frisée), dandelion, radicchio, and watercress complement each other and are particularly good as a base for savory elements such as bacon or grilled or smoked fish or meat, or when you're dressing the salad with a hot vinaigrette. In season, put together a spicy, summer herbal mix of greens based on a mixture of arugula and basil, augmented with other herbs and wild greens. (You can mix between the categories, of course: I offer them as a guide.)

A simple mixture of good-quality wine vinegar and extra virgin olive oil makes the best and simplest sauce for a green salad; there's no need to bother with whisking together a vinaigrette. Dissolve the salt in the vinegar before adding it to the greens so that the salad isn't crunchy with the salt.

Green Salad

1. Soak the salad greens for a few minutes in a bowl of cold water. Gently lift them out of the water with splayed fingers. Repeat as needed, changing the water each time, until there's no grit left in the bottom of the bowl.
2. Gently spin the greens dry in a lettuce spinner.
3. Immediately before serving, drizzle the salad greens with extra virgin olive oil.
4. Put a pinch of salt in one of the spoons you're using for tossing the salad.
5. Pour vinegar into the spoon.
6. Stir the salt around in the vinegar for a few seconds to dissolve it. Drizzle over the salad, grind over fresh pepper, and toss.

Kitchen Notes and Tips

- Wash greens carefully, but never under running water—the force of the water will damage the leaves. Instead, place the leaves in a bowl filled with cold water and very gently move them around in the bowl. Let soak for a few minutes, then gently lift out the greens, leaving the dirt and grit behind, and transfer them to another bowl. Change the water in the first bowl and keep washing the greens until there's no sand or grit left in the bottom of the bowl. Usually two washings is enough, but very sandy or gritty greens may require three.
- There are a number of tricks and gadgets for drying lettuce. Very delicate greens are best gently patted dry between two cloth towels, but for all other greens, a lettuce spinner will do the trick in much less time. Put the greens in the spinner and spin gently. When the lettuce stops spinning, remove the lid, give the leaves a gentle toss to redistribute them, and spin again. Make sure the lettuce is very dry; any moisture clinging to the leaves will dilute the dressing and make the salad taste watery.
- If you want to get organized early in the day, rinse and dry the lettuces and store them in the refrigerator wrapped in a damp towel. If storing for a longer period, wrap the greens in the damp towel and enclose that in a plastic bag.
- Dress the greens at the last minute; the lettuce will wilt quickly once it comes in contact with acidic ingredients such as vinegar or lemon.

To Stem Watercress and Other Greens and Herbs for Salad

Don't waste time removing tiny edible stems from bunches of greens and herbs such as watercress, parsley, and cilantro. Just cut the stems off at the base as shown here.

Cut the stems off about halfway up the bunch, leaving the leaves with the small edible stems attached.

To Seed Tomatoes for Salad

Cut the tomatoes in half vertically first.

1. Cut each tomato half into as many wedges as you like.
2. Run your thumb along both sides of each wedge, pushing the seeds out into a bowl.

Vinaigrette

1. Combine mustard and vinegar in a bowl, and whisk together until smooth.
2. Slowly work in the oil. Extra virgin olive oil is shown here, although the delicacy of finer oils is obscured by the mustard.

HOW TO

Make a Vinaigrette

A vinaigrette is a combination of oil and vinegar that is usually held together—emulsified—with mustard. Making a vinaigrette is much like making a mayonnaise, except that a vinaigrette contains no egg yolks. In fact, most of the time, when you make salads, it isn't necessary to make a vinaigrette—the oil, vinegar, and seasoning can just be tossed with the greens. We generally think of a vinaigrette as a cold sauce for salads, but vinaigrettes, both cold and hot, make excellent sauces for meats, seafood, and vegetables.

Kitchen Notes and Tips

- The type of vinegar and oil you choose depends on your taste. I use extra virgin olive oil for most vinaigrettes, but sometimes a tasteless oil, such as canola, is better for delicately flavored ingredients like carrots, the flavor of which might be overwhelmed by olive oil. Conversely, I sometimes use nut oils to sauce endive, curly chicory (frisée), cabbage, and beets.
- Standard proportions for a vinaigrette are 1 part vinegar (or other acid, such as lemon juice) to 3 to 4 parts oil. It's important to taste as you go, because vinaigrettes are more or less acidic depending on what acid you choose. For example, balsamic vinegar is somewhat sweet, so you'll probably want to use 1 part vinegar to 3 parts oil. Lemon juice, on the other hand, is very acidic, so you'll probably need more oil. The goal is a tangy, but not biting, taste.
- If using mustard in the vinaigrette, start with about half as much mustard as vinegar. Mustardy vinaigrettes are delicious with bitter or strong-flavored ingredients, such as chilled cooked beets or leeks.
- When making a hot vinaigrette, the proportions of oil to vinegar will change, depending on how much you reduce the vinegar; swirl in oil to taste.

Hot Vinaigrette

A hot vinaigrette is based on the same principle as a pan sauce, but olive oil is used instead of butter. The oil won't emulsify into the pan deglazing liquid as butter would. Butter emulsifies easily because it is itself an emulsion of fat and water, but olive oil isn't an emulsion and so remains separate from the liquid. Various hot vinaigrettes can be improvised by substituting infused oils for plain extra virgin olive oil.

1. Deglaze a sauté pan with good-quality wine vinegar.
2. Swirl in a small amount of extra virgin olive oil to finish the sauce. Spoon over sautéed foods such as the piece of red snapper, shown here.

See Also

To make an unemulsified dressing for a green salad, page 35

To make a mayonnaise, page 41

To make infused oils, page 39

Related Glossary Entry

Emulsion

Monter au Beurre

Homemade Wine Vinegar

Because commercial wine vinegars are often of very poor quality or very expensive, it's worthwhile to make your own. Buy a small barrel, like the one shown here of American white oak, from a store specializing in wine- and beer-making supplies. Combine vinegar mother (vinegar that contains the active bacteria that convert alcohol to acetic acid, also available from wine- or beer-making suppliers), or someone else's homemade vinegar, with a small amount of wine and leave the mixture in a warm place. Every few days, for several weeks, add 1 to 2 cups of wine to the barrel, until the barrel is almost, but not completely, full. (If you fill the barrel, the vinegar-making bacteria won't get enough oxygen.) Keep the hole in the top of the barrel clogged with a small piece of cheesecloth, which allows oxygen in but keeps out dust and small bugs. Drain the vinegar off into bottles, a few cups at a time, as you need it and replace with additional wine.

HOW TO

Make Infused Oils

Olive and vegetable oils can be infused with herbs, spices, or other aromatic ingredients (except garlic, which will spoil) to give them a distinctive flavor and color. The simplest way to make infused oils is just to stick whole herbs on the stem into a bottle of oil and let it stand for a couple of weeks, until the oil takes on the taste of the herb. Chopping or puréeing the herb, or heating the oil, speeds up the process so that the oil can be used sooner. Gently heating the oil, as for dried mushroom oil, helps to extract maximum flavor from the ingredient. Heat woody herbs such as thyme, rosemary, and marjoram without losing flavor, but the flavor of fragile herbs such as basil and parsley (any herb that doesn't dehydrate well) is destroyed by heating.

Infused oils can be used in any sauce in which you'd use a plain vegetable or olive oil (such as vinaigrettes or mayonnaises), or as flavorings or sauces in themselves, drizzled over foods (see Grilled Scallions, page 84) instead of a sauce. Infused oils can also be used for gentle sautéing, as for breaded foods, when the heat isn't so high that it would destroy the flavor of the oil.

Basil Oil

1. Combine washed and dried basil leaves in a food processor with just enough extra virgin olive oil to get the mixture to turn around.
2. Purée the mixture for about 2 minutes, scraping down the sides of the processor bowl with a rubber spatula every 20 seconds or so. Transfer to a bowl.
3. Add additional extra virgin olive oil to cover the puréed basil leaves generously. Cover the bowl with plastic wrap and let infuse overnight at room temperature.
4. Strain the oil through a fine-mesh sieve or a strainer lined with a triple layer of cheesecloth.
5. Transfer to glass bottles. Store at room temperature up to a month.

Dried Porcini Mushroom Oil

1. Grind dried porcini mushrooms to a powder in a blender. (If the mushrooms feel at all moist or flexible, dry them out in a low oven before grinding.)
2. Transfer the powdered mushrooms to a heavy-bottomed saucepan.
3. Pour over enough extra virgin olive oil or flavorless vegetable oil to cover generously.
4. Heat gently over low heat, stirring occasionally, for 30 minutes; maintain the oil at about the temperature of a very hot bath—not so hot that you can't stick your finger into it for a second or two. Higher temperatures will destroy the flavor of the mushrooms.
5. Strain through a fine-mesh strainer and transfer to glass bottles.

HOW TO

Make a Mayonnaise

Homemade mayonnaise is a revelation to anyone who has only ever eaten mayonnaise out of a jar. It has real flavor, with hints of mustard and lemon, as opposed to the insipid taste of the jarred version. You can adjust the consistency of homemade mayonnaise depending on what you're using it for. Stiff mayonnaise is good for serving with artichokes and deep-fried and grilled foods, while a looser mayonnaise can be used as a sauce for seafood or hot or cold cooked vegetables.

The process of making mayonnaise is very much like making a vinaigrette, except that the oil is emulsified into an egg yolk–mustard mixture instead of just mustard. The mustard is stirred into the yolk to promote the emulsion, along with a little lemon juice or vinegar for flavor. Tasteless vegetable oils such as canola or safflower oil are used to make all-purpose mayonnaises. Olive oil, or even nut oils, can be used to make more distinctively flavored mayonnaises. Most mayonnaises can be made in a blender, food processor, or by hand, but mayonnaise made with extra virgin olive oil should be always made by hand, using a wooden spoon or mortar with a pestle as when making aïoli (page 43), because the aggressive action of a blender or food processor, or even a whisk, compromises the flavor of the oil and turns it slightly bitter.

If you are concerned about using raw egg yolks, cook them into a sabayon as though you are making a hollandaise sauce and whisk in oil instead of butter.

Basic Mayonnaise (Hand Method)

1. Combine the egg yolks, mustard, and lemon juice or vinegar in a small bowl and whisk until smooth.
2. Start by adding only a teaspoon of oil at a time, pouring it carefully down the side of the bowl and whisking it into the egg yolk mixture a little bit at a time.
3. When the mayonnaise stiffens slightly, you can add the oil more quickly—about a tablespoon at a time.
4. Continue adding oil until the mayonnaise is stiff. If the mayonnaise becomes too stiff to work, add a little more lemon juice, vinegar, or water to loosen it.

Basic Mayonnaise (Blender Method)

1. Combine the egg yolks, mustard, and lemon juice in a blender.

2. With the blender on the lowest speed, pour the oil in a slow but steady stream through the opening in the top of the blender, blending until the mayonnaise stiffens. Season to taste with salt and pepper.

Kitchen Notes and Tips

- Standard proportions for mayonnaise are 1 egg yolk to ½ to ¾ cup oil, 1 teaspoon mustard, and 1 teaspoon lemon juice, or to taste.
- For a looser consistency, thin mayonnaise with water, lemon juice, vinegar or broth.
- Mayonnaise may break—that is, the oil will separate out of the emulsion and the mayonnaise will turn loose and grainy—if the oil is added too fast, especially at the beginning, or if the mayonnaise gets too stiff. If the mayonnaise gets stiff before all the oil is added, add a little water, lemon juice, vinegar, or broth. If mayonnaise does break, it's easy to fix: Just rework the broken mayonnaise into another egg yolk in a second bowl. (If the mayonnaise seemed very stiff before it broke, add a little water before working it into the new yolk).
- Plain mayonnaise can be flavored to create innumerable variations: for example, *sauce andalouse* is mayonnaise flavored with tomatoes and bell peppers; *sauce chantilly* is a mayonnaise into which whipped cream has been folded; *sauce rémoulade* is flavored with herbs and capers; *sauce suédoise* is made sweet and spicy with apples and horseradish; and the gribiche variation shown opposite is flavored with small French sour pickles (cornichons), capers, and finely chopped herbs.
- *Aïoli* is a particularly delicious mayonnaise, made with extra virgin olive oil and flavored with garlic. Because the oil may turn bitter with the rapid action of a whisk, blender, or food processor, aïoli should be worked gently with a wooden spoon or, as shown opposite, in a mortar with a pestle. A mortar and pestle is practical because it allows you to crush the garlic into a paste before adding the other ingredients.
- Color mayonnaise orange with saffron, red with beet juice, and green with chlorophyll (see page 52).

Green Mayonnaise

Add chlorophyll to the mayonnaise and purée until smooth and well blended.

Gribiche Sauce

Stir chopped capers, pickles, parsley, chervil, and tarragon into plain mayonnaise (if you don't have all the herbs, just leave out those you don't have).

See Also

To make a hollandaise sauce, page 44
To extract chlorophyll, page 52
To make a vinaigrette, page 37
To crush garlic to a paste, page 11

Related Glossary Entry

Emulsion

Aïoli

Aïoli (garlic mayonnaise) is a delicious accompaniment to cold or hot grilled vegetables, steamed or boiled artichokes, boiled potatoes, and grilled or baked fish and shellfish. It can be combined with seafood poaching liquid by whisking the hot liquid into a small amount of the aïoli in a bowl, then served around the seafood as a light sauce. Aïoli is also excellent flavored with saffron.

1. Put sliced garlic cloves in a mortar along with a pinch of coarse salt. (The salt helps grind the garlic.) Work to a paste with the pestle. (If you don't have a mortar and pestle, use the side of a chef's knife.)
2. Add the egg yolks and lemon juice or vinegar and work until smooth.
3. Work extra virgin olive oil into the egg yolks a teaspoon at a time. As the aïoli begins to thicken, add the oil more quickly.

Saffron and Garlic Mayonnaise

Soak saffron threads in a teaspoon or two of water for 30 minutes. Stir the saffron and soaking liquid into the aïoli.

HOW TO

Make a Hollandaise Sauce

Hollandaise is a light, airy sauce made by whisking butter and lemon into an emulsion of egg yolks and water. The principles for making hollandaise (and its derivatives, such as béarnaise sauce) are almost the same as for mayonnaise, except that the egg yolk emulsion for a hollandaise is hot, and butter is used rather than oil. A classic hollandaise sauce is made with clarified butter, but whole butter can also be used for a thinner consistency. Clarified butter produces a very thick sauce, almost the consistency of a mayonnaise, because it contains no water. Use clarified butter when the sauce must be thick enough to coat foods like oysters that are to be gratinéed, or to top eggs Benedict, or when the sauce is to be served on top of a steak. Whole butter contains water and so makes a thinner hollandaise. Whole butter can be added as melted butter or whisked into the sauce in chunks, as though you were making a beurre blanc. Use whole-butter hollandaise to sauce seafood and other dishes that are too delicate for a thick sauce.

To make a hollandaise, first make an emulsion of egg yolks and water (professional chefs sometimes call this emulsion a *sabayon*) by beating the egg yolks and water together until frothy, then beating the mixture over heat until barely stiff. Whisk in melted or clarified butter in a constant thin stream (or whisk in chunks of whole butter) until it's all been absorbed by the yolks and the sauce is thick. Once all of the butter has been added, flavor the sauce: A small amount of lemon juice is used to finish a hollandaise, and a strained infusion of tarragon, cracked pepper, shallots, and vinegar flavors a béarnaise, the most famous hollandaise variation.

Hollandaise Sauce

1. Combine 1 tablespoon cold water per egg yolk in a sauce pan with sloping sides (sometimes called a Windsor pan) or in a metal mixing bowl off the heat.
2. Whisk the egg yolks rapidly until frothy, about 45 seconds.
3. Place the pan or bowl over medium heat and continue to whisk rapidly. As you're whisking, the egg yolks will increase in volume. As soon as they start to lose volume slightly and you see streaks on the bottom of the pan, take the pan off the heat.
4. Whisk for about 20 seconds more to cool the pan and keep the yolks from curdling. Whisk in clarified butter, shown here, or whole butter, melted or in chunks.
5. Add lemon juice to taste—about 1 teaspoon for a 4-yolk hollandaise—and season with salt and white pepper.

Kitchen Notes and Tips

- Judging when the egg yolks—the sabayon mixture—are done is the trickiest part of making a hollandaise. As you beat the egg yolks with the water over the heat into a sabayon, they will get very frothy and expand in volume. When the yolks are cooked but before they curdle, the sabayon will stiffen a bit and lose some of its volume. At this point—you may also be able to see the bottom of the pan—immediately remove the sabayon from the heat. Continue whisking for about 20 seconds, so the sabayon isn't overcooked by the heat retained by the pan. If the sabayon does overcook and curdles, it's easy to start over with fresh egg yolks without having wasted any butter.
- Count about 1 tablespoon cold water and 8 tablespoons (1 stick) whole, melted, or clarified butter per egg yolk. A 4-yolk hollandaise will take about 1 teaspoon lemon juice; a 4-yolk béarnaise, 1/2 cup white wine vinegar reduced to 1 to 2 tablespoons.
- The clarified or melted butter should feel hot to the touch but not so hot that it scalds; if the butter is too hot, the sabayon will curdle.
- Make a hollandaise sauce with beurre noisette for a distinctive nutty taste.
- In contrast to mayonnaise, in which the oil must be whisked in drop by drop at the beginning, the hot butter can be whisked into the sabayon in a steady stream, because the sabayon is already emulsified.
- Season a hollandaise with white pepper, so you don't see dark flecks.
- It's easiest to make the sabayon in a special pan with sloping sides, called a Windsor pan, because its shape allows you to reach into every part of the pan with a whisk. If you use a regular saucepan, the egg yolks hide at the edges of the bottom of the pan, are out of reach of the whisk and are likely to curdle. If you don't have a Windsor pan, use a small heatproof bowl—held with a kitchen towel—instead. Don't use a double boiler: It's too hard to control the temperature.

Béarnaise Sauce

1. Combine chopped shallots, sprigs of fresh tarragon, cracked pepper, and white wine vinegar in a small saucepan and place over medium heat.
2. When the mixture has reduced until there are only 1 or 2 tablespoons of liquid left, remove from the heat.
3. Strain the mixture through a fine strainer, pressing against the solids to extract as much liquid as possible.
4. Prepare a hollandaise, as on page 44, and add the strained tarragon infusion to taste in place of the lemon juice. Season with salt only. Some cooks like to finish a béarnaise with chopped fresh tarragon or tarragon butter.

See Also

To make a mayonnaise, page 41
To clarify butter, page 46
To make beurre noisette, page 46
To make tarragon butter, page 47

Related Glossary Entries

Emulsion
Sabayon

HOW TO
Clarify Butter

Because butter contains milk solids (actually, proteins), which burn at relatively low temperatures, it can't be used to sauté at the high temperatures required for browning most meats and seafood and some vegetables. Whole butter also contains water—about 25 percent—that can make certain sauces, such as hollandaise, too thin. To solve both problems, professional cooks often clarify butter, removing the water and milk solids.

Butter can be clarified using one of two methods. The first, used in professional kitchens where large amounts of butter are clarified, consists of melting the butter in a large pot and letting it sit for about half an hour, during which time the water sinks to the bottom and the milk solids float to the top. The milk solids are skimmed off with a ladle and the clarified butter—which is now pure butterfat—is ladled off and saved. This is impractical in home kitchens because it's hard to do with a small amount of butter.

To make a small amount of clarified butter, put two or three sticks of butter in a small heavy-bottomed saucepan. Cook the butter over medium heat for about ten minutes, until the water boils out of the butter and the milk solids turn pale brown, then strain out the milk solids. Not only is butter cooked in this way clarified, but its flavor is enhanced by the caramelized milk solids. Indian cooks call butter clarified this way *ghee*; the French call this butter *beurre noisette* (meaning "hazelnut butter," because of its nutty flavor).

Clarified Butter

1. Melt the butter in a heavy-bottomed saucepan over medium heat.
2. Continue cooking for about 10 minutes, until the froth subsides and the milk solids appear as brown specks on the bottom of the pan.
3. Strain the butter through a strainer lined with a clean kitchen towel, a triple layer of cheesecloth, or a coffee filter.

See Also
To make a hollandaise sauce, page 44

HOW TO
Make a Flavored Butter

A flavored butter, sometimes called a compound butter, is whole butter that has been flavored while cold with herbs or other ingredients such as chopped and cooked mushrooms, chopped truffles, reduced wine, spices, or cooked tomatoes. Small pieces, dollops, or disks of compound butter can be served on top of grilled meats, seafood, or vegetables, in the middle of a bowl of soup, or used to finish hot butter sauces such as beurre blanc. The tarragon butter shown here is rolled into a log to make it easy to store and pretty to serve, but this isn't essential. Logs of herb butters can be wrapped in aluminum foil and frozen for up to a year.

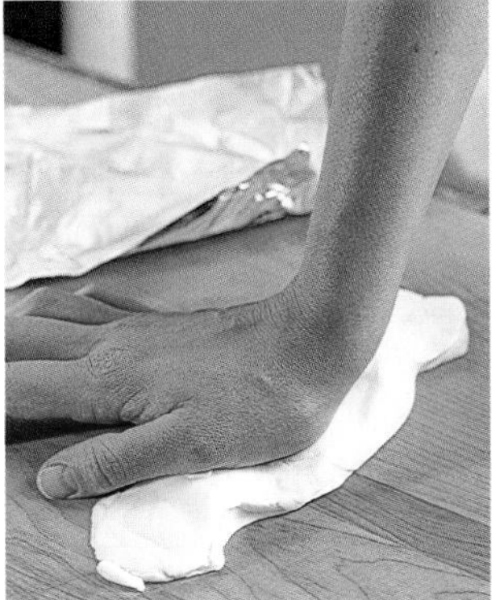

Tarragon Butter

Here, I flavor the butter with tarragon, but herb butters can be made with any fresh herb or combination of herbs.

1. Soften butter by smearing it on a cutting board with the heel of your hand. (Or, to make a lot, work it in a mixer with a paddle blade.)
2. Sprinkle butter with fresh tarragon leaves and begin chopping the tarragon and butter together. (If you're using a mixer, chop the herbs before adding them to butter.)
3. Chop the mixture until the leaves are finely chopped and incorporated into the butter.

See Also
To make a beurre blanc, page 48

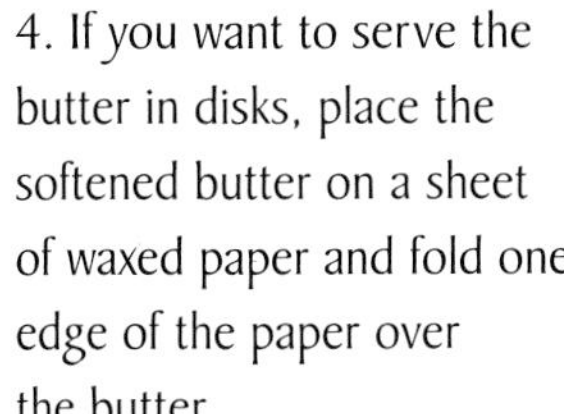

4. If you want to serve the butter in disks, place the softened butter on a sheet of waxed paper and fold one edge of the paper over the butter.
5. Wrap the edge of the paper under the butter and smooth the butter into a log by sliding the fingers of both hands along the waxed paper, then roll the log up in the paper.
6. Twist the ends of the waxed paper in opposite directions to seal. Chill the butter for at least an hour in the refrigerator.
7. Trim the ends off the log with a sharp knife. Remove the waxed paper.
8. Slice the butter into disks.

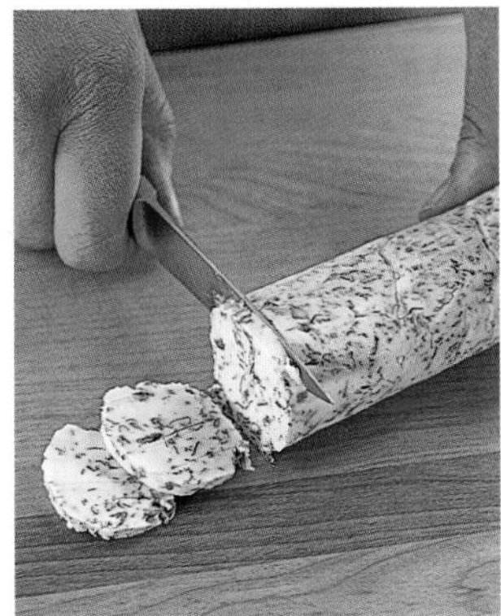

HOW TO

Make a Beurre Blanc

A beurre blanc is a light-textured, creamy, emulsified butter sauce that is made by whisking whole butter into a reduction of white wine, white wine vinegar, and shallots. (Butter itself is already an emulsion of fat and water, held in emulsion by the proteins in the milk solids.) Despite its reputation for being tricky, beurre blanc is quick and easy to make. It also lends itself easily to all kinds of simple variations. Try adding various chopped herbs (or herb butter), curry (cooked first in a little butter), chiles, vegetable purées, and other additions shown on page 49.

Beurre Blanc

1. Combine dry white wine, white wine vinegar, and finely chopped shallots in a heavy-bottomed saucepan. Bring to a simmer over medium heat.
2. When the liquid has reduced to a shiny glaze—so only enough remains in the pan to barely cover the shallots—add 2 tablespoons of heavy cream. Bring to a simmer over medium heat.
3. Add cold butter cut into chunks and turn the heat to high.
4. Whisk continuously until the sauce is smooth and creamy. Don't let the sauce boil, which can cause it to break. Season to taste with salt and white pepper and, if necessary, a few drops of vinegar. If the sauce seems too thick, thin it with a little heavy cream or water. If it tastes acidic, add a bit more butter.

Saffron Beurre Blanc

Soak a pinch of saffron threads in a tablespoon of warm water for 30 minutes and stir the mixture, including the soaking liquid, into beurre blanc.

Tomato and Tarragon Beurre Blanc

1. Whisk a little cooked and strained tomato sauce (coulis) into beurre blanc.
2. Whisk herb butter—tarragon butter is shown here—into the tomato beurre blanc. (Herb butters and other flavored butters can also be whisked into plain beurre blanc.)

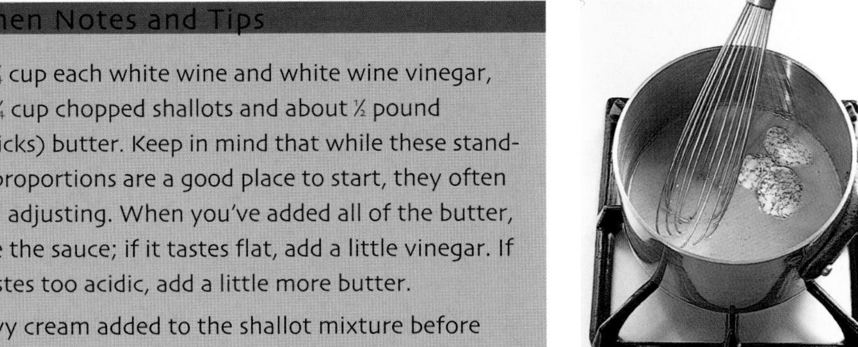

Kitchen Notes and Tips

- For ¼ cup each white wine and white wine vinegar, use ¼ cup chopped shallots and about ½ pound (2 sticks) butter. Keep in mind that while these standard proportions are a good place to start, they often need adjusting. When you've added all of the butter, taste the sauce; if it tastes flat, add a little vinegar. If it tastes too acidic, add a little more butter.
- Heavy cream added to the shallot mixture before adding the butter helps stabilize the sauce.
- Use butter straight from the refrigerator; if the butter isn't chilled, your sauce may have an oily texture.
- The finished sauce should be only slightly thicker than cold heavy cream—no thicker.
- Beurre blanc is fairly stable unless it's boiled, which will break it, or too much butter is added.
- If you have reduced the white wine mixture too much, the sauce may get too thick before you've added all the butter. In that case, add a little water or heavy cream and continue adding the butter.

See Also

To make a flavored butter, page 47

To make tomato coulis, page 50

Related Glossary Entries

Concassée
Coulis
Emulsion
Reduction

HOW TO

Make Tomato Sauce

There are many kinds of tomato sauces, the best known of which is probably bolognese sauce, made by slowly simmering aromatic vegetables, meat, and, of course, tomatoes. Simpler tomato sauces are based on raw or cooked mixtures of chopped tomatoes and tomato purées. Two of the best known are tomato *coulis* and tomato *concassée.* Tomato coulis is made by straining either raw or cooked tomatoes to make a perfectly smooth purée. (Because it is strained, there's no need to peel and seed the tomatoes beforehand.) Tomato concassée, shown here, is made by chopping tomatoes, leaving them raw or cooking them, for a coarse, unstrained sauce. (Because it isn't strained, the tomatoes for a concassée must be peeled and seeded before they are chopped.) Both sauces require flavorful tomatoes.

Raw Tomato Concassée

1. Peel the tomatoes and cut them crosswise in half.
2. Squeeze the seeds out of each half.
3. Slice the seeded halves.
4. Chop the tomatoes to the consistency you like.

Cooked Tomato Concassée

1. Prepare a raw tomato concassée, at left, and put it in a wide pan. Bring to a simmer over high heat, stirring with a wooden spoon.
2. Continue cooking until the moisture released by the tomatoes completely evaporates. Season to taste with salt and pepper.

See Also

To peel tomatoes, page 6

Related Glossary Entries

Concassée
Coulis
Purée (for information on puréeing tomato concassée)

HOW TO

Make Fresh Egg Pasta Dough

Fresh egg pasta dough is made with eggs and flour, but different regions in Italy and different cooks have their own variations—some use egg yolks alone, some add olive oil, others use various combinations of flours. In the recipe below, I use a combination of all-purpose and semolina, or durum, flour. The semolina adds texture and body to the pasta. Pasta can also be made with just all-purpose flour.

To Make Fresh Pasta Dough by Hand

1. Mix the flours together on the work surface with your fingers.
2. Mound the flour and make a well in the center.
3. Place the eggs, any other liquid ingredients called for in the recipe, such as olive oil, and any seasonings in the well of flour.
4. Gradually combine the liquid ingredients with the flour, working the flour into the well with a fork or your fingers.
5. When most of the liquid has been absorbed by the flour, start working the mixture with your hands.
6. Knead the dough until it comes together into a solid mass. It should feel moist and slightly sticky, but it shouldn't stick to your fingers.
7. Continue to knead the dough against the work surface with the heel of your hand.
8. Shape the dough into a ball.

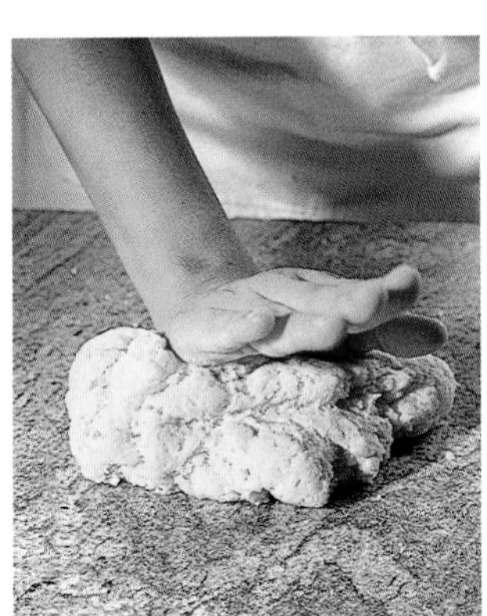

Making Colored Pasta

Fresh pasta can be colored by adding other ingredients along with the eggs. Squid ink—or better, cuttlefish ink—is used for making black pasta; saffron (soaked in a little water for 30 minutes) for orange pasta; beet juice for red pasta; and chlorophyll for green pasta. Of all these, making green pasta is the most elaborate, because it requires extracting the chlorophyll from leafy green plants such as spinach.

TO EXTRACT PURE CHLOROPHYLL FROM LEAFY GREENS

1. Remove the stems from spinach leaves.
2. Push the leaves down into the blender container and add enough cold water to come about halfway up the leaves. Purée for about a minute, until you obtain a green "soup."
3. Strain the green purée through a fine-mesh strainer, working it gently with the back of a ladle, into a small heavy-bottomed saucepan. Discard what doesn't go through the strainer.
4. Heat the purée over medium heat until you see green clumps floating in clear liquid. Immediately drain in a fine-mesh strainer. Be gentle—don't be tempted to push down on the chlorophyll with a ladle. Save the green paste that collects in the strainer.

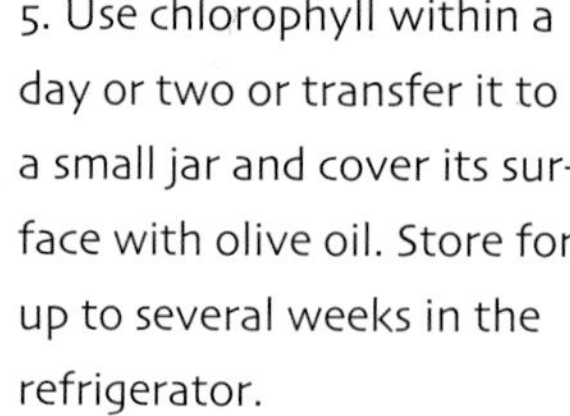

5. Use chlorophyll within a day or two or transfer it to a small jar and cover its surface with olive oil. Store for up to several weeks in the refrigerator.

To Make Fresh Pasta Dough in the Food Processor

A food processor is excellent for making both plain and, as shown here, colored (green) pasta dough.

1. Combine chlorophyll with the other pasta ingredients in the food processor bowl.
2. Process the dough until it has the texture of coarse sand. If it forms a ball, it is too wet and you'll need to add more flour.
3. Knead the dough on a work surface. It should come together into a solid, slightly sticky mass, but it shouldn't stick to your fingers or the work surface. If it doesn't hold together, put it back in the food processor and blend in a little more egg or water; if it's sticky, knead in a little more flour.

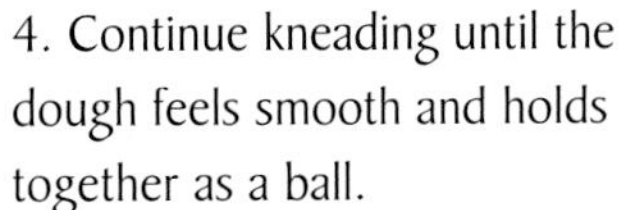

4. Continue kneading until the dough feels smooth and holds together as a ball.

HOW TO

Roll and Cut Fresh Pasta Dough

Use a pasta machine to roll the dough into thin sheets. From there the dough sheets are cut into flat noodles, either using the cutting attachment on the pasta machine or by hand, with a knife. Pasta machines usually give you a choice of two widths of noodles—thick or thin. If you cut by hand, you can cut the noodles as thin or wide as you like.

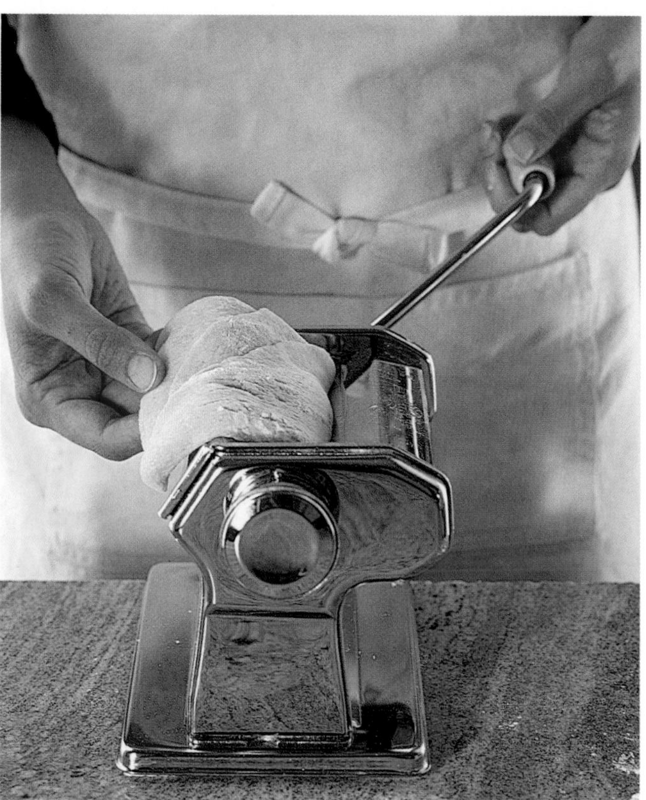

To Roll Out Fresh Pasta Dough Using a Machine

1. Cut the dough into manageable pieces.
2. Flatten the pieces with your fingers, patting them with flour to keep them from gumming up the machine.
3. Attach the pasta machine to the work surface. With the rollers set on the widest setting, run the pasta through the machine.
4. Knead the pasta by folding the strip of pasta over itself once or twice and then running it through the machine again.

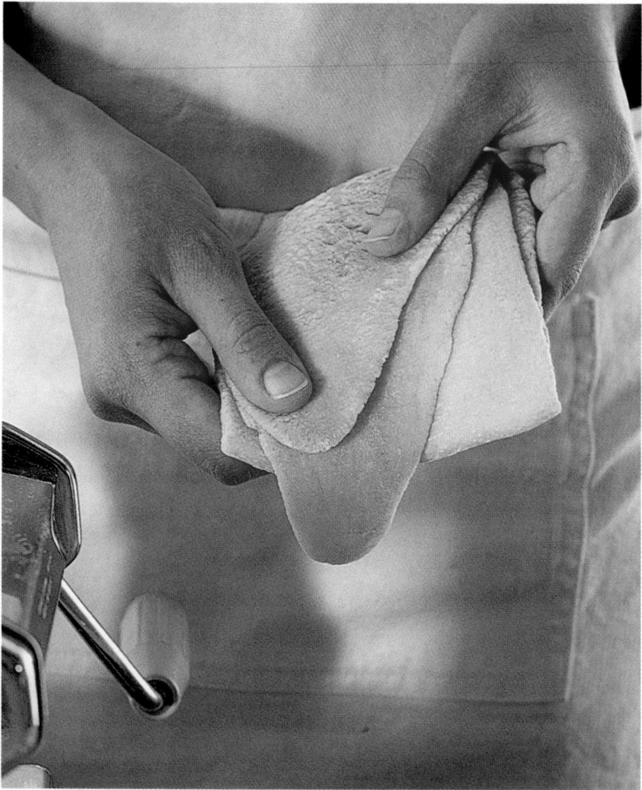

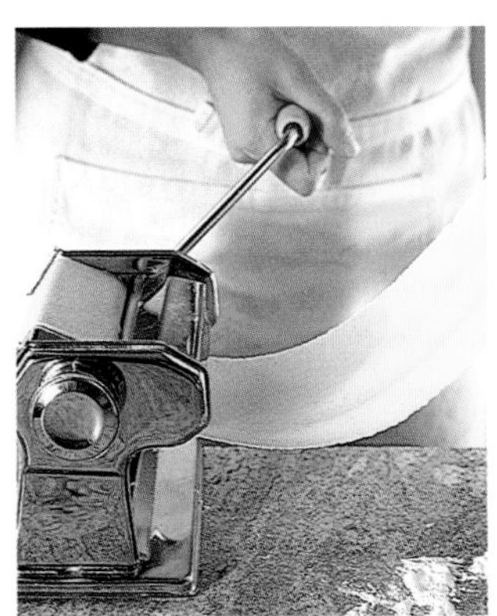

5. Continue kneading in the machine until the dough feels smooth and leathery (it should feel like suede).
6. Support the dough with one hand, gently drawing the dough out, while you crank with the other.
7. Set the machine to the next setting and crank the dough through. Continue rolling the dough through the machine, setting the rollers to the next-thinnest setting each time.
8. If the strips of dough become too long and unwieldy, cut them in half to make them easier to work with.

To Cut Fresh Pasta Dough into Flat Noodles Using a Machine

1. Use the cutting attachment on the pasta machine to cut the pasta into wide strips (fettuccine).
2. Or use the narrow attachment to cut the pasta into thin strips (linguine).
3. Coil the noodles into small nests on a well-floured work surface.
4. Toss the nests with flour to prevent the noodles from sticking to one another.

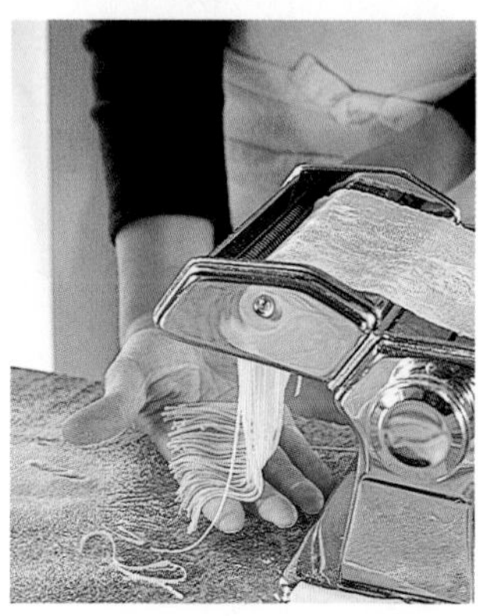

To Cut Fresh Pasta Dough into Flat Noodles by Hand

Cutting sheets of pasta by hand allows you to cut them any width you like—fettuccine (tagliatelle), linguine, pappardelle, etc.—without being limited to the 2 widths on most pasta machines.

1. Flour the sheets of pasta to prevent the noodles from sticking to themselves.
2. Loosely roll up each strip of pasta. Use a chef's knife to cut to the desired width. Cut quickly and cleanly so you don't press the pasta together and cause it to stick to itself.
3. Toss the noodles with flour—semolina flour is best because it's less likely to stick and gum up when you cook the noodles—to keep them from sticking to one another.

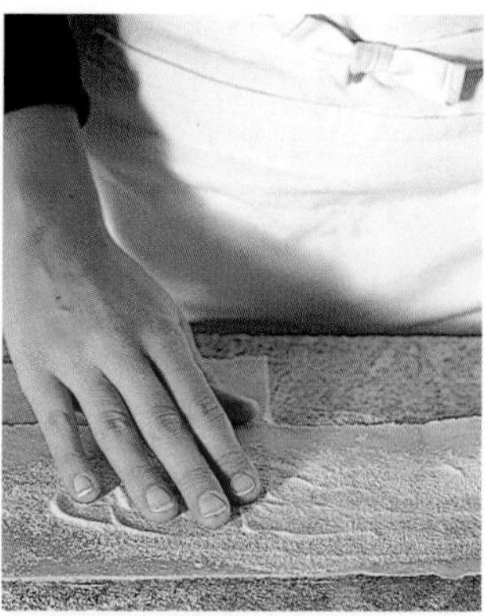

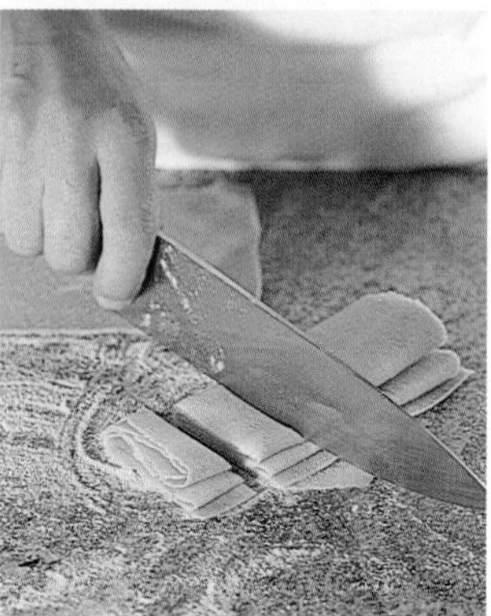

HOW TO

Make Stuffed Pasta Shapes

Once rolled into sheets, fresh pasta is easy to cut into various shapes such as tortelloni and ravioli that can then be stuffed.

To Make Tortelloni

1. Use a fluted cookie cutter to cut rounds out of a sheet of fresh pasta.
2. Pipe (with a pastry bag) or spoon about a teaspoon of filling into the center of each round.
3. Use your fingers to moisten the dough around the filling with cold water.
4. Fold each round in half over the filling.
5. Pinch the edges of each tortellono to seal in the filling.

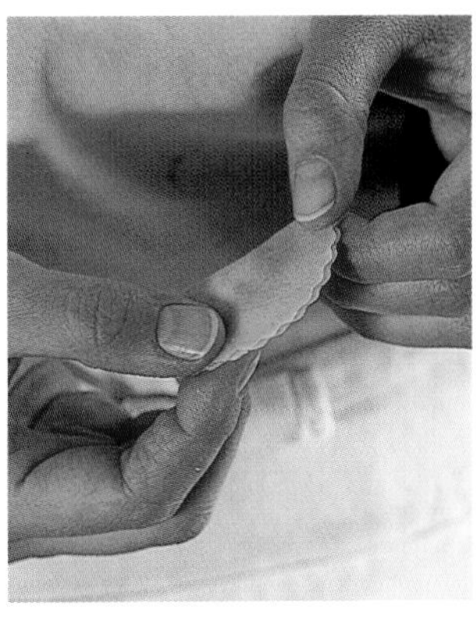

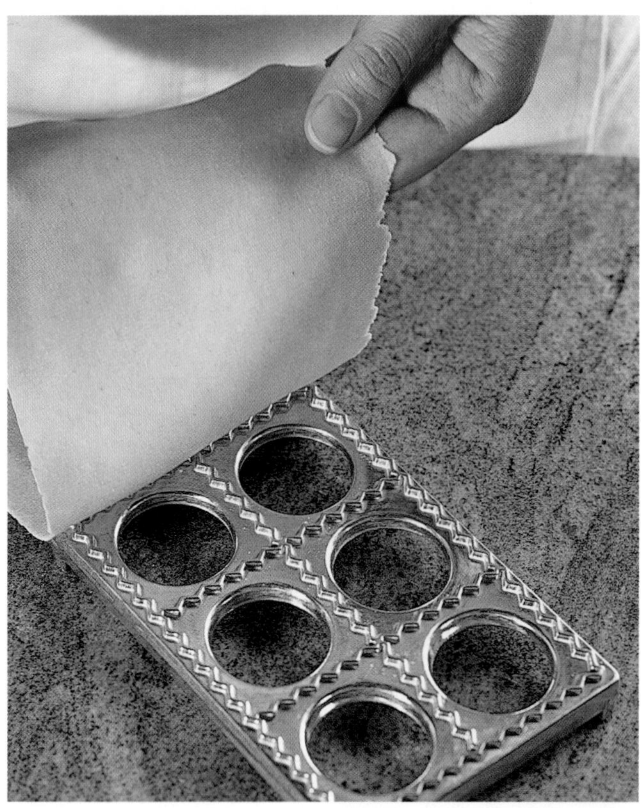

4. Spoon or pipe (with a pastry bag) the filling into each indentation. Brush the dough around the filling with cold water. Lay another sheet of pasta over the first.
5. Roll a rolling pin over the ravioli form, cutting and sealing the ravioli as you go.
6. Gently push out the ravioli.

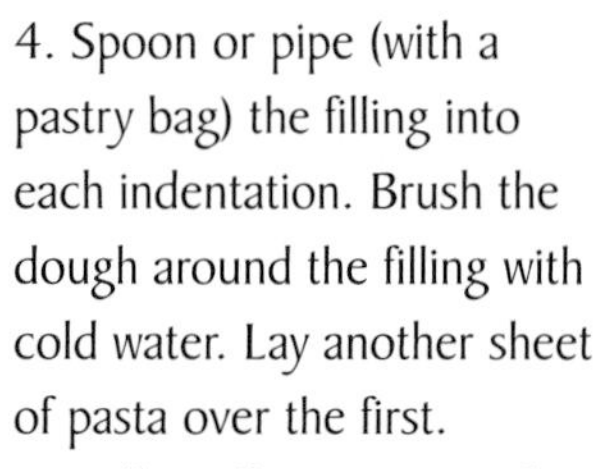

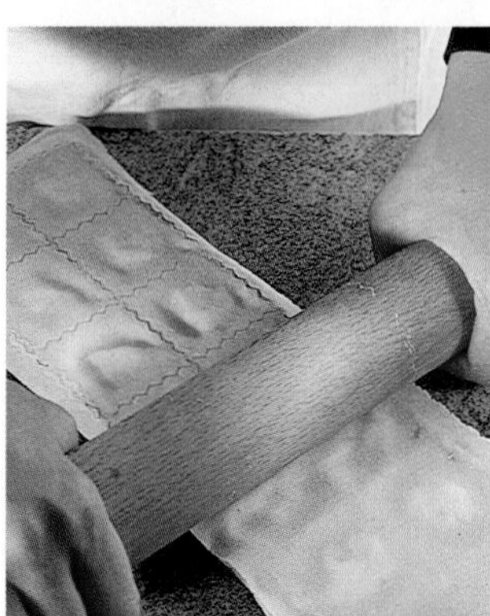

To Make Ravioli

There are a number of gadgets available that make it easier and more efficient to form ravioli. One of the least expensive ravioli makers consists of a metal form and a plastic mold, shown here.

1. Lay a sheet of pasta dough over the ravioli form.
2. Press the plastic mold over the sheet of pasta to form indentations for the filling.
3. Remove the mold.

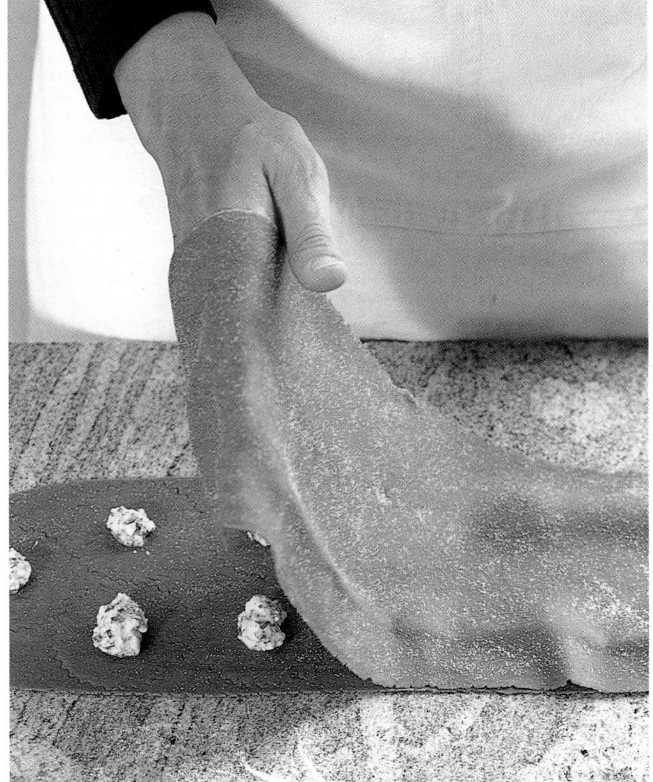

To Make Ravioli with a Hand Pasta Cutter

1. Use a pasta cutter to gently press rounds or squares in a sheet of fresh pasta. Don't cut through the pasta—the markings are just to show you where to put the filling.
2. Pipe (using a pastry bag) or spoon the filling into the center of each round or square. Lightly brush the dough around the filling with cold water. Lay another sheet of pasta over the first.
3. Press the pasta around the mounds of filling, pushing out air pockets and making sure the two sheets of pasta are well sealed together.
4. Cut out rounds or squares of pasta—here, I show both—with the pasta cutter.

See Also
To roll and cut fresh pasta dough, page 54

HOW TO

Make Gnocchi

Gnocchi are starchy dumplings that are made in various shapes. There are two basic types of gnocchi: those based on potatoes (*gnocchi di patate*), shown here, and those based on flour or, occasionally, cornmeal (*gnocchi alla romana*). Once you've poached the gnocchi, toss them with sauce and serve immediately or toss them with olive oil, spread out on a sheet pan, and then reheat them later in the day, in a sauce or in a gratin.

Gnocchi with Garlic and Sage Butter Sauce

Cook thinly sliced garlic and whole sage leaves in butter over medium heat until the butter lightly browns (don't let it burn). Toss drained poached gnocchi in the sauce, heat, and serve.

Gnocchi

1. Prepare mashed potatoes and combine with flour and eggs to make a dough that is softer than pasta dough but doesn't stick to your fingers.
2. Roll the dough into balls about the size of a lemon. Roll the balls in flour to keep them from sticking to the work surface.
3. Roll each ball of dough into a ¾-inch-thick cylinder.
4. Cut the dough into pieces about ¾ inch wide.
5. Poach the gnocchi in simmering salted water for about 5 minutes, or until they float to the top. Remove from the water with a skimmer or slotted spoon and spread out on an oiled sheet pan, or sauce and serve, or even bake in a gratin.

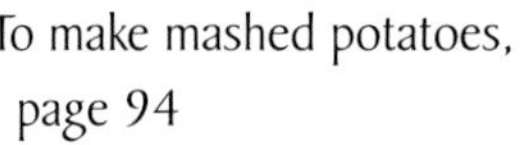

To make mashed potatoes, page 94

HOW TO

Make Blini and Crêpes

Batters for blini and crêpes are similar to pancake batters except that pancakes are usually leavened with baking powder, or, occasionally, beaten egg whites, while blini are leavened with yeast and beaten egg whites, and crêpes aren't leavened at all. There isn't much to making either of these batters, but keep in mind one trick: When combining flour and liquid, start by adding only enough liquid to the flour to work the mixture into a smooth paste. Once the mixture is smooth, go ahead and add the rest of the liquids. This technique prevents the mixture from becoming too lumpy.

Blini are traditionally served with smoked salmon or caviar, but they can also be served the same way as pancakes. I like them with lots of melted butter or with crème fraîche. They have a delicious yeasty flavor that regular pancakes lack. Traditional batters contain half buckwheat flour, but here I use all white flour. When making any yeast-leavened batter, first test, or "proof," the yeast (to make sure it's still alive) by working a pinch (or a small piece, if you're using cake yeast) of it to a smooth paste with a small amount of warm water, sugar, and flour in a small bowl. After ten minutes, the mixture should bubble up slightly and smell yeasty, like stale beer.

Crêpes are made from a very thin batter, about the consistency of heavy cream. The trick to making crêpes is to use a nonstick pan, although a well-seasoned cast-iron pan or skillet will also work. If you make crêpes often, it may be worthwhile investing in more than one pan so you can make more than one crêpe at once.

Blini

1. Proof the yeast by combining a pinch of it with warm water, flour, and a little sugar in a small bowl.
2. In a large bowl, blend the flour with just enough of the milk to form a smooth paste.
3. Stir in the rest of the milk, then add the egg yolks, the proofed yeast, and the rest of the yeast called for in the recipe. Cover and let rise in a warm place until doubled in volume.
4. Just before you're ready to cook the blini, fold the beaten egg whites into the batter.
5. Melt a small amount of butter in a nonstick pan over medium heat. Ladle in about ¼ cup of the blini batter. When bubbles form on top of the blini and break open, turn them over and cook gently on the other side. Serve with smoked salmon, or with any of the accompaniments mentioned previously.

Crêpes

1. In a large bowl, combine eggs, flour, and just enough water or milk to make a smooth paste. Stir in water or milk until the batter has the consistency of heavy cream. If there are any lumps, strain the batter.

2. Whisk in melted butter to add flavor—and to keep the crêpes from sticking, although this is rarely a problem with nonstick pans. (Don't add the butter before straining, or the butter will congeal slightly in the cold batter and then be strained out.)

3. Heat a nonstick crêpe or omelet pan over medium heat. Ladle in just enough crêpe batter to cover the pan with a thin layer and quickly rotate the pan to cover it evenly.

4. Cook over medium heat until the edges of the crêpe curl up and brown slightly. Pick up one edge of the crêpe—or use a spatula—and flip it over.

5. Center it in the pan with your hand.

6. Serve with sweet or savory fillings. Here, crêpes are rolled up with strawberries and whipped cream.

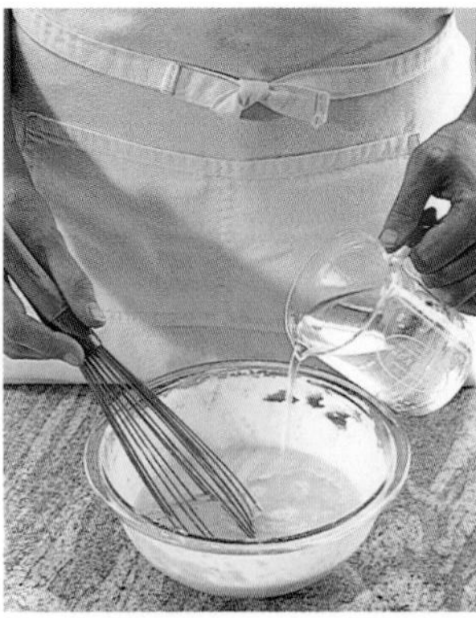

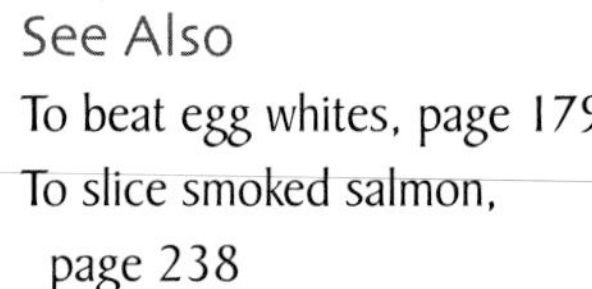

See Also

To beat egg whites, page 179
To slice smoked salmon, page 238

Kitchen Notes and Tips

- To make about sixteen 10-inch crêpes, use the following quantities: 1½ cups flour, 3 large eggs, 2½ cups milk or more to thin to the consistency of cold heavy cream, and 3 tablespoons melted butter.
- To make blini, use the same quantities and ingredients, but ½ teaspoon active dried yeast is proofed and stirred into the batter and the batter allowed to rise.

HOW TO

Cook Risotto, Pilaf, Fluffy Rice, and Paella

Some rice dishes, such as risotto, emphasize the natural starchiness of rice and are designed to help the rice grains cling together in a natural creamy sauce while other dishes, such as pilaf, keep the grains of rice separate and relatively fluffy. Each of the dishes here uses a different kind of rice and a different technique to underline the desired effect.

To make plain boiled rice so that none of the grains sticks together, use firm, long-grained rice, such as basmati, and boil it in a large pot of boiling water as though cooking pasta.

Rice pilaf is made by first cooking long-grain rice in a small amount of fat to cook the starch before the liquid is added. Flavorful ingredients, usually onions and sometimes garlic, are cooked in the fat along with the rice before the liquid is added.

Risotto is a creamy rice dish made with short-grain Italian rice. The rice, usually vialone nano, carnaroli, or arborio, is gently cooked in butter or olive oil. Liquid, usually broth, is then added a small amount at a time until the rice is cooked and bathed in creamy liquid. Risotto must be stirred almost constantly to release the starch from the rice so the starch thickens the broth, giving the dish its characteristic creamy (sometimes even soupy) consistency. The flavoring in a risotto may be very simple (as for a *risotto alla Milanese*) or relatively complex.

Paella is made by cooking Spanish medium-grain rice in a flavorful liquid and then nestling in ingredients such as chicken, sausages (chorizos), seafood, and, in some versions, snails. Traditionally, paella is cooked over an open fire, but it can also be cooked on the stove or in the oven.

Risotto alla Milanese

This classic risotto is flavored with chicken broth, saffron, butter, and finely grated Parmigiano-Reggiano (true Italian Parmesan cheese).

1. Rinse short-grained rice in a strainer.
2. Gently stir the rice in butter over low to medium heat until the grains are all lightly coated with butter.
3. Sprinkle over a pinch of saffron threads and stir in a small amount (about ½ cup) of chicken broth, or enough to just barely cover the rice. Continue stirring until all the broth has been absorbed.
4. Keep adding broth, just enough to barely cover the rice each time, until the risotto has a creamy consistency and the rice grains are cooked through (bite into one to test) about 25 minutes.
5. Stir in freshly grated Parmigiano-Reggiano and butter. Season to taste with salt and pepper and serve immediately.

Boiled Fluffy Rice

To make rice with no hint of gumminess, pour long-grain rice such as basmati or jasmine into a large pot of rapidly boiling water. When the rice is tender—bite into a grain to check—drain in a colander and toss with butter.

Kitchen Notes and Tips

- In addition to the method used to make risotto, there are three other basic methods for cooking rice.
- To cook perfect fluffy rice, add the rice to a large pot of boiling water and cook it just as you'd cook pasta. When the rice is cooked, drain it in a colander and serve it, tossed with a little butter.
- To make rice pilaf, gently cook aromatic ingredients—chopped onions are usually used—in a small amount of butter or olive oil, then stir in long- or medium-grain rice. Cook the rice gently until coated in the butter or oil, then add a measured quantity of water or broth (count 2 cups liquid per cup of rice). When the gently simmering rice has absorbed all the liquid, it is ready. Rice pilaf is served as a side dish.
- A paella is made by adding Spanish medium-grain rice to a flavorful liquid in a paella pan and then simmering—traditionally over an open fire—until the rice has absorbed the liquid. (A paella pan is a wide shallow two-handled pan with sloping sides—it looks as if you could use it to pan for gold.) Ingredients such as chicken, sausages, snails, and seafood are then nestled in the rice as it cooks, with long-cooking ingredients added early on and quick-cooking ingredients added toward the end. There are all kinds of paellas—but traditionally they're made with chicken or fish stock. The one on page 65 is made with shrimp broth. Paella is eaten as a main dish.

Rice Pilaf

1. Rinse long-grain rice in a strainer. Gently cook chopped onions and/or garlic in a small amount of olive oil or butter. Stir in the rice and cook over medium heat, stirring, for about 5 minutes. Add water or broth.
2. Cover with a round of parchment paper or aluminum foil or partially cover with the pan lid.
3. Cook in a 350°F oven or on top of the stove over medium heat for about 20 minutes, until all the liquid has been absorbed and the rice is tender.

Seafood Paella

1. Prepare a *sofregit* by gently cooking chopped onions and garlic in olive oil in a paella pan or wide pot, stirring occasionally, until translucent. Add peeled, seeded, and chopped tomatoes and continue cooking and stirring.
2. When the tomatoes have cooked down into a dry, stiff mixture—the *sofregit*—add broth. Here, I use broth made from shrimp shells and heads.
3. Sprinkle over a pinch of saffron threads and stir in well-rinsed Spanish medium-grain rice.
4. Simmer gently over medium heat (or over an open fire!) until the rice has absorbed most of the liquid. Nestle the seafood in the rice, cover loosely with aluminum foil, and continue cooking on the stove (or over the fire), or finish in the oven, until the seafood is done.

See Also

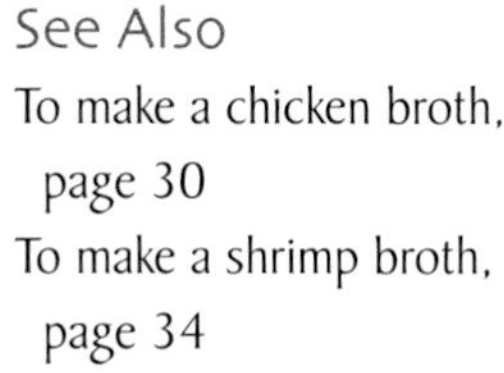

To make a chicken broth, page 30
To make a shrimp broth, page 34

Related Glossary Entries

Mirepoix (for information on *sofregit*)
Parchment Paper or Aluminum Foil Round

HOW TO

Determine Doneness of Foods

Part of becoming a good cook is developing your sensitivity to and intimacy with food—to learn how food changes as it cooks and to recognize the visual and tactile clues that let you know when it's done. There are so many variables at play when you're cooking—reliability of the oven thermostat; size and texture of ingredients; size, material, and type of cooking equipment; stovetop heat—that you can't rely on recipes or cooking times to tell you exactly when the food is done. To cook well, you need to be able to judge how the food is cooking so that you can adjust temperature and timing as you go. Judging doneness by texture and appearance may be difficult at first, but you can practice by looking and touching foods, guessing at how they're cooking, and then confirming your guesswork by cutting into the food or, in some cases, by checking the food's internal temperature with an instant-read thermometer.

To Tell When a Steak Is Done

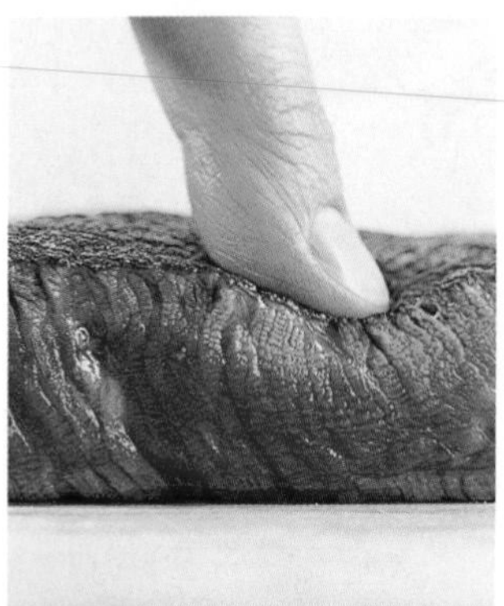

- Rare meat feels fleshy to the touch. As the meat barely approaches being medium-rare, beads of red juices will start to form on its surface.

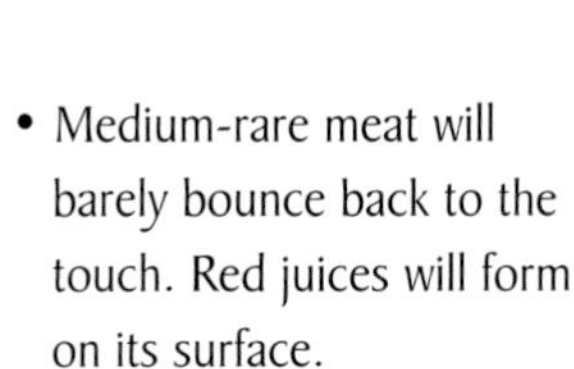

- Medium-rare meat will barely bounce back to the touch. Red juices will form on its surface.
- Medium meat will feel distinctly firm to the touch and pink juices will form on its surface.

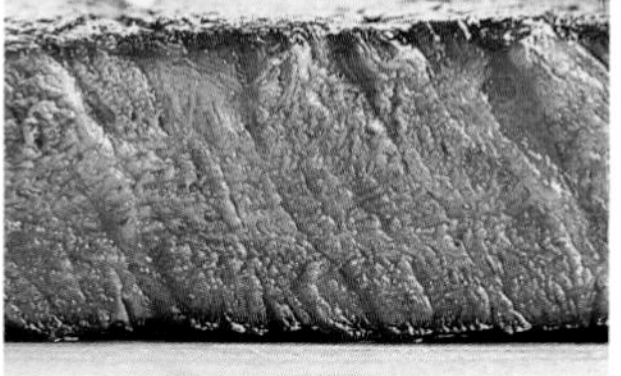

- Medium-well meat will feel very firm. Brown and pink juices will form on its surface.

- Well-done meat will feel hard to the touch and any juices released will be brown.

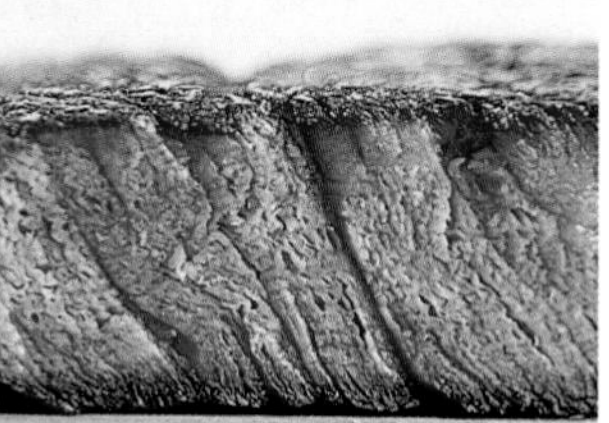

Kitchen Notes and Tips

ROASTED MEATS

- Roasts can be tested with an instant-read thermometer, but professional chefs often just insert a skewer into the meat and then touch it to their lip to determine doneness. Train yourself to do this by first checking the temperature on an instant-read thermometer, then immediately touching the end of the thermometer to your lower lip: You'll quickly learn what 120°F, or 140°F, feels like on your lip. Tender cuts of meat that are poached, such as tenderloin for *boeuf à la ficelle,* can be tested in the same manner. When checking the internal temperature of a roast, remember that the temperature will rise about 5 degrees while the roast rests.

STEAK

- It's awkward to use a thermometer to check the doneness of steak. Other than cutting into the meat and judging its color, the best way to determine doneness is to press on the meat with your finger and feel its texture. (At later stages of cooking, you can also judge the meat's doneness by the amount and color of juices it releases.) Raw and very rare meat feels fleshy and soft and releases no juices. As soon as the meat begins to spring back ever so slightly and tiny beads of red juice form on its surface, it is rare to medium-rare. Meat cooked to medium springs back completely, feels firm to the touch, and releases larger amounts of pink juices. As meat cooks beyond medium, it feels increasingly firm to the touch and starts to release large amounts of brown juice.

BRAISED AND POACHED MEATS

- A meat thermometer is never used to determine the doneness of long-braised meats, because the temperature is irrelevant: The meat reaches maximum temperature (say, 180°F) long before it's cooked to fork-tender, which is what you want. The best way to determine when long-braised, stewed, or poached meat is done is to stick a knife or skewer into the meat. If it slides in and out easily, with no resistance, the meat is done. However, the doneness of short-braised or poached dishes, such as sweetbreads or *boeuf à la ficelle*, is determined by temperature or texture in the same way as for roasts and steaks.

POULTRY AND YOUNG RABBIT

- Check doneness of cut-up poultry and tender rabbit as you would a steak, by pressing on the flesh with your finger to feel the texture. Cook chicken until the flesh springs back when you press on it, and there's no hint of a fleshy feeling. Duck breasts, however, should be cooked to between rare and medium-rare—just to the point where there's a slight hint of firmness and a less-fleshy feeling when you press on them.

FISH

- A general rule of thumb is to cook fish for 7 to 10 minutes per inch of thickness, but you can judge the doneness of fish steaks and fillets by texture. Press the top of the fish with your finger. During the first few minutes of cooking, the fish will feel fleshy. As soon as the fish begins to feel firm, it is usually perfectly done. (Tuna is an exception, since it is best cooked very rare and will still feel fleshy when it's ready.)
- You can also check the doneness of whole fish by sliding a knife into the back of the fish along the backbone and peeking in. If the flesh has lost its translucency and can be pulled away from the bone, the fish is done. A thermometer can also be slipped into the back of a whole fish or into a thick fish steak or fillet. Perfectly done fish has an internal temperature of 135°F (again, tuna is an exception).

FLANS, CUSTARDS, AND SOUFFLÉS

- It's sometimes hard to tell when baked liquid or airy mixtures such as flans and soufflés are done. Professional cooks judge doneness by giving the mold or pan a gentle back-and-forth shake. If a flan mixture or custard is still runny and undercooked, it will slosh around in the mold or ripples will be visible on the surface. As the mixture cooks, the sloshing stops and any ripples restrict themselves to the center. When the mixture is done, there are no ripples. Soufflés are tricky because even the raw mixture is fairly stiff. It is possible, with practice, to see the moment when the mixture has just barely stiffened on the inside—and the soufflé is done. If you cut into it and it's still too runny inside—it should be somewhat runny in the center—slide it back into the oven. Unless overcooked, soufflés are surprisingly stable.

Vegetables and Fruits

HOW TO

Roast Vegetables

Roasting pulls the water out of vegetables and concentrates their flavor. (Taste a roasted carrot next to a boiled carrot, and you'll see how roasting emphasizes the vegetable's natural sweetness.) Roasting works best for root vegetables, such as carrots, turnips, potatoes, and onions, and for vegetables that contain a great deal of moisture, such as tomatoes and mushrooms. I sometimes coat these softer vegetables with bread crumbs to add texture, as in a gratin.

Sometimes you'll want to roast root vegetables in their skins: russet potatoes because we like to eat the skins, beets because they bleed and dry out once they're peeled, and baby vegetables because their thin skins are entirely edible. But usually we roast vegetables that have been peeled beforehand. Cut the peeled vegetables into sections or wedges, or turn them, and then lightly coat with olive oil or melted butter to prevent them from drying out in the oven.

Vegetables can be roasted alone or in combination. Most of the time, all you need to do to roast vegetables is to slide them into the oven and turn them over from time to time so they brown evenly. A nice touch, however, is to pour a little good meat or chicken broth into the roasting pan about ten minutes before the vegetables are done. The broth quickly reduces in the heat of the oven and glazes the vegetables.

Vegetables being roasted alone are shown here, but they can also surround roasted meats or poultry—leg of lamb, roast beef, or roast chicken, for example. When you roast them this way, drippings from the roast mingle with and flavor the vegetables.

To Roast Mixed Root Vegetables

1. Same-size vegetables cook evenly: Here, carrots are peeled, sectioned, and cored (for an elegant presentation, they can even be turned). The spring onions are trimmed and left whole (or, if very large, quartered), the turnips are peeled and quartered, and the peeled parsnips are cut the same way as the carrots. Toss the vegetables in the roasting pan with a little extra virgin olive oil or melted butter.

2. Roast the vegetables at 400°F until they start to brown on top, about 20 minutes. Gently stir so they will brown evenly, and continue roasting for about 20 minutes more, until the vegetables are evenly browned and a knife penetrates easily. If desired, add broth and continue roasting until the broth has evaporated and the vegetables are coated with a shiny glaze.

Roasted Beets

1. Cut off the greens, leaving a ½- to 1-inch stem attached to the beet. If you cut into the flesh, the juices will leach out. (Save the greens and cook them.)

2. Wrap beets individually in aluminum foil to keep them from drying out. (Smaller beets can be grouped together.)

3. Because beets release juices while they roast, they should be roasted on a sheet pan, not directly on the oven rack like potatoes. Roast large beets at 400°F for about 1 hour and 15 minutes, until a skewer inserted into the center (just poke right through the foil) penetrates easily. Unwrap the beets.

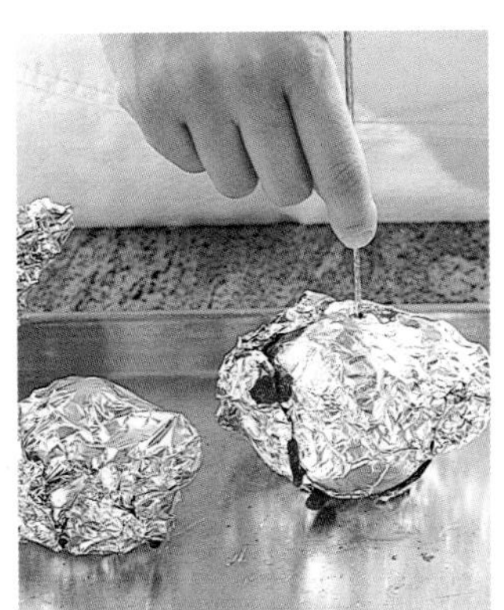

To Peel Roasted Beets

Beets are easiest to peel when still hot. Holding the beet in a kitchen towel, cut off the stems and pull away the peel in strips.

Kitchen Notes and Tips

- Roast root vegetables and most other vegetables, both whole and cut up, at about 400°F. Roast very moist vegetables, such as mushrooms and tomatoes, at about 350°F; a higher temperature may cause the juices released by the vegetables to burn. If a vegetable browns before the inside is cooked, turn the oven down.
- Wrapping vegetables in foil traps moisture: Do wrap beets before roasting to keep them from drying out and leaking juices. Don't wrap sweet potatoes, yams, or russet potatoes; you want the skin to dry and crisp, rather than steam, and the flesh to give up its moisture so that it becomes fluffy rather than dense.
- Choose a roasting pan just large enough to hold the vegetables in a single layer. If the pan is too big, the juices released by the vegetables may burn; if it is too small, the vegetables may steam in these same juices.
- To roast cut-up vegetables along with roasting meats and poultry, choose a roasting pan large enough to hold both and work out the timing so the roast and the vegetables are done at the same time. (You may need to start one or the other first.) Because the vegetables insulate the roast from the heat, they may increase the meat's cooking time slightly and slow down browning. Turn roasting meats halfway through the cooking so that they roast and brown evenly. The juices released by the meat will coat and flavor the vegetables.

See Also

To turn vegetables, page 13
To make fresh bread crumbs, page 164
To steam beet greens, page 87
To roast meats, pages 184 and 191
To roast chicken, page 146
To make a chicken broth, page 30
To core carrots, page 21
To cut roasted beets in bâtonnets, page 18
To cut turnips into wedges, page 22
To seed tomatoes, page 36

Related Glossary Entries

Bake
Glaze
Roast

Baked Tomatoes with Garlic and Fresh Basil

Many recipes for baked tomatoes recommend relatively high heat and a short baking time, but gentle heat and long baking will better concentrate their flavor. Serve with roasted or grilled meats and poultry.

1. Arrange unpeeled seeded tomato halves cut side up in an oiled baking dish just large enough to hold them in a single layer. Stuff with finely chopped garlic, basil, parsley, and fresh bread crumbs.

2. Dribble extra virgin olive oil into the openings in the tomatoes. Bake at 350°F for about an hour or longer, until the tomatoes shrivel and any liquid in the bottom of the pan has evaporated.

HOW TO

Make a Vegetable Gratin

A gratin is a great way to bind ingredients together and cook them under what becomes a crisp, golden brown crust. I bake root vegetables in a mixture of grated cheese, cream, and milk that reduces over the vegetables to make a thick rich sauce. Potatoes are particularly marvelous in this style of gratin, because they're such wonderful foils for cream and cheese, and their starchiness thickens the sauce. Turnips and celery root are good in combination with potatoes, because the potatoes add starch, which helps hold the gratin together, and softens the aggressive taste of the other vegetables. Parsnips can be used on their own, because they have a high starch content and their flavor is milder than turnip and celery root.

Because watery vegetables such as zucchini, summer squash, eggplant, and mushrooms contain so much liquid of their own, their moisture should be cooked out to concentrate their flavor. In the zucchini gratin, the zucchini are first sautéed and then layered with a fairly thick tomato sauce (coulis) and cheese.

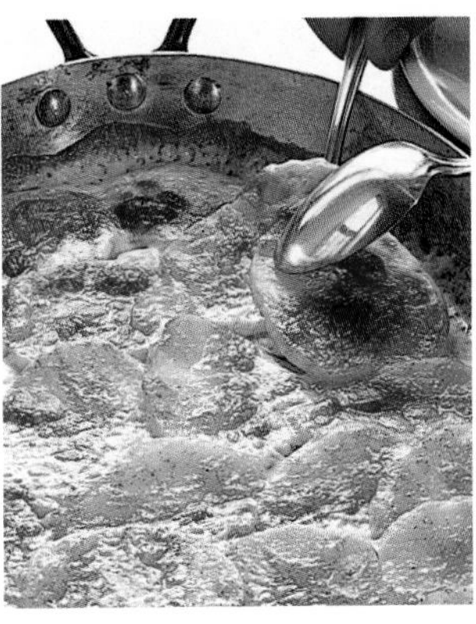

Potato Gratin

1. Pour a thin layer of the cream and milk mixture into a gratin dish. Season with salt, pepper, and nutmeg and arrange a single layer of potato slices on top. Heat on the stove—use a Flame Tamer if the dish is porcelain or ovenproof glass—until the liquid simmers.
2. Make alternating layers of grated cheese and potatoes, sprinkling each layer with the cream mixture and finishing with a cheese layer. Season with salt, pepper, and nutmeg.
3. Bake at 375°F until the liquid is absorbed, the potatoes are soft, and the top is a crusty gold.

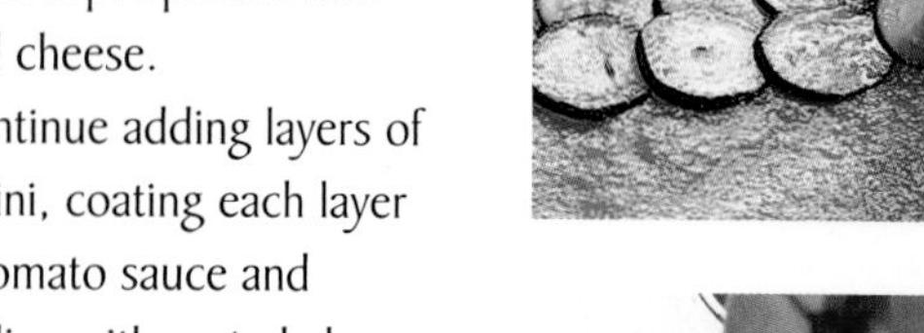

Zucchini Gratin

1. Coat the bottom of a gratin dish with a layer of cooked tomato coulis.
2. Arrange a layer of sautéed zucchini slices in overlapping rows on top. Sprinkle with grated cheese.
3. Continue adding layers of zucchini, coating each layer with tomato sauce and sprinkling with grated cheese.
4. Bake at 375°F until golden brown on top.

Kitchen Notes and Tips

- When making a root vegetable gratin, add just enough liquid so that all but the topmost layer is covered and when you press down on it, the liquid oozes up around and barely covers the top layer. The proportion of cream to milk is up to you. Using very little cream, however, increases the possibility that the milk will curdle and give the gratin a grainy texture. A proportion of half cream and half milk makes the gratin creamy but not too rich. For a completely lean gratin, use broth instead of milk or cream.
- The thinner and wider the gratin, the greater the proportion of caramelized, crispy crust (which is, remember, the whole point).
- The moister the vegetable, the thinner the gratin should be, so the moisture in ingredients like zucchini will evaporate and the vegetable's flavor will be concentrated. Root vegetable gratins can be somewhat thicker. In general, a gratin should be about 1 to 2 inches deep before it is cooked.
- Bake gratins at 375°F.
- The gratin is done when it is no longer soupy and the surface is browned and caramelized. Monitor the heat to make sure the gratin is cooking evenly: If the top browns too fast, turn the oven down. If the liquid isn't bubbling or the vegetables are sitting in a puddle of their own juices, turn the oven up.

See Also

To make a cooked tomato coulis, page 50

To sauté vegetables, page 89

Related Glossary Entries

Bake

Gratin

Reduction

Sauté

HOW TO

Slow-Cook (Braise) Green Vegetables

Though we are all fans of quickly cooked, bright green vegetables, some green vegetables, such as cabbage, green beans, and broccoli, and hardy greens, such as kale and chard, are actually more flavorful when cooked slowly in a covered pot (braised). They lose some of their bright green color, but the loss is more than compensated for by their deep and satisfying flavor, especially when they are cooked with ingredients such as garlic, hot chiles, and bacon.

Kitchen Notes and Tips

- Start with enough water or broth to come about one quarter of the way up the vegetable. This will be just enough liquid so that the vegetable cooks in, and is flavored by, its own juices.
- Monitor the heat so that the liquid stays at a gentle simmer. The idea is to control the rate of evaporation so that the liquid completely evaporates by the time the vegetable is completely cooked, but not before. If the liquid is evaporating too quickly, turn down the heat or add more liquid as needed. If it's not evaporating quickly enough, turn up the heat and/or remove the lid.
- The vegetable is done when the liquid has completely evaporated and the vegetable has a melting texture.

See Also

To glaze root vegetables, page 76

To make a chicken stock, page 30

To fillet anchovies, page 236

To julienne bell peppers, page 13

Related Glossary Entries

Braise

Glaze

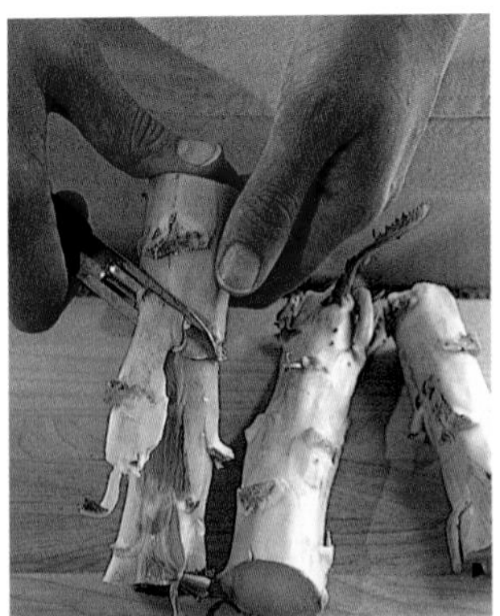

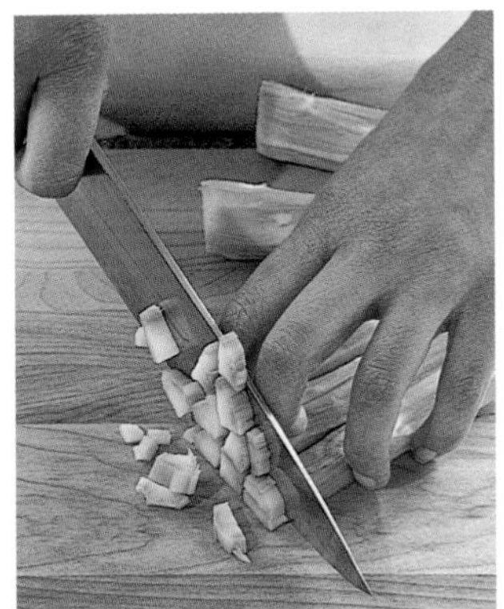

Braised Broccoli

1. Cut the stalks off the florets and peel the stalks with a vegetable peeler.
2. Cut the stalks lengthwise into quarters. Group the strips together and cut across into pieces.
3. Gently cook sliced garlic in extra virgin olive oil. Stir in the chopped broccoli stems and the florets and add enough water or broth to come about one quarter of the way up the broccoli.
4. Cover and cook over low to medium heat for about 30 minutes, stirring every 5 minutes and checking to make sure the pan isn't dry. (Add a little more liquid if necessary.) If there's any liquid left in the pan after 30 minutes, cook, uncovered, for about 10 minutes more to eliminate moisture.
5. Braised broccoli served on toasts and garnished with anchovy fillets and strips of grilled bell pepper makes a savory bruschetta hors d'oeuvre.

HOW TO

Glaze Root Vegetables

Root vegetables are often cooked using a special technique called glazing. Glazing means to cook vegetables in a small amount of liquid, usually with a tiny bit of butter and sugar, in a partially covered pan or with a round of parchment paper or aluminum foil placed directly over them. As the vegetables cook, they release their savory juices into the surrounding braising liquid (usually water or broth). The liquid reduces and thickens as the vegetables cook, so that when tender, they're coated with a shiny, savory glaze that tastes of the vegetable.

Root vegetables, here pearl onions, can be "white-glazed" or "brown-glazed." (Traditionally only onions are brown-glazed, but in fact, you can brown-glaze any root vegetable.) White-glazed onions are cooked only long enough for the liquid to evaporate and lightly glaze the onions. Brown-glazed onions are cooked slightly longer, until the glaze on the bottom of the pan lightly caramelizes and browns. A small amount of water or broth is then added to dissolve the caramelized juices so they will coat the onions. Cream used for this stage results in creamed onions.

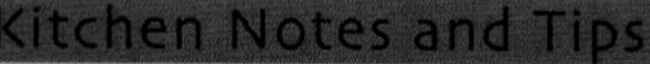

Kitchen Notes and Tips

Successful glazing depends on the right timing and temperature. If the heat is too high or not enough liquid is added to the vegetables at the beginning, the liquid will evaporate before the vegetables are cooked. If this happens, just add more liquid and turn down the heat. If, on the other hand, too much liquid is added at the beginning or the heat is too low, the vegetables will overcook before the liquid cooks down to a glaze. If the vegetables seem to be cooked but there's a lot of liquid left in the pan, turn up the heat and remove the paper or foil round so the liquid boils away.

See Also

To peel pearl onions, page 5

To glaze roasted vegetables, page 70

Related Glossary Entries

Braise

Glaze

Parchment Paper or Aluminum Foil Round

Brown-Glazed Pearl Onions

1. Put peeled onions in a pan just large enough to hold them in one layer. Add a pat of butter and pour in water or broth to come halfway up their sides. Cover with a round of parchment paper or aluminum foil.
2. Simmer gently until the onions are easily penetrated with a knife and the liquid has evaporated and formed a brown glaze on the bottom of the pan. Add just enough water to dissolve the glaze.
3. Simmer gently until the liquid cooks down to a glaze and coats the onions.

HOW TO

Deep-fry Vegetables

Deep-frying is a way to cook vegetables so that they are piping hot, crisp on the outside, and moist on the inside. Juicy vegetables such as zucchini, eggplant, and mushrooms should be coated with a light batter or bread crumb crust to keep them from absorbing too much oil. Potatoes can be fried without a batter or coating because they contain less water and brown well on their own.

On the following pages are examples of two styles of coatings: a bread crumb coating and a lighter flour and club soda (or water) batter. A bread crumb coating makes a very substantial crust; because it absorbs juices, it works particularly well with very wet vegetables such as tomatoes. Liquid batters, like one of flour and club soda, coat vegetables with a crisp and delicate crust. Tempura batter (page 122) makes a delicate but crunchier crust than club soda batter and works particularly well for absorbent vegetables like mushrooms and tomatoes. Since tempura batter is substantial, it protects the vegetables from absorbing oil.

Fried Zucchini Slices

Use this method for thinly sliced vegetables such as eggplant, fennel, mushrooms, and okra.

1. Cut the zucchini into thin slices and put them, several at a time, in club soda and flour or plain water and flour batter (page 78).
2. Arrange the slices on a spider or in a deep-fry basket (you can also use a slotted spoon, or drop them in with your fingers—but be careful) and lower them into 360°F oil.
3. Break the slices up while they're frying—here, I use tongs—to keep them from sticking to each other.
4. Take the slices out of the oil when they've barely begun to brown and have turned crispy, and drain on baking sheets lined with paper towels.

Light Frying Batters

By simply mixing water and flour, you can make a good all-purpose frying batter that will coat vegetables with a light, crisp crust. The carbonation in club soda will give you an even more fragile and delicate crust. When making either of these batters, don't overwork the flour: Stir just until the liquid is incorporated into the flour and the batter is smooth. Overworking develops gluten, which would cause the batter to shrink as it fries, leaving part of the food exposed.

To make the batter, whisk just enough liquid into the flour to make a smooth paste. (Too much liquid added at the beginning makes it impossible to work the lumps out of the flour.) Let this "starter" batter rest at room temperature for at least 1 and up to 2 hours to give the gluten in the flour a chance to relax. Shortly before frying, gently stir in club soda or water until the batter has the consistency of heavy cream. Club soda batter must be used immediately, before it loses its carbonation.

Kitchen Notes and Tips

- Deep-fry most vegetables at 360°F.
- Use "pure" olive oil or vegetable oil for frying. Don't use extra virgin olive oil; it's too expensive.
- To keep the oil from splattering, use a spider, deep-fry basket, or slotted spoon to lower the vegetables into the oil.
- Fried foods with no coating or those coated with a light batter should be cooked just to a pale ivory color or they will lose their delicate flavor. Foods coated with bread crumbs can be deep-fried until the coating turns golden brown.

Flour and Club Soda Batter

This batter can also be made with plain water instead of club soda, but the coating's texture won't be quite as light.

1. Use a whisk to work club soda or seltzer into flour in a small bowl. Use the least amount of liquid you need to make a smooth paste. Let this "starter" rest for 1 to 2 hours.
2. Just before frying, gently stir in club soda until the batter has the consistency of heavy cream.

Fried Tomatoes

Select tomatoes that are relatively firm. Don't peel them; slice them into ¼-inch-thick rounds. Squeeze the seeds out of each round.

1. Coat the tomatoes on both sides with flour and pat off the excess.
2. Dip the tomatoes into beaten egg seasoned with salt and pepper, coating both sides.
3. Coat the tomatoes on both sides with fresh bread crumbs.

4. Arrange the tomatoes on a spider, shown here, or in a frying basket and gently lower into 360°F "pure" olive oil or vegetable oil.
5. Fry the tomatoes until golden brown, about 3 minutes.
6. Take the tomatoes out with the spider or basket and drain on paper towels. Sprinkle with salt and serve immediately.

See Also

To make bread crumbs, page 164
To bread chicken breasts, page 162
To make a tempura batter, page 122
To make potato chips and French fries, page 80

Related Glossary Entries

Bread Deep-fry
Gluten
Spider

HOW TO

Make Potato Chips and French Fries

Potatoes are perfect for deep-frying. When cut thick, they turn crisp on the outside and soft, almost purée-like on the inside. When cut thin, they become fragile, delicate crisps. Potatoes are commonly fried in three shapes—French fries, the thinner straw potatoes, and potato chips. The technique for frying all of them is essentially the same except that straw potatoes and chips are simply fried in hot oil, while the thicker French fries must be fried twice—a preliminary frying in medium-hot oil to cook the potatoes through without browning, and then a second cooking in hotter oil to give them their crisp, golden crust. (Double frying is necessary because oil that is hot enough to brown the potatoes will overbrown raw potatoes before they're cooked through.)

Potato Chips

Potato chips are fried in a single stage in the same way as straw potatoes (page 81). Here, I am making waffled potato chips; plain rounds are cooked in the same way.

1. To make regular potato chips, just slice the potatoes into thin rounds with the regular blade on a mandoline or a vegetable slicer. To make the waffle potatoes shown here, use the wavy blade on the mandoline. After each slice, give the potato a 90-degree turn. Adjust the thickness so the tiny holes in the potato slices have the diameter of a pin.
2. Arrange the potatoes on a spider or in a deep-fry basket.
3. Plunge the potatoes into 350°F oil. Fry for about 4 minutes, until golden brown. Remove and drain on paper towels. Sprinkle with salt.

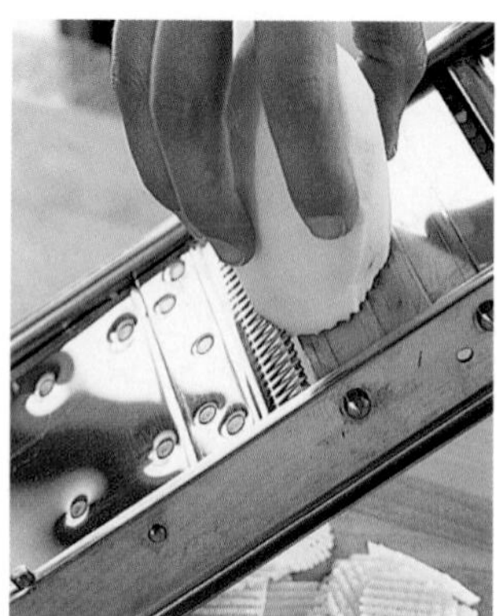

Straw Potatoes: Single-Stage Frying

Straw potatoes are fried only once.

1. Use the julienne attachment on a mandoline to cut the potatoes into julienne strips about ⅛ inch thick or slice and julienne the potatoes by hand (see Box, page 82).

2. Plunge the potatoes into 350°F oil and stir while they fry to keep them from sticking to each other or to the sides of the pot.

3. When the potatoes have browned, after 3 or 4 minutes, remove them from the oil and drain on a sheet pan covered with paper towels. Sprinkle with salt.

Kitchen Notes and Tips

- The julienne blade on a mandoline is the easiest gadget for making straw potatoes, but you can also slice the potatoes with a plastic vegetable slicer and then cut the slices by hand into thin fries.
- An electric frying pan is good for frying potato chips and small numbers of French fries and straw potatoes because the built-in thermostat makes it easy to regulate the temperature.
- You'll need a mandoline to make the waffled potatoes shown on page 80, but plain sliced potatoes can be sliced on a plastic vegetable slicer.
- If straw potatoes and chips have browned but are limp when you take them out of the oil, turn down the oil to lengthen the frying time before you add the next batch—this will allow more time for the moisture in the potatoes to evaporate and will make them crisper.
- For single-stage frying, heat the oil to 350°F. For double-stage frying, fry the potatoes first at 320°F and a second time at 360°F.
- I recommend russet potatoes for French fries and straw potatoes, but other root vegetables also make excellent chips.

See Also

To cut vegetables into julienne, page 13

Related Glossary Entries

Deep-fry
Slicer
Spider

French Fries: Double-Stage Frying

The French fries shown here are between ⅛ and ¼ inch thick (3⁄16 inch) and are cooked in two stages.

1. Cut the ends off the potatoes so the French fries will be of equal length and trim the sides so you don't end up with little irregular pieces once you start slicing (this is optional).

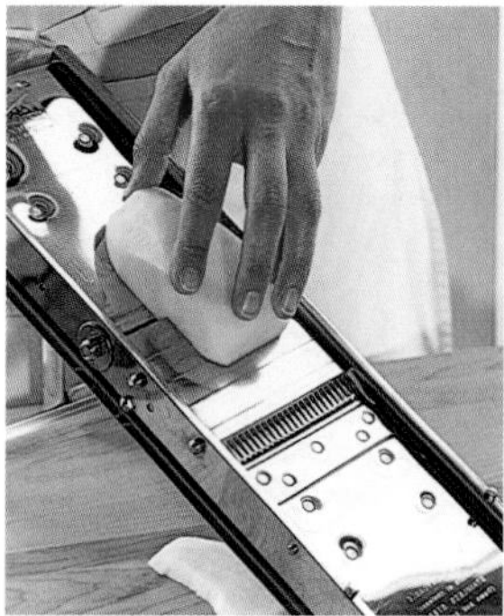

2. Cut the potatoes into 3⁄16-inch-thick slices. Here, I use a mandoline. Be careful with your fingers; as you get near the blade, use the guard.

3. With a chef's knife, cut the slices into 3⁄16-inch-thick French fries (so all four sides are the same).

4. With a spider or deep-fry basket, plunge the French fries into 320°F oil.

5. Fry the potatoes, stirring once or twice at the beginning to prevent them from sticking, for about 5 minutes. If they start to brown sooner, turn down the heat.

6. Scoop the potatoes out of the oil—they should show no sign of browning—and pinch one between your fingers. It should crush easily and be purée-tender inside. If not, return the potatoes briefly to the oil.

7. Heat the oil to 360°F (if you're making a lot of fries, it's easier to use two pots of oil, one hotter than the other) and plunge the French fries in for 3 to 4 minutes, or until golden brown.

8. Take the potatoes out of the oil and spread them on a sheet pan covered with paper towels. Sprinkle with salt.

HOW TO

Grill Vegetables

Grilling gives vegetables a lightly smoked flavor, it doesn't take much preparation, and best of all, you can do it outdoors. Mushrooms and other small vegetables can be grilled whole. Larger vegetables just need to be sliced or cut into wedges. All vegetables are brushed lightly with olive oil before grilling to add flavor, promote browning, and keep them from drying out and sticking to the grill. Grilled vegetables are usually served as a side dish with other grilled foods, but they can also be served as a first course, drizzled with plain or flavored olive oil. When you can't grill outside, use a grill pan on top of the stove to give vegetables a light grilled taste indoors.

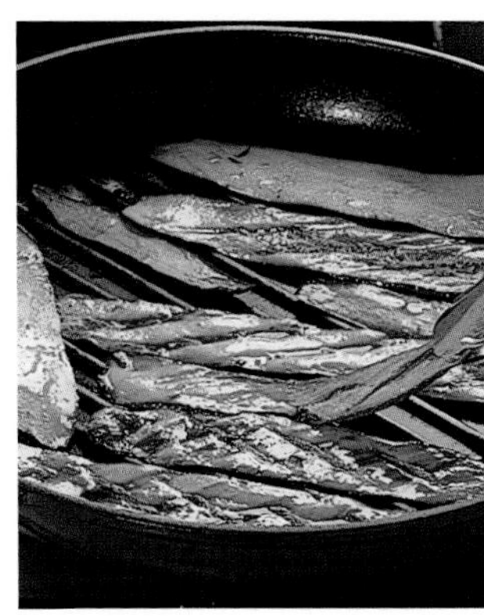

Grilled Zucchini or Summer Squash

Slice zucchini and summer squash lengthwise—a plastic vegetable slicer is great for this—so the slices are easy to turn and don't fall through the grill. Brush the slices with olive oil and sprinkle with herbs such as thyme or marjoram.

Grill the strips in a grill pan over high heat or on an outdoor barbecue. Turn the slices when they are well browned, cooking for about 5 minutes on each side.

Grilled Assorted Vegetables

1. Large vegetables are cut into slices and wedges; larger mushroom caps can be left whole.
2. Brush vegetables with olive oil before and during grilling to prevent them from sticking to the grill and drying out, and grill until tender.
3. If you like, you can brush vegetables with an herb-flavored oil or olive oil containing chopped herbs just before serving.

Grilled Scallions

Scallions, baby leeks, and ramps are all delicious grilled.

1. Grill scallions until lightly charred on the outside and softened all the way through, 10 to 15 minutes.
2. Here, grilled scallions are drizzled with dried porcini and basil oils, but plain extra virgin olive oil is also delicious.

Kitchen Notes and Tips

- Thinly slice firm, slow-cooking vegetables such as fennel or potatoes so the heat can penetrate to the center before the vegetable overcooks and chars on the outside. You can also partially cook slow-cooking vegetables, such as potatoes, ahead of time and then grill them just long enough to heat them through; this is a particularly good trick when there is limited grill space and you're cooking other grilled foods, such as meat and seafood, at the same time.
- Cut sturdy head lettuces such as Treviso and round red radicchio and endive in half or into wedges through their base.
- Large mushrooms or mushroom caps, such as those from portobellos, can be grilled whole, but other mushrooms, small vegetables such as baby onions, and small pieces of vegetables should be threaded onto two parallel skewers to make them easier to turn and to keep them from falling through the grill.
- Brush vegetables with olive oil and sprinkle with salt and pepper before grilling. If the surface of the vegetable begins to dry out during grilling (eggplant is likely to dry out), lightly brush with olive oil.
- Use herbs to flavor grilled vegetables in four ways: Sprinkle chopped fresh or dried pungent woody herbs such as thyme, marjoram, savory, and oregano over raw vegetables before grilling. Chop more delicate herbs such as basil, tarragon, chives, parsley, and chervil and mix with enough olive oil to make them easy to brush on, then brush them on grilled vegetables before serving. Use bundled branches of herbs such as dried thyme, rosemary, savory, or sage as a brush to brush olive oil on the vegetables during grilling. Or as a last method, put a small, moistened bundle of dried herbs such as thyme or rosemary on the coals so it produces smoke and scents the vegetables.
- Vegetables are done when they are lightly browned, or marked with grill marks, and tender. If the vegetables are browning too fast, move them away from the hottest part of the fire.

Grilled Mixed Vegetable Kebabs

Serve each guest his or her own skewer, or slide the cooked vegetables off the skewers onto plates or a serving platter either alone or with other grilled foods.

1. Thread the vegetables onto 2 skewers to make them easy to turn. If you're using wooden skewers, wrap the ends in aluminum foil to keep them from burning and make sure the vegetables are touching each other so none of the skewer is exposed to the flame.
2. Arrange the skewers about 8 inches away from the coals. Lightly brush the vegetables with olive oil during grilling. Here, I use a bunch of dried thyme as a brush to add flavor.

See Also

To make dried basil and porcini oils, pages 39 and 40

Related Glossary Entries

Grill
Slicer

HOW TO

Steam and Boil Vegetables

Steaming is a great method for cooking vegetables because the vegetables' nutrients aren't leached out into the surrounding liquid, something that may happen when vegetables are boiled or poached. Steaming is also very gentle, so that fragile vegetables, potatoes for instance, that might be damaged by the movement of simmering water, are left intact.

Gadgets for Steaming

Steaming is simple. Liquid, usually water but occasionally wine or vegetable stock (court bouillon), is brought to a rapid boil, food to be steamed is suspended over the liquid, and the pot covered.

There are many steamers and related gadgets available.

- The least-expensive steamers are circular folding steamers with perforated metal leaves. You just unfold the steamer inside a pot with a little liquid in it so the ends of the leaves meet the sides of the pot. These folding steamers work perfectly well with leafy vegetables or small amounts of green or root vegetables.

- A gadget that works well for larger quantities looks like a bucket with holes in it. The bucket has little feet that keep it about an inch above the bottom of a pot—just enough so the boiling liquid doesn't get into the steamer through the holes in the bottom. Just bring ½ inch of water to a boil in a pot, arrange the food to be steamed in the bucket, put the bucket in the pot, and put the lid on (see page 87).

- Chinese bamboo steamers are inexpensive and easy to use. They look like drums with thin bamboo slats held in a thick wooden ring with a snug-fitting lid. An advantage of bamboo steamers is that you can stack them on top of each other so you can steam a

larger amount of food or you can steam different foods with different cooking times. Start with a layer of slower-cooking foods and then add layers of quicker-cooking foods later. Originally, Chinese steamers were designed to use in a wok, but a pot will work just as well. Make sure that it has the same diameter as the steamer so the steam is forced upward.

To Steam Greens

1. Bring about an inch of water to a rapid boil in a pot large enough to hold the steamer insert. Place the greens (here, spinach) in the steamer insert and lower it into the pot with the boiling water. Cover and steam for 1 minute.
2. Turn off the heat, remove the lid, allow about 15 seconds for the steam to dissipate, and remove the steamer insert. Unless you're using the spinach right away, refresh the spinach by rinsing under cold running water, or submerging in a bowl of ice water, as shown here.
3. Squeeze excess water out of the refreshed spinach.

To Boil Greens

Green vegetables are excellent when steamed, but some cooks prefer to boil green vegetables because they cook faster and boiling better preserves their bright green color. When boiling green vegetables, use a lot of salted water and boil uncovered. If you're not serving the vegetables right away, immediately rinse them under cold running water in a colander or plunge them in ice water.

1. Plunge the cleaned greens (here, spinach) into a large pot of boiling salted water and stir.
2. As soon as the spinach melts, about 30 seconds, drain in a colander and rinse under cold running water or plunge into a bowl of ice water.
3. Gently squeeze the excess water out of the spinach.

Boiled spinach can be reheated by lightly sautéing it in olive oil or butter, or it can be creamed.

See Also

To slow-cook hardy greens, page 75
To stem greens, page 8

Related Glossary Entries

Boil
Poach
Steam

Creamed Spinach (and Other Leafy Greens)

Once cooked, greens can be served as is or perhaps sauced with lightly reduced cream. (Creamed spinach is delicious when made with a minimum of cream and lightly cooked spinach.) When you cream greens, they must be completely dry so that their moisture doesn't dilute the cream and cause it to run out onto the plate. And the cream must be reduced until so thick that it almost breaks and turns oily. The moisture in the vegetables will reconstitute the cream.

1. Simmer about 2 tablespoons heavy cream in a heavy saucepan until very thick. Season with salt and pepper.
2. Add a well-squeezed bunch of steamed or boiled and refreshed spinach (or other greens) and heat through, stirring with a wooden spoon.

HOW TO

Sauté Vegetables

Sautéing is a high-heat cooking method that concentrates and enhances the flavor of vegetables by evaporating their water and caramelizing them so that they are savory and flavorful on the outside and meltingly tender on the inside. The fat you use—butter, oil, or rendered animal fat—adds additional flavor.

Small vegetables or vegetable slices and pieces are sautéed by tossing in a wide pan with sloping sides. Tossing is better than stirring because it's gentler and even delicate stirring can crush some vegetables as they cook. Tossing can be intimidating at first, but with a little experience (tossing dried beans is good practice), it becomes second nature and is easier than stirring. Vegetable pieces that are too large to toss—such as potatoes, long slices of zucchini or eggplant—are sautéed in a single layer until browned, then turned with a pair of tongs or a spatula. Watery vegetables such as sliced tomatoes may also be coated with flour or a breading mixture before sautéing. The coating absorbs the moisture given off by the vegetable as it cooks and helps it brown; it also adds flavor and keeps the vegetable from absorbing fat.

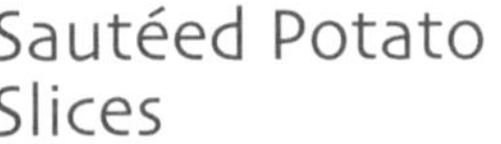

Sautéed Potato Slices

1. Slice peeled russet potatoes into ⅛- to ¼-inch-thick rounds. Rinse thoroughly in cold water to eliminate some of the starch. Drain and pat dry on kitchen towels. (Paper towels will stick and tear.)
2. Cook the potatoes in a single layer in hot clarified butter or olive oil over medium heat. Turn them gently with a spatula as they brown.
3. Transfer the potatoes to a serving dish and sprinkle with salt.

Château Potatoes

French château potatoes are traditionally made with large potatoes turned to small, perfect egg shapes, but it's easier and less wasteful to use peeled, whole, small waxy potatoes (here, I use Peruvian purple potatoes).

1. Put the peeled potatoes in a pot with cold water to cover. Bring to a simmer over low to medium heat, adjusting the heat so that the water takes about 15 minutes to come to a simmer. Remove the potatoes with a slotted spoon or drain in a colander.
2. Sauté the potatoes in vegetable oil in an ovenproof skillet over medium-high heat until lightly browned. Add whole butter to the pan and roast the potatoes in a 375°F oven until well browned and easily penetrated with a knife, about 15 minutes.

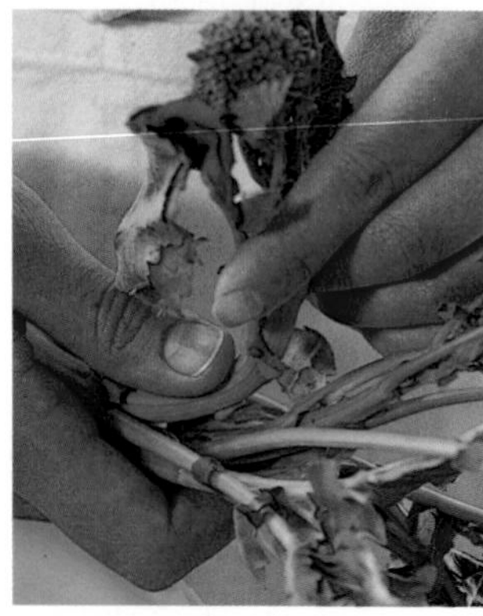

Sautéed Broccoli Rabe with Garlic

It's pointless to sauté most greens, because they release so much water into the pan when they hit the hot oil or butter that they steam instead of sauté. I do, however, sauté broccoli rabe, which gives up less water than other greens. Even broccoli rabe releases enough moisture to steam, however, so it steams and is flavored with the hot olive oil in the same operation. Flavorful ingredients such as chopped or sliced garlic, ginger, chiles, or cubes of pancetta or bacon can be used to flavor the hot oil before the vegetables are added.

1. Pull the leaves and flowers away from the thick central stems. Leave small tender stems attached to the flowers and leaves.
2. Cook sliced garlic in olive oil over medium heat until the garlic barely begins to turn blond.
3. Add the trimmed broccoli rabe and stir it around with a wooden spoon until it becomes limp.
4. Continue cooking over medium heat until the broccoli rabe has the texture you like, about 5 to 10 minutes. (If you like it well cooked, add a little liquid—broth or water—cover, and cook 5 to 10 minutes more.)

Sautéed Eggplant

Here, the eggplant is cut lengthwise, but it can also be cut across, into rounds.

1. Cut the stem ends off the eggplant and peel (optional). Slice the eggplant with a plastic vegetable slicer, as shown here, or by hand.
2. Coat the eggplant slices with flour, pat off the excess, and dip in beaten egg seasoned with salt, pepper, and fresh thyme leaves.
3. Sauté the eggplant slices in olive oil or whole butter over medium-high heat until golden brown on the first side. Turn gently with tongs and brown on the other side. Drain on paper towels.

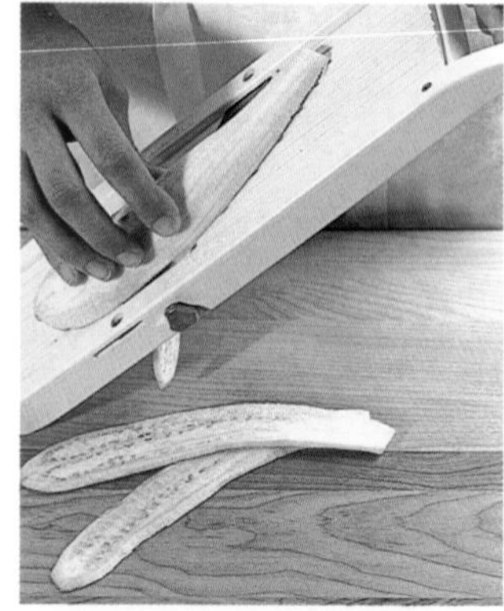

Sautéed Zucchini with Parsley and Garlic

Flavor sautéed vegetables at the end of cooking with the mixture of parsley and garlic called a persillade.

1. Toss the zucchini in olive oil over high heat until the zucchini turns golden brown and smells fragrant. Gently stir in a few spoonfuls of persillade.
2. Continue tossing for a minute or two, until the smell of garlic fills the room. Serve immediately.

Kitchen Notes and Tips

- Sauté vegetables in butter (whole or clarified), olive or vegetable oil, or rendered animal fat. When choosing which fat to use, think of the character of the dish: I use olive oil, for example, with sautéed zucchini, because it is southern French or Italian. Use oil or clarified butter for sautéing over high heat; you cannot cook over high heat with whole butter—it will burn. For foods that are not floured or breaded, heat oil or clarified butter until the fat ripples in the pan but is not smoking. Sauté breaded vegetables in clarified butter, because, although whole butter will work, its milk solids will darken as they cook and dot the breading with dark specks.
- If you want the flavor of butter but don't want to go to the trouble of clarifying it, sauté the vegetable in a small amount of oil and add whole butter at the end of cooking.
- Watery vegetables, like zucchini, eggplant, and mushrooms, can be sautéed over high heat without burning.Denser vegetables, like potatoes and other root vegetables, need medium-high, or sometimes medium, heat.
- For floured or breaded vegetables, use medium-high heat rather than high, because flour browns at a lower temperature than the vegetable itself. You can use whole butter as well, because the heat is gentler.
- Potatoes can be sautéed whole, sliced, or cut into small regular cubes. Sliced potatoes are hard to toss because the starch in the potato causes them to stick together—use a spatula to turn them one by one. It's easier and quicker to sauté cubes than slices, but they don't look as pretty. Large pieces of potatoes or whole potatoes must be blanched before sautéing. (With the exception of potatoes, I don't sauté root vegetables. I'd rather glaze or roast them.)
- Sauté mushrooms over very high heat so that their water, released into the pan as soon as the mushrooms get hot, evaporates the instant it hits the pan. And add mushrooms to the hot pan only a handful at a time so the pan temperature isn't lowered or too much liquid released. (I prefer cremini mushrooms to regular cultivated mushrooms because they are less watery and more flavorful.)
- For most sautéing, use enough fat to coat the bottom of the pan. When sautéing a floured or breaded vegetable, use more fat, because the coating absorbs some of it.
- Keep an eye on the vegetable to ensure that the outside doesn't get too brown and the oil doesn't burn before the inside cooks through. (If the vegetable browns too fast, lower the heat.)

See Also

To clarify butter, page 46
To turn vegetables, pages 13 and 21
To dice vegetables, pages 13 and 17
To coat with eggs and bread crumbs, page 162
To peel eggplant, page 3

Related Glossary Entries

Bread
Panfry
Persillade
Sauté
Slicer
Sweat (for the difference between sautéing and sweating)

HOW TO
Cook Artichokes

Boil artichokes in water to cover by several inches with a tablespoon of olive oil until the bottom of the artichoke is easily penetrated with a paring knife. (Bring the water to a boil before adding the artichokes.) Artichokes will darken if cooked in aluminum or exposed to air during cooking, so use a nonaluminum pot and put a plate or kitchen towel on top of the artichokes to keep them submerged. Also, to keep them from darkening, raw artichokes are rubbed with lemon; the oil in the water helps protect them from exposure to oxygen, too. Serve cooked whole artichokes with homemade mayonnaise (homemade aïoli is fantastic with artichokes) or vinaigrette.

Artichokes are sometimes trimmed of their leaves and choke (a technique called "turning") and the cooked bottoms served whole—as a container for small vegetables such as peas—or cut into wedges and served on their own as a vegetable. Baby artichokes have a slightly milder flavor than bigger artichokes and they're easier to prepare, because the immature chokes are so small that you don't need to remove them.

To Prepare and Cook Whole Artichokes

1. Cut the stem off the artichoke just above the small leaves at the top of the stem.
2. Whole artichokes are gently simmered in water containing a dribble of olive oil to keep the artichokes from turning dark. Cover the artichokes with a damp towel or a plate to keep them moist during cooking. Boil until a paring knife slides with only slight resistance into the base, 25 to 30 minutes.

To Prepare and Cook Baby Artichokes

If you're serving the artichokes as a garniture for a stew, cut off the stem flush with the bottom. If you're serving as a vegetable side dish, you can peel the stem, removing the tough fibers, and leave it attached to the artichoke.
1. If the end of the stem is dark or dried out, trim it off. Cut off the top half of the leaves.
2. Rotate the artichoke bottom against the blade of a very sharp small knife to trim off the outermost dark green leaves.
3. Trim off and discard the tiny leaves at the base. Toss the artichokes in a bowl with oil and lemon juice. Boil for about 30 minutes.

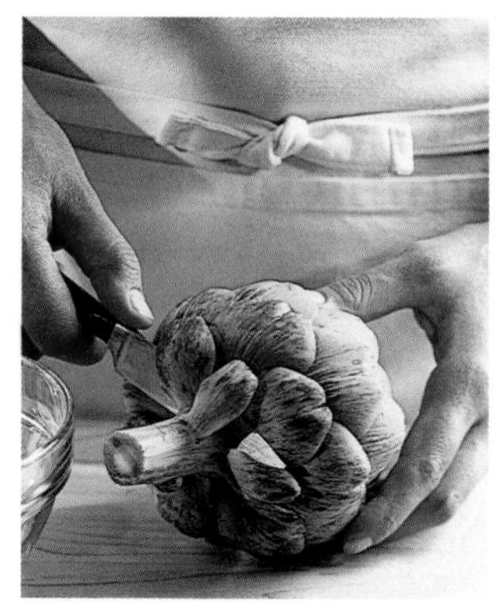

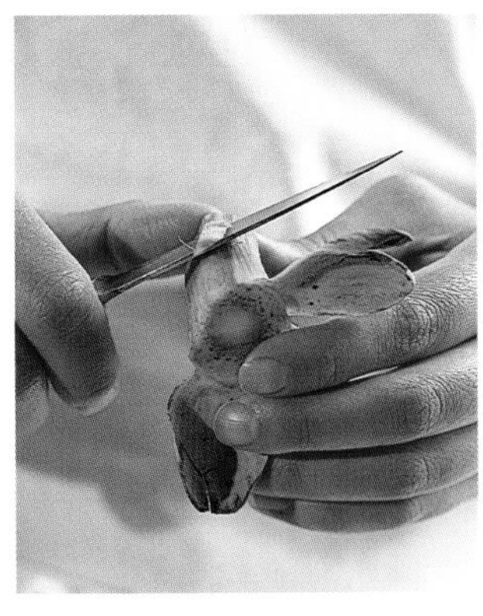

To Turn Artichokes

The stems from large artichokes can be trimmed and boiled and served in a little dish on the side, sliced and layered into a zucchini gratin, or used in stuffings.

1. If you're using the stems, peel off the tough outer layer and outer fibers with a paring knife. Rub the stem with lemon juice.
2. Rotate the artichoke against a very sharp paring knife, keeping the blade perpendicular to the base of the artichoke, until you see the pale green flesh on the sides of the base.
3. Hold the artichoke so the base is facing the knife at an angle and rotate the artichoke, trimming the leaves off the bottom.
4. Hold the artichoke upside down and trim off any last patches of green.
5. Cut the leaves away from the base. Be careful not to cut off any of the base—it's better to err in the direction of leaving too many leaves attached to the base; they can be trimmed later.

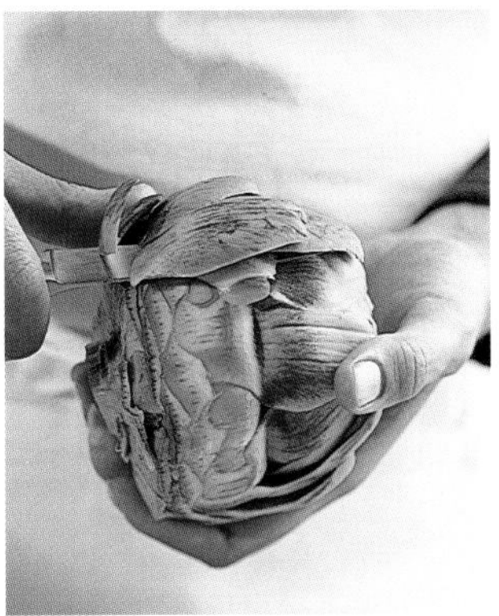

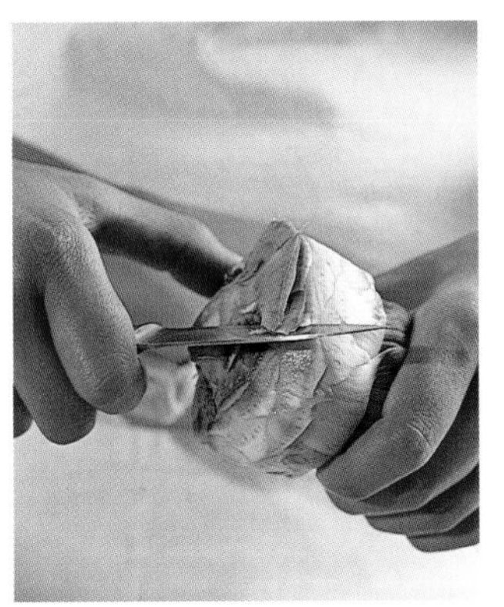

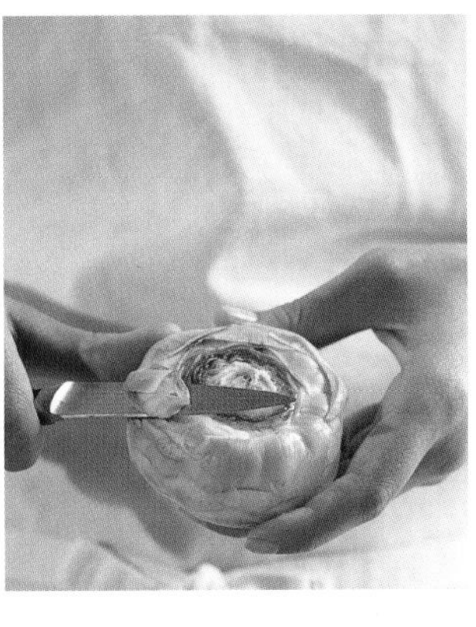

6. Again, rotate the artichoke against the knife, trimming off any dark patches that are still attached to the top of the base. Rub with lemon juice to prevent darkening. Then cook the hearts as you would whole artichokes (but don't bother with the towel or plate, because they don't bob up as much as the whole vegetables).

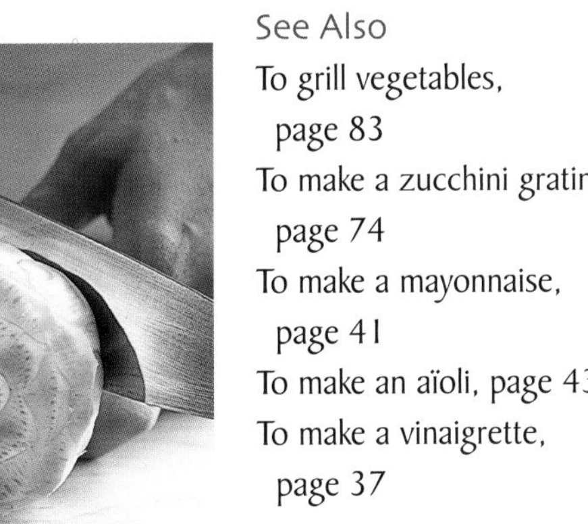

See Also

To grill vegetables, page 83

To make a zucchini gratin, page 74

To make a mayonnaise, page 41

To make an aïoli, page 43

To make a vinaigrette, page 37

To Remove the Choke from Cooked Artichoke Bottoms

The choke can be cut out of raw artichoke bottoms, but it's easier to cook the artichoke first, for about 20 minutes, and then scrape the choke out with a spoon.

1. Scrape along the inside of the artichoke with a spoon. Don't dig or cut into the artichoke bottom—just scrape and pull the choke away from the flesh.
2. The chokeless bottom can be used whole—in formal presentations it can be used to hold buttered peas or fava beans—or cut into wedges and served as a vegetable.

HOW TO

Make Mashed Potatoes and Other Vegetable and Fruit Purées

A purée is a food that has been mashed or sieved to make it smooth and soft, like mashed potatoes. The smoothest purées are made by working the cooked vegetables through a drum sieve, which makes very fine purées and gives the finished purées a silky-smooth consistency. But since most cooks (outside of restaurant professionals) don't own drum sieves, most can get by using either a ricer—a gadget that presses cooked vegetables through small holes—or a potato masher. The ricer produces a purée that is only slightly less smooth than a drum sieve. A masher may leave some lumps, but it's very easy to use. Never purée white-fleshed potatoes in a food processor or blender. These machines overwork the starch in the potatoes and you'll end up with a gummy, gluey purée.

Unless they're very stiff, many vegetables and fruits *can* be puréed in a food processor. A regular-mesh strainer or a food mill will purée most vegetables regardless of texture.

Kitchen Notes and Tips

- Unless they are to be part of a soup or sauce, vegetable purées should be thick enough to hold their shape on the plate, but other than that, the consistency is up to you.
- To make mashed potatoes, work the cooked potatoes through a ricer or drum sieve, or use a potato masher. Thin the purée with a little of the potato cooking liquid (it thins without adding fat), and enrich the mixture with cream and/or milk and butter to taste. Season with salt and pepper.
- For other vegetable purées (such as acorn squash or root vegetables), purée the cooked vegetable, add butter or broth, and season with salt and pepper.
- For applesauce or any other cooked fruit purée, purée the fruit and add sugar and lemon juice to taste.
- All vegetable and fruit purées can be reheated in a saucepan over low heat. Stir so that the purée doesn't burn.

To Use a Ricer to Purée Potatoes

1. Place the peeled and cooked potatoes in the ricer. Set the ricer over a bowl.

2. Squeeze the ricer handles together, forcing the pulp through the tiny holes.

To Mash Potatoes with a Potato Masher

1. Mash boiled peeled potatoes with cream and butter, as shown here, or with lighter liquids such as milk, broth, or the potato cooking liquid.

2. Mashed potatoes are sometimes flavored by adding vegetables such as celeriac, garlic, or fennel to the potatoes before they are pureed. Here, pesto is stirred into the mashed potatoes just before serving.

To Use a Food Mill to Make Applesauce

1. Toss sliced apples with a tablespoon of fresh lemon juice to keep them from turning dark and then put them in a heavy-bottomed pot with about ½ cup of water. The water generates steam, which helps cook the apples; it also helps keep them from burning.
2. Cover the pot and cook over low to medium heat until the apples have softened, 15 to 30 minutes, depending on the apples. (Check every now and then to make sure that there's liquid in the pot. Add a little more water as necessary.)
3. Uncover the pot and continue cooking, stirring, until all of the liquid evaporates.
4. Set the food mill over a bowl. Add the apple slices and crank the food mill, forcing the apple mixture through the grid.

To Use a Coarse-Mesh Drum Sieve to Purée Acorn Squash

1. Cut the squash crosswise in half.
2. Scoop out and discard the seeds. Set the squash cut side up on a baking sheet and bake at 375°F until soft.
3. Set the drum sieve on a clean surface or a sheet pan and scoop the squash pulp onto the sieve. Work the pulp through the sieve with the back of a spoon or a plastic pastry scraper.
4. Scrape off any pulp clinging to the underside of the sieve, adding it to the rest of the purée.

To Use a Strainer and a Fine-Mesh Drum Sieve to Purée Chestnuts

Instead of puréeing cooked chestnuts in a food processor, which incorporates pieces of the dark inner peel into the purée, work the chestnuts through a strainer or drum sieve, eliminating the pieces of the peel while puréeing. Here, the chestnuts are worked first through a coarse strainer and then through a fine-mesh drum sieve. Serve chestnut purée with game or meat with red wine sauce.

1. Braise the peeled chestnuts in a covered pan with a small amount of broth, port, or water. Use a slotted spoon to scoop the cooked chestnuts into a coarse-mesh strainer set over a bowl. (Reserve the braising liquid.)
2. Work the chestnuts through the strainer with the back of a ladle.
3. Scrape the purée clinging to the outside of the strainer into the rest of the purée.
4. For a very fine purée, work the strained mixture through a fine-mesh drum sieve with the back of a spoon or wooden spatula.
5. Scrape off the purée clinging to the underside of the drum sieve, adding it to the rest of the purée.

6. Thin the purée to the consistency of creamy mashed potatoes with the reserved braising liquid plus additional broth, and if you like, butter or cream.
7. Stir until smooth. Season to taste with salt and white pepper.

See Also

To thicken with vegetable purées, page 286
To cook potatoes, page 89
To make pesto, page 99
To make a chicken broth, page 30
To use vegetable purées for vegetable flans, page 97
To make a puréed vegetable soup, page 100
To peel chestnuts, page 4

Related Glossary Entries

Braise
Purée (also for information on equipment for puréeing)

HOW TO

Make a Vegetable Flan

A vegetable flan is a savory baked custard made by holding liquids together with eggs. A quiche is a flan with a crust. Flans are a great way to turn leftover cooked vegetables and soups into something different. Vegetable flans can be made with whole eggs, egg yolks, or egg whites (or sometimes a combination), depending on how rich you want the mixture to be, and usually contain cream or milk to give the flan a smooth, melting texture and to keep it from being rubbery. Flans are baked in a *bain-marie* (water bath) so they cook evenly, don't overcook or curdle, and become creamy and smooth.

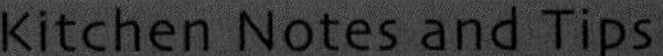

Kitchen Notes and Tips

- To make a flan mixture from leftover cooked vegetables, purée the vegetables and then add enough milk or cream (or a combination of both) to give the purée the consistency of thick soup.
- Bind ¾ cup of flavorful soup or thinned vegetable purée with 1 whole egg, 2 egg whites, or 2 egg yolks. (The more yolk, the richer the mixture will be.)
- If you're using a hot liquid, whisk it into the eggs rather than the other way around. Eggs whisked into very hot liquid will curdle.
- Cook flans at 350°F in a *bain-marie* until the mixture no longer ripples on the surface when the flan is jiggled.
- To make a quiche from a flan mixture, pour the mixture into a prebaked pastry shell and bake at 300°F until set, about 40 minutes.

Carrot Flan

1. Whisk hot carrot purée, diluted with milk, cream, or a combination—essentially the carrot soup on page 100 but without the potatoes—into beaten eggs.
2. Line a baking pan with a triple layer of parchment paper to protect the ramekins from the direct heat of the stove. Fill buttered ramekins with the flan mixture and pour hot water into the pan to come halfway up the sides of the ramekins. Bring the water in the pan to a simmer over high heat. Transfer to the oven and bake at 350°F for about 45 minutes, until the mixture has set.
3. To unmold the flans, place a small plate upside down on each mold, turn the whole assembly over, and give it a quick shake up and down to release the flan.
4. Remove the mold.

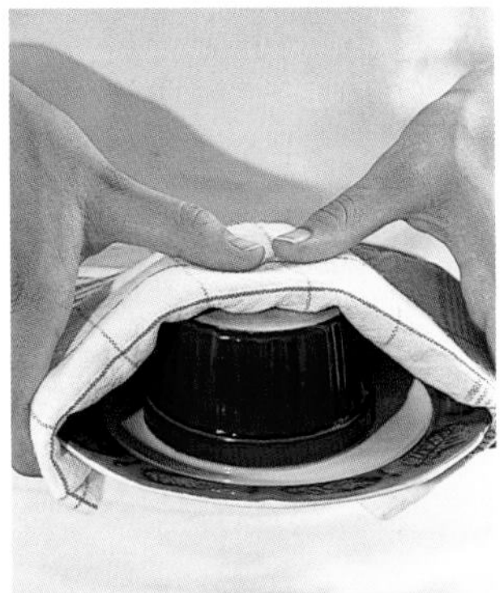

See Also

To purée vegetables, page 94
To determine doneness, page 66
To make Puréed Carrot Soup, page 100

Related Glossary Entries

Bain-marie
Purée

HOW TO

Make a Chunky Vegetable Soup

Most of the world's best vegetable soups are made in the same way, by simmering chopped vegetables in water or broth. Different vegetables are used, depending on what's available and what's in season, but the basic method is almost always the same. Sometimes starchy ingredients such as rice or pasta are added to the soups to make them more substantial.

There are two tricks for elevating a simple vegetable soup into something sublime. One is to cook cubes of preserved pork, such as pancetta or prosciutto ends, in the pot before adding the vegetables. If you're using prosciutto, you'll need to add a little olive oil to the pan, since the prosciutto itself releases very little fat. A second trick is to stir a flavorful mixture into the soup just before serving or to pass it at the table for guests to help themselves. The mixture can be a simple as a little crushed garlic and chopped parsley or it can be more elaborate. Two of the most famous examples of this method are Ligurian *minestrone col pesto* and Provençal *soupe au pistou*—vegetable soups finished with pastes of crushed garlic, basil, Parmesan cheese (or pecorino), and pine nuts (in the Italian pesto) or tomatoes (in the French pistou).

Many of the same tricks used to enhance the flavor and color of creamy soups are also applicable to chunky soups. Sweat aromatic vegetables in a small amount of fat before adding liquid (along with prosciutto as mentioned above if you're using it); add green vegetables and quick-cooking vegetables near the end of cooking; and precook hard-to-peel vegetables such as acorn squash before adding them to the soup.

Chunky Vegetable Soup

1. Cut prosciutto ends, shown here, or pancetta into ¼-inch dice.
2. Stir the prosciutto in a small amount of olive oil in a heavy-bottomed pot over low to medium heat until fragrant, about 10 minutes. If you're using pancetta, don't bother with the olive oil—pancetta supplies its own fat as it cooks.

3. Add chopped vegetables such as leeks, onions, garlic, carrots, turnips, parsnips, and/or potatoes and cook gently for about 10 minutes, until the vegetables soften slightly and release their fragrance.
4. Add moist or quick-cooking ingredients, such as the tomatoes and precooked dried beans shown here. Add broth or water and simmer until all the vegetables are completely soft. Just before serving, add green vegetables, such as the string beans used here, and simmer for about 10 minutes.

5. Spoon the soup into warmed bowls. Here, I've placed a piece of toast rubbed with garlic in the bottom of each bowl to add substance and flavor to the soup—and so the vegetables form an attractive mound on top of the soup.
6. Pass pesto sauce at the table so guests can spoon it into their soups.

To Make Pesto Sauce

In this basic pesto sauce, garlic and basil are crushed to a paste in a mortar with a pestle and the mixture combined with grated Parmesan cheese and olive oil. It can also be made in a food processor, puréeing the ingredients as on page 39. Traditional Ligurian versions contain pine nuts, and the French *pistou* contains tomatoes.

1. Combine thinly sliced garlic with coarse salt—the salt helps grind the garlic—in a mortar and work to a smooth paste.

2. Work in basil leaves, a handful at a time, and continue grinding to a smooth paste. Combine with olive oil and freshly grated Parmesan cheese.

See Also
To make a chicken broth, page 30
To make a creamy vegetable soup, page 100

HOW TO

Make a Creamy Vegetable Soup

Traditionally, creamy vegetable soups were usually thickened with a roux and then enriched with cream or butter. You can make a simpler light, creamy vegetable soup by puréeing vegetables with broth, water, or milk. (Milk is a little tricky because it can curdle when boiled, but you can stabilize it by adding puréed vegetables.) Then, if you like, you can enrich the soup with butter or cream.

To make almost any creamy vegetable soup, start by sweating aromatic vegetables such as leeks or onions in a little butter, so they release their flavor, before adding liquid. If you're using green vegetables such as spinach, broccoli, peas, or chard, add them near the end so they don't lose their color. Some vegetables, such as asparagus, can be cooked in two stages—the stalks simmered in the soup for about ten minutes before the soup is puréed, and the tips quickly blanched and added to the soup just before serving. Purée soups with a food mill, blender, immersion blender, or strainer. Don't use a food processor or the liquid will run out through the hole under the blade.

Puréed Leek and Potato Soup

1. Gently sweat sliced leeks in butter over medium heat until they soften and turn translucent, about 20 minutes.
2. Add peeled and sliced potatoes. Pour in liquid such as broth, milk, or water and simmer until the potatoes have completely softened.
3. Purée the soup by working it through a coarse strainer, as shown here, or through a food mill. If you want it even smoother, strain it again through a fine-mesh strainer. Whisk heavy cream or butter into the soup (optional).

Puréed Carrot Soup

Practically any vegetable can be added to a leek and potato soup to give the soup that vegetable's flavor and color.

1. Add carrots or other slow-cooking vegetable when you add the liquid and potatoes.
2. Carrot soup is better finished by whisking in butter instead of cream.

See Also

To make a chicken broth, page 30
To make miso soup, page 143

Related Glossary Entries

Purée
Sweat

HOW TO

Roast Fruit

Roasting intensifies the taste of fruit and is an excellent technique for most fruits, with the exception of berries or kiwis, which are so delicate that they turn to mush in the oven.

Very juicy fruits, such as pears and peaches, release a lot of liquid as they roast. The juices cook down and caramelize in the bottom of the pan along with added butter and sugar. I use this mixture to make a pan sauce—much like a meat "jus" or gravy made from pan drippings—by deglazing the pan with cream and simmering until smooth. (Unlike the method used for making a jus or gravy, however, in which fat in the pan is removed before deglazing, here the butter remains in the pan and is emulsified into the sauce.) For a perfectly smooth sauce, strain to remove any dark specks.

Bananas and apples don't release much liquid, so I treat them more like a gratin. Sprinkle bananas or sliced or cut up apples with butter and sugar and roast them until they turn golden brown. Flambéed rum, poured over just before serving, combines with the caramelized butter-sugar mixture to make the sauce.

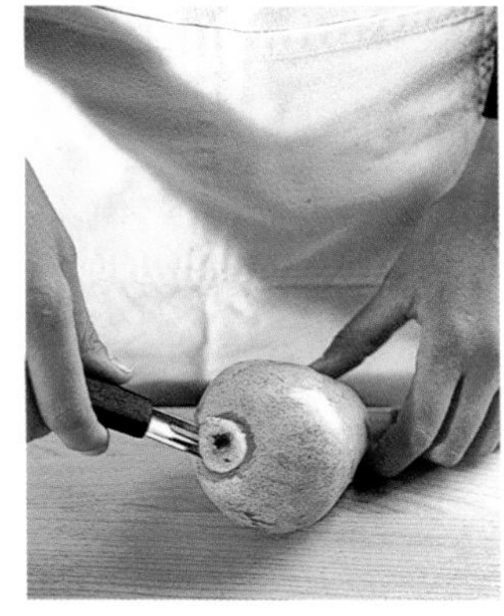

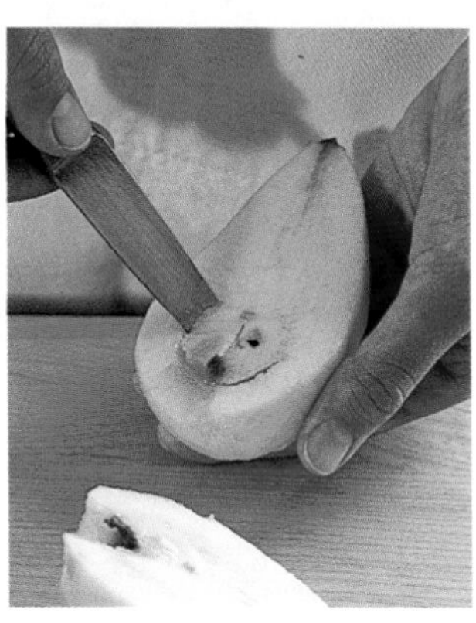

Roasted Pear Halves with Cream

To peel pears

1. Cut out the dark blossom end of the core at the bottom of the pear by inserting a peeler deep into the pear and rotating it around the core.
2. Peel by rotating the pear against the blade of the vegetable peeler.

To core and seed pear halves

3. Cut the peeled pears vertically in half and then use a paring knife to cut out the stem.
4. Cut out the seeds from each half with the paring knife (or use a melon baller).

7. Transfer the pears to a serving dish or individual plates. Heat the roasting pan over medium to high heat and pour in heavy cream.
8. Simmer, stirring with a wooden spoon, until the caramel dissolves and the mixture forms a smooth sauce. Strain, if desired, and ladle the sauce over the hot pears as shown on page 101.

To roast pears

5. Spread the pear halves in a heavy pan just large enough to hold them in a single layer. Add chunks of butter and coat liberally with sugar.
6. Roast at 375°F until the pears are soft, the juices have caramelized to a nutty brown glaze on the bottom of the pan, and the butter has separated and is floating on top, 30 to 45 minutes.

Kitchen Notes and Tips

- For juicy fruits such as pears: For 6 pears, use 1 cup sugar and ½ pound (2 sticks) unsalted butter, with ¾ cup heavy cream to finish. Cook the pears until the juices are caramelized and the pears are soft.
- For bananas and similar fruits: For 4 bananas, use 8 tablespoons (1 stick) unsalted butter, ½ cup sugar, and ½ cup dark rum.

Baked Bananas with Rum

1. Sprinkle peeled and halved bananas with sugar and dot with butter. Bake at 350°F until the bananas have browned and the sugar has lightly caramelized, about 30 minutes.
2. Flambé dark rum in the kitchen. When the flames die out, spoon the rum over the bananas and serve. You can also flambé in the dining room.

See Also
To flambé, page 269
To make a jus from roasted meats, page 187

Related Glossary Entries
Deglaze
Emulsion
Gratin
Jus
Roast

HOW TO

Poach Fruit

Poaching is a great way to deal with out-of-season or underripe fruits that are too hard or haven't developed enough natural sugar to be tasty on their own. The fruit is poached in water, wine, fruit juice, spirits such as whiskey or rum, or some combination of these, almost always sweetened with sugar. (The sugar is necessary even when poaching ripe, sweet fruits, because without it, the poaching liquid will pull out the fruits' natural sugars.) The liquid can also be flavored with spices such as cinnamon, cloves, or vanilla. After poaching, the cooking liquid is often reduced so that the flavor of the fruit is concentrated in it, and then it is served along with the fruit.

A delicious way to poach all kinds of fruit is to cook the fruit in water sweetened with sugar, reduce and cool the syrup, and then flavor it with an appropriate fruit brandy or other alcohol that underlines the taste of the fruit. Pears are often poached in sweetened red wine that is then reduced, cooled, and served as a sauce for the pears.

Poached Strawberries and Apricots

Here, strawberries and apricots are poached separately in a light sugar syrup. The syrup from each fruit is then reduced to concentrate its flavor, allowed to cool, and flavored with an appropriate fruit brandy.

1. Pour water over the fruit in each saucepan to cover, add sugar, and simmer until the fruit is soft.
2. Use a slotted spoon to transfer the fruit to a bowl. Boil the poaching liquid down to a thick syrup. Let cool, then flavor with a fruit brandy or other alcohol, such as rum, brandy, or whiskey.
3. Let each fruit macerate in its own flavored syrup for at least an hour and as long as several days in the refrigerator. Serve in stemmed glasses or bowls, or spoon over ice cream.

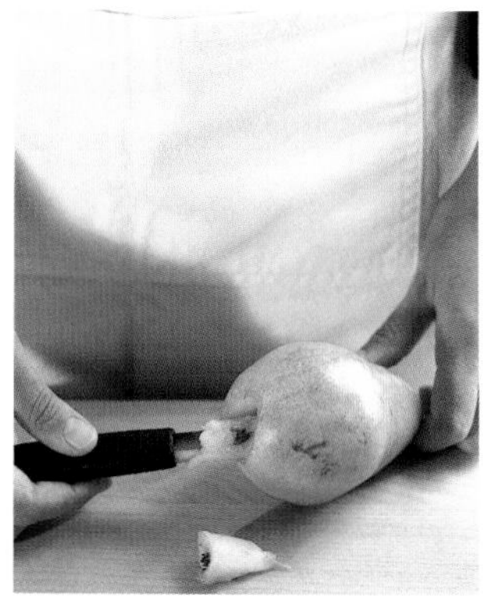

Poached Pears in Red Wine

To core whole pears

1. Remove the core from the bottom of the pear with a nonswivel peeler, a corer, or a paring knife.

To poach pears

2. Pour red wine over to completely cover cored and peeled pears in a saucepan and sprinkle generously with sugar.
3. Poach at a bare simmer until the pears are easily penetrated with a paring knife.
4. Drain the pears and reduce the poaching liquid until it is the consistency of thin syrup. Cut the pears in half and slice each half into a fan shape.
5. Serve hot or cold in shallow bowls, spooning the sauce around.

Kitchen Notes and Tips

- Sweeten the poaching syrup lightly so that when it reduces, it doesn't become too sweet.
- When using spirits to flavor the poaching liquid (eaux-de-vie, fruit brandies, rum, whiskey, brandy), poach the fruit in a sugar syrup first and add the spirits only after the syrup has reduced and cooled. Reduce the syrup to a fairly thick consistency (it will be sweeter than you like), because the alcohol will thin the consistency as well as cut the sweetness of the syrup.
- As you get adept at poaching, you may want to adjust the amount of sugar in the syrup to the sweetness of the fruit. But here are some basic proportions to get you going:

  For pears only: (for 6 pears) 2 bottles red wine to 1 cup sugar. Flavor with 1 vanilla bean, split, and 2 cinnamon sticks (optional).

  For all fruits: 2 cups water to ½ cup sugar.

See Also

To hull strawberries, page 28
To peel pears, page 101

Related Glossary Entries

Fruit brandy
Poach

Fish and Shellfish

HOW TO

Poach a Big Fish

Poaching is a great way to cook a big whole fish, particularly one that you will be serving cold, because poaching cooks without fat, which would congeal on the fish when it cooled. Poaching makes the skin of the fish easy to remove, leaving the flesh underneath smooth and intact, even-colored, and pretty looking. Best of all, poaching doesn't alter the delicate taste of the fish.

Fish is traditionally poached in a court bouillon, a vegetable broth flavored with white wine, but I often simplify things by just combining water, white wine, salt, and a bouquet garni in the pan with the fish.

You need a fish poacher or a large deep roasting pan to poach a big fish. A poacher is a long narrow lidded pot with handles at either end that is fitted with a two-handled rack. A fish poacher is easier to use than a roasting pan because the rack makes it easy to pull the fish out of the hot water without its falling apart. And the shape of the poacher allows you to use a minimum of liquid.

I most often poach salmon or its smaller relative, Arctic char, but occasionally I'll poach a large striped bass.

To Poach in a Fish Poacher

Here, an Arctic char, a fish closely related to trout and salmon, is poached in a court bouillon that has been strained and allowed to cool.

1. Place the char in the fish poacher and ladle over enough cooled court bouillon to completely cover the fish. Bring to a simmer over medium heat.
2. Simmer the fish gently until done. Lift the rack out of the poacher and set it on an angle on top of the poacher. To remove the skin, cut through it at the base of the head.

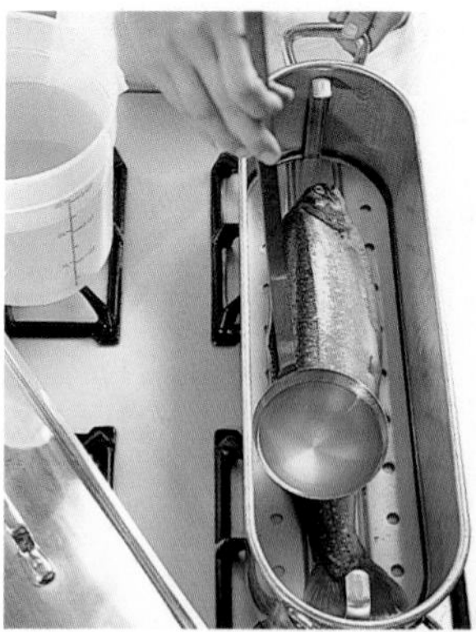

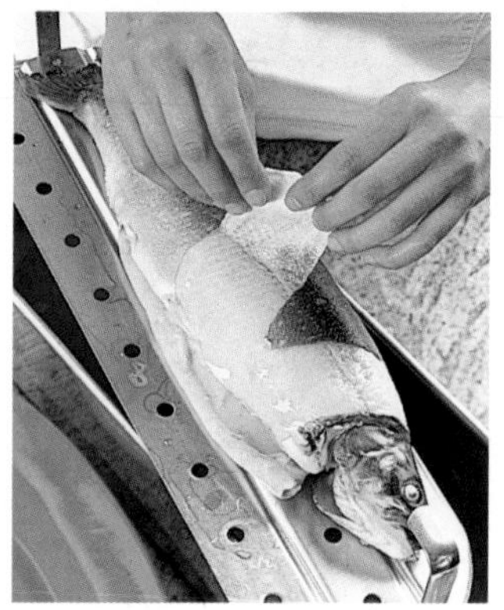

3. Peel off the skin with your fingers and discard. Gently turn the fish out onto a serving platter and peel the skin off the other side. If the fish is too large or awkward to handle, leave the skin on the bottom and discard when serving.

To Serve

1. Insert 2 spoons (or a fish knife) in the dark line that runs along the center of the top of the fish. Gently separate the 2 halves of the top fillet.
2. Cut the fillets into sections with one of the spoons—here, the top fillet is sectioned into sixths, but for larger fish, you'll need to cut more pieces.
3. Continue sectioning the fillet and transfer the pieces to hot plates.
4. Lift the spinal column to detach it from the bottom fillet.
5. Break the spinal column where it joins the head and set it and the head aside on the platter.
6. Pull away any bones that remain attached to the bottom fillet.
7. Separate the bottom fillet into sections, leaving the skin behind if you haven't already removed it, and serve.

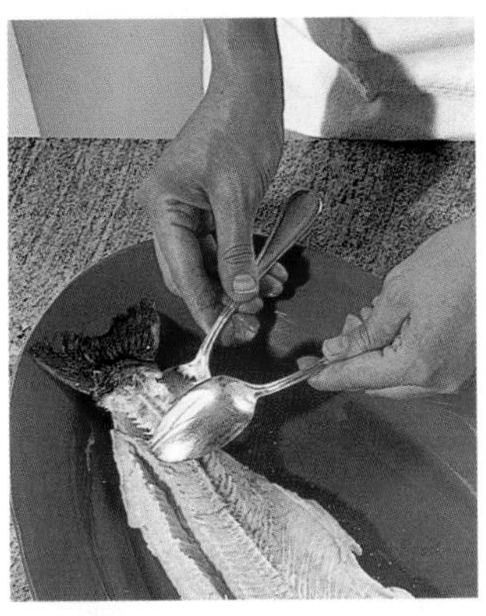

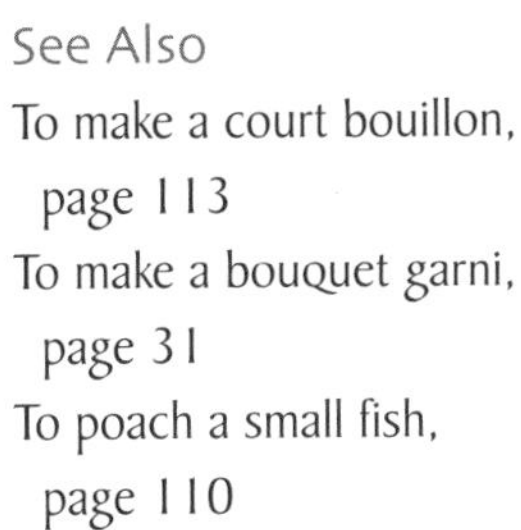

See Also

To make a court bouillon, page 113

To make a bouquet garni, page 31

To poach a small fish, page 110

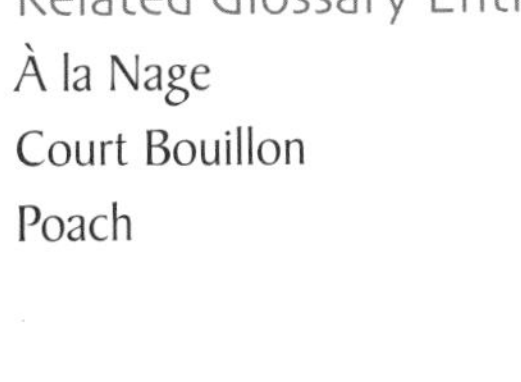

Related Glossary Entries

À la Nage

Court Bouillon

Poach

Kitchen Notes and Tips

- Fish poachers come in different sizes; obviously, the larger the fish, the larger the poacher you'll need. But if the fish is too large for your poacher, ask your fish retailer to cut off the head and the tail.
- It's best to heat the poacher over two burners.
- Poach fish in a court bouillon, or for simplicity, in salted water with a splash of white wine and a bouquet garni.
- Start the fish in cold liquid so that the outside of the fish doesn't overcook before the inside is cooked through. (Smaller fish are poached in hot liquid. See page 110.)
- Poach fish for 7 to 10 minutes per inch of thickness. Start timing the cooking once the liquid has come to the simmer. Begin checking doneness after cooking for 7 minutes per inch by lifting the rack out and setting it on an angle on the rim of the poacher. Make a small cut down to the bone, parallel to the backbone, in the middle of the fish and peek in. The flesh should pull away from the bone and have lost most of its translucency. Or test by sticking an instant-read thermometer into the back of the fish, again along the backbone—the thickest part of the fish. It's done when it reaches 135°F.
- The skin of poached fish has an unpleasant texture and should be peeled off as soon as the fish is cooked or it will stick.

HOW TO

Poach a Small Fish

I poach small fish for all the same reasons I poach a large fish—because poaching doesn't interfere with the fish's delicate flavor and requires no fat. You don't need a fish poacher for small fish; you can use any sauté pan or baking dish that is deep enough to submerge the fish. A small fish can be poached on the bone, but I often bone the fish and stuff it. I also poach fish steaks and fillets.

Wrapping a whole fish in cheesecloth makes it easy to pull it out of the hot poaching liquid. The cheesecloth wrapping also helps a boned whole fish hold its shape, keeps the sides of the fish from curling up, and holds a stuffing in.

Trout is the fish I most like to stuff and poach, but this poaching technique can be used for any small whole or boned fish, such as black sea bass and small red snapper. (Fish is best boned through the back, but if the fish has been gutted already, bone it through the stomach.)

Kitchen Notes and Tips

- If you bone and stuff fish, wrap it in cheesecloth before poaching. The wrapping is not critical for bone-in fish, but makes the hot fish easier to handle.
- Poach fish in a court bouillon, or for simplicity, in salted water mixed with a splash of white wine and flavored with a bouquet garni.
- Use any pan just large enough to hold the fish in a single layer.
- Although large fish are started in cold liquid, when poaching small fish, you should bring the liquid to a simmer before adding the fish.
- The poaching liquid should just cover the fish. If you don't have quite enough, baste the fish every 30 seconds with a ladle.
- Boneless stuffed fish will cook slightly faster than fish on the bone; begin checking for doneness after cooking for about 7 minutes per inch of thickness.
- Remove the skin of the fish while the fish is still hot, even if you're serving it cold. Once the fish is cool, the skin will stick.

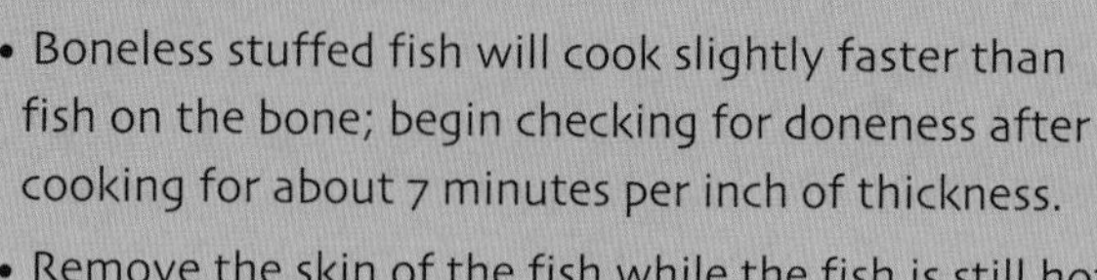

To Poach in a Pan

Here, a stuffed trout is poached in salted water and white wine that has simmered with a bouquet garni.

1. Rub the inside of the boned trout with chopped herbs or stuff with duxelles.
2. Wrap the trout in a double layer of cheesecloth.
3. Tie the cheesecloth at both ends with string.
4. Slide the trout into an oval sauté pan with just enough simmering liquid to cover and poach until cooked through.
5. Transfer the cooked trout to a cutting board.
6. Cut away the ends of the cheesecloth and unwrap.

To Serve

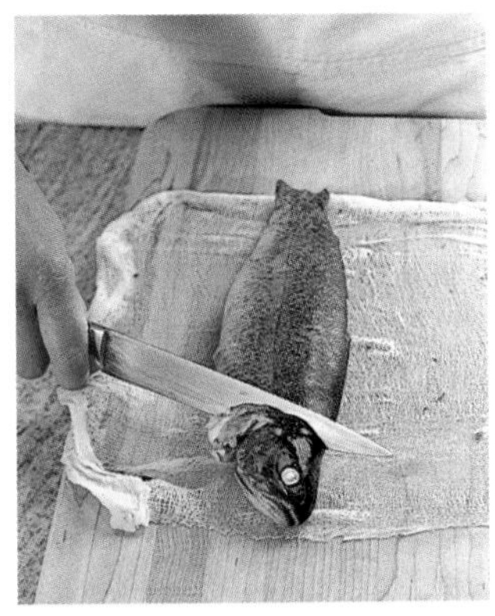

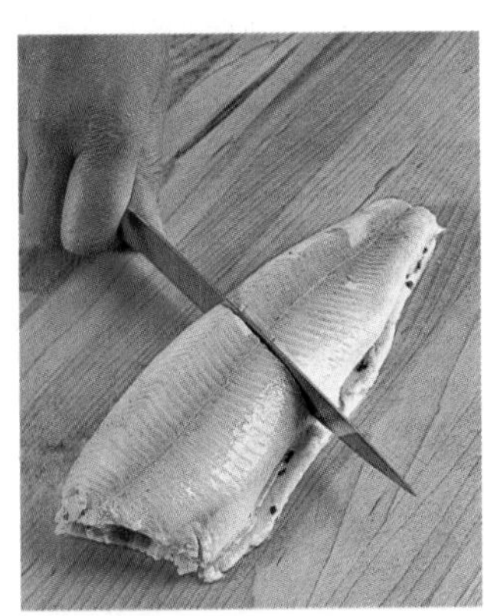

Serve the trout with a light sauce or in a wide bowl surrounded with a little of the trout's poaching liquid.

1. Cut the head off the trout.
2. Peel off the skin with your fingers.
3. Cut off the tail. Use a small knife or spoon to pull out any small bones that you can feel running along the back of the trout. Then cut the trout in half at a slight angle.
4. Poached trout is especially good with a butter sauce such as the saffron beurre blanc shown here.

To Make Duxelles, or Mushroom Stuffing

This is a great way to use mushroom stems, which can be stored in the freezer until needed.

1. Melt about a tablespoon of butter in a wide skillet and stir in chopped mushrooms or mushroom stems. Cook over medium heat until the mushrooms release their liquid. Turn up the heat to high and continue cooking until the liquid in the pan evaporates.
2. Sprinkle with parsley or other chopped herbs.
3. Add heavy cream and reduce until the cream thickens slightly (optional).

See Also

To bone a whole trout through the stomach, page 226

To bone a whole fish through the back, page 228

To make a court bouillon, page 113

To chop mushrooms, page 14

To make a beurre blanc, page 48

To poach a big fish, page 108

To poach and serve a small fish *à la nage*, page 112

To determine doneness, page 67

Related Glossary Entries

Beurre Blanc

Poach

HOW TO

Poach Fish Steaks and Fillets, Small Whole Fish, and Shellfish

Fish steaks and fillets, small whole fish, and shellfish such as scallops, shrimp, crayfish, and lobster all can be poached. One of the best ways to cook a fish steak or fillet, small whole fish, or shellfish is *à la nage*, which means that the fish is served surrounded with court bouillon and the vegetables used to make the court bouillon. The poaching liquid serves as a light, delicate, fat-free sauce that allows you to taste all of the subtle flavor of the fish. Because the poaching liquid is served with its vegetables, the vegetables are cut into pretty, presentable shapes, often julienne.

Kitchen Notes and Tips

- Poach fish steaks, fillets, and small whole fish for 7 to 10 minutes per inch of thickness. Start checking for doneness after cooking for about 7 minutes per inch by feeling the fish's texture or by making a small cut into the center of the thickest part of the steak or fillet. The flesh should have lost most but not all of its translucency.
- Poach in court bouillon, or for simplicity, in salted water flavored with white wine and a bouquet garni.
- Use a sauté pan or other pan large enough to hold the fish in a single layer.
- Bring the poaching liquid to a simmer before adding small fish, steaks, or fillets.
- I like to bone salmon steaks and tie them into medallions; not only is the fish easier to eat without bones, but the neat round shape looks pretty on the plate.
- Serving seafood *à la nage* is a light alternative to using a rich sauce, but a lovely compromise is to whisk the poaching liquid into an equal amount of beurre blanc. The beurre blanc gives the poaching liquid a buttery flavor and texture, but the dish will be much lighter than if beurre blanc alone were used. Any beurre blanc variation can be used in this way. The lightened beurre blanc is then ladled around the fish in wide soup plates.

Poached Salmon Medallions

To bone and tie a salmon steak into a medallion

1. Pull any pin bones out of the salmon steaks with a small pair of pliers. Slide a paring knife along the inside of the bones lining the stomach flaps.
2. Cut along the small bones running up toward the back of the salmon steak. Cut all the way to the back of the steak up to, but not through, the skin.
3. Repeat on the other side of the steak so that the central bone is completely separated from the two halves of the steak.
4. Carefully cut off 2 inches of the skin that wraps around one of the stomach flaps and fold the flap up in toward the center of the steak.
5. Wrap the remaining stomach flap around the outside of the steak and tie into a round, or medallion, with string.

To Make a Court Bouillon

A court bouillon is a vegetable broth flavored with white wine. Simmer chopped or sliced aromatic vegetables (shown in the top photograph) and a bouquet garni in water in a covered pot for 20 minutes, add salt to taste and a cup of white wine per 2 quarts of water, and simmer for 20 minutes more. Strain the court bouillon and discard the vegetables and bouquet garni. There is no fixed rule about quantities of vegetables, but I use 2 large carrots and onions for every 2 quarts water. (You can use leeks in place of onions, and skip the carrot; the only vegetable that's essential in the broth is onion or leek.) If you come up short on court bouillon, just add water.

If you are using the court bouillon to serve seafood *à la nage,* cut the vegetables into perfect slices or into julienne (shown in the bottom photograph). Cook and strain the court bouillon as usual, but reserve the vegetables. Reheat the vegetables in the strained broth just before serving. (The vegetables could be left in the liquid while the seafood is poaching, but the seafood throws off scum that may cling to the vegetables and look unattractive.) I use leeks or onions and determine how many vegetables to use on the basis of the number I'm serving.

6. Place the medallions in a pan or pot just large enough to hold them in a single layer and pour over enough strained, simmering court bouillon to cover. If you're serving the salmon *à la nage* as shown here, make the court bouillon with julienned vegetables and reserve the vegetables. If you're not serving the salmon *à la nage,* make a regular court bouillon using chopped vegetables and discard the vegetables.

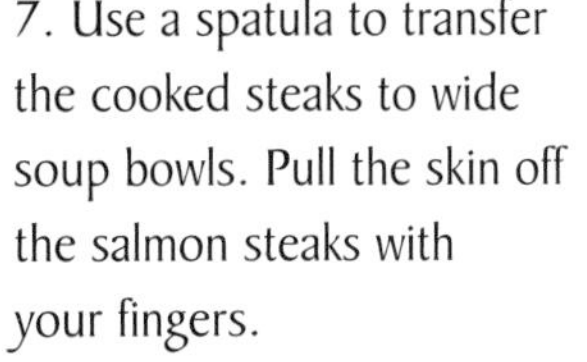

7. Use a spatula to transfer the cooked steaks to wide soup bowls. Pull the skin off the salmon steaks with your fingers.

8. If you're serving the salmon *à la nage,* surround each steak with hot julienned vegetables and ladle over the vegetable broth. Serve immediately.

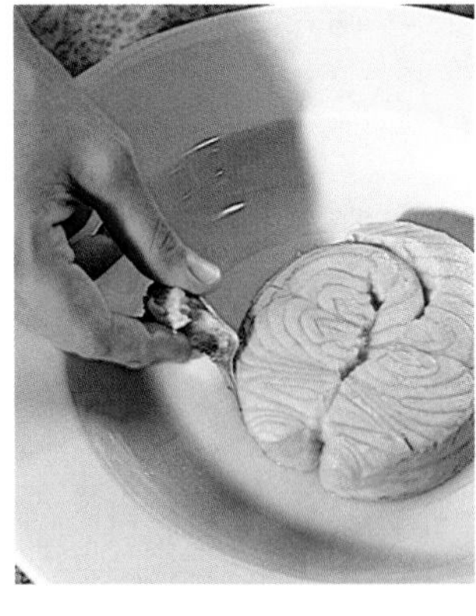

See Also

To julienne vegetables, page 13
To make a bouquet garni, page 31
To make a beurre blanc, page 48
To poach a small fish, page 110
To poach a big fish, page 108
To determine doneness, page 67

Related Glossary Entries

À la Nage
Poach

Kitchen Notes and Tips

- Judging the doneness of fillets cooked en papillote is a bit tricky because you can't probe or even look at the fish in the package during cooking. But the fish is usually done when the paper or foil packet is completely puffed up. It takes the same time to cook en papillote—7 to 10 minutes per inch of thickness—as with other cooking techniques.

HOW TO

Cook Fish Fillets en Papillote

Cooking *en papillote* combines the techniques of baking, braising, and steaming. Fillets are sealed in a parchment paper or aluminum foil packet along with an herb butter, sometimes a vegetable, and usually a sprinkling of a liquid such as wine, and then baked. In the heat of the oven, the liquid turns to steam and, depending on the amount of liquid, braises or steams the fish. The butter melts and bathes the fish in the flavor of butter and the herbs. While cooking en papillote is a dramatic, professional cooking method, it's also surprisingly practical, because it allows you to prepare everything ahead of time—and there are fewer dishes to clean because the meal cooks in a packet. Traditionally, the papillotes are opened in front of the diners (sometimes right under their noses) so they can savor the fragrance of the hot seafood.

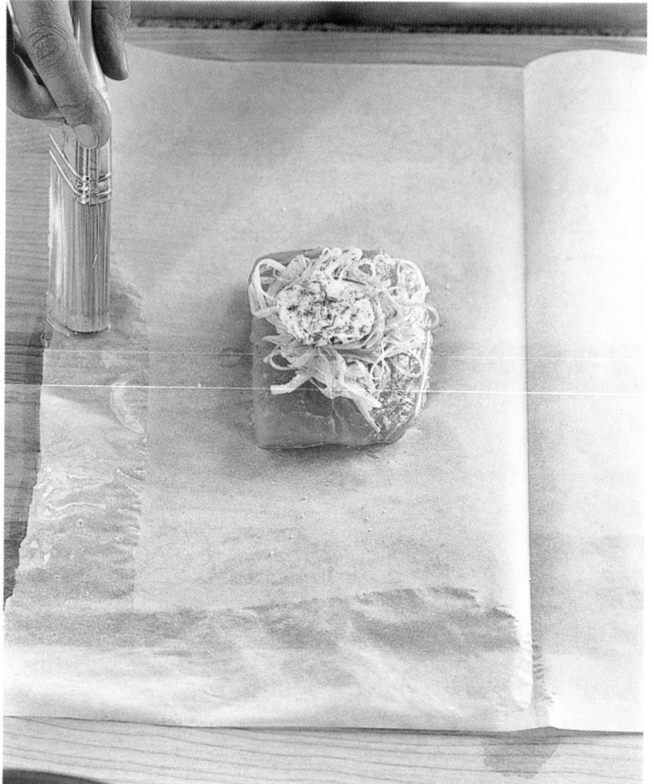

Salmon en Papillote

1. Cut a square of parchment paper, fold it in half to crease it, and unfold it. Center a piece of salmon fillet on the half to your right. Top the salmon with sweated julienned leeks.
2. Place a slice of tarragon butter on top and sprinkle the salmon with white wine.
3. Brush the edge of the right half of the parchment paper with lightly beaten egg white. (If using aluminum foil, this isn't necessary.)
4. Fold the left half of the parchment paper over the salmon. Press along the edges to seal the paper and brush the edge again with egg white.
5. Make a series of straight folds along the outer edge of the papillote, pressing firmly on each fold to help seal the paper. Bake at 375°F for 7 to 10 minutes per inch of thickness of the fish, or until the bag is completely puffed up.
6. Cut the bag open with scissors in the kitchen or at the table.
7. Spoon the salmon and all of the juices into hot bowls and serve. (Or place unopened papillotes on plates in front of the diners and let them cut open their own papillotes.)

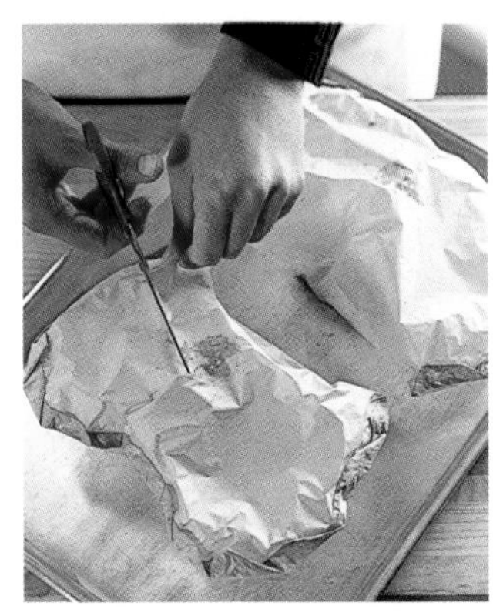

See Also

To make an herb butter, page 47
To julienne leeks, page 20
To fillet a salmon, page 224

Related Glossary Entries

Bake
Braise
Steam
Sweat

HOW TO

Bake Fish and Make a Sauce at the Same Time (Braise)

Baking in a small amount of aromatic liquid, called braising, is a simple and practical way to cook whole fish, fillets, or steaks. The fish flavors the surrounding liquid as it cooks, so that the liquid can be used to make quick, savory sauces.

The technique is simple: Butter a baking dish or pan just large enough to hold the fish in a single layer. Sprinkle the bottom of the dish with chopped aromatic ingredients—shallots, garlic, mirepoix of vegetables, or finely chopped raw mushrooms. Place the fish on top (in a single layer, if you're cooking fillets or steaks) and season with salt and pepper. Add enough liquid—wine, fish broth, or concentrated red-wine fish broth—to come halfway up the side of the fish. Loosely cover the pan or dish with parchment paper or foil, bring to a simmer on top of the stove, transfer to the oven, and bake until done. (Or skip the aromatics and just pour enough simmering liquid over the fish to come halfway up the sides of the fish, cover with parchment, and bake.) Remove the fish and serve with the cooking juices as they are, or thickened (see Box, page 117).

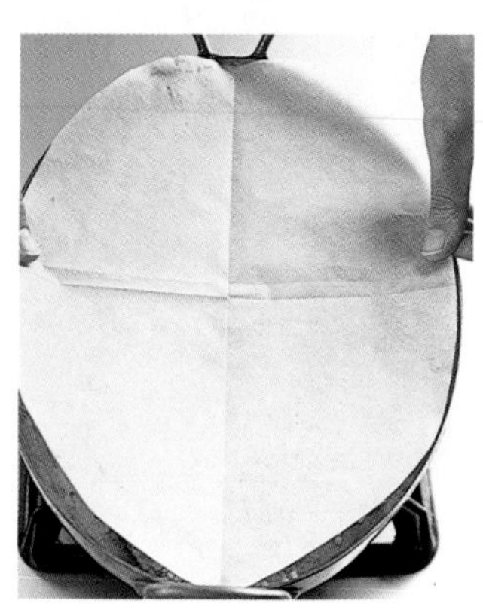

Whole Flounder Baked with White Wine and Shallots

1. Sprinkle minced shallots generously over the bottom of an ovenproof oval pan and place the whole flatfish—top skin removed and the bottom skin scaled—on top.
2. Pour over wine and fish broth to come halfway up the sides of the fish.
3. Place the pan on the stove and bring the liquid to a simmer over high heat. Place an oval of parchment paper or aluminum foil over the fish and bake at 375°F until the fish is cooked through, 7 to 10 minutes per inch of thickness.
4. Place the pan on the stove over medium heat, remove the parchment paper, and use a wide spatula to transfer the fish to a plate or platter.
5. Whisk butter into the cooking liquid in the pan.
6. Season the sauce with salt and pepper and spoon over the fish. Serve whole, or fillet the fish at the table as shown on page 127.

Baked Whole Snapper with Red-Wine Fish Broth

1. Place the scaled and cleaned fish in a baking dish, preferably oval, just large enough to hold it comfortably. Ladle over simmering concentrated red-wine fish broth and slide the fish into a 350°F oven.
2. Bake the fish, basting every few minutes, until done. Transfer the fish to a plate.
3. Whisk butter or another thickener into the hot braising liquid in the dish. (Or transfer the cooking liquid to a saucepan, heat, and whisk in the butter.) Season to taste with salt and pepper.
4. The fish can be served whole or filleted, as it is here. Spoon the sauce over the fish.

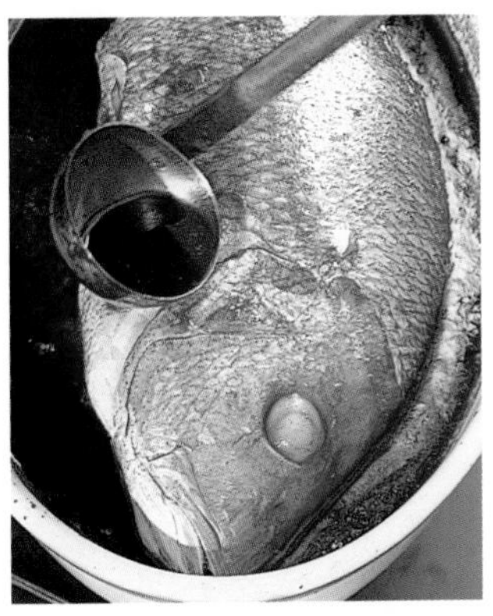

Kitchen Notes and Tips

- Remove the skin from fillets before baking; the skin gets rubbery.
- Scale and trim whole flatfish such as sole and flounder before cooking. Remove the top dark skin from most flatfish. Flounder skin is difficult to remove from the raw fish; peel it off in strips, or remove it after the fish is cooked.
- Clean and scale whole fish before baking. Unlike *roasted* whole fish (page 118), which can be cooked with the scales on, whole fish *baked* in liquid must be scaled.
- The cooking liquid must be simmering before the fish goes into the oven; if the liquid is cool to start, the top of the fish will cook more quickly than the bottom.
- Bake large whole round fish such as snapper uncovered, basting every few minutes with the cooking juices.
- The simplest way to serve the cooking liquid is just as it is, broth-like, spooned around each serving of fish in wide soup plates. The liquid can also be reduced slightly and mounted with butter; other thickeners, such as heavy cream, vegetable purées, and beurre manié, can be whisked in to thicken the sauce. Often, especially when using heavy cream, the sauce will need to be reduced to finish thickening.

See Also

To clean and skin a flatfish, pages 230 and 234
To clean a round fish, page 220
To skin a fillet, page 233
To fillet a cooked sole or flounder, page 127
To make a concentrated red-wine fish broth, page 33

Related Glossary Entries

Braise
Garniture
Mirepoix
Monter au Beurre
Parchment Paper or Aluminum Foil Round
Thickener (for information on thickening the sauce)

HOW TO

Roast a Whole Fish

One of the most flavorful ways to cook fish is to roast it whole. Because the skin and bones are left intact, the flavor and juiciness of the fish are sealed in. Roasted fish, and whole fish in general, are neglected in the United States because many of us don't know how to eat them—but the flavor and texture of whole fish is incomparable. My favorite fish to roast are red snapper, sea bass, striped bass, Arctic char, and small salmon.

Serve roasted whole fish sprinkled with extra virgin olive oil and a few drops of lemon juice or good wine vinegar—or just pass the oil and vinegar or lemon wedges at the table for guests to help themselves.

To Roast and Carve Whole Fish

1. Rub the cleaned fish (here, scaled sea bass) with olive oil and season it with salt and pepper. Place the fish in a 425°F oven and roast for about 7 to10 minutes per inch of thickness.
2. Using a fish knife and fork or 2 spoons, break through the skin down the back of the fish.
3. While holding the fish with the fork or one of the spoons, slide the knife or other spoon against the tiny bones that run along the ridge of the back, pushing the bones out into the roasting pan.
4. Break through the skin along the center and the top fillet with the knife or spoon until you run into bone. Continue along the whole length of the fish from the tail to the back of the head, dividing the top fillet in half.
5. Break through the skin at the back of the head, separating the head from the top fillet.

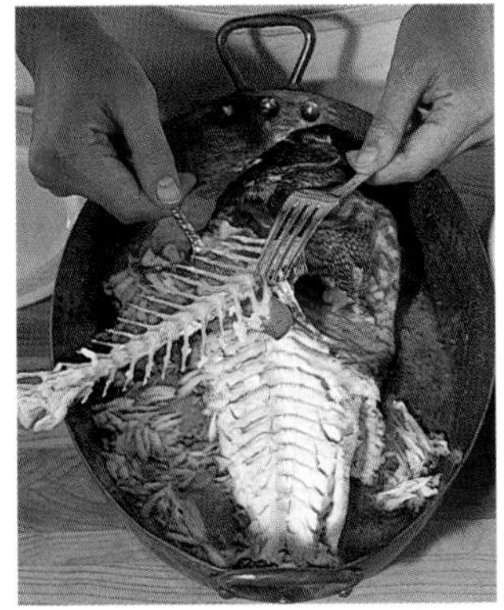

6. If the fish is fairly large, cut the upper fillet half crosswise into 2 pieces.
7. Lift out the 2 pieces of the fillet with the knife or spoon.
8. Use the knife and fork or the spoons to pull out any small bones along the edge of the fish's back.
9. Cut the fillet half crosswise into 2 pieces and lift out with the knife or spoon.
10. Slide the knife under the backbone.
11. Gently lift the backbone away, and set it aside.
12. Pull off the head.
13. Gently pull away any ribs still attached to the bottom fillet.
14. Divide the bottom fillet into 4 pieces in the same way as the top fillet.
15. Serve on a hot platter or on individual plates.

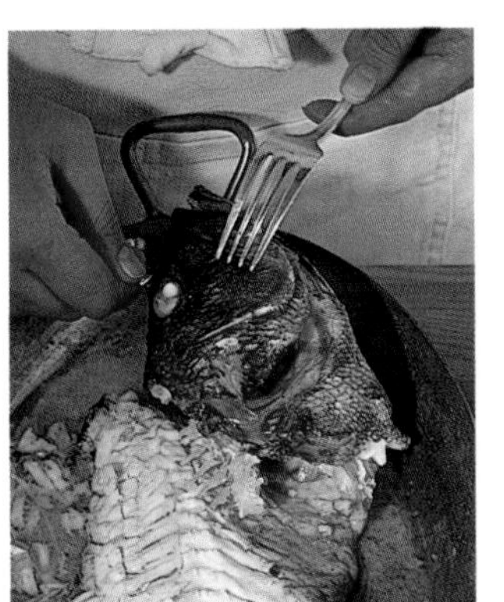

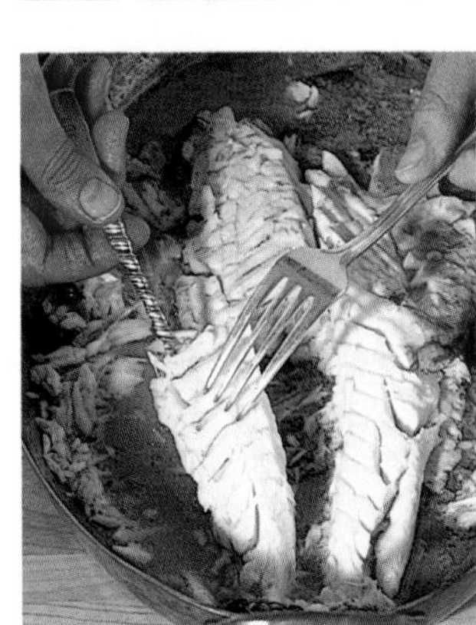

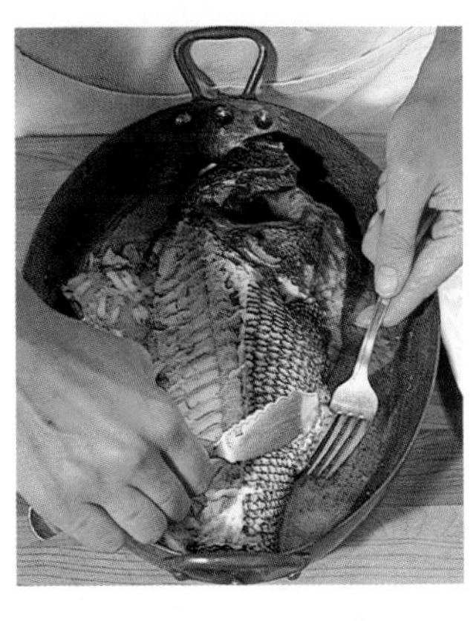

To Remove the Skin from a Whole Fish Roasted with the Scales On

Unless you want to eat the crispy skin, you can roast many whole fish with their scales attached.

1. Work a small knife (here, I use a fish knife) down the back of the fish, cutting through the skin.
2. Pull the skin away in one piece. Remove the backbone and carve the fish as shown on page 119.

See Also

To clean and scale whole round fish, page 220
To determine doneness, page 67

Related Glossary Entry

Roast

Kitchen Notes and Tips

- Roast fish that weigh 5 pounds or less at 425°F. Roast fish that weigh 5 pounds or more at 350°F; the lower temperature ensures that the skin won't burn and the outside of the fish won't dry out before the heat penetrates the fish.
- To test for doneness, slide an instant-read thermometer into the fish through the back, parallel with the backbone. The fish is ready when the thermometer reads 135°F. If you don't have a thermometer, slide a knife through the back along the backbone, lift the knife slightly, and peek inside. If the flesh holds fast to the bone and still looks translucent, cook the fish a bit longer. If the flesh comes away but clings very slightly, the fish is done. Don't cook fish beyond this point, or the flesh will dry out.
- Figure on 1 pound of whole fish per person.
- A whole fish must be cleaned before roasting, but it doesn't necessarily need to be scaled: The scales help seal in the flavorful juices and make it easy to remove the skin in one piece. If you're planning to remove the skin before serving, don't bother to scale the fish; you can easily pull away the skin, scales and all, from the cooked fish. If you want to serve the fish with the skin on (the skin can be delightfully crispy), do scale the fish before roasting.

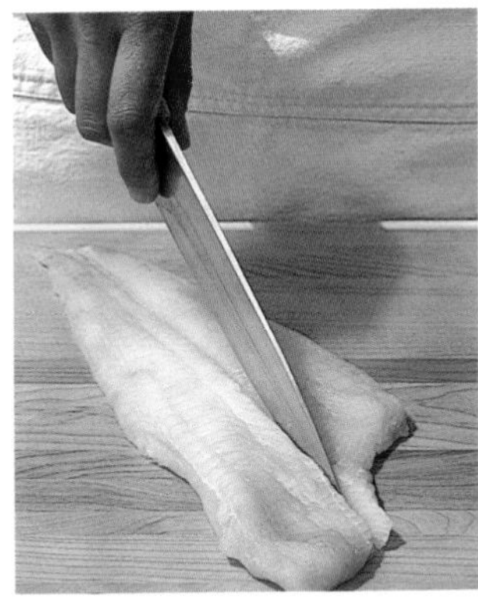

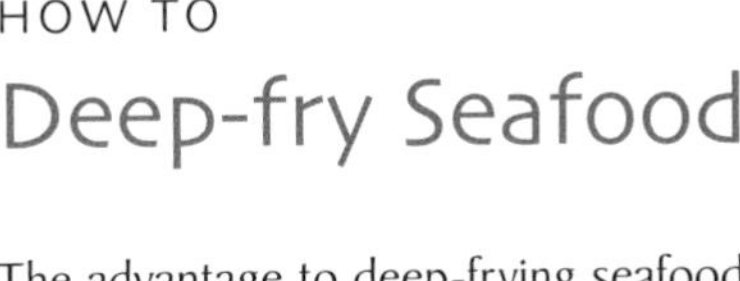

HOW TO

Deep-fry Seafood

The advantage to deep-frying seafood is that it comes out of the oil intensely hot, crisp, and flavorful. No other cooking method creates such a satisfying and distinct contrast between the moist interior and the fragile, crunchy crust. Lean white-fleshed fish fillets are excellent deep-fried, as are shrimp, squid, and baby octopus.

Prepare seafood for frying by coating it with something that produces a crust: flour, a bread crumb coating, a light flour and water (or club soda) batter, or a tempura batter. Flour results in a subtle crust that is barely noticeable; you taste more of the fish. Breading and batters make a more apparent, crunchy outer coating. Tempura batter makes the crunchiest coating of all. If you want to emphasize the fish, use a flour coating. If you want to emphasize the crust, use a breading or batter. For lots of crunch, use a tempura batter.

Tempura batter is fundamentally different from other flour-based deep-fry batters. While other batters are mixed until perfectly smooth (and perhaps strained) and then given a rest period to allow the gluten to relax before frying, tempura batter is mixed together at the very last minute. The ingredients are just barely blended together (and therefore contain lumps) and so quickly that the gluten in the flour is never activated.

Fried Flounder Goujonettes

A goujonette is a thin strip of fish cut from a larger fillet, intended to look like a tiny fried fish. (*Goujon* is the French word for "minnow.") Serve fried goujonettes with tartar or gribiche sauce or sprinkled with malt vinegar, fish-and-chips style, as a first course.

1. If the fillets are attached in the center, cut them apart along one side of the thin gristly strip that runs down the middle.
2. Cut the strip off and discard it.
3. Cut the fillets crosswise on the diagonal into strips about ½ inch thick and 3 inches long. (Those from the ends of the fillets will be shorter.)
4. Just before you're ready to fry, toss the goujonettes in flour to coat.
5. Then toss over a drum sieve set over a sheet pan or in a large strainer to get rid of the excess flour.
6. As soon as they are floured, fry the goujonettes in 370°F oil for about 5 seconds. Be careful not to overcook: Goujonettes cook very quickly. Drain on paper towels and serve immediately.

Shrimp Tempura

Japanese cooks usually serve shrimp tempura with a simple dipping sauce made by combining dashi, mirin (a sweet wine used for cooking), soy sauce, and ginger. Leave the small tail flippers attached when you peel the shrimp.

1. Lightly combine egg yolks and ice water with chopsticks. Don't worry if the yolks aren't fully blended. Pour in flour all at once and stir for a few seconds with the chopsticks until the batter barely comes together in a lumpy mass.
2. Just before frying, dip the shrimp into the batter.
3. Gently lower the shrimp, holding the tail flipper with tongs, one at a time into 370°F oil. Fry for about 1 minute.
4. Take the shrimp out of the oil with a spider, as shown here, or slotted spoon. You can also use a wire frying basket. Drain on paper towels and serve immediately.

Kitchen Notes and Tips

- Deep-fry seafood at 370°F.
- Fillets of lean white-fleshed fish such as cod, scrod, sole, and flounder can be cut into thin strips called goujonettes. Goujonettes should be thin; if your fillet is thicker than 3/4 inch, cut it horizontally into 2 layers.
- You can cut fish into goujonettes several hours in advance and refrigerate them, but don't flour until just before frying.
- Tempura batter should be mixed only until the ingredients are barely combined, so as not to overwork the flour. Expect some lumps of dry flour in the batter, as well as dry flour remaining on the sides of the bowl. Japanese cooks like to mix tempura batter with chopsticks to avoid overworking it.
- Serve deep-fried seafood as soon as it is cooked, while it is very hot.

See Also

To coat with bread crumbs, page 162
To make a light frying batter, page 78
To peel and devein shrimp, page 131
To fillet a flounder, page 231
To make gribiche sauce, page 43
To make dashi, page 143

Related Glossary Entries

Bread
Deep-fry
Goujonette

HOW TO

Grill Seafood

Grilling is the only cooking method we still use regularly that cooks with a live fire. It adds a light, smoky flavor to seafood and like sautéing, also sears food, giving it a crisp, savory outer crust. I like to grill whole fish, firm-fleshed steaks or fillets, shrimp, and scallops. During the winter, I sometimes use a grill pan so I can grill indoors on the stove. A grill pan resembles a heavy cast-iron skillet but it has a ridged surface that simulates the effect of cooking on an outdoor grill. Mollusks such as oysters and mussels are sometimes grilled in the shell, but I don't recommend it. While the heat from the grill causes the mollusk to open, grilling does little to enhance the mollusk's flavor.

The key to grilling seafood is keeping it from sticking to the grill rack. Whole fish such as snapper, pompano, and sea bass must be handled carefully so they don't stick and fall apart. Firm fish steaks such as tuna, swordfish, and shark are particularly good on the grill because they hold together well and don't stick, and they are especially flavorful when grilled.

Grilled Shrimp

Grilled shrimp are tastiest when the shell is left on (of course, this means everyone must peel their own) and even tastier when the heads are left on, as shown here.

Lightly sprinkle the shrimp with salt and grill them, in their shells, until the shells turn pink, about 5 minutes. Serve piping hot.

To keep fish from sticking to the grill, make sure the grill rack is clean and very hot before you start to grill. Rub it quickly with a paper towel dipped in a little oil before you put the seafood on the grill.

To Use a Grill Pan to Grill Pompano

A grill pan gives seafood a light smoked flavor and cooks it with virtually no fat. Because pompano is a firm, rich fish, it takes especially well to grilling. Pompano should be cleaned before grilling, but it has no scales to worry about.

Cut the tail off the pompano so that it will fit into the grill pan, then rub with olive oil. Grill over high heat for about 5 minutes, then give the fish a 90-degree turn and grill for 5 minutes more to give the fish a crosshatch pattern on one side. Turn the pompano over and grill until cooked through, 8 minutes more, depending on its thickness.

Kitchen Notes and Tips

- When grilling whole fish, leaving the scales attached will provide natural protection against sticking and help seal in savory juices. When you're ready to serve, just peel off the skin, scales and all.
- If your whole fish has already been scaled, a grill basket makes the fish easy to handle: Instead of trying to turn over the fish on the hot grill, you just turn over the grill basket. A grill basket has legs on each side that enable you to set the basket directly over the coals, or you can fold the legs in and set the grill basket right on the grill.
- One way to grill fish fillets is to dip skin-on fillets skin side down in coarse salt. The salt forms a barrier between the fish and the grill rack and keeps the skin from sticking. The excess salt can be brushed off or the skin removed entirely before serving, but I leave the skin on because the salty skin—especially salmon skin—is crispy and delicious.
- When lifting fish steaks or fillets off the grill, don't slide a spatula under the fish or you may tear the skin or flesh. Instead, slide 2 chopsticks or a 2-pronged sauté fork under the fish and gently lift the fish off the grill. Then, slide a spatula under the fish for turning or transferring to plates or a platter. Use tongs for shellfish such as shrimp.

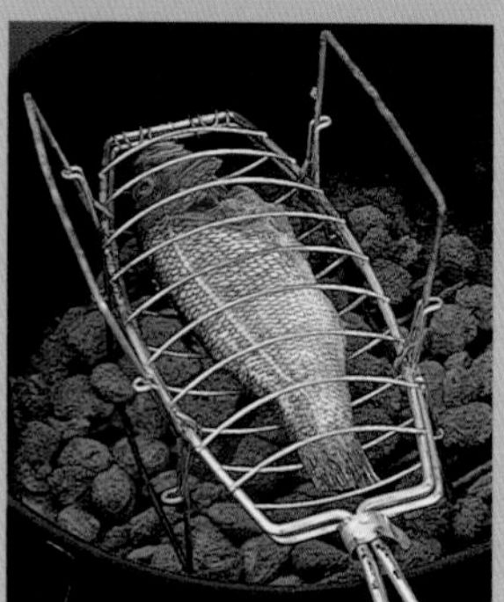

See Also

To prepare a whole round fish, page 220

To carve a whole fish, page 118

To clean shrimp, page 131

To remove skin and scales together, page 120

Related Glossary Entries

Broil (also for information on quick-broiling)

Grill (also for information on grill pans)

HOW TO

Sauté Seafood for a Crisp Crust

The purpose of sautéing seafood is to give it a crisp, lightly browned crust. The seafood is cooked in butter (clarified is best because it doesn't burn over high heat) or oil over intense heat, so that the outside of the food browns quickly before the inside overcooks. It's easiest to cook small shellfish such as scallops or shrimp by tossing them in a pan with sloping sides; the sloping sides make the tossing motion easier. Whole fish, fish fillets, and steaks would fall apart if tossed that way, so they are browned on one side and then carefully turned with a spatula.

Fish steaks, thick fillets, and small thin whole fish such as sole or trout are the simplest to sauté because they cook through in about the same amount of time it takes the exterior to brown. Thin fillets, especially from fragile fish such as flounder, fall apart if overcooked by even a second, so watch them carefully.

I cook most fillets with the skin on, because the skin holds the fillet together, tastes deliciously crispy, and looks good. (Exceptions are fish with thick or leathery skin, such as grouper and blackfish.) But skin tends to stick, so use a nonstick pan or a well-seasoned skillet. Fish skin also contracts when hot, causing the fillet to curl. To prevent curling, start the fillet flesh side down, cooking it for a minute or two to allow the flesh to contract. Then turn the fillet skin side down and press down with the back of a spatula as it cooks to prevent it from curling and to keep the skin in contact with the bottom of the pan so its entire surface browns.

Sautéing *à la meunière* is an excellent way to prepare almost any small whole fish or fillet. The fish is coated with flour and then sautéed in butter (preferably clarified). Flouring—or breading—is particularly useful when cooking thin fish such as Dover sole, because the flour speeds up browning (flour and breading brown faster than the unadorned fish itself would) and so prevents the fish from overcooking. Once cooked, the fish is transferred to a platter or plates and sprinkled with lemon juice. The butter used for sautéing is discarded and fresh whole butter is cooked in the pan until it barely begins to brown—at which stage it is called "noisette"—and spooned over the hot fish.

Sautéed Skin-on Red Snapper Fillets

1. The small pinbones running down the head end of the fillet can be pulled out with pliers, but this is laborious and often tears the flesh. To avoid this, cut along each side of the strip of pinbones and remove the whole strip.
2. Cut the fillets into 2 equal pieces of similar shape.
3. Season the fillets with salt and pepper. Cook the fillets flesh side down in hot oil or butter for 1 to 2 minutes.
4. Turn the fillets over and press down with the back of a spatula while sautéing the skin side. (This prevents the skin from contracting and causing the fillet to curl.) If necessary, turn over again and finish cooking on the flesh side. Transfer to serving plates.

After sautéing the fish, some cooks like to prepare a sauce by deglazing the sauté pan. One method is to make a hot vinaigrette by deglazing the pan with good-quality wine vinegar, olive oil, and herbs. Another method is to cook butter in the pan as in the Whole Dover Sole *à la Meunière*. The pan also can be deglazed with a little wine and/or fish broth and a small amount of cream or a chunk of butter added to the liquid to turn it into a sauce.

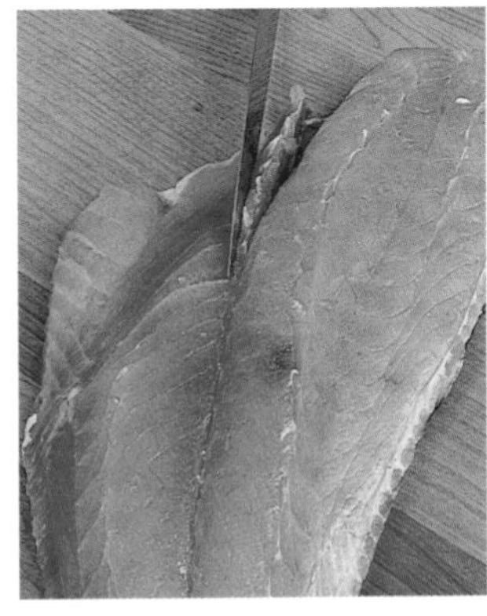

Kitchen Notes and Tips

- To prepare whole flatfish for sautéing, scale the white skin. Remove or scale the black skin.
- Cut large fillets into manageable pieces. Cut large fillets crosswise into individual portions. Flatfish fillets that are joined in the center should be divided and the thin gristly strip that held them together removed. Fish steaks can be boned and tied into medallions.
- Sauté seafood fillets over medium to medium-high heat, depending on their thickness: The thinner the fillet, the higher the heat. Floured or breaded fish can be cooked over lower heat because the coating will brown faster over lower heat than the unadorned fish would.
- Cook fish for 7 to 10 minutes per inch of thickness.
- Sautéing is easiest in a nonstick pan or well-seasoned cast-iron skillet.
- To prevent fragile seafood from breaking apart when turned, use a spatula that's large enough to support the whole fish or fillet.

Whole Dover Sole *à la Meunière*

1. Season the cleaned and prepared sole with salt and pepper and coat it on both sides with flour. Pat off any excess flour. Sauté the fish in oil or clarified butter over medium heat, top side (the side that had the dark skin) down first.

2. Turn the fish over when it is golden brown on the first side, after about 5 minutes, and cook for about 5 minutes longer. Serve the fish whole or fillet the fish and arrange it on plates (see page 127). Sprinkle the fish with lemon juice.

3. Pour off and discard the butter in the pan used to sauté the fish, wipe out the pan, and heat fresh whole butter in it (or heat the butter in a small saucepan). When it has barely begun to brown, spoon it over the fish. Serve immediately.

How to Fillet a Cooked Sole or Flounder

1. Using a knife and fork or 2 spoons, push away the small bones—the fringe bones—that line the outside of the fish.

2. Slide a knife or spoon down the center of the fish, between the 2 top fillets, separating them slightly from the bone.

3. Slide a knife—here, a fish knife is used—or a spoon under each of the fillets, detaching them from the backbone.

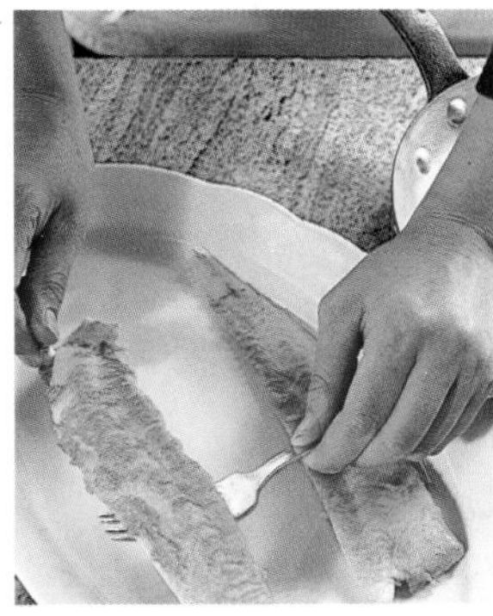

4. Transfer the fillets to a platter, placing them toward the outer edge.

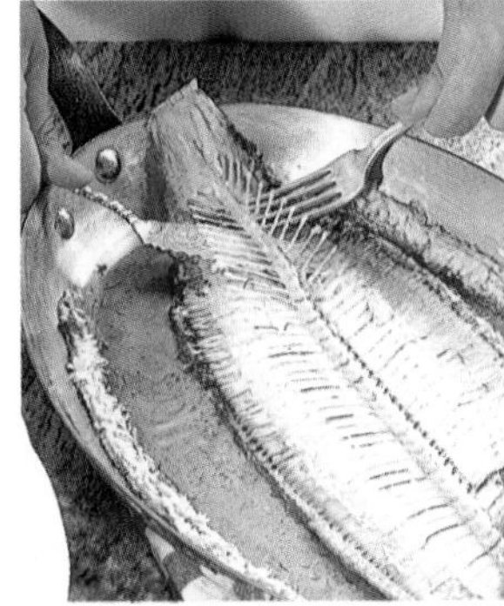

5. Slide knife or spoon under the backbone. Lift it away from the bottom fillets.

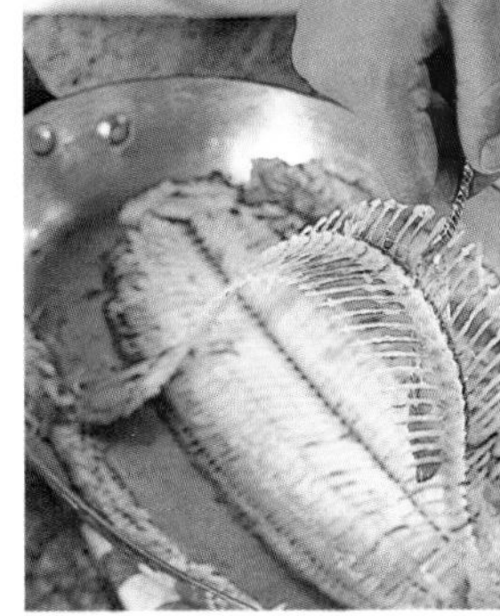

6. Detach head and backbone and push them gently to the side of the pan.

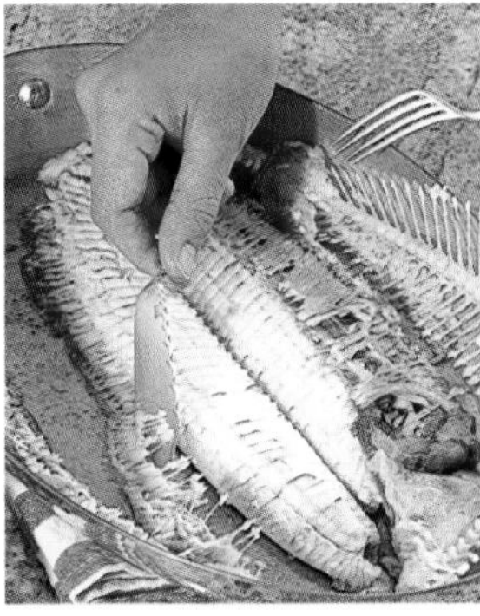

7. Push away the small bones surrounding the fillets with knife or spoon.

8. Lift the bottom fillets and place them in the center of the platter.

9. Place the top fillets over the bottom fillets.

See Also

To clarify butter, page 46

To make a hot vinaigrette, page 38

To make a fish broth, page 32

To sauté soft-shell crabs, page 138

To prepare a whole flatfish, page 230

To fillet a snapper (same as for a striped bass), page 222

To make fresh bread crumbs, page 164

To remove the fringe bones before filleting, page 230

Related Glossary Entries

Bread

Monter au Beurre

Panfry

Sauté

HOW TO

Cook Squid (and Other Tentacled Creatures)

Squid (along with other cephalopods, such as octopus and cuttlefish) is treated differently from most seafood because it toughens as it cooks. Squid can be either cooked very briefly—until just cooked through, or it will be tough—or long-cooked, stewed past the point of toughening until it becomes tender again.

Short-cooking methods are the same as for other seafood: Squid can be deep-fried, sautéed, or stir-fried. It also takes well to cooking as a quick stew: First sauté or stir-fry it in a little oil or butter, then add a small amount of flavorful liquid such as white wine. The liquid reduces into a light sauce during the minute or two it takes to cook the squid through. (This is technically called short-braising.) Be careful not to cook the squid more than one or two minutes, though, or it will toughen.

Octopus and cuttlefish take longer to cook than squid because they are thicker and tougher. Cuttlefish can be stewed in the same way as squid, but cook it covered for thirty minutes before uncovering, as shown here, and then cook for forty-five minutes to one hour more. Cook octopus as you would a beef daube.

Long-cooking, or stewing (technically called long-braising), squid takes forty-five minutes to an hour. The squid is cooked with aromatic vegetables and liquid to cover. Red wine is one of the best liquids to use for stewing squid, octopus, and cuttlefish because its full body and flavor match their flavor. Most stews are cooked covered, but squid, because it releases a lot of liquid and cooks relatively quickly, is cooked uncovered so that the stewing liquid reduces and concentrates while the squid is braising.

Squid is usually first separated into bodies, sometimes called hoods, and tentacles. The bodies are sliced into rings before cooking.

Squid Stewed with Red Wine

Any liquid can be used to stew squid, but here, I use red wine and chopped tomatoes. I serve the squid with aïoli and small slices of toasted French bread.

1. Prepare a flavor base by gently stirring chopped shallots and garlic or other aromatic vegetables in a small amount of olive oil over medium heat until the vegetables lightly caramelize, about 10 minutes.
2. Add the squid and enough liquid (here, the seeded and chopped tomatoes) to come halfway up the sides of the squid.
3. Add a bouquet garni and pour over enough red wine to cover the squid.
4. Bring to a simmer and cook, stirring from time to time, until the squid is tender and only a small amount of liquid remains in the bottom of the pan, 45 minutes to an hour.
5. Serve with toasts and aïoli (optional).

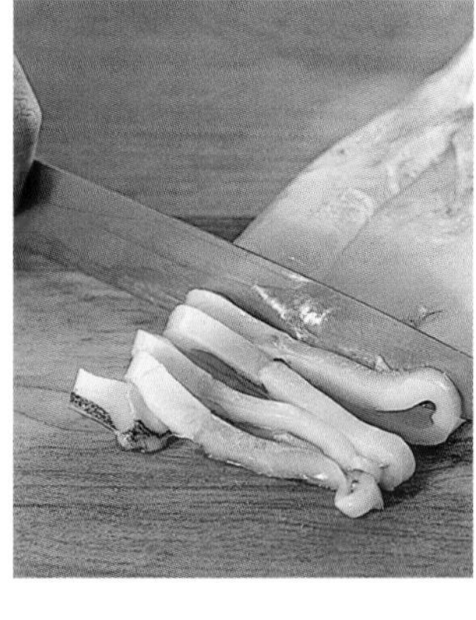

To Clean Squid

1. Cut the tentacles off just below the eye. Don't cut them too far down, or they will come apart.
2. Fold back the tentacles slightly and push out the "beak" and any grit caught in the small center opening.
3. Pull the innards out from the hood. Reach into the hood and pull out any remaining innards. Rinse out the hood.
4. Pull out the small plastic-like "quill" that runs along the inside of the hood.
5. Cut off the small fin on one side of the hood and cut it into strips.
6. Removing the purple skin makes the squid more attractive but less flavorful. To remove it, start by scraping the covering off with a knife. Continue peeling the skin off with your fingers.
7. Unless you're stuffing the hood, slice it into rings.
8. If the tentacle bunches are large, cut them into two or more pieces through the top.

See Also

To make a stew without browning, page 210
To seed and chop tomatoes, pages 36 and 50
To make aïoli, page 43
To deep-fry seafood, page 121
To sauté seafood, page 125
To stir-fry seafood, page 130

Related Glossary Entries

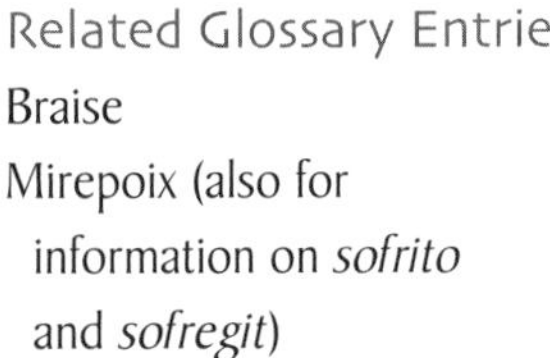

Braise
Mirepoix (also for information on *sofrito* and *sofregit*)

HOW TO

Stir-fry Seafood in a Wok

Stir-frying is like sautéing in that its purpose is to cook food quickly over high heat in a small amount of fat. The sloping sides of the wok make it easy to stir and toss the food with a spoon, wooden spatula, or a pair of chopsticks. To cook a stir-fry, heat a small amount of oil—just enough to lubricate the food—in the wok over high heat. Add aromatic ingredients, such as garlic, ginger, and/or chiles, and cook for a minute or two to infuse the oil with their flavor. (These ingredients can then be removed with a slotted spoon when they begin to brown, or left in the oil.) Add the seafood and other ingredients in stages—longer-cooking ingredients before quicker-cooking foods—and stir rapidly, still over high heat. Once the ingredients are cooked, you can add broth and/or other flavorful liquids to make a quick sauce that coats the foods. In Chinese cooking, a thickener, usually cornstarch moistened with water, may be stirred in to bind the sauce. Coconut milk also makes a lovely addition to Asian, especially Thai, stir-fries.

Stir-fry any firm-fleshed seafood, such as scallops, shrimp, squid, and crayfish tails. Don't sauté delicate fillets—they'll fall apart. A wok stand, a metal ring that sits on the stove burner and supports the bottom of the wok, will help to keep the wok stable.

Stir-fried Shrimp with Cashews

1. Heat peanut or vegetable oil in a wok. Add aromatic ingredients—here, slices of ginger and garlic—to flavor the hot oil and remove with a slotted spoon as soon as they begin to brown.
2. Add the remaining ingredients, stirring rapidly as you go. Here, shrimp, cashews, chopped jalapeño chiles, and julienned bell peppers are all added at the same time. Cook until just cooked through. Serve immediately.

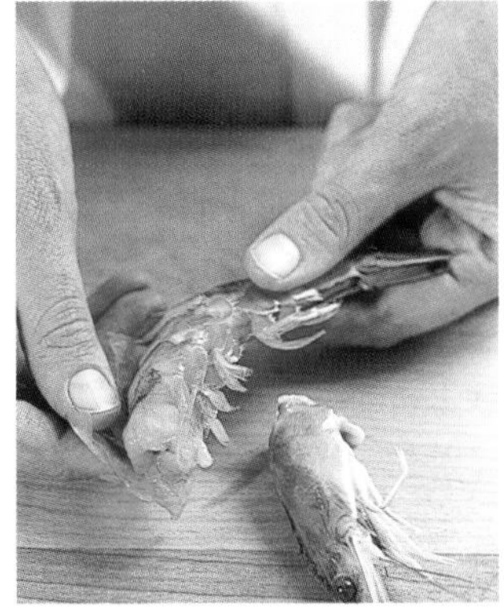

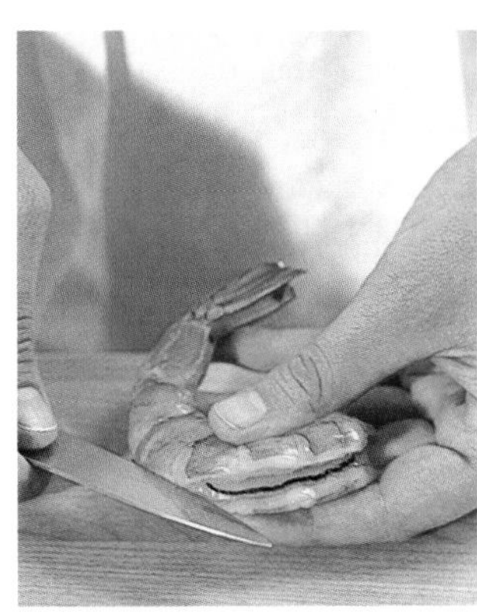

To Peel and Devein Shrimp

You need to devein shrimp only if the intestine is full of grit. To see if deveining is necessary, devein a couple of shrimp and inspect the intestines. If they are clean, don't bother with the rest.

1. If the shrimp have heads, twist them off. The heads can be frozen and used later for making soups, sauces, and stocks.
2. Peel off the shells (optional). If guests will be picking the shrimp up with their fingers, leave the tiny tail flaps attached.
3. If you do need to devein, cut down the back of the shrimp with a small paring knife, exposing the "vein" (actually, the intestine).
4. Pull the intestine out with the knife or your fingers.

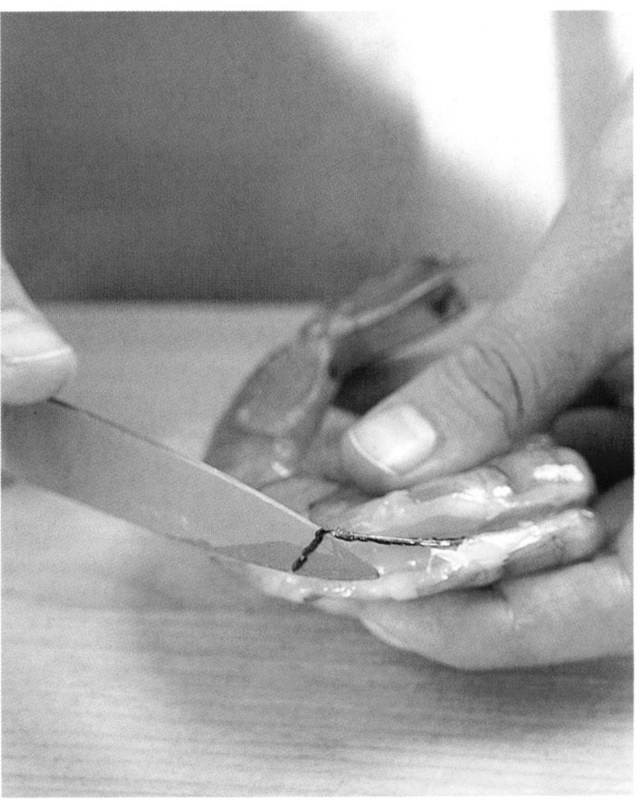

See Also

To make a fish broth, page 32
To make a shrimp broth, page 34
To grate coconut for its milk, page 29

Related Glossary Entries

Sauté
Thickener

HOW TO

Steam Shellfish

I steam lobsters and mollusks such as mussels, clams, and cockles by placing the shellfish directly in a pot with a small amount of liquid. I don't bother to use a steamer insert or rack. Mussels, clams, and cockles are typically steamed in white wine flavored with aromatics such as shallots, garlic, and parsley. Once the shellfish is cooked, the steaming liquid is served as a broth along with the shellfish, to be mopped up with crusty French bread, or it is used as a base for a sauce for the seafood. The briny steaming liquid can also be combined with olive oil or butter and used, along with the shellfish, as a sauce for pasta.

Mussels usually open after about five minutes, cockles about seven minutes, and clams about ten minutes. Lobsters are done when they turn completely red, usually in about twelve minutes. Many recipes call for longer cooking times, but even slight overcooking leaves lobsters tough and dry.

Lobsters can be steamed in the same way as mollusks—in a large covered pot containing a small amount of boiling liquid, usually wine or water flavored with herbs and/or shallots. (If this seems inhumane, kill the lobsters before steaming.) If several lobsters are stacked in a large pot, use tongs to move those on top to the bottom and vice versa in the pot, being careful of the steam, after about six minutes.

Steamed Mussels with White Wine and Parsley

1. Add the liquid and aromatics to a pot large enough to hold the mussels after they've opened. Here, I use white wine, shallots, and parsley. Bring to a gentle simmer.
2. Add the mussels to the pot, cover, and turn the heat to high. Steam until all the mussels have opened, about 5 minutes. Remove the mussels with a slotted spoon.
3. To eat the mussels, pull apart the 2 shells and, using 1 shell as a spoon, scoop out the mussel and pop it into your mouth.

Kitchen Notes and Tips

- Steam mollusks (mussels, cockles, and clams) in about ½ inch of liquid in a covered pot just until they open.
- Steam whole lobsters in about ½ inch water or white wine in a covered pot until the lobster turns red. At this point, the lobster flesh will still be very slightly translucent. If you like your lobster more cooked, steam 2 to 3 more minutes. Check the liquid once or twice during steaming to make sure it doesn't boil dry.

Cleaning Mussels

Wild mussels may be encrusted with dirt or barnacles, and so you will have to scrub them with a stiff brush or scrape them clean with a dull knife. But today many mussels are cultivated, already very clean and requiring only a quick rinse before they're ready to cook. Traditionally, the "beard"—the clump of fibers attached to the mussel meat that sticks out from the shell—is yanked out before cooking, but it's easier to remove the beards once the mussels are cooked. You don't need to debeard mussels raw unless you're serving them whole, in the shell—and even then, if the dinner is casual, most guests won't mind pulling off the beards themselves. Cultivated mussels, such as those shown here, have such tiny beards that it's hardly ever necessary to remove them.

To Clean Mussels

1. Rinse the mussels under cold running water while rubbing them vigorously between your fingers. If the mussels are very dirty, scrub with a stiff brush or scrape them with the back of a knife.
2. If you do want to remove the beard, pull it out with your fingers. If it's especially stubborn, grab it with a kitchen towel and pull.

See Also

To kill a lobster humanely, page 135

Related Glossary Entry

Steam

HOW TO

Shuck Oysters

You're likely to encounter two kinds of oysters: elongated oysters such as blue points and Kumamoto oysters, which are the most common, and round, relatively flat oysters, such as Belons, a European variety that is growing in popularity. Elongated oysters are most easily shucked by working an oyster knife through the hinge, while round oysters are usually easier to open through the side. Place the oyster on the counter to help steady it while shucking.

To Shuck Elongated Oysters

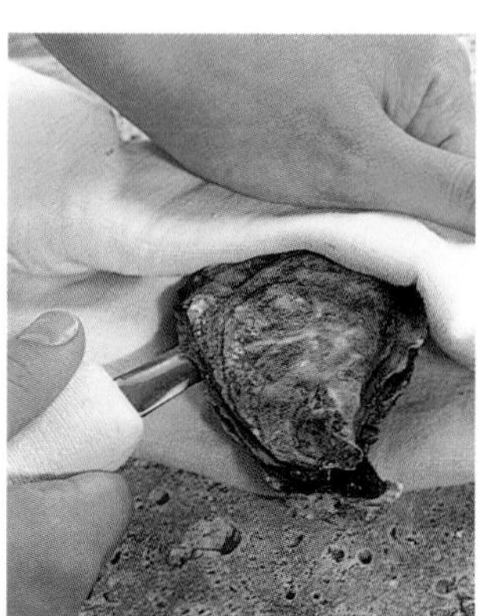

1. Hold the oyster in a kitchen towel, with a fold of the towel between the hand holding the oyster and the knife blade. Twist the blade in the hinge until the top shell loosens.
2. Slide the knife along the underside of the top shell. Press against the shell but don't cut into the oyster. Cut the oyster away from the top shell.
3. Pull off the top shell. Holding the knife firmly against the inside of the bottom shell, slide the knife along the shell to cut through the muscle that attaches the oyster to the shell.

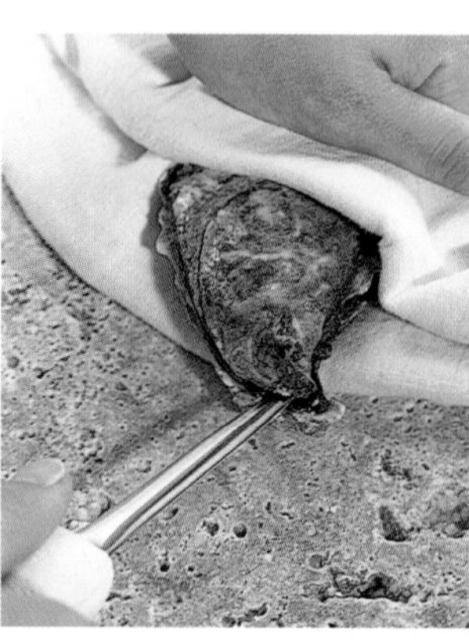

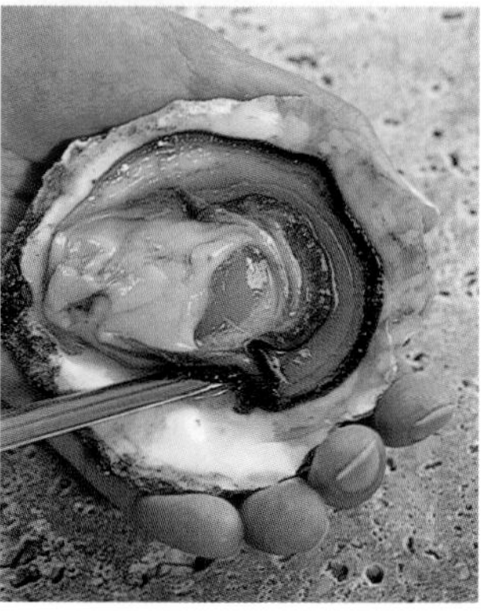

To Shuck Round Oysters

1. Slide an oyster knife into the side of the oyster. You may have to search for an opening between the 2 shells. Then, keeping the knife pressed against the underside of the lid, slide the knife along the top shell to detach the oyster. Be careful not to cut into the oyster.
2. Slide the knife along the bottom shell to cut through the muscle that attaches the oyster to the shell.

HOW TO

Prepare Lobster

If lobster is simply going to be steamed and served whole, it needs only a quick rinse to ready it for the pot. For more elaborate recipes, however, you may need to pry the cooked meat from the shell or cut up the lobster while it is raw, by either splitting it lengthwise or cutting it into sections.

To Select a Lobster

A number of lobster dishes call for lobster roe, found only in females. To judge a lobster's sex, turn the lobster upside down and look at the small flippers attached to the tail where it joins the head. Those on a female are flexible and soft; those on the male are hard.

Female

Male

To Kill a Lobster Humanely

Sometimes you'll need to cut up the lobster before cooking it to extract the maximum flavor from the shell, roe, and tomalley. Some recipes call for cutting the lobster in half, while others say to cut it into sections. Regardless of how you will cut the lobster up, you need first to kill it humanely. Hold a chef's knife directly over the lobster's head. Quickly push the knife all the way down to the cutting board and rapidly pull the knife forward, cutting the front part of the lobster's head in half and killing it instantly.

To Cut a Raw Lobster in Half

After killing the lobster, turn it around and split it in half from the head to the tail. Remove the small grain sac from each side of the lobster's head (it'll feel rough when you run your fingers along the inside of the head) and discard. Occasionally the vein that runs down the top of the tail contains grit; if it does, pull it out.

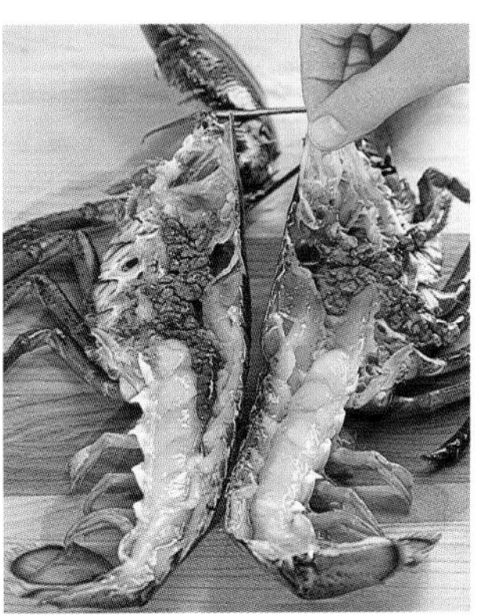

To Cut a Raw Lobster into Sections

Often a lobster is cut up raw for soups and stews or to get at the tomalley (the liver) or roe. The tomalley (which is a light grayish-green) is found in both male and female lobsters; the roe (which is dark green, almost black) is only found in females. Both tomalley and roe can be pressed through a strainer and used to thicken, flavor, and color sauces.

1. After killing the lobster, snap off the claws where they join the head (thorax).
2. Hold the head firmly in one hand and twist off the tail with the other.
3. Reach into the head with your forefinger and scoop out any tomalley or roe into a strainer set over a bowl containing a teaspoon of wine vinegar or cognac.
4. Work the tomalley or roe (tomalley is shown here) through the strainer with the back of a ladle. You can also work it through with the tips of your fingers.

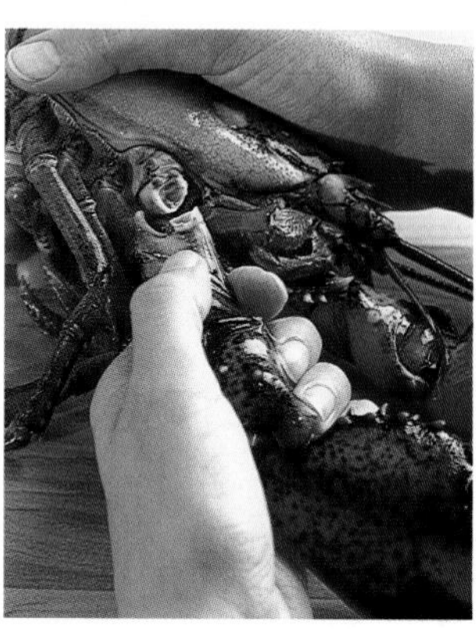

5. Finish cutting the head in half.
6. Pull the grain sac out of either side of the head and discard. Pull out any remaining coral or tomalley and work it through the strainer.

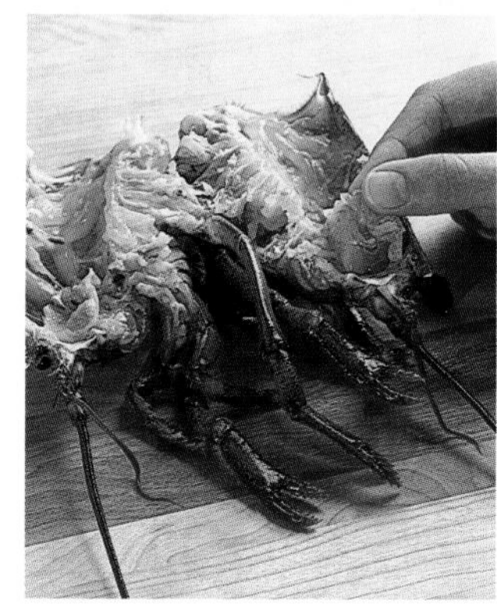

To Remove Cooked Lobster Meat from the Shell

This method of shelling cooked lobster is designed for working quickly in the kitchen and can be used for any recipe calling for cooked lobster meat.

1. Snap off the lobster claws where they are attached to the head (thorax).
2. Grip the head and tail firmly in both hands and twist off the tail.
3. Snap off the flipper at the end of the tail.
4. Place the tail on its side and press gently on it with the heel of your hand until you feel the shell crack and hear a gentle

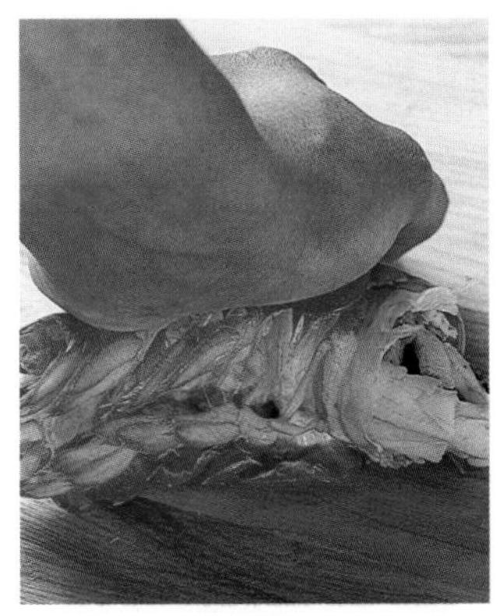

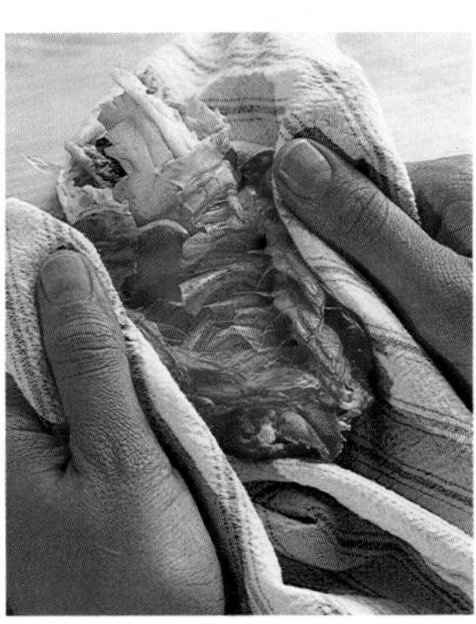

crunch. Don't push too hard or you will mangle the meat.

5. Place the tail upside down in a kitchen towel and pull away the sides to release the tail meat.

6. The tail can be cut lengthwise in half, cut into cubes, or, as shown here, sliced.

7. Gently move the claw pincers from side to side, then bend them away from the claw while pulling them out. The small feather-shaped piece of cartilage that's imbedded in the claw should come away with the pincer.

8. Hold the claw "thorny" side up. Give a quick whack with a chef's knife (preferably an old one, since the shell can damage the blade; you could also use a cleaver, if you handle it carefully) so the knife goes in about ½ inch, without cutting into the meat.

9. Rotate the knife to crack open the claw.

10. Use the chef's knife to crack through the small hinge at the base of the claw.

See Also

To steam lobster, page 132

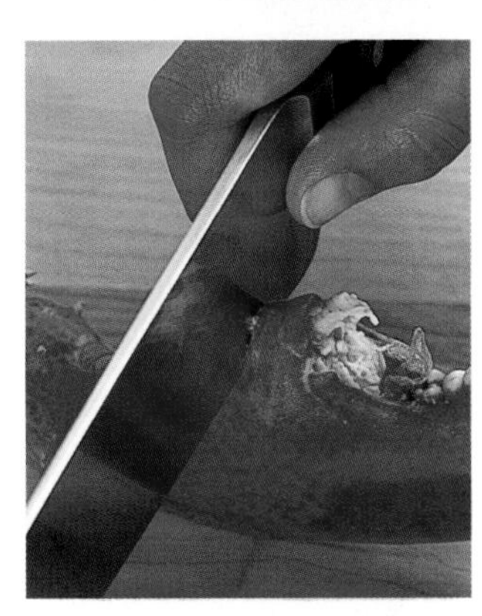

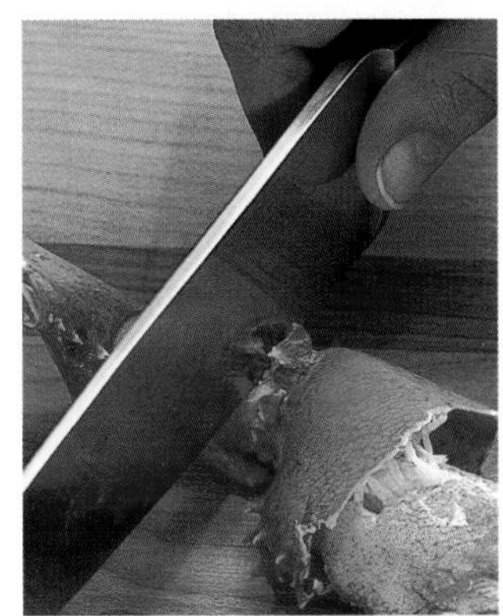

11. Use a pair of kitchen scissors to cut through the shells of the "knuckles" that connect the claws to the body. Pull the meat out of the claw and knuckles with your fingers.

12. Cut the head in half with the chef's knife.

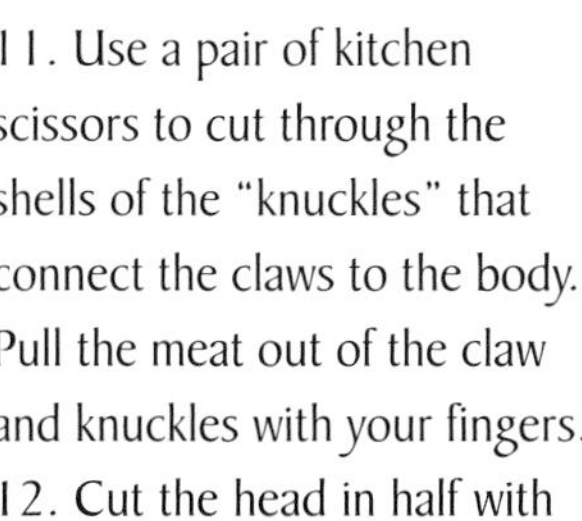

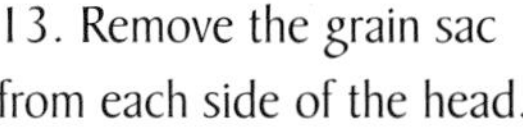

13. Remove the grain sac from each side of the head.

HOW TO

Prepare Soft-shell Crabs

Most crabs are sold cleaned, cooked, and cracked, but soft-shell crabs are sold alive and are so perishable that it's best to clean them no more than an hour or two before they are cooked.

1. Rinse the crabs. Cut off the very front part of each crab—the spiky part with the eyes—with scissors.
2. Turn the crab on its back and pull open the "apron" (the tail flap). Twist it, pull it off, and discard.
3. Turn the crab right side up and pull up the shell on each side.
4. Pull away the rough gills (sometimes called dead man's fingers) on each side of the crab.

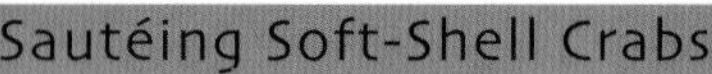

Sautéing Soft-Shell Crabs

A coating of flour gives soft-shell crabs a crisp, brittle exterior.

Clean the crabs. Just before cooking, pat the crabs with flour. Heat whole butter or olive oil in a nonstick or well-seasoned cast-iron sauté pan over medium-high heat. Sauté the crabs on both sides until crisp, about 3 minutes on each side.

HOW TO

Cook Crayfish

Like lobsters, crayfish should be alive when you buy them. Before cooking, sort through them and throw out any that are dead. When handling crayfish, pick them up from behind the head, holding them between thumb and forefinger, so they don't pinch you.

One way to cook crayfish is just to toss them in a pot of boiling water for five minutes or so. (Southern cooks flavor the water with herbs and spices; French cooks use a court bouillon.) Here, I sauté them and use their shells to make a sauce.

Sautéed Crayfish

Here, the crayfish are sautéed with carrot and onion because the crayfish shell–vegetable mixture will be used to make a sauce. If you're not making a sauce, omit the vegetables.

1. Rinse the crayfish in a colander. Gently sweat chopped carrots and onions in olive oil in a heavy-bottomed pan. Add live crayfish and stir over high heat.
2. Cook until all the crayfish turn red, about 7 minutes.

Crustacean Sauces, Bisques, and Butters

Any crustacean—crayfish, shrimp, lobster, or crab—can be used to make an excellent sauce or bisque using fundamentally the same technique. Sauces and bisques are based on a stock made by simmering the cooked shells in various liquids. Often the only difference between the two is a matter of degree: Bisques are usually thinner than sauces because they are eaten with a spoon and there's no need to thicken them so they coat foods. Cooked rice or, sometimes, bread crumbs may be puréed into a bisque to give it body. Sauces are more concentrated, because their flavor must contrast or complement the foods they're served with. Sauces are likely to be enriched with more cream and butter than soups, fine when you're eating only a couple of tablespoons, but daunting when you're eating a whole bowl. However, any bisque recipe can be converted into a sauce by leaving out the rice, using less liquid, reducing the crustacean broth, and adding a little cream or butter at the end. Conversely, any sauce can be converted into a bisque by adding more liquid to thin it and some puréed cooked rice or bread crumbs, not reducing the broth, and using less butter or cream.

To make a crustacean stock, the whole crustaceans are typically sautéed with a few chopped aromatic vegetables, usually carrots and onions, and a sprig of thyme. When the shells turn red, the meat is removed from the shells and then the broken-up shells are simmered in liquid to extract their flavor. Most crustacean stocks are made with tomatoes, because tomato reinforces not only the flavor but also the color of the crustaceans. Because much of the flavor and color contained in the shells are soluble in fat but not in water, some crustacean stocks are made with heavy cream so that the fat in the cream extracts the flavor and color of the shells and emulsifies it into the rest of the liquid.

A crustacean butter is made by slowly cooking butter with the broken-up crustacean shells. Crustacean butter is whisked into soups and sauces.

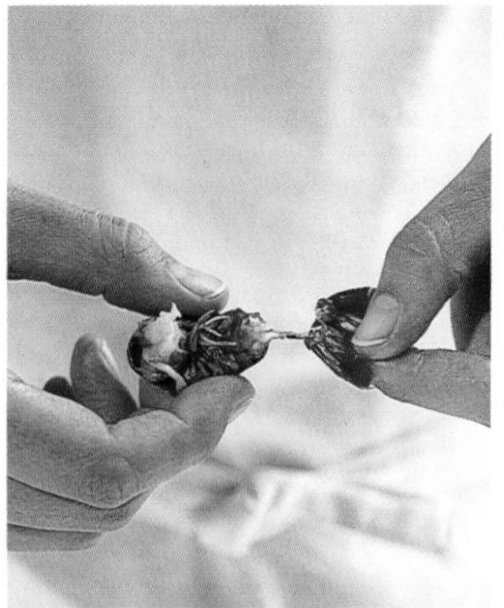

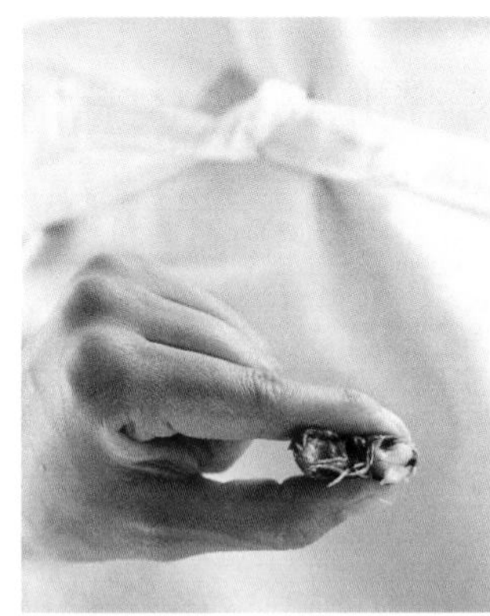

To Take Cooked Crayfish Meat out of the Tails

Most of the meat in crayfish is in the tails. If you like, you can crack the claws and remove the meat, but this is very labor-intensive and will yield only a small amount of meat.

1. Gently twist the tail of each cooked crayfish away from the head.
2. Firmly pinch the tail flipper where it joins the rest of the tail and pull it off. The intestine should come out with it. If it doesn't, the tail meat can be deveined in a similar way as shrimp.
3. Pinch the tail between your thumb and forefinger until you feel the shell crack slightly.
4. Pull the shell away from the tail meat. If the intestine didn't come out in Step 2, push the thin covering of meat that covers the vein sideways with your thumb so that it opens, revealing the vein. Pull the vein out with your fingers.

To Use the Shells for a Crayfish Sauce

Here, the heads and shells from sautéed crayfish (page 139) are used to make a sauce.

1. Snap the claws off the sautéed crayfish (they're very hard and would damage the food processor blade). Shell the tails (see page 140) and reserve the meat. Grind the heads and the tail shells for about 1 minute in the food processor.
2. Crush the claws with the end of a European-style rolling pin or mallet.
3. Combine all the shells, including the claws, in a heavy-bottomed saucepan and add chopped tomatoes, cognac, and heavy cream. Simmer, stirring occasionally, until the liquid turns orange, about 45 minutes.
4. Strain through a coarse strainer, pushing hard against the shells to extract the maximum amount of liquid, then strain again through a fine-mesh strainer or cheesecloth. If the sauce is thin, reduce it—cook it down—to thicken it slightly.
5. Here, the crustacean tails and sauce are served with a salmon mousseline.

See Also

To devein shrimp, page 131
To make a salmon mousseline, page 276
To make a crustacean broth, page 34

Related Glossary Entries

Mousseline

Reduction

HOW TO

Use Salted Anchovies

The best preserved anchovies come packed in salt. These anchovies are whole and must be partially desalted and filleted before they can be used. Because salted anchovies are sold in one-and-a-half pound or larger cans, it's easiest to desalt them all at once and repack them in extra virgin olive oil, to be used as needed. Whole salted anchovies can also be bought in small amounts from specialty food shops, but these often come from cans that were opened too long ago and the anchovies are stale and fishy. Keep your own repacked anchovies in the refrigerator for up to a month.

To Desalt and Repack Anchovies

1. Dissolve the salt at the top of the can by soaking the can for a few minutes in cold water and then quickly rinsing off the salt under cold running water.

2. Turn the can over and shake out the anchovies in a clump into a bowl of cold water. Soak for about 10 minutes, then gently separate the anchovies one from another, a few at a time.

3. When all of the anchovies have been freed, soak them for 20 minutes in a fresh bowl of cold water.

4. Snap off the heads (the method is similar to taking the heads off fresh sardines) and gently push the fillets away from the backbone with your thumbs and forefingers.

5. Soak the fillets in fresh cold water for 5 minutes, then transfer to cloth kitchen towels to drain. (Don't use paper towels, which would stick and tear.)

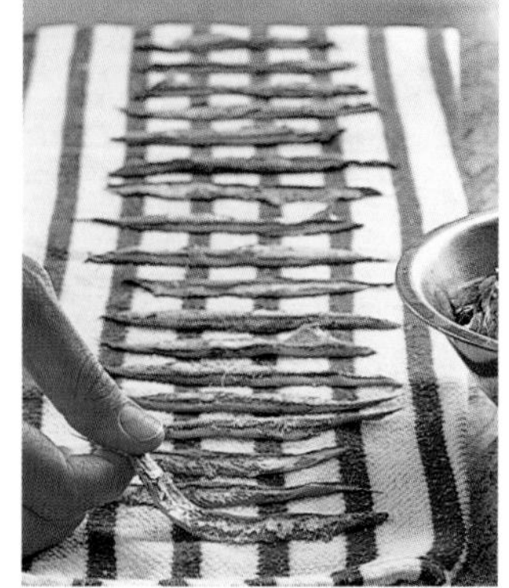

6. Pack the fillets in jars and pour over enough extra virgin olive oil to cover. Press down on the fillets to push out any trapped air and add more olive oil as needed to cover completely.

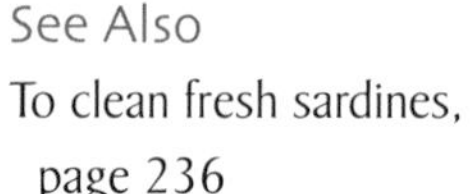

See Also
To clean fresh sardines, page 236

HOW TO

Make Miso Soup

Miso soup is made by flavoring Japanese-style fish and seaweed broth, called dashi, with a paste of fermented soybeans. It is completely different in style and technique from European soups, and is more akin to making tea.

Dashi is made by steeping a special variety of kelp, called konbu, and finely shaved flakes from dried bonito (a tuna-like fish) in hot water. The dashi is then strained and whisked with enough miso paste—a thick paste of fermented soybeans—to flavor the soup without making it too salty. The soup can be garnished with cubes of tofu, shellfish, vegetables, pieces of seaweed, lemon zest, or noodles. Simmer quick-cooking garnishes such as shellfish, tofu, lemon zest, leafy greens, or finely julienned vegetables directly in the soup. Cook noodles separately and place in each bowl.

Miso paste comes in many different varieties, from mild and very pale brown to strong and salty and such a dark red-brown that it looks almost black. It is available in Asian markets and even some supermarkets. For beginners, a medium-dark miso works perfectly well.

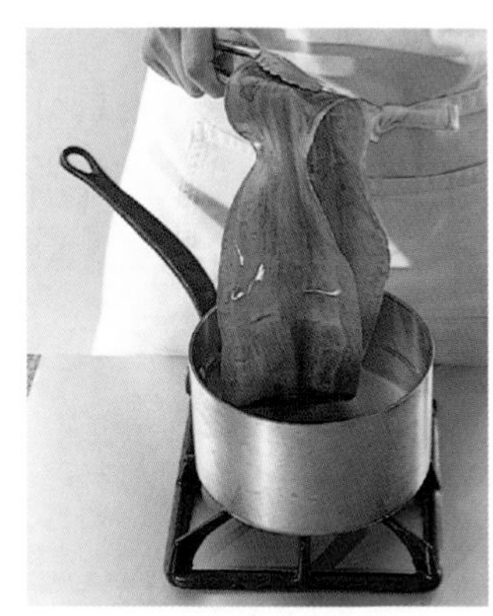

Dashi

Dashi is the base for many Japanese soups and sauces.

1. Add a strip of konbu to a pot of cold water. Bring the water to a simmer over low to medium heat. It should take about 15 minutes to simmer, to give the konbu time to infuse.
2. Remove the konbu from the water as soon as the water comes to the boil.
3. Bring the infused water (konbu dashi) back to the simmer, toss in a handful of shaved bonito flakes, and remove from the heat. Leave the flakes in the water for 1 minute.
4. Strain the bonito flakes out of the liquid.

Miso Soup

1. Whisk just enough dashi into a small amount of miso paste to make a smooth paste.
2. Whisk this paste back into the dashi and return to the simmer.
3. Ladle the miso soup into hot bowls containing whatever garniture you've chosen.

Kitchen Notes and Tips

- Use an 18-inch strip of konbu (folded over or broken, so it fits in the pan) or equivalent for each 5 cups water.
- Count 2 to 4 tablespoons miso paste per quart of dashi.

Poultry and Eggs

HOW TO

Roast a Chicken

One of the quickest, easiest, and best-tasting ways to prepare a chicken is to roast it whole and serve it with the pan juices. You don't need a roasting pan or a rack—in fact, I caution against using a rack because the juices will burn in the pan underneath and you'll lose your sauce. A baking or gratin dish large enough to hold the bird works perfectly well. Nor do you need to baste the chicken, because the skin keeps the chicken moist by slowly releasing fat that bastes the meat throughout roasting. (The fat ends up on the bottom of the roasting pan and is skimmed off.) Breast meat cooks faster than thigh meat, so to equalize the cooking time, place a folded and buttered sheet of aluminum foil over the breasts during the first fifteen minutes in the oven to slow their cooking.

Cooks often ask whether it's really necessary to truss a chicken. It's not necessary, but I recommend it. Trussing doesn't affect the way the bird cooks but a trussed chicken is easier to handle. Trussing also gives the bird an attractive shape, which is important if you're carving it at the table. With practice, it takes less than a minute to truss a bird.

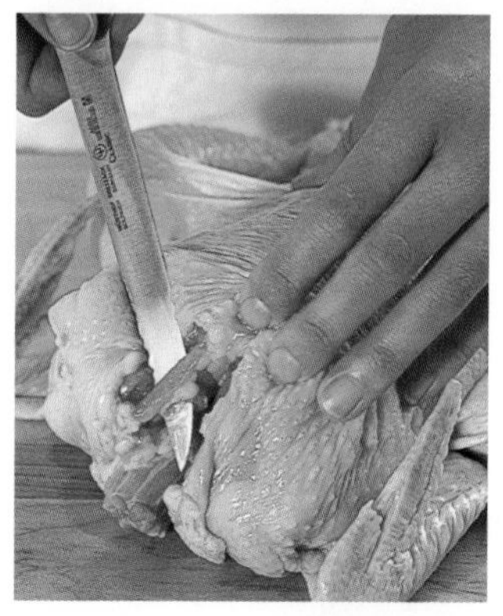

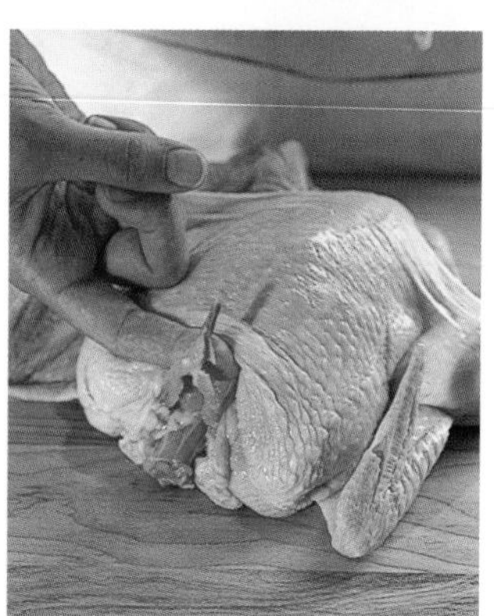

To Prepare a Chicken for Roasting

1. To make carving easier, remove the wishbone: Pull the skin up out of the way and slide the knife along the underside of the wishbone.
2. Continue cutting around and under the wishbone until it's separated from the flesh.
3. Pull the wishbone out with your fingers.
4. To truss the chicken (optional), slide the center of a 2½-foot length of string under the tail end of the chicken by about an inch.
5. Cross the ends of the string over the drumsticks, making sure that each of the drumsticks is caught by the string.

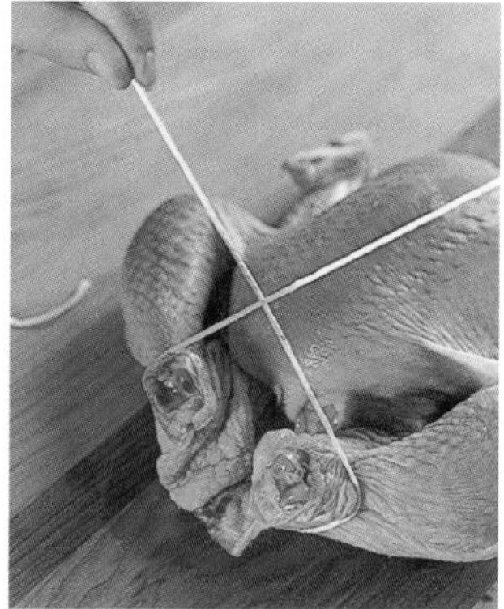

6. Tuck the left end of the string under the right drumstick and the right end under the left drumstick, making an X.
7. Pull tight so the drumsticks come together.
8. Pull the string back along the breast and over the wings.
9. Stand the chicken neck side up so the string hooks on top of the wings.
10. Turn the chicken over, pull the string tight over the wings, and tie into a knot. Fold under the end of each wing so that it hooks under the back of the chicken and stays in place.

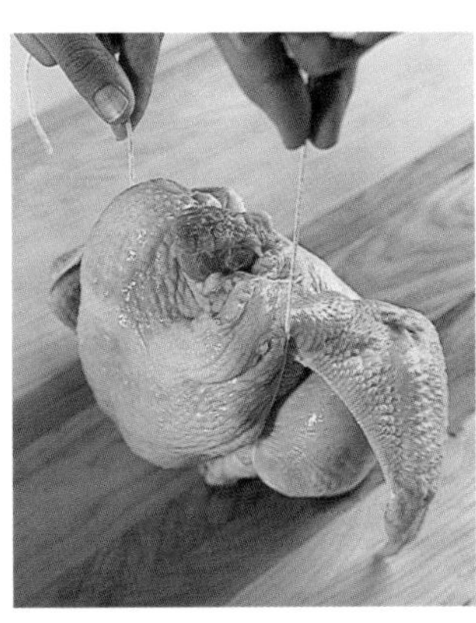

Kitchen Notes and Tips

- A 3½-pound chicken takes 45 minutes to an hour to roast at 425°F. Count on slightly more time for larger chickens.
- Cornish game hens and other small birds won't brown well enough in the oven in the time it takes to cook them through. Before roasting, brown the birds on each side in a pan on top of the stove over high heat. Once browned, Cornish game hens will roast in about 30 minutes.
- The method on page 148 will give you the simplest of all possible sauces—a tablespoon or so of pan juices, or "jus," per person. If you want to make a slightly more complicated jus that is flavored with roasted vegetables, see the Glossary.

Roast Chicken

1. Preheat the oven to 425°F. Place the trussed chicken in a small roasting pan or oval baking dish. Loosely cover the breasts but not the thighs with a buttered triple sheet of aluminum foil, buttered side against the chicken, and roast for 15 minutes. (The foil slows the cooking of the breasts so they don't dry out before the thighs are cooked.) Remove the foil and continue roasting until a thermometer inserted between the thigh and breast reads 140°F.

Remove the trussing string, cover the entire chicken loosely with aluminum foil, and let rest in a warm place such as the back of the stove or the oven on the lowest setting (however, if the oven has been used at a higher temperature, let it cool down with the door open before putting the chicken inside) for 20 minutes.

2. Use a wooden spoon stuck into the cavity of the chicken to transfer it to a platter (or a cutting board with a moat to catch the juices), tilting the chicken as you lift it so any juices in the cavity spill into the roasting dish.

3. Pour any juices that accumulate on the platter into the roasting pan. Tilt the roasting pan and skim the fat off the top of the jus with a spoon.

4. Carve the chicken and serve the jus at the table in a sauceboat, or spoon it over each serving.

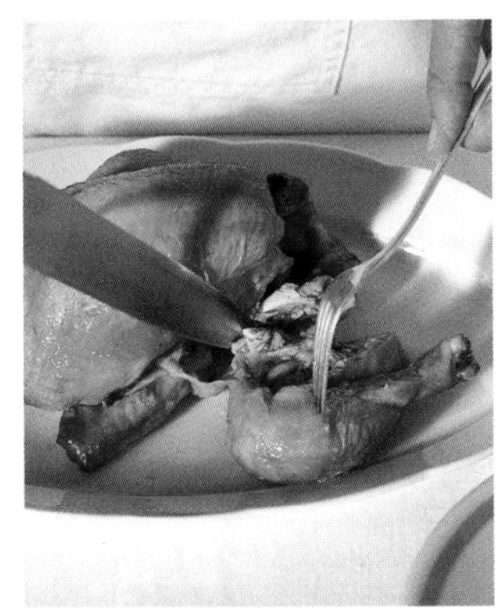

To Carve a Roasted or Poached Chicken

1. Hold the chicken steady with a fork inserted in the cavity. Cut through the skin separating the thigh and breast down to the bone at the base of the thigh that connects the thigh to the back.
2. Push the thigh down and away from the chicken so the small bone at the base of the thigh snaps out.
3. Slide the knife along the side of the chicken where the thigh connects to the back and separate the thigh completely from the chicken, leaving as little meat as possible attached to the back.
4. Cut into the breast just above the wing and locate the joint where the wing joins the rest of the chicken. (The joint is deeper inside the chicken than it appears from the outside.) Fold the wing out from the breast and cut through the joint, detaching the wing.
5. Slide the knife along one side of the breastbone, as close to the bone as possible, pushing the breast meat away from the bone with the back of the knife.
6. Continue sliding the knife along the breastbone, pushing the breast meat away from the bone with the back of the knife, and cut the breast off the carcass. Turn the chicken around and repeat on the other side.

See Also

To roast vegetables with the chicken, page 70

To test the internal temperature of poultry, page 167

Related Glossary Entries

Degrease
Gravy
Jus
Roast

HOW TO

Poach Chicken in a Pot

Poaching is a great method for cooking chicken and other poultry because it's light—no fat is added—and it makes its own savory broth that can be served with the carved chicken as a delicate, fat-free, and pure-flavored sauce. Root vegetables such as carrots, leeks, and turnips poached along with the chicken make the dish a one-pot meal. Cut vegetables into relatively large pieces so they cook at the same rate as the chicken. Here, carrots are sectioned and cored and turnips cut into wedges. Remove the wishbone and truss the chicken before poaching, so that it cooks to an attractive shape and is easy to lift in and out of the poaching liquid.

Kitchen Notes and Tips

- Once the poaching liquid has come to a simmer, a 3½-pound chicken cooks in about 35 to 45 minutes.
- Start the chicken in cold broth or water. Starting in hot liquid will give you a cloudy broth.
- Poach the chicken, uncovered, at a gentle simmer.
- Pull the cooked chicken out of the poaching liquid by hooking a fork onto the trussing string and lifting the chicken out.

Chicken in a Pot *(Poule au Pot)*

1. Place the trussed chicken in a pot just large enough to hold it but deep enough to completely cover it with liquid. Add aromatic vegetables, such as the cored carrot sections and turnip wedges shown.
2. Cut rinsed leeks in half. Tie together with string so they don't float up and interfere with skimming. Add them to the pot.
3. Put a bouquet garni in the pot and pour over enough broth or water to cover. Simmer gently, skimming off any fat or scum that floats to the top with a ladle, for 35 to 45 minutes.
4. Transfer the chicken to a serving dish. See if it's done by inserting a skewer into the thickest part of the thigh, right where it joins the drumstick. If the liquid runs clear, not pink, it is ready.
5. Pull off and discard the skin.
6. Carve the chicken and serve with the vegetables in wide soup plates, ladling over the broth.

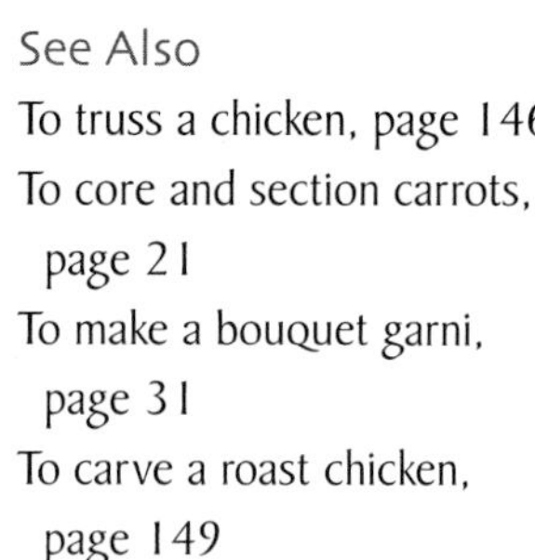

See Also

To truss a chicken, page 146
To core and section carrots, page 21
To make a bouquet garni, page 31
To carve a roast chicken, page 149

Related Glossary Entry

Poach

HOW TO

Cut Up a Chicken

Use cut-up chicken in stews and sautés, and for frying and grilling. For family-style cooking, when you can pick up and eat chicken wings with your fingers, cut off the wings, cut the rest of the chicken into quarters (which actually yields two servable legs, two servable breasts, and the back in addition to the two wings), and cook the wings too. For a more elegant restaurant-style presentation, cut the chicken into six pieces: Trim off and discard the last two joints of the wings, leaving the first meaty joint attached to the breast (this not only makes use of the most edible part of the wing, but it also looks attractive) (see Box, page 153) and cut the legs in half into thighs and drumsticks. To cut the chicken into eight pieces, cut the breasts in two. Cutting the chicken into eight pieces allows you to serve four people a piece of white and dark meat each. Chicken backs and wing tips can be frozen and used for chicken broth.

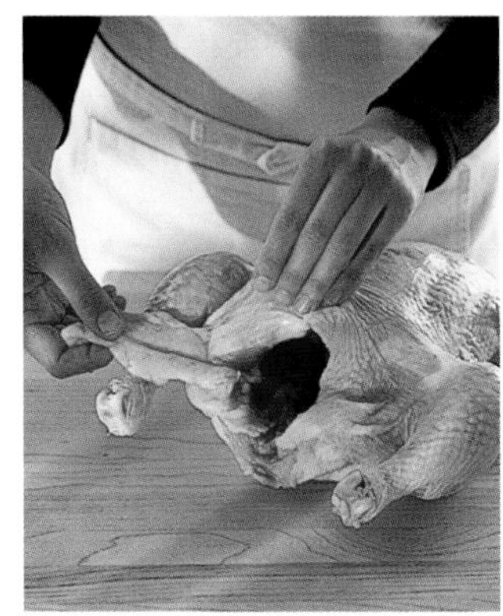

To Cut a Chicken into Quarters (plus Wings or Wing Tips and Back)

1. Cut off the tail (optional).
2. Pull out any large clumps of fat from the cavity opening.
3. Pull one wing out from the body and cut through the joint where the wing joins the body. Repeat with the other wing.
4. Pull one thigh forward so that when you cut off the thigh, the breast stays well covered with skin.
5. Cut through the skin between the thigh and breast all the way to the back. Follow the natural line of fat running along the edge of the thigh.

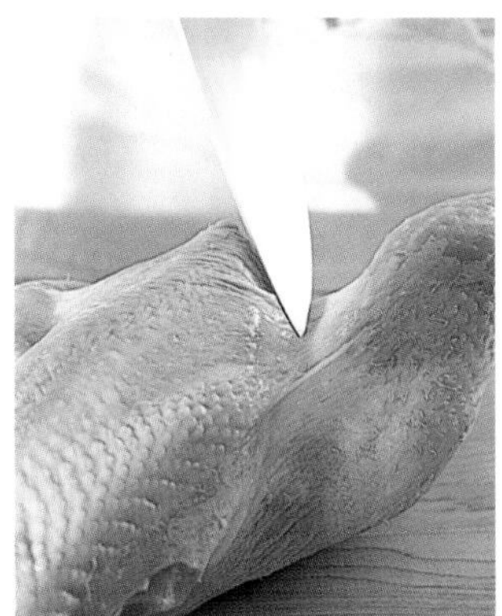

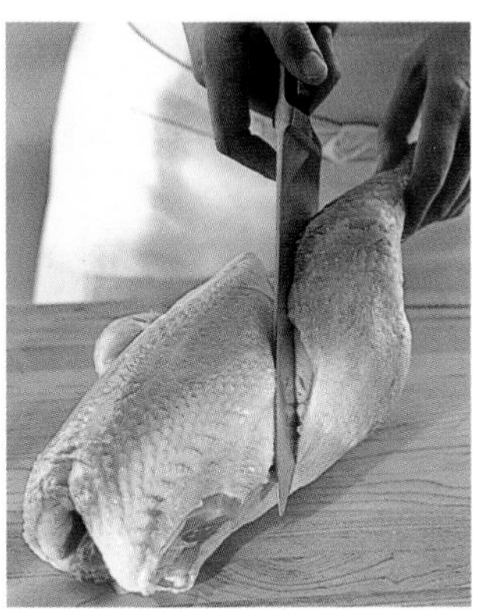

6. Hold your finger under the joint where the thigh connects to the rest of the chicken and snap open the thigh. You'll feel the joint snap out.
7. Slide the knife along the back, keeping the knife against the bone and pulling on the thigh with the other hand as you go. Be sure to cut under the small morsel of meat ("the oyster") imbedded in the back so that you leave it attached to the thigh.

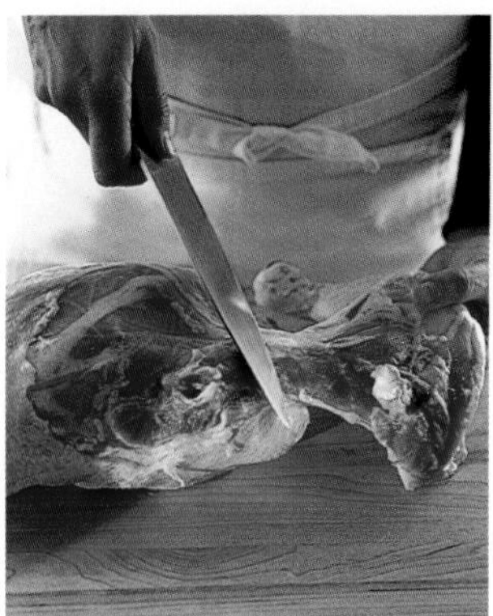

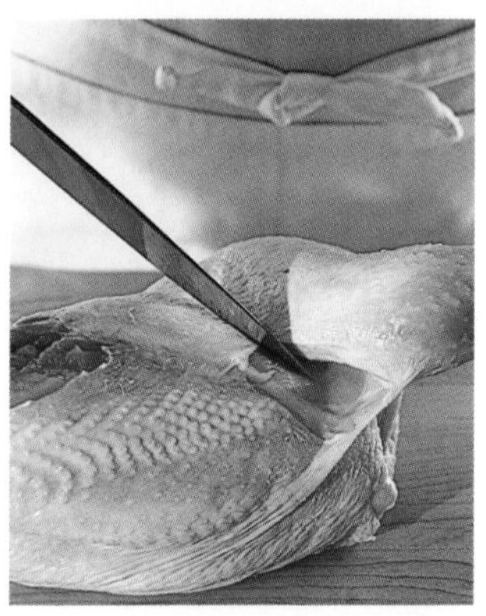

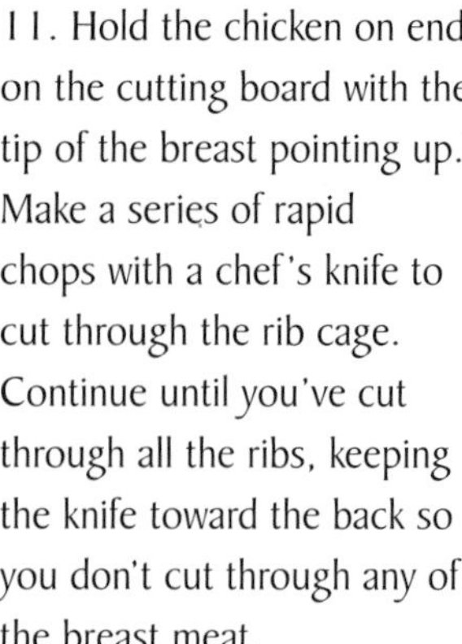

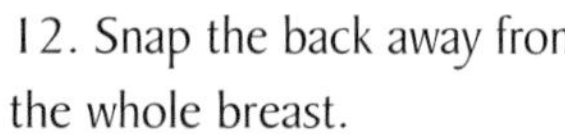

11. Hold the chicken on end on the cutting board with the tip of the breast pointing up. Make a series of rapid chops with a chef's knife to cut through the rib cage. Continue until you've cut through all the ribs, keeping the knife toward the back so you don't cut through any of the breast meat.
12. Snap the back away from the whole breast.
13. Cut through the joints that attach the breast to the back and separate the breast from the back.

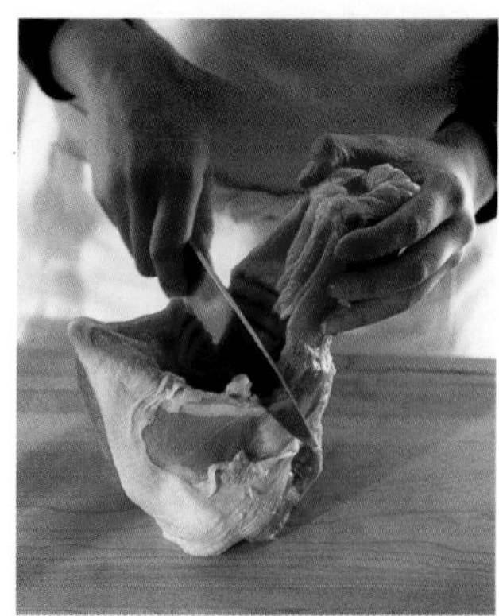

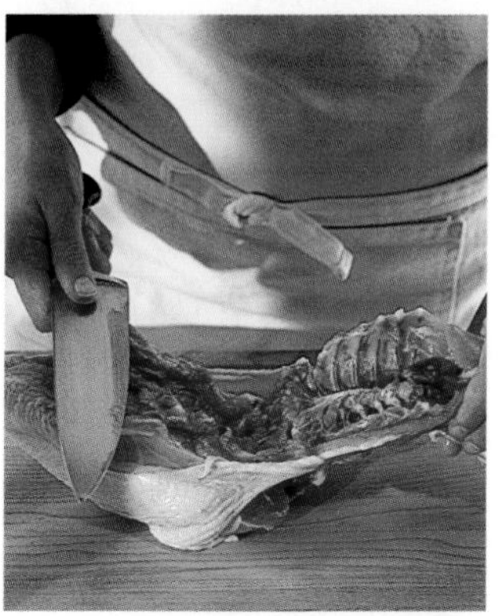

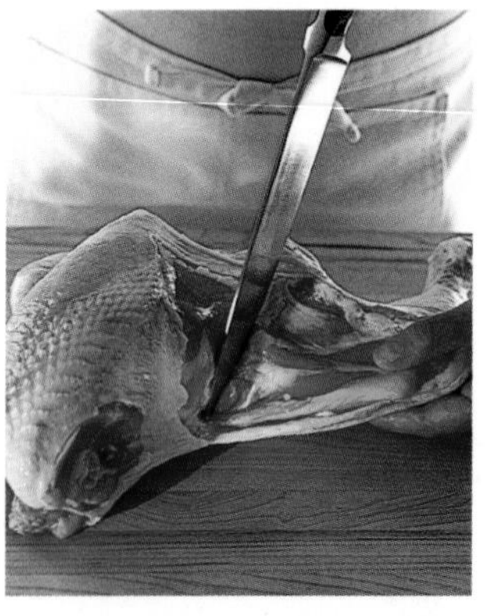

8. Continue sliding the knife along the backbone while pulling on the thigh until the thigh comes away.
9. Turn the chicken onto its other side and repeat.
10. Remove the other thigh.

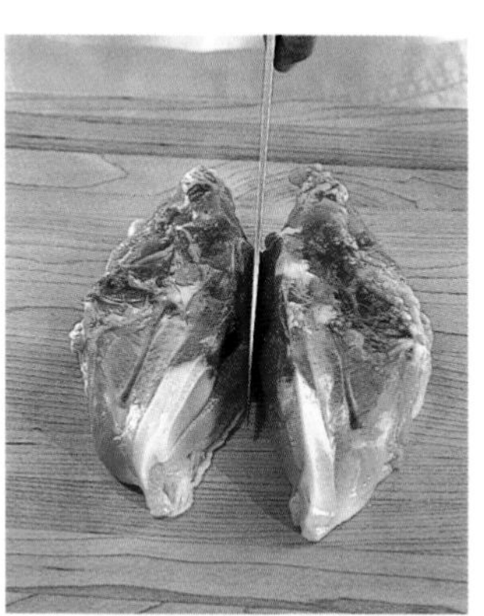

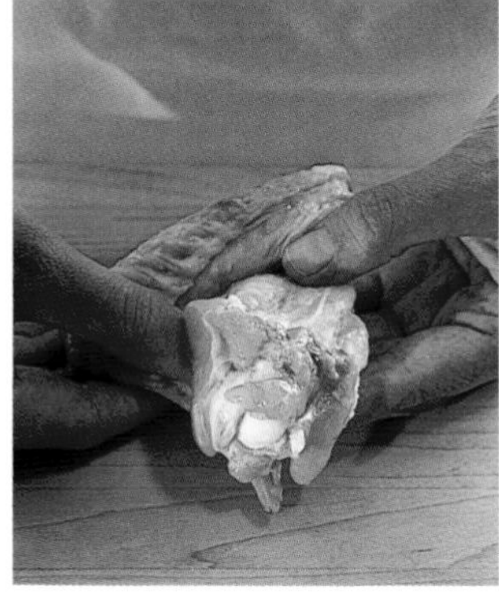

14. Split the breast by placing it skin side down on the cutting board and cutting straight down through the center of the breastbone. Pull the knife toward you to split the back part of the breast.
15. Turn the breast around and cut in the other direction, separating the 2 halves.
16. To cook wings for family-style eating, hook the tips of the wings under the rest of the wing to make a more compact shape.
17. If desired, cut off the ends of the thigh bones with a quick whack of the chef's knife. Use the very back end of the blade so you don't damage the edge.

See Also

To make a chicken stew, page 154
To make a chicken sauté, page 157
To grill chicken, page 161
To fry chicken, page 160

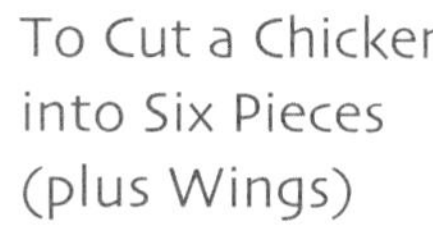

To Cut a Chicken into Six Pieces (plus Wings)

First cut the chicken into quarters as instructed on pages 151 and 152. Then place 1 leg skin side down on the cutting board. Locate the joint between the drumstick and thigh with your fingers and cut through with the chef's knife. Repeat to split the other whole leg.

To Cut a Chicken into Eight Pieces (plus Wings)

First cut the chicken into 6 pieces as instructed above. Then cut through the breast with the chef's knife, pressing firmly on the back of the knife to cut through the bone.

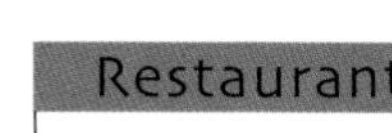

Restaurant-Style Chicken Breast

In fine restaurants the first joint of the wing is sometimes left attached to the breast and the rest of the wing saved for making stocks. Pull the wing away from the chicken and cut it away by slicing through the second joint. Use a chef's knife or a cleaver to hack off the unattractive little nub that's left on the second joint.

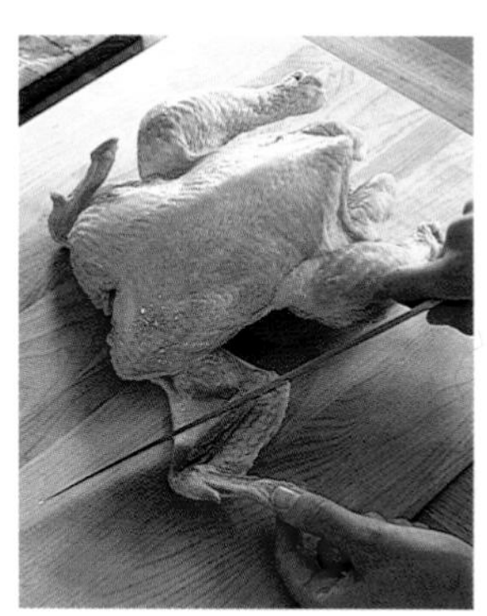

HOW TO

Make a Chicken Stew

Chicken stews (*fricassées* in French cuisine) are made by first cooking chicken pieces in a small amount of butter, olive oil, or other fat, then adding a liquid such as broth, wine, or vinegar and cooking, covered, until the chicken is tender. Once the chicken is done, the stewing liquid is usually thickened to make a sauce, but it is occasionally served, broth-like, around the chicken. A garniture may be cooked along with the chicken, or cooked separately and added at the end. Chicken stews differ from chicken sautés in that stewed chicken is cooked in liquid that is eventually bound to make the sauce, while sautéed chicken is cooked all the way through in fat alone (butter or oil). For a chicken sauté, liquid is added to the pan to make a sauce only after the chicken has been removed. Stewed chicken has a milder flavor than sautéed chicken and the skin is soft, not crispy. (Technically speaking, chicken stews are short-braises, because chicken is tender and lean enough that it need only be braised for a short time.)

Fricassées offer myriad possibilities for the creative cook. Liquids and garnitures can be varied almost endlessly to change the character of the basic stew. But beyond a change in ingredients, the way the chicken is cooked also substantially changes the flavor of the dish. So-called white fricassées are stews in which the chicken is cooked in the fat just long enough to cook the skin but not to brown it, producing a stew with a light-colored sauce and a delicate chicken flavor. In a brown fricassée, the chicken is thoroughly browned before liquid is added; this additional caramelization deepens the flavor of the chicken and results in a darker-colored, stronger-flavored sauce. Brown fricassées can accommodate more assertive ingredients, such as red wine or vinegar, that would overpower the taste of chicken that has not been browned.

When I want a delicate-flavored, light-colored chicken dish with a creamed or herbed sauce, I make a white fricassée. When I'm looking for a deeper, more concentrated chicken flavor, I make a chicken sauté or a brown fricassée.

White Chicken Fricassée with Wine Vinegar

This stew is garnished with glazed assorted vegetables, added at the end.

1. Gently cook the chicken pieces in butter on both sides until the skin no longer looks raw. Pour over enough liquid to come a quarter of the way up the sides of the chicken; here, I use sherry vinegar.
2. Cover and simmer over low to medium heat until the chicken pieces feel firm to the touch, about 15 minutes. Transfer the chicken to plates or a platter and keep warm.
3. Tilt the pan so the liquid collects at one side. Spoon off any fat floating on top of the liquid. Discard the fat.
4. Reduce the liquid slightly to thicken it. Pour in heavy cream and continue to reduce until the liquid has a sauce-like consistency.

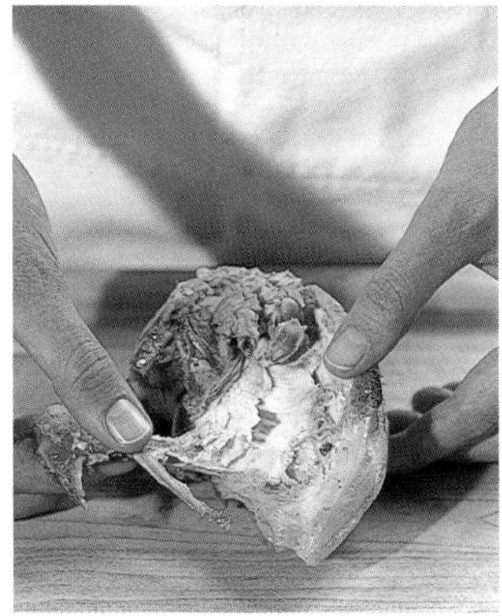

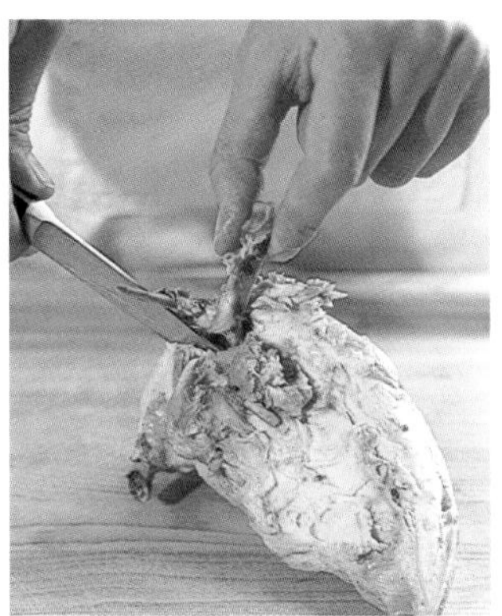

5. Pull the ribs and other small bones away from the inside of the chicken breasts.
6. Cut off the small bone attached to each breast near the wing.
7. Garnish with glazed vegetables. Season the sauce with salt and pepper and spoon over the chicken.

Kitchen Notes and Tips

- Cook chicken stews on top of the stove or in the oven.
- Keep the liquid at a bare simmer during cooking.
- Cook the chicken in butter if the sauce will be finished with cream; use olive oil with Mediterranean ingredients such as tomatoes.
- As a refinement for any chicken stew, after cooking, pull the ribs and other small bones away from the inside of the chicken breast and cut off the small bone that attaches to the breast near the wing. (I leave these bones attached during cooking because they equalize the cooking time of the breasts and legs and help seal in flavor.)
- You'll need 2 to 3 tablespoons fat to cook a chicken for either a white or brown stew. Keep in mind that this fat, plus additional fat rendered by the skin, will be discarded.

Making Bacon Lardons

Many French dishes call for strips of unsmoked bacon cut into strips called *lardons*. Because American bacon is always smoked, our lardons must be blanched to get rid of some of their smokiness. Otherwise, the smokiness will take over the flavor of subtle dishes such as coq au vin and boeuf à la bourguignonne.

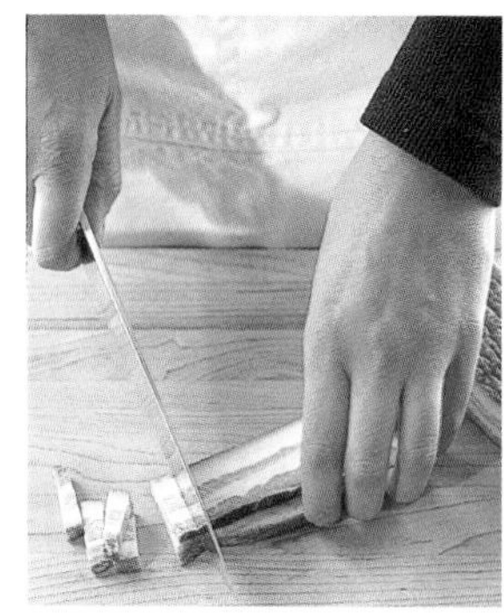

1. Cut thick slices of bacon crosswise into strips.
2. Put the strips in a pan, cover with cold water, and bring to the boil. Remove the lardons with a slotted spoon or drain in a colander.

3. Cook the lardons gently, without additional fat, as you would bacon, until they barely begin to turn crispy.

Chicken with Red Wine

Chicken with red wine—*coq au vin*—is traditionally made by simmering a cut-up rooster in red wine for 3 hours and finishing the braising liquid with the rooster's blood. Nowadays, because roosters are hard to find, chickens are often used instead. Because chickens are tender and cook quickly, the dish is prepared like a brown fricassée. The garnish of baby onions, lardons, and sautéed mushrooms is cooked separately and added to the stew at the end.

1. Cut the chicken into 8 pieces and marinate it with aromatic vegetables (here, carrots and onions) and enough red wine to cover for 4 hours or overnight in the refrigerator. Take the chicken out of the marinade and strain the marinade, reserving the vegetables and the liquid separately.
2. Blanch and gently cook lardons (see Box, page 155). Brown the blanched lardons in a sauté pan and remove with a slotted spoon; reserve for the garniture. Add the chicken to the pan and brown it in the fat rendered by the lardons, then remove from the pan.
3. Discard all but a tablespoon of the fat left in the pan. Brown the reserved vegetables over medium heat for about 10 minutes. Stir in flour and continue stirring for about 2 minutes.
4. Stir in the strained marinade and bring to a gentle simmer.
5. Add the chicken. Nestle a bouquet garni in the pot, cover, and cook very gently on top of the stove or in a 325°F oven for about 20 minutes, until the chicken is firm to the touch. Strain the braising liquid, then reduce and degrease it, with the pan moved to one side of the burner so it's easier to skim off the foam and fat.
6. Serve the chicken with the lardons, glazed onions, and sautéed mushrooms—here, I use wild mushrooms—and ladle the sauce over it.

See Also

To cut up a chicken, page 151
To glaze root vegetables, page 76
To make a bouquet garni, page 31
To make a chicken broth, page 30
To make a chicken sauté, page 157

Related Glossary Entries

Blanch
Braise
Degreasing
Fricassée
Garniture
Thickener

HOW TO

Make a Chicken Sauté

A chicken sauté is intensely flavorful because the chicken pieces are cooked entirely in a small amount of fat such as butter or olive oil on top of the stove. Sautéing the chicken pieces this way leaves them well caramelized, crispy, and very flavorful. When the chicken is done, serve it as is or make a sauce out of the caramelized juices that are left clinging to the bottom of the sauté pan. Classic and imaginative garnitures can be added for more complexity and to vary the flavor (see Box, page 159).

Kitchen Notes and Tips

- Sauté chicken in whole butter, extra virgin olive oil, or rendered duck or bacon fat. The choice of fat should be consistent with the character of the dish and the garniture (for example, use olive oil with Mediterranean ingredients such as tomatoes, butter for cream sauces).
- You'll need 2 to 3 tablespoons fat to sauté 1 chicken.
- Sauté over medium to high heat.
- Sauté skin side down first and serve the chicken skin side up, because this side is more attractive. Sautéing the skin side first diminishes the risk of sticking and saves you turning the pieces over again when serving.
- Test the doneness of the chicken by pressing gently with your finger on the thickest part. When the chicken is done, the meat springs back. If the chicken is underdone, the meat will feel fleshy.
- After discarding some or all of the fat, deglaze the pan with wine, stock, spirits, cream, chopped tomato, and/or a combination (see Box, page 159).
- Unlike steaks and chops, chicken doesn't need to be started in an extremely hot pan in order to brown well. Because it takes longer to cook through, the chicken will brown well over medium heat. The skin, which browns and releases its fat, forms a crispy coating that seals in the chicken's juices.
- Sauté chicken mostly skin side down so the fat in the skin has a chance to render and the skin to turn crispy.
- To keep the chicken from sticking, use a nonstick pan or well-seasoned skillet. If the skin sticks to the bottom of the pan as you're trying to turn the chicken, wait a minute or two. Often, as the fat in the skin continues to render, the skin will come loose from the pan.

Sautéed Chicken Breasts and Thighs with Mushroom Sauce

1. Heat butter in a heavy-bottomed pan just large enough to hold the chicken in a single layer. Season the chicken with salt and pepper and place it skin side down in the pan.
2. Cook for about 15 minutes, until the skin turns golden brown. Turn the chicken pieces over.
3. Cook on the flesh side for about 10 minutes, or until the flesh springs back when you press on it. Transfer the chicken to a plate or platter.
4. Pour out all but about a tablespoon of the fat left in the pan. Place over high heat, add shallots, and stir for about a minute, until they release their fragrance.
5. Add sliced mushrooms and continue to cook until the mushrooms brown and any liquid they release has completely evaporated.
6. Add white wine and simmer over high heat until it reduces to about 2 tablespoons.
7. Add brown chicken broth and reduce to a lightly syrupy consistency.
8. Whisk in butter and season with salt and pepper. Spoon the sauce over the sautéed chicken as shown on page 157.

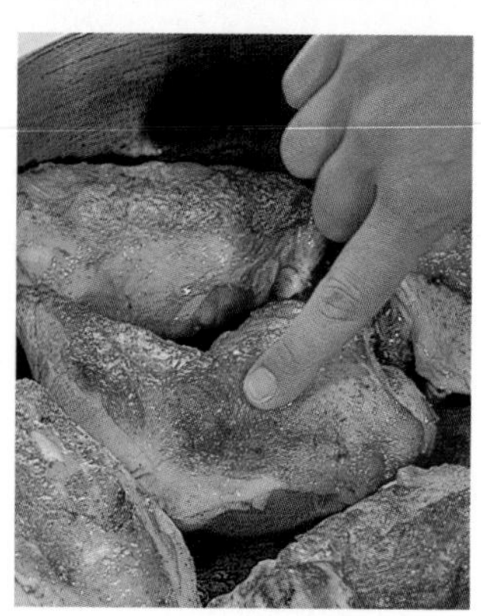

See Also

To cut up a chicken, page 151
To make a brown chicken broth, page 30
To make a chicken stew (and for the difference between a stew and a sauté), page 154
To determine doneness, page 66
To turn vegetables, page 13
To thicken with vegetable purées, page 286

Related Glossary Entries

Deglaze
Garniture
Monter au Beurre
Sauté
Sweat
Thickener

Classic Sauces for Sautéed Chicken

Because of its delicate flavor, chicken lends itself to an almost infinite number of sauces and garnitures. Escoffier, in the 1902 edition of his *Le Guide Culinaire,* lists more than seventy dishes based on sautéed chicken. However, for all this seeming complexity, the basic techniques—sautéing the chicken, deglazing the pan, adding flavorful liquids—remain the same. You can prepare classic dishes or make up your own just by plugging in different ingredients. Here are a few French classics:

- SAUTÉED CHICKEN ALGÉRIENNE: Deglaze the pan with white wine. Add crushed garlic and chopped tomato. Garnish with turned sweet potatoes.
- SAUTÉED CHICKEN ARCHIDUC: Sweat chopped onions in the cooking pan. Add Cognac and finish the sauce with cream, lemon juice, and Madeira. Pour over the chicken.
- SAUTÉED CHICKEN ARLÉSIENNE: Deglaze the pan with white wine and reduced veal stock. Garnish with fried onion rings and eggplant slices and stewed tomatoes.
- SAUTÉED CHICKEN ARTOIS: Deglaze the pan with Madeira and reduced veal stock. Finish with butter. Garnish with glazed turned carrots and pearl onions.
- SAUTÉED CHICKEN BERCY: Sauté chopped shallots in the pan used for the chicken. Deglaze with white wine, meat glaze, and lemon juice, then add mushrooms. Finish with butter.
- SAUTÉED CHICKEN BORDELAISE: Deglaze with chicken broth. Garnish with sautéed artichoke quarters, sautéed sliced potatoes, fried onion rings, and fried parsley.
- SAUTÉED CHICKEN À LA BOURGUIGNONNE: Deglaze with red wine, adding a crushed garlic clove. Finish with butter. Garnish with lardons and sautéed mushrooms.
- SAUTÉED CHICKEN WITH CÈPES: Sweat chopped shallots in the pan used for the chicken. Deglaze with white wine and finish with butter. Garnish with sautéed cèpes (porcini).
- SAUTÉED CHICKEN DORIA: Deglaze the pan with veal stock. Garnish with turned cucumbers.
- SAUTÉED CHICKEN WITH FINES HERBES: Deglaze the pan with white wine and reduced veal stock. Finish the sauce with chopped chervil, parsley, tarragon, and chives.
- SAUTÉED CHICKEN À LA HONGROISE: Brown chopped onion with a pinch of paprika in the pan used for the chicken. Add chopped tomatoes and cream. Reduce the sauce, strain, and pour over the chicken.
- SAUTÉED CHICKEN MARENGO: Deglaze the pan with white wine, adding chopped tomatoes and crushed garlic. Garnish with croutons, crayfish, and fried eggs. (Nowadays the crayfish and fried eggs are often left out.)
- SAUTÉED CHICKEN À LA NORMANDE: Deglaze the pan with Calvados. Garnish with apple slices gently cooked in butter.
- SAUTÉED CHICKEN WITH OYSTERS: Sauté the chicken with finely chopped onions, mushrooms, and chopped celery. Deglaze the pan with veal stock and strain the sauce. Poach oysters in the sauce and spoon over the chicken.
- SAUTÉED CHICKEN PARMENTIER: Deglaze the pan with white wine and veal stock. Garnish with turned potatoes cooked in butter.
- SAUTÉED CHICKEN TARRAGON: Deglaze the pan with white wine and reduced veal stock. Add chopped tarragon.
- SAUTÉED CHICKEN SAINT-LAMBERT: Deglaze the pan with white wine and mushroom cooking liquid. Thicken the sauce with a purée of cooked carrots, turnips, onion, and mushrooms.
- SAUTÉED CHICKEN VICHY: Deglaze the pan with veal stock. Garnish with glazed turned carrots.

HOW TO

Make Fried Chicken

Fried chicken, deservedly one of our most popular fried foods, is not technically deep-fried, because it isn't completely submerged in the oil. Rather, it is cooked by the method called shallow-frying, in which food is fried in enough oil or other fat to come halfway up its sides. Frying gets the chicken piping hot and very crispy—when you want a really great crust, it's the best method.

Cooks debate endlessly about how to coat chicken to get the best crust. I just dredge the chicken parts in flour. Since chicken skin browns perfectly well on its own, it needs only a little help to get really crisp. (I save more substantial batters made with flour, water, oil, and sometimes eggs, to deep-fry moist foods like vegetables that don't have a skin and so need an additional something to produce a crispy outer layer.) Don't use a bread-crumb coating for frying chicken—the breading just gets oily. (Breaded chicken breasts are better sautéed.) Two to four hours in a white wine marinade before frying will add enough flavor to the chicken so that it won't need a sauce. But if you like, serve fried chicken with a salsa or a flavored mayonnaise such as aïoli or gribiche.

Kitchen Notes and Tips

- Fry chicken at 360°F.
- An electric frying pan is good for frying chicken because the built-in thermostat makes it easy to regulate the temperature.
- Most cooks use vegetable oil for frying chicken, but "pure" olive oil (not extra virgin, which is expensive) will give it an even better flavor.

Fried Chicken

1. Cut the wings off a chicken and then cut it into 8 pieces. If desired, marinate the chicken for 2 to 4 hours in a mixture of chopped garlic, sliced onions, white wine, and a little olive oil.
2. Just before frying, toss the (drained) chicken pieces in flour and pat off the excess.
3. Heat the oil in an electric frying pan or large heavy pot to 360°F. Gently lower the chicken pieces into the oil with tongs. Start checking the chicken after 5 minutes.
4. When the pieces have browned on one side, turn them over. The chicken is done when the pieces feel firm to the touch with no fleshiness, about 10 to 15 minutes in all. Drain on paper towels.

See Also

To make an aïoli or gribiche sauce, page 43
To cut a chicken into 8 pieces, page 153
To sauté breaded chicken breasts, page 162

Related Glossary Entries

Bread
Deep-fry
Marinate

HOW TO

Grill Chicken

Grilling is a great method for cooking chicken because the skin crisps on the grill and grilling adds a savory, gently smoky flavor. Unlike when sautéing, when it's best to start with the skin side down first, start by grilling the chicken pieces skin side up over high heat. The flesh side is less likely to cause flames and the charcoal will have a chance to burn down somewhat before you turn the chicken skin side down. If the fire does flare up, move the chicken around on the grill.

A good way to prepare small poultry such as Cornish hens or squab for grilling is to cut out the backbone, spread the bird open, and insert the legs into small incisions made in the skin. This is a practical way to handle small whole birds, because it flattens them so that they grill evenly and quickly. Grill small birds just as you grill chicken. Cornish hens take about ten minutes on each side. Cook red-meated birds such as squab only until the meat is rare to medium-rare, about six minutes on each side.

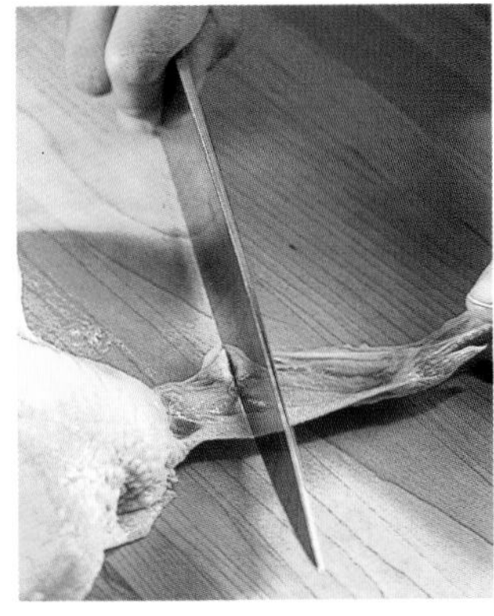

Grilled Chicken

Quarter a whole chicken, or cut it into 6 or 8 pieces. If desired, marinate the chicken in white wine with sliced onions, garlic, and thyme.

Grill the chicken pieces skin side up until the flesh side is well browned, at least 10 minutes. Turn and grill until the skin is crisp and brown and the chicken feels firm to the touch, with no fleshiness.

See Also

To cut up a chicken, page 151
To marinate chicken, page 156
To roast a chicken, page 146
To determine doneness, page 66

Related Glossary Entries

Grilling
Marinate

To Prepare Cornish Hens for Grilling

1. Cut off the last 2 sections of the wings or leave them on and fold them under.
2. Slide a heavy chef's knife into the cavity. Cut through just to the left of center.
3. Spread the bird open. Cut off the other side of the backbone. (You can also cut out some ribs for easier eating.)
4. Turn skin side up and make small slits on both sides.
5. Tuck the drumstick ends into the slits.

HOW TO

Sauté Breaded Chicken Breasts

Breading and sautéing in butter is an excellent way to prepare boneless skinless chicken breasts. The breading traps the delicious lightly browned, hazelnut-flavored butter and flavors the mild-tasting white meat. Breading also allows you to brown over a relatively low heat (breading browns at a lower temperature than the flesh), which makes it easier to brown the breasts without overcooking and protects them from drying out. Boned chicken breasts can usually be found at the supermarket, but you'll get more for your money if you start with a whole chicken or whole bone-in chicken breasts and bone the breasts yourself. In any event, breasts should be lightly pounded to an even thickness so that they cook evenly.

Kitchen Notes and Tips

- Breaded chicken breasts require a fair amount of fat to brown evenly. Add enough butter or oil to the pan to come to a depth of about ⅛ inch.
- Sauté over medium—not high—heat. If the breading browns too quickly, turn the heat down; if not quickly enough, raise the heat slightly.
- Sauté in whole or clarified butter; with clarified butter, there won't be any dark specks of milk solids clinging to the breading. Extra virgin olive oil can also be used.
- Serve the breasts with lemon wedges, a flavored butter, or beurre noisette.
- You'll get the best results if you use fresh bread crumbs (page 164).
- For a different flavor, replace the flour with porcini powder or grated Parmesan cheese, or a mixture of half bread crumbs and half grated Parmesan.

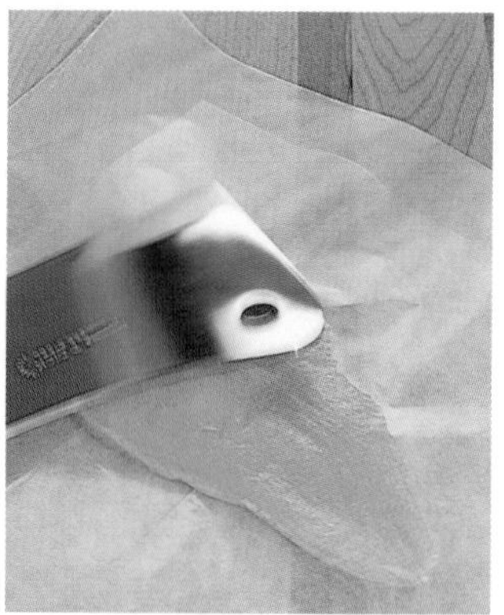

Sautéed Boneless Chicken Breasts

1. Place each chicken breast between 2 sheets of waxed paper or plastic wrap and gently flatten the thick end with the side of a cleaver so the whole breast is of the same thickness. Don't overdo it; if the chicken is too thin, it will dry out.
2. Coat each breast on both sides with flour and pat off the excess.
3. Dip the chicken in beaten egg that has been well seasoned with salt and pepper.
4. Coat the breasts on both sides with fresh bread crumbs.
5. Sauté the breaded chicken breasts in clarified butter or extra virgin olive oil over medium heat, until golden brown and firm to the touch, 3 to 4 minutes on each side, turning once. Turn gently with tongs so you don't tear the breading.

To Prepare Chicken Breasts for Sautéing

Whole double chicken breasts can be split in two and cooked with both skin and bone left attached or they can be skinned and boned, as shown here, and sautéed with or without a coating.

It's less expensive to buy bone-in double chicken breasts and bone them yourself than to buy already boned breasts. The tenderloin, the small muscle that runs along one side of the boneless breast, is usually left attached. But for some dishes, such as the breaded boneless chicken breasts, it's best to cook the tenderloins separately so they don't fall off the rest of the breast during cooking. The small tendon that runs along the tenderloin is removed because it's chewy and rather unattractive.

Skin-on chicken breasts can be sautéed almost in the same way as steaks, except over somewhat lower heat and almost entirely on the skin side to get the skin to release a maximum of fat.

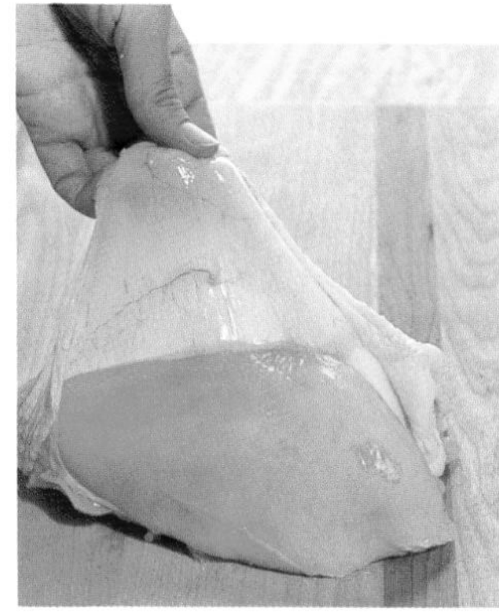

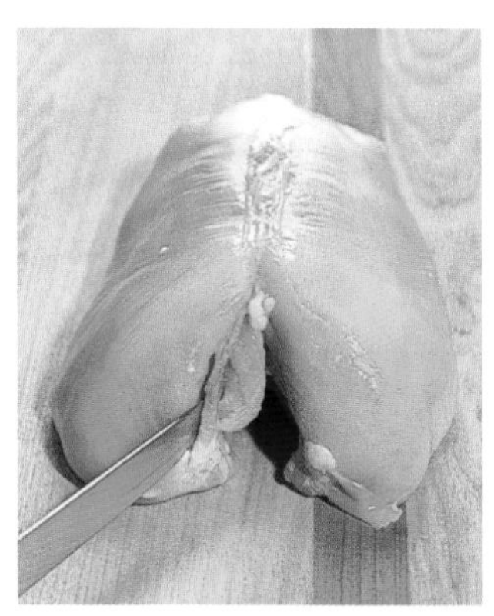

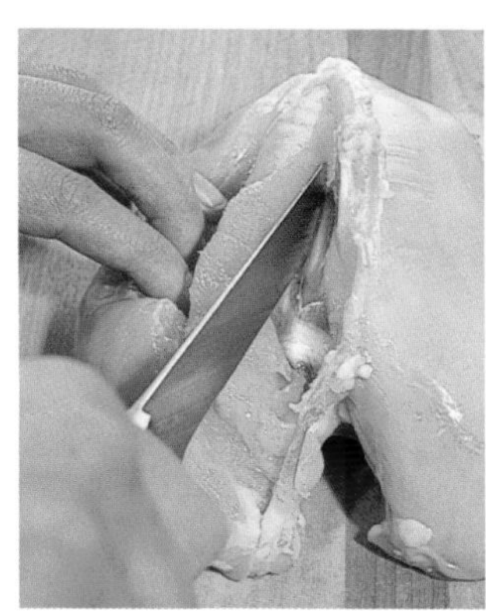

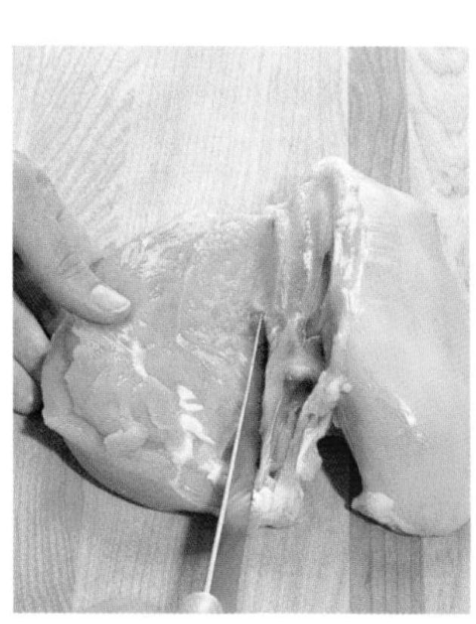

To make two boneless breasts

1. Peel off the skin.
2. Slide a small paring or boning knife under the wishbone on one side to free it from the meat.
3. Working on the same side, slide the knife along the breastbone, keeping the knife against the bone and pulling the meat away from the bone.
4. Continue sliding the knife against the bone until you've completely detached the boneless breast. Repeat on the other side.

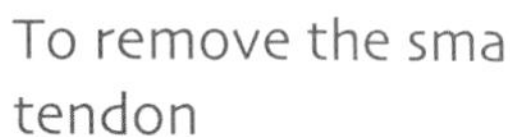

To remove the small tendon

1. Pull the tenderloin away from each boneless breast.
2. Slide a boning or paring knife under the end of the small tendon at the thicker end of the tenderloin.
3. Place the tenderloin tendon down on the cutting board. With the knife against the tendon, pull on the tendon, moving it gently from side to side with your other hand, until it comes away.

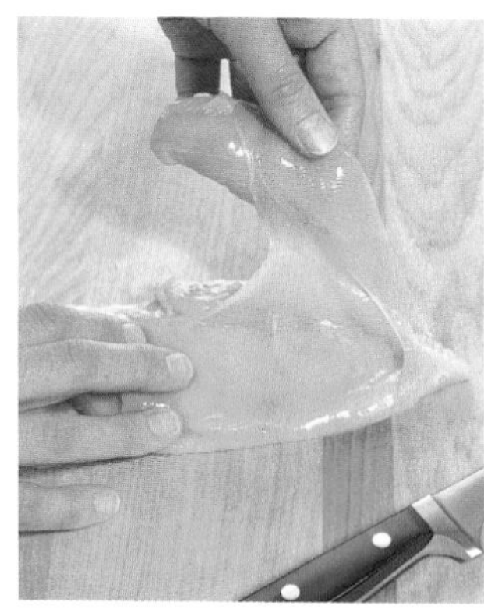

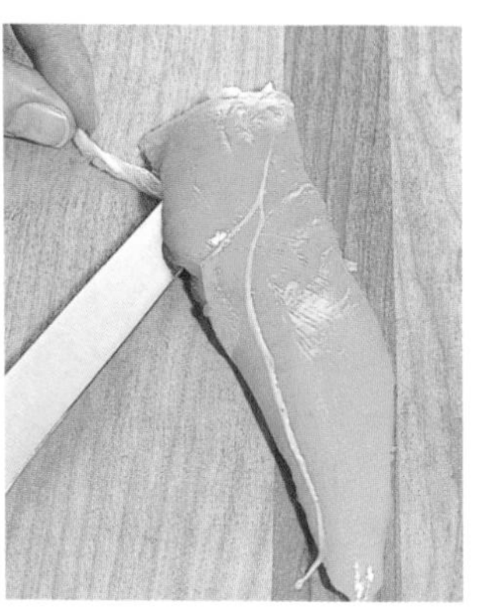

See Also
To cut up a chicken, page 151
To cut up a duck, page 170
To sauté a steak, page 195
To make a beurre noisette, page 46

Related Glossary Entries
Confit
Sauté

To Prepare Porcini Dust

Porcini dust can replace flour and other coatings when sautéing poultry, seafood, veal, and sweetbreads. Before beginning, unless the dried porcini feel perfectly dry and hard to the touch, dry them thoroughly on a sheet pan in a 250°F oven for 15 to 45 minutes, depending on how moist they are.

1. Finely grind in a food processor.

2. Work the dust through a fine-mesh strainer with the tips of your fingers. Return any chunks that don't go through the strainer to the food processor, grind again, and strain once more.

To Make Fresh Bread Crumbs

Because bread crumbs out of a box are usually stale and too dry for coating foods with a delicate coating, it's well worth the effort to make fresh bread crumbs.

1. Cut the crusts off fresh white bread. Use a white bread with a dense crumb, such as Pepperidge Farm. Tear the bread into pieces.

2. Work the bread in a food processor and then work the crumbs through a fine-mesh strainer or drum sieve with your fingertips.

See Also

To cut up a chicken, page 151
To clarify butter, page 46
To make a flavored butter, page 47
To make a beurre noisette, page 46
To sauté sweetbreads, pages 216 and 217

Related Glossary Entries

Bread
Purée (for information on sieves and strainers)
Sauté

HOW TO

Make a Chicken Liver Mousse

Chicken livers are delicious just sautéed and served with a port-wine-and-shallot pan sauce. But if you're game for a bit more work, one of the best ways to prepare the livers is in a mousse. Chicken livers have a full rich flavor and, once cooked and puréed, a smooth texture. There are several ways to make a chicken liver mousse. One basic technique is to purée the cooked livers with butter so that the resulting mixture has the texture of smooth pâté. In the recipe here, I go a step further and fold the butter/liver mixture with whipped cream to make it airy and light.

It's important that the pan used to sauté the livers be preheated over very high heat. If the pan isn't hot enough, the livers will steam instead of sauté; they'll never brown, and the mousse will have an unpleasant gamy flavor. Cook the livers until they just spring back when pressed with your finger, or cut into them to check their color—they should be barely pink (medium) with no trace of rawness. (Overcooked livers will make the mousse grainy.) The mousse can be served in small ramekins or shaped into quenelles.

Chicken Liver Mousse

1. Pat the livers dry with a clean kitchen towel and season with salt and pepper. Sauté in clarified butter or olive oil in a preheated heavy-bottomed pan over very high heat, turning once, until the livers feel firm to the touch. Stand back—they spatter as they cook.
2. Transfer the livers to a bowl and pour the burned fat out of the pan. Add chopped shallots, garlic, and fresh thyme to the pan and whisk for about a minute, until they smell fragrant. Pour in port or Madeira and reduce to about 2 tablespoons.
3. Add chunks of butter to the bowl with the warm livers, to soften the butter, and scrape in the port mixture. Purée the mixture in a food processor until smooth.
4. Work the purée through a drum sieve to make it perfectly smooth.
5. Fold the strained mousse with whipped cream to lighten it. Season to taste with salt and pepper. Serve in ramekins or shape into quenelles.

Related Glossary Entry
Quenelle

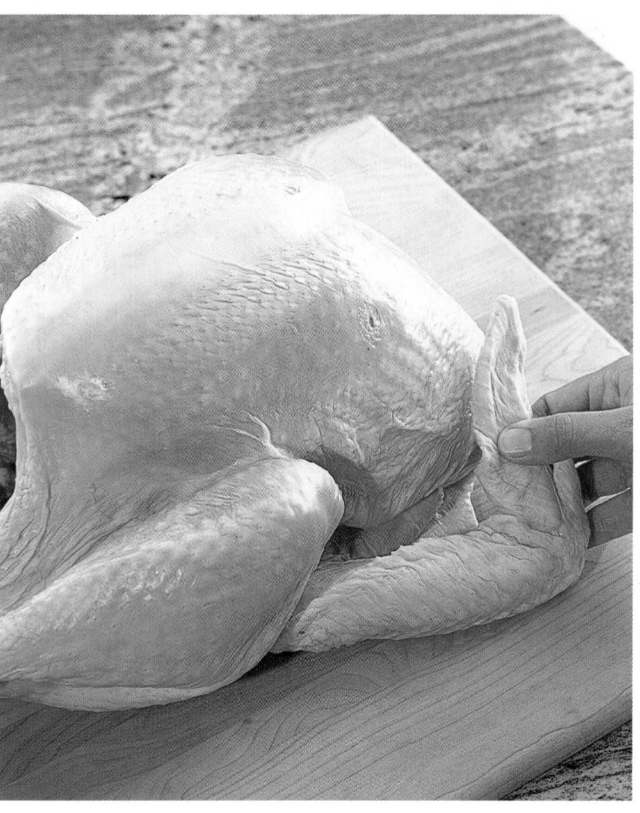

Roast Turkey

1. Fold the outer joints of the wings under the turkey.
2. Spread a few coarsely chopped vegetables and the turkey tail, cut in half, in a heavy-bottomed roasting pan. These prevent the turkey from sticking to the pan and also provide flavor. (The giblets could be added too, but here they're used for the gravy.)
3. Place the turkey in the roasting pan and tie the ends of the drumsticks together with a piece of string.

HOW TO

Roast a Turkey and Make Giblet Gravy

A turkey is roasted the same way as a chicken except that the cooking time is longer because turkeys are larger and need to be roasted at a lower temperature than chicken to prevent the skin from browning too much before they cook through. Exact cooking times and oven temperatures depend on the size of the turkey, but a very large turkey is usually roasted at a lower temperature than a small one. As when roasting a chicken, cover the turkey breast with a buttered tripled sheet of aluminum foil; remove the foil after an hour of roasting. The foil slows the cooking of the breast and prevents the breast meat from overcooking and drying out before the legs are done.

It isn't necessary to remove the wishbone or truss the turkey; just tuck the wings under as for a chicken and tie the drumsticks together with string so they don't flop open during roasting. I never stuff a turkey because getting the stuffing to cook through usually requires overcooking the turkey.

4. Roast the turkey, breast covered with a buttered sheet of tripled foil, at 350°F for about 1 hour. Remove the foil.

5. Continue roasting until an instant-read thermometer inserted between the thigh and breast reads 145°F. Remove the turkey from the oven, cover loosely with foil, and let rest in a warm place, such as the turned-off oven, for 30 minutes.

Kitchen Notes and Tips

- I don't recommend a roasting rack, because it holds the bird above the roasting pan so the juices released by the turkey are likely to burn when they hit the hot pan. The bird may also stick to the rack, causing the skin to tear. Instead of using a rack, sprinkle a few coarsely chopped vegetables and, as shown at left, the turkey's tail, cut in two, over the bottom of the roasting pan to prevent the turkey from sticking to the pan. The vegetables will also contribute their flavors to the pan juices.
- The turkey is done not when the little plastic timer pops up, but before—when an instant-read thermometer inserted between the thigh and breast (the coolest part of the bird), reads 145°F.
- For unstuffed turkeys, count on about 8 minutes per pound at 350°F for larger turkeys and 10 minutes per pound for smaller turkeys.
- For stuffed turkeys, count on about 10 to 12 minutes per pound at 350°F. When you remove the foil after an hour of cooking, check to see how well the turkey is browning: If the skin isn't browning, turn up the oven. If it's browning too much, turn the oven down.
- To move the cooked turkey from the roasting pan to the carving platter, insert a sturdy wooden spoon into the cavity and lift up the turkey.
- Figure on about 1½ tablespoons each flour and fat (butter or the turkey fat from the roasting pan) to bind about 1 cup turkey juices into a light gravy.

4. Slice the "second joint" dark meat off the thigh and transfer it to the platter. This meat is juicier than the "first joint" meat on the drumstick.
5. Make a slight diagonal cut in the turkey just above the wing. This will allow the breast meat slices to come away as you carve the breast.
6. Slice the breast meat.
7. Use the carving fork to aid slicing.
8. Continue slicing until you reach the carcass. At this point, you will see the wing joint. Insert a knife into the joint and remove the wing. If the wing is large, the meat on the wing can be sliced.

To Carve a Roast Turkey

Before carving, transfer the turkey to a platter. Set up a cutting board—preferably one with a trough to trap juices—in the dining room with the platter next to it.
1. Cut through the piece of crispy skin that joins the thigh and breast.
2. Continue cutting down, pulling the thigh away from the turkey with the fork, until you reach the joint where the thigh meets breast. Cut through the joint and remove the leg.
3. Place the leg on the cutting board and cut apart the thigh and drumstick. (The joint is farther into the drumstick than you might think.)

See Also

To roast a chicken, page 146
To make a chicken broth, page 30

Related Glossary Entries

Deglaze
Degrease
Gravy
Thickener

Preparing a Traditional Giblet Gravy

Giblet gravy is an exception to the rule that liver should never be included in a stock or broth.

1. While the turkey is roasting, combine the giblets—the gizzard, neck, liver, and heart—in a small saucepan with a few cloves of garlic, a small peeled onion, and a small bouquet garni. Add water or chicken broth to cover and simmer gently, skimming every now and then, for about 1½ hours.

2. Remove the giblets from the broth with a slotted spoon and reserve the broth. Peel the meat off the neck and combine it with the other cooked giblets. Discard the neck bone.

3. Chop the giblets medium-fine. Don't chop them too fine, or they won't contribute enough texture to the gravy.

4. Pour 1 cup of the giblet broth into the roasting pan and scrape the bottom of the pan with a wooden spoon to dissolve any juices that may have caramelized.

5. Strain the juices into a degreasing cup or glass pitcher and allow a few minutes for the fat to float to the top.

6. Pour about 1½ tablespoons of turkey fat into the roasting pan for every cup of gravy you want. Sprinkle in the same amount of flour. Stir this roux over medium heat for about 2 minutes.

7. Pour in the turkey juices, leaving the fat behind. Add additional chicken broth if you need to make more gravy, but be aware that this will weaken the gravy's turkey flavor.

8. Stir in the chopped giblets and season to taste.

HOW TO

Cut Up a Duck

Because most ducks are covered with a rather thick and fatty skin, they are difficult to roast in the same way as other birds such as chicken. In order to get the skin to release most of its fat, and for the duck to turn "crispy," the duck has to be roasted for such a long time that the meat is invariably overcooked. To solve this problem, separate the duck into thighs, breasts, and carcass bones. The thighs can be braised, cooked into confit, or grilled—they're tougher than the breasts and require longer cooking—and the breasts can be sautéed so the skin turns crispy, but the meat remains pink (see page 157). The carcass bones can be used for making duck broth.

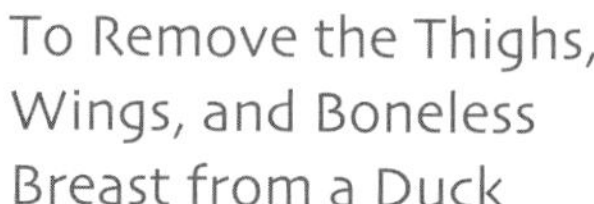

To Remove the Thighs, Wings, and Boneless Breast from a Duck

1. Turn the duck on its breast and cut off the wings where they join the body. Be careful not to cut into the breast meat.
2. Turn the duck on its back and pull one thigh forward and out. Cut through the skin between the thigh and the breast, keeping the knife blade against the thigh. Follow the strip of fat that lies under the skin and leads along the side of the thigh down to the back.
3. Fold the thigh back and, with your thumb against the base of the thigh, snap the thigh out of the joint.
4. Slide the knife along the side of the duck where the thigh meat attaches to the back. Follow the contours of the backbone, leaving the meat attached to the thigh. Detach the thigh. Repeat to cut off the other leg.

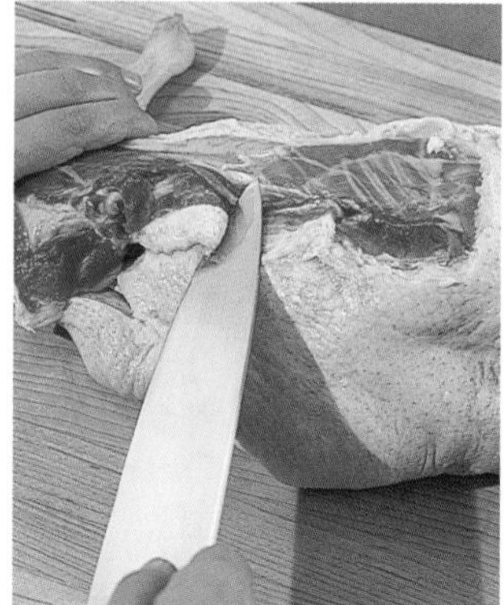

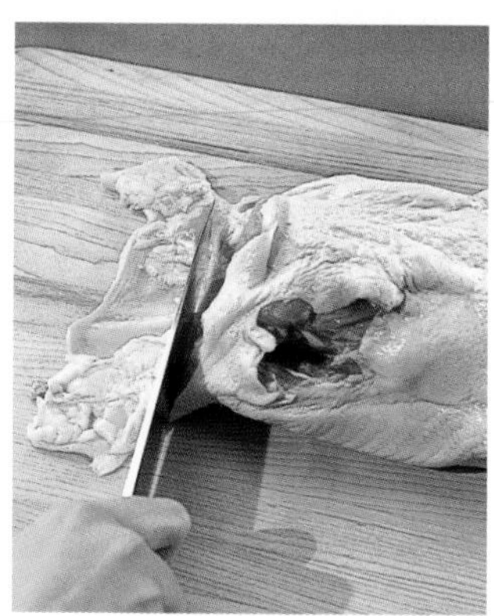

5. Cut off the large flap of fat and skin at the neck end of the duck. This can be discarded or rendered for its fat. (Duck provides excellent and flavorful cooking fat.)
6. Turn the duck on its back. Cut along one side of the breast bone, keeping the knife flush against the bone, until you have detached the breast along the entire length of the backbone.
7. Peel the breast back, away from the bone, with your fingers and slide the knife under the wishbone, detaching it from the breast.
8. Continue sliding the knife against the breastbone, keeping the knife against the bone so you don't cut into the breast meat until you completely detach the boneless breast.
9. Place the breast skin side down on the cutting board and cut away excess skin and fat. (This can also be rendered for duck fat.) Repeat with the other breast.

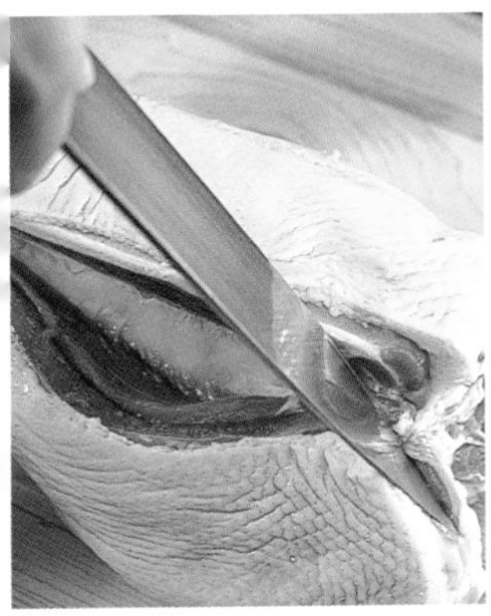

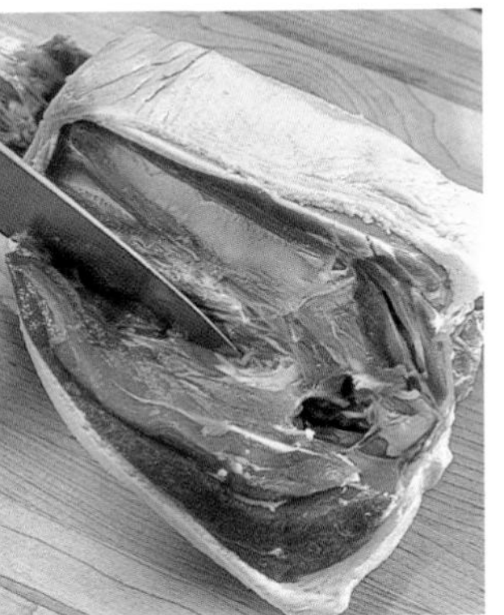

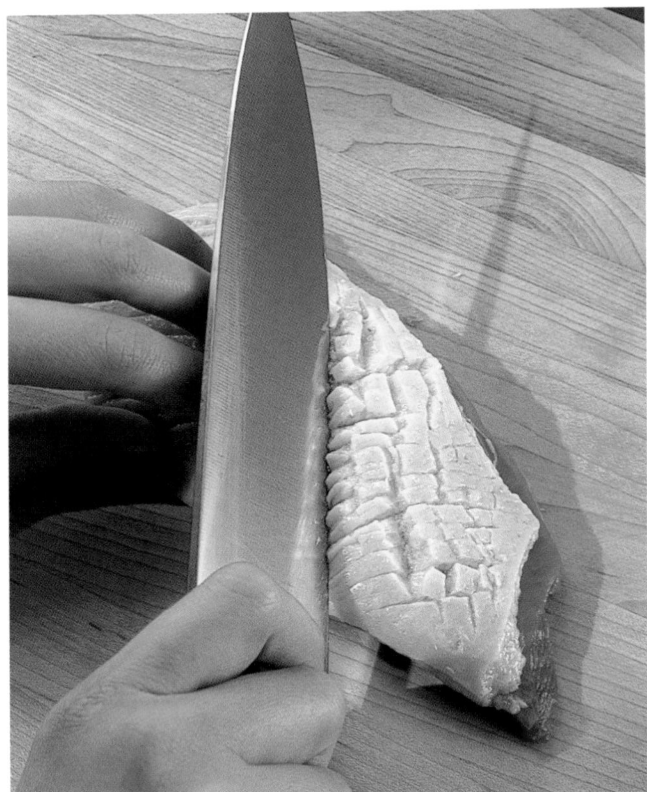

To Prepare a Duck Breast for Sautéing

Because most duck breasts are covered with a thick layer of fatty skin, the skin is sometimes removed, an unfortunate solution, since the skin is very flavorful. A better method is to finely score the skin so that its fat quickly renders in the sauté pan and the skin turns crispy before the meat overcooks.

1. Use a sharp chef's knife to make a series of about 20 fine parallel cuts in the fatty skin, without cutting into the meat. Keep the knife at an angle so that you cut sideways into the skin, exposing more fat.
2. Give the breast a 90-degree turn and make a second series of cuts at right angles to the first.

See Also

To make brown chicken broth, page 30

To prepare chicken breasts, page 163

Related Glossary Entry

Confit

Sauté

HOW TO

Boil Eggs

The best way to soft- and hard-boil eggs, both to get consistent results (so that a three-minute egg is always a three-minute egg) and to keep the shells from sticking to the eggs (making them hard to peel), is to start the eggs in boiling water and then turn the heat down to maintain a gentle simmer. Once the eggs are cooked, scoop them out into a bowl of ice water to stop the cooking if they are to be served cold. For soft-boiled eggs, skip the ice water and serve immediately.

When hard-boiled eggs are overcooked, the outside of the yolks turn an ugly dark green and the sides are pale and dry. Because of this, most recipes calling for hard-boiled eggs are best made with "medium-boiled" eggs (what the French call *oeufs mollets*), cooked for between six and eight minutes, so that the yolks are still moist and a bright, shiny yellow.

To Soft-boil and Hard-boil Eggs

Here, I boil cold eggs that have come straight out of the refrigerator. If your eggs are at room temperature, the cooking times will be slightly shorter.

1. Use a pin to poke a tiny hole in the rounder end of each egg. This allows trapped air to escape during boiling and helps prevent the shell from cracking.
2. Gently lower the eggs into rapidly boiling water and start timing. When the water returns to the boil, turn the heat down to maintain a gentle simmer and cook to the desired doneness.

A 3-minute egg

A 4-minute egg

A 6-minute egg is firm enough that the yolk will hold its shape when you cut into the egg.

An 8-minute egg still has a shiny yellow yolk and a moist center.

A 10-minute egg has a completely firm yolk but is still shiny.

Kitchen Notes and Tips

- The exact cooking times for boiled eggs depend on the temperature of the egg when you put it into the boiling water, the number of eggs, and the amount of water in the pan. The times shown are for 4 to 6 eggs, taken right from the refrigerator. If you're cooking a larger number of eggs, count on slightly longer cooking times.
- For consistent timing, always use just enough water to cover the eggs by about 2 inches.

If you're serving the eggs cold, immediately plunge them into ice water and let them sit for 5 minutes before peeling. The ice water helps prevent the shells from sticking to the eggs.

HOW TO

Poach Eggs

Poaching eggs is simple—just remember to keep the water at a very low simmer, so that it barely murmurs. If the water simmers too briskly, the egg whites will break apart rather than firming around the yolks. (You can trim the whites after cooking for a perfect oval shape.) A tiny bit of vinegar added to the water helps to coagulate the whites. The eggs should be cooked until the whites are set and opaque; if you're unsure, carefully lift one of the eggs out of the water with a slotted spoon and touch the white—it should feel firm. If you're poaching eggs for a crowd, cook them ahead of time and save them in a bowl of cold water in the refrigerator. When you're ready to serve them, carefully drain off the cold water, pour boiling water over the eggs, and let stand about a minute, just long enough to reheat them.

To Poach Eggs

1. Crack the eggs and open the shells over a pan of simmering water containing a teaspoon of vinegar. Open the eggs as close to the surface of the water as possible so the eggs don't break apart.
2. Or, break each egg into a little cup and then pour the egg from the cup into the water, so that you don't burn your fingers.
3. When the whites are set and opaque, remove the eggs from the water with a slotted spoon.
4. Cut off any irregular or foamy white with a knife. Serve the eggs right away, or put them in a bowl of ice water as described above and refrigerate until needed.

HOW TO

Bake Eggs

Oeufs en cocotte, eggs baked in individual porcelain ramekins with mixtures such as cooked tomato concassée, mushroom duxelles, or creamed spinach, under a drizzle of heavy cream and a grating of cheese, can be superb. The white of the egg firms and the barely cooked yolk mixes with the cream to make a rich, delicious sauce, flavored with the other ingredients. The whole thing is soft enough that you can eat it with a spoon and toast wedges dipped into the egg. Baked eggs are a practical way to use up leftover vegetable mixtures, ham or prosciutto, and cooked shellfish such as shrimp, crab, or lobster. *Oeufs en cocotte* are baked in a *bain-marie* to keep the whites tender and ensure that the eggs cook evenly.

To Make *Oeufs en Cocotte*

1. Place a tablespoon of a vegetable mixture or other ingredients in each buttered porcelain ramekin. (Here, I use cooked tomato concassée, duxelles, and creamed spinach.) Break an egg into each ramekin.
2. Pour a tablespoon or two of heavy cream on top of each egg. Season with salt and pepper and sprinkle with Parmesan cheese.
3. Place the ramekins in a pan or baking dish just large enough to hold them. Pour in enough boiling water to come halfway up their sides.
4. Bake in a 350°F oven just long enough to set the egg white but leave the yolk runny, about 10 minutes. Serve with toast wedges.

See Also

To make a cooked tomato concassée, page 50

To make duxelles, page 111

To make creamed spinach, page 88

Related Glossary Entry

Bain-marie

HOW TO

Make an Omelet

Omelet making has acquired a certain mystique, but a dozen eggs and a little practice are enough to master the technique. For a classic French omelet, the eggs should be completely cooked on the outside but creamy and custardlike on the inside.

How you stuff an omelet, if you stuff it at all, depends on the filling. Simple chopped ingredients such as herbs can be beaten into the raw eggs. Ingredients such as cheese, which can make the omelet stick to the pan, should be sprinkled over the cooked omelet just before it is rolled up. To stuff an omelet with a more elaborate filling—such as lobster or wild mushrooms—heat the filling separately, then make a shallow slit down the top of the finished omelet and gently spoon the hot filling over and into the slit.

Plain Omelet

1. Heat a small amount of butter in a nonstick or well-seasoned omelet pan over high heat until the butter froths and the froth subsides. Add 3 beaten eggs, seasoned with salt and pepper, and beat vigorously with a fork.
2. When the eggs are loosely scrambled and very little liquid remains, tilt the pan away from you and gently fold the omelet away from you, so the edge of the omelet forms a gentle downward arc.
3. Give the pan handle a quick whack to jerk the omelet up slightly over the rim of the pan.
4. With a fork, fold the part of the omelet that comes up above the rim into the rest of the omelet.
5. Lift the pan (you'll want to switch hands for this) and turn the omelet out onto a hot plate.

Truffled Eggs

A good trick for getting more truffle for the buck: Store your truffles overnight in a tightly sealed container in the refrigerator with whole eggs in the shell. Use the "truffled" eggs in the next day or two to make omelets.

HOW TO

Make a Soufflé

A soufflé is made by folding stiffly beaten egg whites into a savory or sweet mixture and baking the mixture in a metal or porcelain soufflé mold or dish. Most savory soufflés, such as the one below, are based on béchamel sauce, but dessert soufflés are usually based on pastry cream or a light sabayon made with beaten egg yolks and a flavoring. Because soufflés contain very little (sometimes no) flour, they are relatively unstable (unlike a cake, which will hold its shape) and fall quickly once out of the oven. For this reason, most soufflés are served the instant they're done.

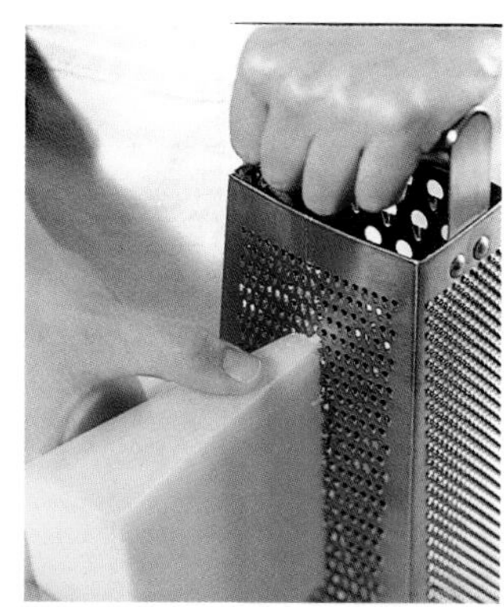

Cheese Soufflé

To line the soufflé dish and make a collar

1. Brush the inside of the soufflé dish with softened or melted butter. If you use melted butter, chill the buttered dish in the refrigerator and brush a second time to ensure that there's a thick enough layer of butter.
2. Fold a strip of aluminum foil long enough to wrap around the soufflé dish lengthwise into thirds. Brush the part of the collar that will rise above the rim of the soufflé dish with softened or melted butter. Wrap the collar around the soufflé dish. Attach it with a paper clip or by pinching it together.
3. Finely grate hard cheese, such as Parmesan, for coating the soufflé dish. (Or use flour.)
4. Put the grated cheese in the soufflé dish. Rotate the dish so the inside of both dish and collar is coated with a layer of cheese.

To Separate Eggs

HAND METHOD

Crack open the egg. Hold your (well-washed) hand over a bowl and pour the egg out into your hand. Let the egg white drip through your fingers.

SHELL METHOD

Crack open the egg and transfer the egg yolk back and forth over a bowl between the 2 halves of the shell until all of the egg white has dripped into the bowl. Work carefully so that you don't break the yolk.

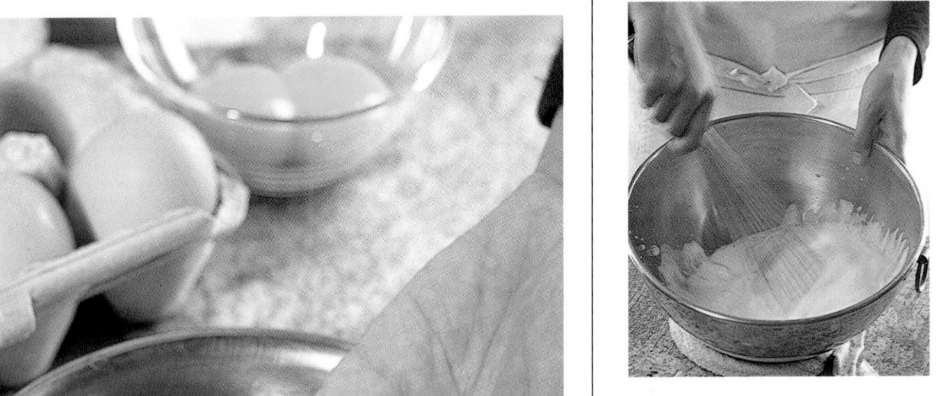

To beat the egg whites

5. If using a copper bowl, swirl distilled vinegar and salt around in the bowl to eliminate tarnish. Rinse the bowl with hot water and dry thoroughly with a clean towel. Wrap a moist kitchen towel around the base of the bowl to hold it in place.
6. Separate the egg whites and yolks as directed on page 178. (If using an electric mixer, add a pinch of cream of tartar to the whites before you start beating.) Or, as shown here, break up the egg whites by twirling a balloon whisk between your hands in the whites for about 30 seconds.
7. Start beating slowly and gently and gradually build up speed. (If you can, switch arms as you get tired of beating.)
8. The egg whites have reached stiff peaks (the proper stage for a soufflé) when they stick straight out from the side of the whisk. Start on low speed and gradually increase the speed to high. Beat to stiff peaks, as opposite.

To fold egg whites into the soufflé base

The base is flavored with Italian Parmigiano-Reggiano and Swiss Gruyère.
9. Prepare a béchamel sauce as directed on page 180. Then, off the heat, whisk egg yolks—usually about 2 fewer than the number of whites you're using—into the béchamel sauce. Continue to whisk until smooth.
10. Whisk half of the grated cheese into the béchamel mixture.
11. Whisk in about one quarter of the beaten egg whites.
12. Use a large rubber spatula to fold the soufflé base into the rest of the egg whites. Slide the spatula around the sides and bottom of the bowl, lifting up the egg whites and folding them over as you go.

13. Continue folding, being careful not to deflate the egg whites but rather to cut through them, until the mixture is smooth and homogeneous but not overworked.
14. Scoop the mixture into the prepared soufflé dish.

To Make a Béchamel Sauce

1. Combine equal parts flour and butter (see Box, page 181) in a heavy-bottomed saucepan.

2. Stir with a small whisk over medium heat until the mixture—called a roux—is smooth and smells toasty, about 3 minutes. Don't let it brown.

3.Whisk milk into the hot roux.

4. Continue whisking until smooth. The sauce will become thinner as you add more milk. Be sure to bring the sauce to the boil so it thickens as much as possible.

To bake and serve the soufflé

15. Place the soufflé on a sheet pan, slide it into a 375°F oven, and bake until it rises but still jiggles slightly (a soufflé should be slightly runny in the center) when you move it back and forth. A 4- to 6-serving soufflé will take from 35 to 50 minutes. Remove the collar in the kitchen, as shown on page 177, present the soufflé, and serve immediately.
16. Use a large spoon to spoon the soufflé onto hot plates.

Kitchen Notes and Tips

- Soufflé dishes must be coated with butter. Dishes for savory soufflés are then coated with a thin layer of flour or finely grated dry cheese (such as Parmesan) to keep the mixture from sticking to the dish, which would prevent it from rising. For dessert soufflés, the dishes are coated with butter and sugar.
- An aluminum foil collar holds the soufflé mixture in place as it puffs up over the rim of the dish and prevents the top of the soufflé from falling off. The collar should be coated the same way as the dish.
- When separating large numbers of eggs, work over a smaller bowl and transfer the whites a few at a time—or, if you're being really careful, one by one—into a large bowl. This way, if you accidentally break an egg yolk into the whites, you don't ruin the whole batch.
- When beating egg whites, it's essential that no trace of egg yolk, grease, or moisture comes in contact with the whites. Fat and moisture keep the whites from rising, so be sure your hands, bowl, and any utensils are perfectly clean and dry.
- A copper bowl is traditionally used for beating egg whites because the copper interacts with the whites so that, once beaten, they stay firm and hold their shape. A copper bowl must be cleaned of tarnish each time before it's used. The traditional way to clean the bowl is to swirl distilled vinegar and salt around in it, then thoroughly rinse and dry it.
- Add a pinch of salt to egg whites before beating to help them rise. If you're not using a copper bowl, add a pinch of cream of tartar to the whites to help stabilize them.
- Beat the whites with a large whisk or an electric mixer, preferably one with a planetary motion and a whisk attachment.
- To keep the soufflé mixture airy and light, the egg whites must be folded into the soufflé base mixture properly: First lighten the base by beating in about one quarter of the beaten egg whites. Then fold in the rest.
- The cheese for a cheese soufflé must be dry and flavorful; if the cheese is too mild, you'll need too much to give the soufflé flavor and the soufflé will be heavy.
- Standard proportions for an 8-cup soufflé dish

  Roux: 4½ tablespoons butter and 4½ tablespoons flour

  Béchamel: made by adding 1½ cups milk to the roux

  Eggs: 6 large egg yolks, added to the béchamel

  8 large egg whites, beaten to stiff peaks and folded in

  Grated cheese (or other flavoring): 1½ cups (or more or less, depending on the ingredients)

Related Glossary Entries

Sabayon
White Sauce

Meat

HOW TO

Roast a Leg of Lamb

A leg of lamb makes a big roast that's a satisfying and less expensive alternative to the elegant saddle or rack. Some cooks bone the leg completely before roasting, but I only partially bone it—or have the butcher do it—to make the leg easier to carve. I leave at least two bones in the leg because the bone adds flavor and makes for an attractive presentation. I tie the leg in three places to secure the flaps of meat around the hip, so that the roast cooks evenly.

To roast a leg, just set it in a heavy-bottomed roasting pan, with no roasting rack, in a hot oven. When the lamb is cooked, you can skim the fat from the juices left in the pan and serve them as a simple jus. Or, you can make more—and more flavorful—jus if you roast the leg on a bed of lamb bones and trimmings (from the leg itself), and a handful of unpeeled garlic cloves—or chopped onion or shallot and carrot. (The bones and trimmings also serve to keep the leg from sticking to the pan.) Then deglaze the pan with broth or water and strain the juices. You could go a step further and thicken the jus with the puréed garlic from the roast.

Kitchen Notes and Tips

- A whole leg of lamb with the hip bone (pelvis) left in should weigh from 7 to 8 pounds; the lamb should be no more than a year old.
- If you buy a leg of lamb from the butcher, he or she will remove the large piece of pelvis and tailbone, but if you buy a leg of lamb at the supermarket, you may have to do this yourself.
- The roasting temperature is determined by how long it takes to brown the meat without overcooking it. Because leg is relatively large, it is roasted at a lower temperature (400°F) than rack of lamb.
- Because the leg cooks for a long time, chances are the bones and trimmings will be well browned by the time the leg comes out of the oven. If not, brown them a bit more in the roasting pan on top of the stove before deglazing the pan.

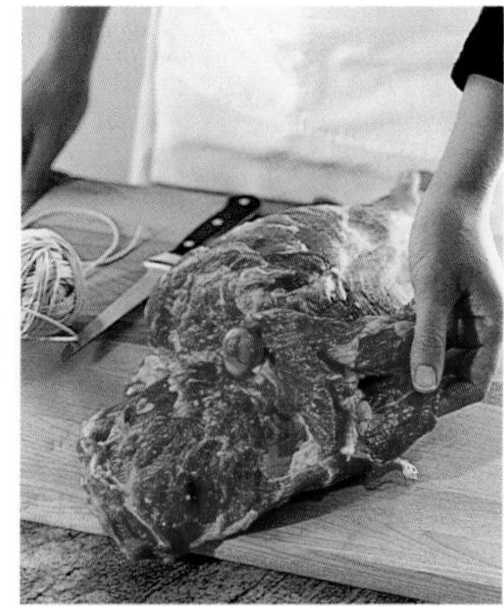

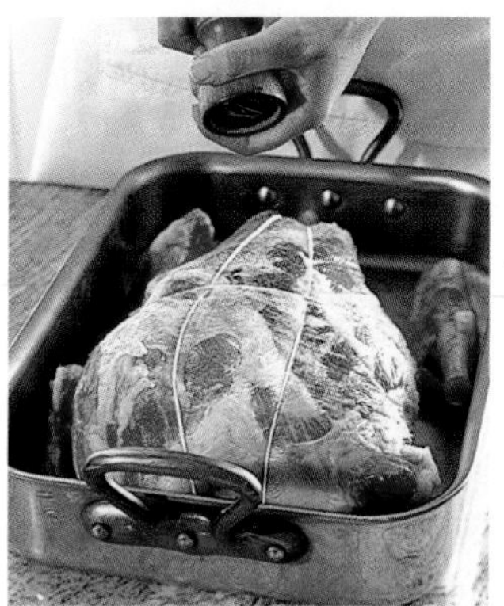

Roast Leg of Lamb

1. Fold up the loose flaps at the end of the leg of lamb.
2. Tie two lengths of string lengthwise around the leg of lamb, hooking them on both sides of the shank on one end and over the loose flaps at the other. Then tie a length of string crosswise around.
3. Place the leg in a heavy-bottomed roasting pan, season with salt and pepper, and surround with the bones and any small meat trimmings.
4. Roast in a 400°F oven for about 50 minutes to 1 hour, or until a thermometer inserted into the thickest part of the leg reads from 120° to 130°F for rare to medium-rare, or more, depending on your tastes. Twenty minutes into the roasting, surround the rack with the cloves from 2 broken-up heads of garlic.

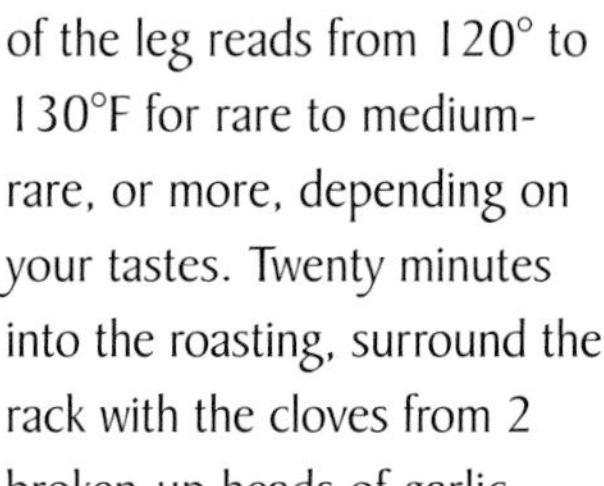

5. When the leg is done, take it out of the roasting pan. Cover it loosely with aluminum foil and let it rest for 20 to 30 minutes. Pour brown chicken, lamb, or beef broth into the pan. Put the pan on top of the stove and simmer gently while scraping the bottom of the pan with a wooden spoon.
6. Strain the cooking juices, reserving the garlic, and degrease the "jus" by skimming off the fat with a ladle or with a degreasing cup. Transfer the garlic cloves to a strainer or a food mill fitted with the finest attachment. Work the garlic cloves through the strainer with the back of a ladle, as shown here, or purée them through the food mill.
7. Whisk the degreased jus into the garlic purée, pour into a sauceboat, and pass the jus at the table.

To Carve a Leg of Lamb

Because American legs of lamb tend to be larger than European ones, two different carving methods have evolved. The American method, shown below, calls for carving the lamb with the knife almost perpendicular to the bone, leaving the slices attached to the bone. The slices are then detached from the bone by slicing right along the bone where the slices are attached. The European method is somewhat more straightforward: Just hold the leg at an angle and slice at a slight angle, almost parallel to the bone. In both the European and American systems, this is the method used for slicing the smaller side of a large leg of lamb.
1. Place the leg on a cutting board with a moat. Slice up and down along the end of the leg.
2. Continue slicing until you encounter the bone and can't slice anymore.
3. Transfer the slices to a heated platter as you carve.
4. Continue slicing the meat down to the bone. The slices will stay attached at the point where they meet the bone.

5. Slice along the top of the bone to detach the slices.
6. Turn the leg over, tilt it upward, and slice at an angle along the top side of the leg. (This method can also be used to slice the thicker side of the leg—the European method.)
7. Transfer the slices to the platter.

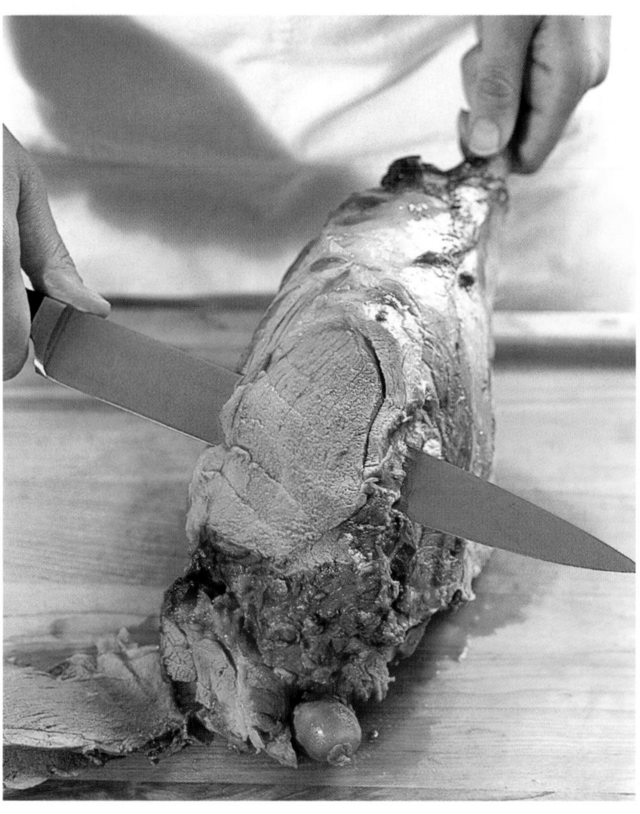

See Also

To remove the large piece of pelvis and tailbone from the leg and to cut off the shank, page 242
To brown trimmings for jus on top of the stove, page 188
To make a brown chicken broth, page 30
To determine doneness, page 66

Related Glossary Entries

Deglaze
Degrease
Jus
Roast (also for a discussion of resting)
Thickener

HOW TO

Roast a Rack of Lamb and Make a Jus

Roasting is the best way to cook rack of lamb, a tender, tasty, and quick-cooking piece of meat that is also one of the most expensive. To roast rack of lamb, simply put it in a hot oven and cook it until the outside is brown and crisp and the interior is rare.

Rack of lamb is traditionally served with a jus—the juices that are released by the lamb as it cooks. Because rack of lamb is cooked rare or medium-rare, however, it releases very little of its own juices; therefore, to stretch the juices, the pan is often deglazed with broth or water. This deglazing also dissolves juices that have caramelized and that are left adhering to the bottom of the pan. Since the addition of liquid dilutes the flavor of the jus, the rack is often roasted on a layer of coarsely chopped bones and meat trimmings (from the roast, if possible) and aromatic vegetables. This layer browns along with the roast and when extra liquid is added to the roasting pan, releases its flavor into the liquid.

Kitchen Notes and Tips

- When buying a single rack at a butcher's, make sure that the central backbone—called the chine bone—has been removed; if you don't take this precaution, the rack will be impossible to carve. Cooperative butchers may also be willing to French the rack, or you can do it yourself. The ribs on a Frenched rack are trimmed of meat and fat so that the clean rib bones stick out decoratively above the meat, as pictured at left.
- As for any roast, a rack of lamb is best roasted in a roasting pan just large enough to hold it, and with no roasting rack. If the pan is too large, the juices released by the lamb may run to the edges of the pan and burn. The juices are also more likely to burn if the meat is roasted on a rack because they will drip down onto the bare hot roasting pan that the meat isn't touching.
- If you plan to make a jus, you'll need lamb trimmings. Ask your butcher for a handful of trimmings from the rack or saddle, or for pieces of lamb stew meat or shoulder chops, cut into strips or small pieces so they cook quickly. You can also use the defatted trimmings from Frenching the rack.
- Because the trimmings need to roast for 45 minutes to release their flavor, and the rack for only 25, the trimmings must either be roasted for 20 minutes before adding the rack (see page 188) or be caramelized by leaving them in the oven or by placing them on top of the stove after the rack has cooked and then by stirring them over the heat with a wooden spoon. (When caramelizing the trimmings after removing the cooked rack, you need to keep the roast warm.)
- Let the rack rest for 10 to 20 minutes in a warm place before carving.

See Also
To French a rack of lamb, page 246
To butcher a double rack of lamb, page 244
To make a brown chicken broth, page 30
To roast a saddle of lamb, page 250
To roast a rack of pork, page 189
To determine doneness, page 66

Related Glossary Entries
Aromatic vegetables
Deglaze
Degrease
Jus
Mirepoix
Roast

Roast Rack of Lamb

As shown in the photograph on page 187, the trimmings and garlic are preroasted for the jus.

1. Preheat the oven to 425°F. Place the trimmings and garlic in a roasting pan and roast for 20 minutes. Place the rack on top of the trimmings and roast until the temperature in the middle of the loin reaches 125°F, about 25 minutes. (You can also determine doneness by pressing on either end of the rack. When the meat just begins to spring back, it's done.) Transfer the rack to a platter and keep it warm.
2. If the trimmings aren't thoroughly browned, put the roasting pan back on the stove for a few minutes. Stir with a wooden spoon so the trimmings brown evenly. Tilting the pan, spoon off and discard any fat floating on top of the jus.
3. Stir a cup of brown lamb, chicken, or beef broth into the roasting pan.
4. Put the roasting pan over high heat and stir for about 5 minutes to extract the flavor from the trimmings. Strain the jus and pour into a sauceboat.
5. Slice the rack between the ribs and serve with the jus.

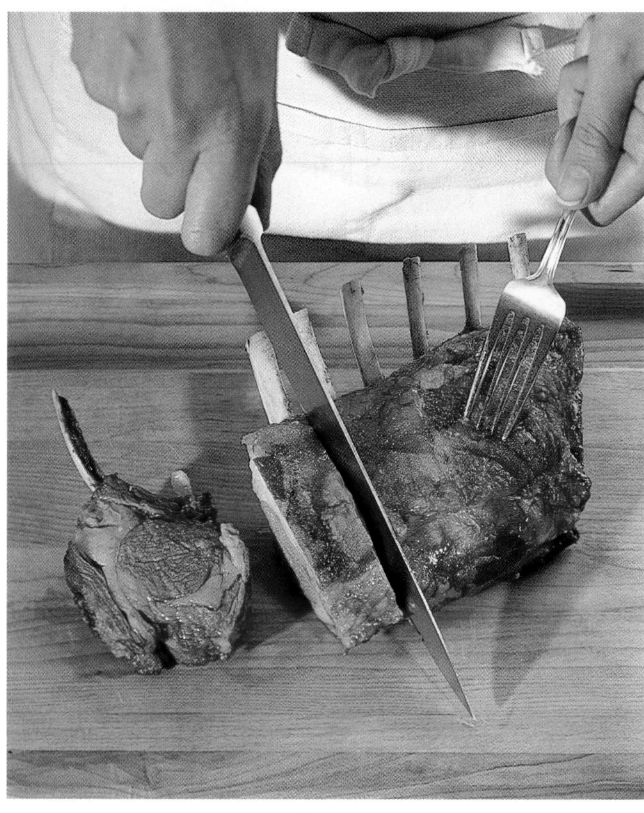

HOW TO

Roast a Rack of Pork

A rack of pork (also sold as a bone-in pork loin roast) is the rib section from the pork loin. When buying a rack of pork, ask for a center-cut rib section of the loin. Specify the number of ribs you want, counting one per serving. Ask the butcher to cut off the chine bone—which will make it easier to carve the roast—and save it for you. Pork loin is often sold boneless. Boneless loin cooks more quickly and doesn't, of course, require Frenching, but it's less dramatic to look at and isn't quite as flavorful, because there are no bones to help hold in the juices. A rack of pork can be Frenched and then roasted just like a rack of lamb in a heavy-bottomed roasting pan with no roasting rack, with or without pork trimmings, and served with its jus. (Frenching the rack will give you trimmings that can be used, along with the chine bone, for the jus.) Because rack of pork is quite lean and will dry out if over-cooked, it should be cooked only to medium, so the meat is just barely pink. (This is true for rack of veal as well.)

The easiest and most obvious way to carve a rack of pork is the same method used for carving a rack of lamb or veal—the chops are simply sliced so that each person gets a whole chop. For thinner slices, remove the ribs entirely and slice the meat to the desired thickness (or roast a boneless pork loin).

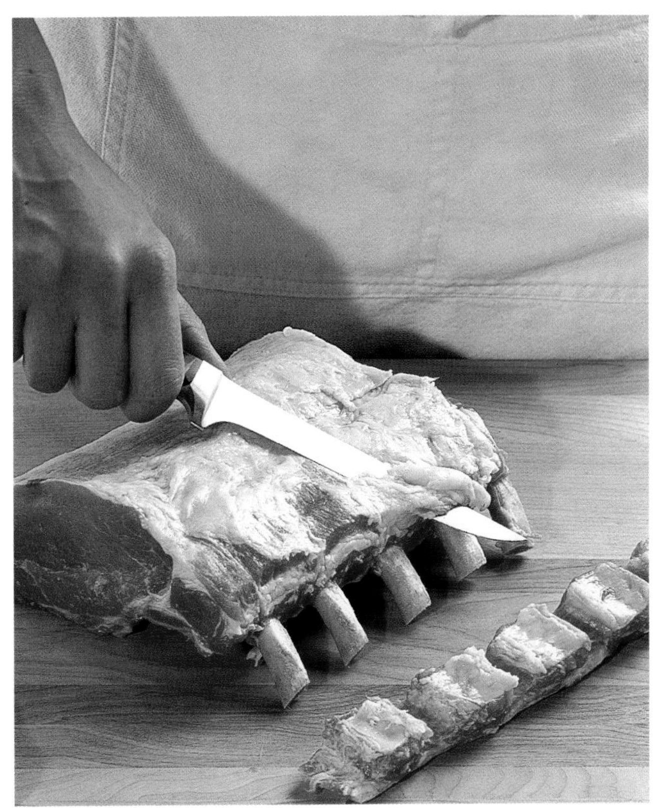

Roast Rack of Pork

Here, I roast a 5-rib rack, consisting of the ribs nearest the loin end (the rear) of the animal.

1. Trim off the excess fat near the top of the ribs, but don't cut down to the fleshy loin muscle. Roast in a 400°F oven for about 45 minutes, to an internal temperature of 140°F. The meat will be barely pink.

2. Judge the doneness of the meat with an instant-read thermometer or, as shown here, by pressing on the outside ends of the roast: When there's no fleshy feeling and the roast feels firm, it is done. Let the roast rest, loosely covered with aluminum foil for 15 minutes (its internal temperature will rise about 5 degrees).

(A roast rack of pork and roast vegetables is pictured on pages 182 and 183.)

To Carve a Roast Rack of Pork

Method 1 (for whole chops)

1. Hold the rack with a towel or fork.
2. Slice the rack between each rib, giving each guest a whole rib chop.
3. Here, an individual serving is shown with Baked Tomatoes with Garlic and Fresh Basil.

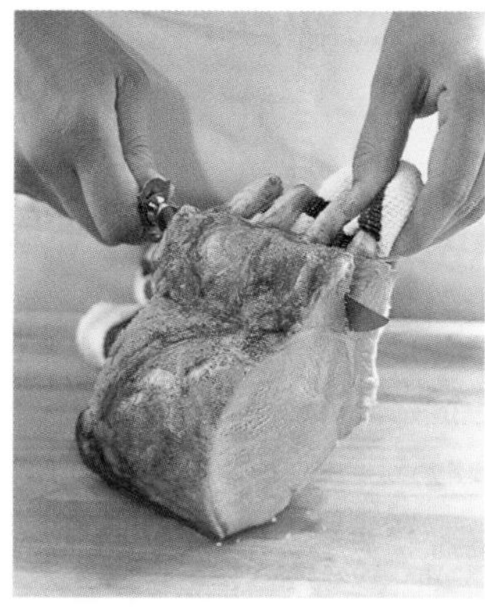

Method 2 (for thin slices without ribs)

1. Slide the knife against the inside of the ribs.
2. Pull away the ribs, keeping the knife against the bones. (Be sure to keep the ribs for nibbling.)
3. Slice the meat into the desired thickness.

Kitchen Notes and Tips

- A whole pork loin is a large cut of meat that extends from the base of the shoulder to the top of the leg. Roughly, the loin is divided into two sections—the rib section and the section without ribs, toward the hindquarters. When cut into chops, the rib section of the loin yields the familiar-looking center-cut rib chops. The section of the loin closer to the leg yields loin chops, which contain two major muscles (loin and tenderloin) and look like miniature T-bone steaks. The ribs closest to the loin are called "center-cut" ribs and are slightly leaner and neater looking than those toward the shoulder. The ribs that are closer to the shoulder are fattier and have smaller, less decorative ribs.

See Also

To make a simple jus, page 272
To augment the jus using bones and trimmings, page 188
To French a rack of lamb, page 246
To roast a rack of lamb, page 187
To determine doneness, page 66
To make Baked Tomatoes with Garlic and Fresh Basil, page 72

Related Glossary Entries

Jus
Roast

HOW TO

Roast a Prime Rib of Beef

A prime rib of beef is roasted in exactly the same way as a pork or lamb rack, in a heavy-bottomed roasting pan without a roasting rack, and traditionally served with a jus. The beef rib roast can be cooked on its own or, for more jus, on top of trimmings (use the trimmings from the ribs themselves or buy beef stew meat and cut it into very small pieces).

A standing beef rib roast is too large to be cut into chops like a lamb or pork rack. To carve a cooked roast, either lay it on its side and slice toward the bone, detaching the slices from the ribs as you go, or cut the meat completely away from the bones and then slice the meat.

Roast Rib Roast

1. Tie the roast between the ribs to help pull the meat into an even round that will cook more evenly.

2. Roast at 400°F until browned, about 45 minutes, then turn the oven down to 350°F and continue roasting until the temperature in the center of the roast reaches 120° to 125°F for rare, or 125° to 130°F for medium-rare.

3. Professional chefs often insert a skewer into the roast and touch it to their lip to determine doneness. You can train yourself to do this by using an instant-read thermometer, checking it and touching it with your lip.

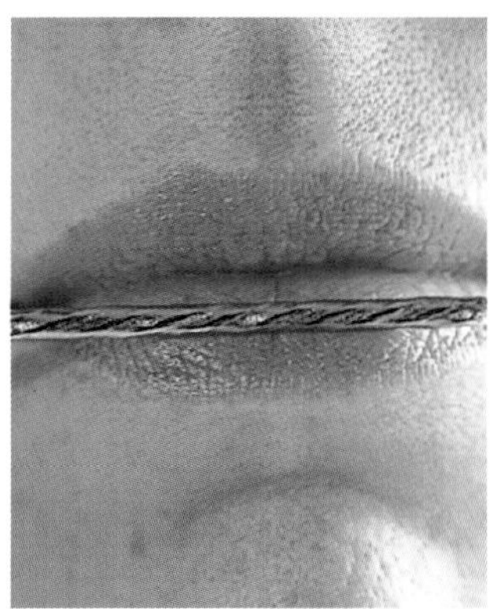

Kitchen Notes and Tips

- Order rib roasts by the rib. One rib makes a generous serving for 2 people, so a three-rib roast will easily serve 6.
- The section of ribs taken from the loin end has less fat than one taken from the shoulder end.
- Because a rib roast is relatively large, it is best to brown it at a relatively high temperature (400°F) and then continue roasting at a lower temperature (350°F). A 5-pound roast will take about 45 minutes to brown at 400°F and then about 40 minutes to finish cooking to rare at 350°F.
- When the roast is cooked, set it on the back of the stove or in another warm place, loosely covered with aluminum foil, and let it rest for 20 to 30 minutes before serving.
- Other cuts of beef can be roasted in the same way as a rib roast, but the timing will be somewhat different. When timing any roast, don't blindly follow weight/temperature guidelines (so many minutes per pound), because the shape of the roast affects the cooking time. A long thin roast, such as a tenderloin, will cook faster than a rectangular roast (such as a standing rib roast) of the same weight.

Beef tenderloin cooks very quickly—25 minutes or less, depending on size—because it's a thin elongated cut, quickly penetrated by the oven heat, and because it's typically served rare. The major issue in cooking tenderloin is that it be in the oven long enough to brown before it overcooks. Unless you're sure that your oven gets hot enough to brown the roast before it cooks through, brown it on top of the stove and then roast at 400°F. Before roasting, fold the skinny tail end of the tenderloin under itself and tie it to equalize the thickness of the meat.

Top round roast and eye of the round are less tender cuts than rib or tenderloin, but they are relatively inexpensive and excellent thinly sliced for sandwiches. Eye of the round, because it is relatively small, should be browned on all sides on top of the stove before roasting. Roast at 400°F until rare. Top round roast may be roasted in the same way as rib roast.

To Carve a Rib Roast

Method 1

1. Make a slice along the top rib, separating it from the meat.
2. As you slice the meat, the slice will come away.
3. Slice sideways toward the bone, transferring the slices to a platter or individual plates.

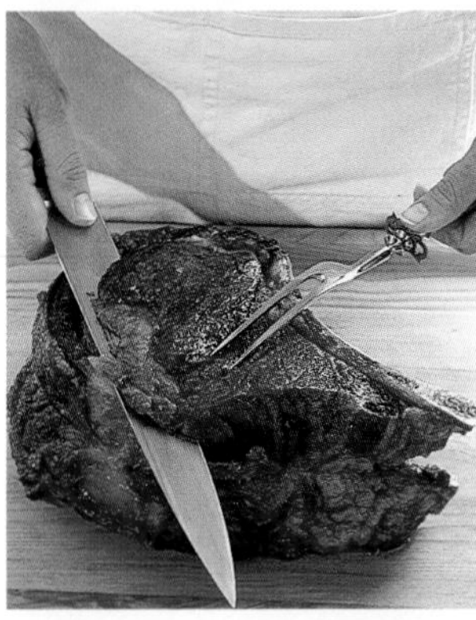

Method 2

1. Hold the roast upright with a towel and slice along the inside of the ribs.
2. Keep the knife against the ribs so you don't cut into meat. Remove the ribs.
3. Slice the meat and transfer it to plates or a platter.

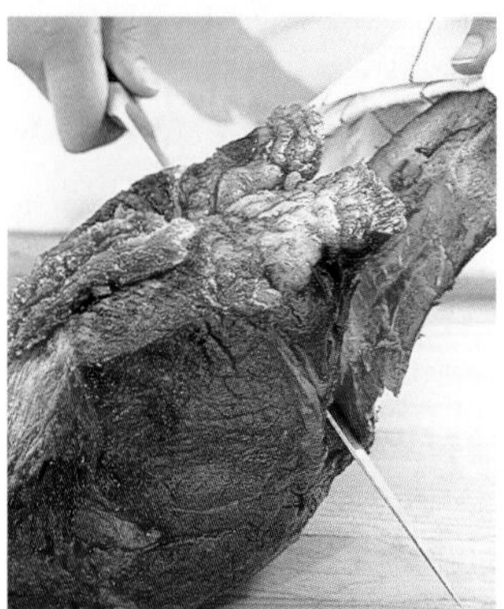

See Also

To make a simple jus, page 148
To augment a jus with bones and trimmings, page 188
To sear on top of the stove before roasting, page 195
To roast a rack of lamb, page 187
To roast a rack of pork, page 189

Related Glossary Entries

Jus
Roast (also for determining doneness of roasts of various sizes and a discussion of resting)

HOW TO

Grill (or Broil) Chops and Steaks

Grilling gives steaks and chops a light, smoky flavor that no other technique can. The intense heat of the grill sears the meat so it develops an exceptionally flavorful crust, with no added fat. In France, grilled steaks and chops are traditionally served with a compound butter or béarnaise sauce, but they are also delicious with mayonnaises, salsas, or vinaigrettes. Choose a sauce with some tangy acidity so it both balances and contrasts with the richness of the meat.

You can also grill larger pieces of meat, such as a butterflied leg of lamb or a whole beef tenderloin. Large cuts are treated differently from small cuts because they take longer to cook. Brown them over the hottest part of the fire to get a good crust on both sides, then finish over lower heat so the heat has time to penetrate without the meat burning on the outside.

Like grilling, broiling cooks meat with intense heat and minimal fat, but broiling cooks from above rather than below. Broiling doesn't usually brown and flavor foods as well as grilling does, but it's convenient when the weather's uncooperative. Following, I show broiling a mixed grill, which could, of course, also be prepared on a grill. When you place the food under the broiler, start by positioning the broiler rack close to the heat source and then lower it if the foods start to brown too quickly.

Grilled and broiled meats should be lightly rubbed with oil before cooking to prevent them from sticking to the grill rack or broiler pan.

Grilled Strip Steaks

A grill pan is a useful alternative to a grill when it's too cold or too wet to grill.

1. Preheat the grill or a grill pan. Rub the grill or grill pan and the steaks lightly with oil. Grill the steaks for 2 to 4 minutes, depending on how done you like your meat.
2. Give the steaks a 90-degree turn and grill for 2 to 4 minutes more to give them a decorative crosshatch pattern.
3. Turn the steaks over and grill on the other side to desired doneness.

Broiled Lamb Chops and Pork Chops

1. Spread the lightly oiled and seasoned chops on the broiler rack.

2. Turn the meats over as necessary to control browning. Remove the lamb chops before the pork chops (or start them later) because lamb chops will take less time to cook.

Kitchen Notes and Tips

- When cooking several different kinds of meat at once, keep in mind that pork chops are cooked more than lamb chops and other red meats. Unless the pork chops are cut very thin, you may want to get them started before adding the other meats. Pork chops must be cooked to 140°F for medium. Lamb chops can be cooked rare (125°F) or medium-rare (130°F).
- Meats that are well marbled and/or rimmed with a layer of fat are likely to cause flare-ups as they grill because their fat drips down onto the coals and often catches fire. There are several methods for controlling flare-ups:

  Make sure that steaks and chops are trimmed of excess fat.

  Use a squeeze bottle to spray a thin jet of cold water into the areas of the coals that start to flare up.

  If the fire starts to flare up, move the pieces of meat to a different spot on the grill.

  If you're cooking in a covered barbecue, move the coals to one side and arrange the food on the other so the rendered fat doesn't drip down into the coals. (If there's room, you can even arrange a pan of water under the food to catch the dripping fat and keep it from smoldering and creating smoke and soot that will give the food an unpleasant flavor.)

See Also

To make a flavored butter, page 47

To make a béarnaise sauce, page 45

To make a mayonnaise, page 41

To make a vinaigrette, page 37

To season steaks and chops, page 195

To determine doneness, page 66

Related Glossary Entries

Broil

Grill (also for information on grill pans)

HOW TO

Sauté Steaks, Chops, Noisettes, and Medallions (and Make a Pan Sauce)

Sautéing is an excellent way to cook steaks and other relatively small pieces of meat such as chops and medallions. The high heat forms a savory crust on the outside of the meat and browns the meat quickly enough that the inside stays juicy and rare. When sautéing steaks, don't keep turning or tossing them in the pan as you might smaller pieces of foods such as mushrooms or scallops, but, instead, brown them completely on one side before turning. (Turning the steaks or chops over and over again doesn't give the meat a chance to brown.)

An added advantage to sautéing steaks or chops is that it gives you caramelized juices that can be deglazed with a variety of liquids and lightly thickened to make a quick pan sauce. Any relatively tender steak or chop, or a London broil cut, can be sautéed and sauced in the same way as the flank steak here.

When serving more than a couple of tenderloin steaks, it's more economical to buy a whole beef tenderloin and trim and slice it into steaks yourself. Pork and veal tenderloin can be trimmed, thickly sliced, and sautéed in the same way.

Medallions, Noisettes, and Scallopini

We're all familiar with steaks and chops. A steak is a relatively thick slice of meat, usually beef, that comes with or without a bone. Chops always have bones and are usually from animals other than beef. Smaller boneless cuts, such as slices of pork or veal loin, are sometimes called medallions. Medallions are round, about 3 inches in diameter, and about ½ inch thick. Very small slices of meat, taken from the smallest boneless cuts such as pork or veal tenderloin, are sometimes called noisettes. Noisettes are usually about an inch in diameter and between a ½ inch and an inch thick. Scallopini are very thin slices, usually of top round of veal, that are larger but thinner than medallions and noisettes. They are usually about 5 to 6 inches long, 3 inches wide, and ⅛ to ¼ inch thick.

Kitchen Notes and Tips

- Salt draws moisture out of meat and makes the surface moist, which may prevent browning. If possible, season the meat an hour before you plan to cook it and then pat dry before sautéing. If you're in a hurry or forget, season steaks and chops immediately before or after cooking.
- Sauté over high heat in oil (or rendered duck fat, if you have it). If at any point the meat or pan starts to burn, reduce the heat.
- Heat the oil until it barely begins to smoke, add the steak, and cook on the first side until completely browned, then turn and cook to the desired doneness.
- Once the steak is removed, finely chopped shallots or other aromatic ingredients such as garlic or finely chopped onions, carrots, and celery may be added to the pan and cooked briefly before deglazing for added flavor.
- To make a sauce, deglaze with water or broth, or wine first and then broth, reducing after each addition until slightly syrupy. (If you're not using broth, the liquid won't actually get syrupy—just reduce it until about 1 tablespoon per serving remains.) Unless your stock is already very concentrated, use 1 part wine to 2 parts broth, counting on ¼ to ½ cup wine for 4 people. Thicken by whisking in cold pieces of butter or by adding cream.

Sautéed Flank Steaks with Red-Wine Pan Sauce

1. In a heavy-bottomed pan just large enough to hold the steak, heat a small amount of oil over high heat. Pat the meat dry, season it (unless you seasoned it earlier), brown on both sides, and cook until done to your liking.
2. Pour out and discard the fat from the pan.
3. Pour liquid—such as broth, water, or, shown here, wine—into the hot pan.
4. Scrape the bottom of the pan with a wooden spoon to dissolve the caramelized juices. Reduce the wine until only a couple of tablespoons are left.
5. Add beef or brown chicken broth and reduce again until the sauce is lightly syrupy.
6. Swirl in butter until the sauce is thickened to the consistency you like and season to taste.
7. Slice the flank steak across the grain and at an angle into thin strips. (This is a good technique for tougher cuts of meat. Because they're thinly sliced, they seem more tender in the mouth.)
8. Spoon the sauce over each serving or pass it in a sauce boat at the table.

Sautéed Beef Tenderloin (Fillet) Steaks with Green Peppercorn Sauce

1. Brown the steaks on both sides in a small amount of oil over very high heat. Cook the steaks until they are done to your taste. Remove and keep warm.
2. Pour out and discard the fat in the pan. Add finely chopped shallots and stir for about a minute, until the shallots release their fragrance.
3. Deglaze the pan with wine—here, I use a sweet Madeira—and simmer until only a couple of tablespoons remain.
4. Add beef broth or brown chicken broth and reduce the sauce until it is slightly syrupy.
5. Add green peppercorns, and a little Cognac if you like, and crush the peppercorns with a fork.
6. Whisk in cubes of cold butter. If the sauce gets too thick, thin it with a little broth. Season to taste with salt.
7. Spoon the sauce over the steaks and serve.

See Also

To make a brown chicken broth, page 30
To determine doneness, page 66

Related Glossary Entries

Caramelize
Deglaze
Degrease
Monter au Beurre
Panfry
Sauté
Thickener (for thickening with butter and cream)

To Cut a Beef Tenderloin (Fillet) into Steaks

Slice the trimmed tenderloin as thin or thick as you like.

To Trim and Cut a Pork Tenderloin into Noisettes

1. Trim the thin silverskin off the tenderloin by sliding a knife under it, pulling the silverskin taut, and slicing while keeping the knife pointed very slightly upward toward the silverskin.
2. Slice the tenderloin into noisettes about 1 inch thick.

HOW TO

Sauté a Small Whole Loin of Pork, Veal, or Venison

Small loins of pork, veal, and venison can be cut into medallions and sautéed like steaks, or they can be sautéed whole and then sliced as you would a small roast. The loin is served with a sauce made from the deglazed pan juices.

Sautéed Venison Loin

1. Slide a small sharp knife under the thin membrane—the silverskin—that covers the loin. Move the knife toward the end of the loin, keeping the blade facing up against the membrane.
2. Turn the knife in the other direction and, while pulling on the membrane, slide the knife all the way to the other end of the loin. Detach the strip of membrane. Repeat to remove all the membrane.
3. Brown the loin on all sides in a heavy pan, just large enough to hold it, then continue cooking to the doneness you like. If you want the loin cooked to more than rare (not recommended), finish it in a 400°F oven.
4. Slice the loin.
5. Serve the loin, here shown with roast vegetables and a sauce made by deglazing the pan with a small amount of port and thickening it with heavy cream.

See Also

To determine doneness, page 66
To sauté steaks and noisettes, page 195
To make a pan sauce, page 195
To roast vegetables, page 70

Related Glossary Entries

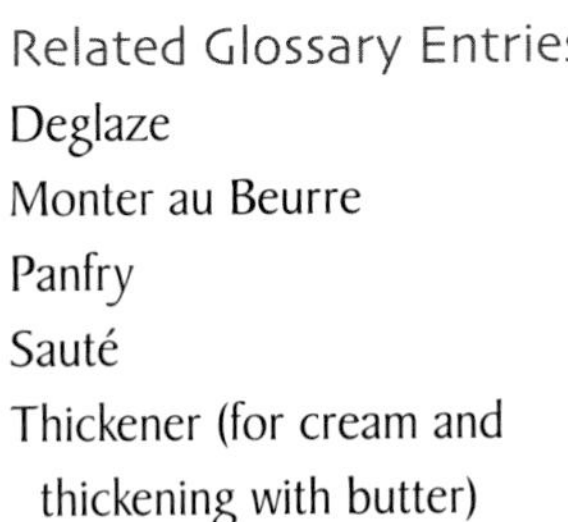

Deglaze
Monter au Beurre
Panfry
Sauté
Thickener (for cream and thickening with butter)

HOW TO

Make Pot-au-Feu and Other Boiled Dinners

The cuisines of most Western countries include a poached meat dish: France has *pot-au-feu;* Italy, *bollito misto;* and Spain, *cocido.* (The United States equivalent is a New England boiled dinner, which is slightly different from the dishes mentioned above because the meat, corned beef, is cured, while the meats in the other dishes are fresh.) Though every country has its own variation and cuts of meat, the techniques are essentially the same: Meat, aromatic vegetables, and a bouquet garni are gently simmered in water or broth until the meat and vegetables become meltingly tender. Many of these dishes were traditionally designed to provide two courses, the rich broth served as a first course, followed by a plate of meat and vegetables. In practice, the broth can also be served with the meat on a plate or in shallow bowls. Or you can choose not to serve the broth at all, but save it for making soups or sauces.

A traditional pot-au-feu requires several cuts of beef—usually chuck, shank, and short ribs. All of these cuts are relatively tough and gelatinous and require long, moist cooking, making them perfect not only for pot-au-feu, but for stews, daubes, and pot roasts. Poaching is the purest way to cook these flavorful cuts of meat; because the meat is not browned, its taste is little altered. There's a wonderful simplicity about a pot-au-feu and a satisfaction to tasting the meat and vegetables in such an unadorned, natural form. Pot-au-feu is also the lightest, least-rich way to eat these meats, because poaching requires no fat and the broth isn't thickened with rich ingredients.

Kitchen Notes and Tips

- Poaching is a great way to cook any relatively tough cut of meat—in addition to the beef chuck, shank, and short ribs mentioned here, you might also try veal shanks and lamb shoulder. Except for lamb shoulder, which has a strong flavor that takes over the flavor of the broth, cuts of meat from different animals can be poached and served together. For a luxurious touch, add a chunk of beef tenderloin to a pot-au-feu about 15 minutes before it's done.
- When buying beef chuck, you're likely to run into several different shoulder cuts, labeled differently depending on what part of the country you're in. Ask your butcher for a cut that is good for a pot roast.
- Use a pot just large enough to hold the meat, so that you can use as little liquid as possible, making the broth more concentrated (this is particularly important if you're using water to moisten).
- Start meats for pot-au-feu in cold liquid to allow the heat to penetrate the meat evenly and to produce a clear broth. Cook the meats at a low simmer. Never allow the liquid to boil, which will make the broth greasy and the meat dry.
- Cut the vegetables into large pieces—carrots sectioned and halved; parsnips cored (the center is sometimes woody or bitter), sectioned, and halved; turnips halved; leeks halved lengthwise and tied together so it's easier to pull them out of the pot.
- Add the vegetables only after the poaching liquid has been skimmed of any froth and is clear, so that the scum doesn't stick to the vegetables. (The vegetables also take less time to cook than the meat.)
- The meat is done when it is fork-tender—it offers no resistance to a knife.
- Remove the cooked meat with a slotted spoon, or tie it up as for *boeuf à la ficelle* and hook it with a fork.
- Pot-au-feu doesn't need to rest before serving. Cut the meat into fairly thick slices; it will be so tender that it will fall apart if you try to slice it thin.

Pot-au-Feu

Here, a chuck roast alone is used to prepare a simple version of a traditional pot-au-feu. In France, a pot-au-feu is served with mustard, coarse salt, and the little pickles called cornichons.

1. Place the meat in a pot just large enough to hold it.
2. Pour over enough cold water or broth to cover and bring to a gentle simmer. Skim off any froth or scum that floats to the top during the first 30 minutes of poaching.
3. When the broth is clear, and the meat partially cooked, after about 1½ to 2 hours, add a bouquet garni and the vegetables. The meat is done when it is easily penetrated with a knife or skewer, 1 to 3 hours more, depending on the size of the roast and the cut.
4. Transfer the meat and vegetables to a serving platter. Serve plates or bowls of sliced meat and the vegetables; the broth can be served over or around the meat.

See Also

To make *boeuf à la ficelle*, page 202
To clean leeks, page 9
To section and core carrots, page 21
To determine doneness, page 66

Related Glossary Entries

Braise
Poach
Stew

HOW TO

Poach a Tender Cut of Meat

Sometimes I poach a tender cut of meat such as a beef tenderloin—a cut that is usually roasted—to enjoy the pure flavor of the meat, unaltered by crust or caramelization. A tenderloin can be poached as one of the cuts in a pot-au-feu, to add luxury and contrast to the dish. It is poached for a shorter period of time than the tough cuts, because it should be cooked only to rare or medium-rare. Tender cuts can also be poached as the sole meat in a flavorful broth, with vegetables as for a pot-au-feu, or without. Meats that are cooked in this way are sometimes described by the words *à la ficelle*. *Ficelle* means "string" and refers to the method of tying up the meat to make it easier to fish out of the simmering broth.

Kitchen Notes and Tips

- Any tender cut of meat can be poached: eye of round, small legs of lamb, duck breasts, and the tenderloin shown below all work well. (Eye of round is slightly tougher than tenderloin, so it should be sliced thinner than shown here.)
- Unlike long-cooking tough cuts of meat, tenderloin should be cooked in broth rather than water, because the meat doesn't cook long enough to produce its own flavorful broth.
- Start tenderloin and other tender cuts in simmering broth.
- If you're poaching the meat with vegetables, remember that the vegetables take longer to cook than the meat. Start the vegetables first and cook them until almost tender—30 to 40 minutes—then add the meat.
- Test doneness just as you would if you were roasting—by touch, or with an instant-read thermometer: 120°F for rare.

Boeuf à la Ficelle

1. Tie a piece of string around a setion of beef tenderloin and submerge it in barely simmering broth until cooked rare, 15 to 20 minutes.
2. Slice the meat.
3. Serve the meat on a platter or in individual soup plates, surrounded with the vegetables poached in the broth in the same way as for pot-au-feu. Ladle some of the broth around the meat on the platter or around each individual serving.

See Also

To make a pot-au-feu, page 200

To determine doneness, page 66

Related Glossary Entry

Poach

HOW TO

Make a Pot Roast

A pot roast offers one way (along with stews, daubes, and pot-au-feu) to cook a tough, gelatinous cut of meat such as beef chuck or lamb or veal shoulder. The meat can be marinated for added flavor (in France, the beef is traditionally marinated in red wine for *boeuf à la mode,* but in the United States pot roast typically isn't). The meat is browned and simmered (technically, braised) for a long time in a small amount of wine, broth, or water until completely tender. The cooking liquid is strained and degreased, returned to the pan with the meat, and used to baste the meat as it reduces, coating the meat with a dark, shiny, flavorful glaze.

Cooking in this way dramatically concentrates the flavors of the meat and the broth. The juices released by the meat mingle with the broth, to be reduced and then reabsorbed by the meat during the final glazing. The technique concentrates and melds the flavors of broth, meat, herbs and aromatic vegetables into a sapid and flavorful whole. Although both dishes may use the same cut of meat, pot roast is very different from a pot-au-feu: The point of pot-au-feu is to preserve the essential flavors of the ingredients, while pot roast involves an alchemical process by which new flavors are created from the marriage of the meat with herbs, aromatic vegetables, and sometimes wine.

Red-Wine Pot Roast

1. Marinate the chuck roast overnight in red wine to cover, with chopped onions and carrots. Use a larding needle to insert strips of fatback into the meat (optional).
2. In a heavy pot just large enough to hold it, brown the meat over high heat in a small amount of oil.
3. Strain the marinade, reserving the vegetables and wine separately. Pour the oil used for browning the meat out of the pot and add a little new oil. Add the vegetables and stir over medium heat until browned.

4. Add the browned meat to the vegetables and pour over the wine from the marinade.
5. Pour over enough beef or chicken broth or water to come halfway up the sides of the roast. Nestle a bouquet garni in the vegetables. Bring to a slow simmer over medium heat.
6. Cover the pot with aluminum foil. Push down the center of the foil so the moisture that accumulates inside the pot will condense on the underside of the foil and drip down on the roast and baste it. Put in a 325°F oven for 3 hours.
7. Insert a skewer into the meat. If the skewer slides out easily, the meat is done. If the meat isn't done, cook for another 30 minutes and check again.
8. Take the meat out of the pot and strain the cooking liquid. (Leave the oven on.) Discard the vegetables or purée them and use them to thicken the braising liquid. Degrease the liquid and gently reduce it for 10 minutes. Place the meat in a clean pot (you can wash out the first one) and pour over the cooking liquid. Add fresh vegetables—here, carrots, sectioned and halved, and peeled boiling onions.
9. Heat the pot over medium heat until the liquid comes to the simmer. Cover the pot with foil and the lid and bake for 30 minutes more. Remove the lid and continue baking, basting the meat every 5 or 10 minutes.
10. Bake until the pot roast is covered with a shiny glaze and the braising liquid is slightly syrupy, about 30 minutes longer.
11. Slice the pot roast (cutting perpendicular to the strips of fatback if you larded the meat) and arrange the slices in individual soup plates or on a platter.
12. Spoon over the cooking liquid and vegetables.

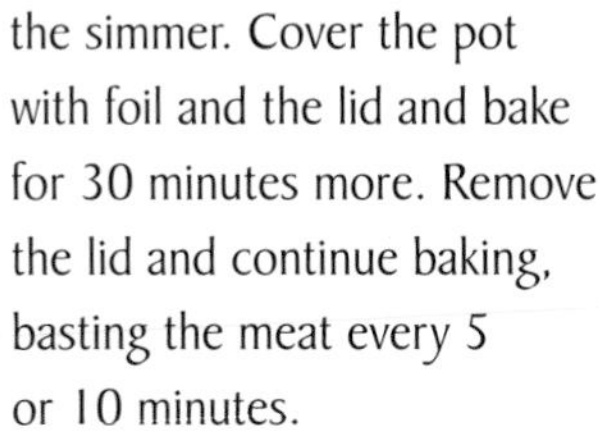

Kitchen Notes and Tips

- You can lard the meat as shown on page 203. (This step is optional, but it will give the meat an incomparable moistness, particularly if the meat is not well marbled.)
- Cook pot roast in red or white wine, broth, a combination of wine or wine vinegar and broth, or, in a pinch, water.
- A vegetable garniture is optional. For the most basic vegetable garniture, serve the vegetables used for marinating and cooking. In the method here, fresh vegetables are added near the end of cooking, a refinement that allows you to control their cooking time. You can also garnish a pot roast with vegetables that have been cooked separately, such as glazed root vegetables or even blanched green vegetables such as shell beans, string beans and peas, adding them to the pot roast just before serving.
- Use a concave aluminum foil cover under the lid so that moisture condenses on the underside of the foil and drips down onto the roast to baste it; without the foil, the condensation would drip down the sides of the pot.
- Bring the pot roast to a simmer on top of the stove slowly, over medium heat, so it takes 15 to 20 minutes to reach the simmer. (This allows the heat to fully penetrate the meat and shortens the time in the oven.)
- The pot roast should cook at a bare simmer, so that a bubble breaks the surface about every 3 seconds.
- Start the pot roast in a 325°F oven. Lift the lid and foil after about 15 minutes: If no bubbles are rising to the surface, raise the oven temperature to 350°F; if the bubbles are rising too quickly, lower the heat to 300°F.
- Reducing the braising liquid over the roast while basting gives the liquid more flavor than if you simply reduce the liquid separately.
- The intensely flavored braising liquid that remains in the pan is typically thickened by reduction alone, but if you like, you can thicken it with cornstarch or puréed vegetables.

See Also

To make a stew, page 206
To make a beef daube, page 210
To make a pot-au-feu, page 200
To section and core carrots, page 21
To make a chicken broth, page 30
To purée braised vegetables, page 207

Related Glossary Entries

Braise
Degrease
Glaze
Lard
Marinate
Reduction
Thickener

Long-Braised Beef Stew

A classic *boeuf à la bourguignonne* is garnished with mushrooms, glazed onions, and bacon, but other ingredients, such as baby artichokes, green beans, glazed carrots, glazed turnips, stewed cucumbers, and/or wild mushrooms can replace the classic garniture used here.

1. Trim connective tissue and any large pieces of fat off the meat (here, a chuck roast), and cut the beef into chunks about 1 by 2 inches.

2. Marinate the beef for 3 to 5 hours in red wine with onions, carrots, celery, and a bouquet garni. The individual pieces of meat can also be larded for extra moisture (see page 210).

Drain the meat, reserving the marinade, and pat dry on towels. Brown in oil over high heat, adding only several pieces at a time. (If the meat is added too quickly, it will cool the pot, release too much liquid, and never brown.)

3. Sprinkle with flour (optional). Cook a few more minutes on all sides to brown.

4. Remove the meat from the pan and pour out the fat. Put all the meat back in the pan, along with the wine, vegetables, and bouquet garni from the marinade. Pour over more wine to barely cover.

HOW TO

Make a Stew

A stew is another excellent way to cook tough, gelatinous cuts such as beef chuck to melting tenderness. A stew is technically a braise, like a pot roast, but it's made with meat that has been cut into smaller pieces. Sometimes meat for stew is marinated with wine and aromatic vegetables for added flavor, but this isn't essential. Usually the meat is first browned and then simmered in a liquid or combination of liquids with aromatic vegetables and herbs. Browning and long simmering concentrate and layer flavor into the stew, producing a delicious, complex taste. Stews made without browning the meat (sometimes called *daubes*) taste slightly less concentrated. The cooking liquid in stews is usually bound, or thickened, with some form of thickener. Stews are usually garnished with a combination of vegetables and other ingredients, such as small strips of bacon.

Bring to a gentle simmer on top of the stove. Cover the pot and cook in a 325°F oven for 2½ hours, or until the meat is easily penetrated with a skewer or small knife. Take the meat out of the pot.

5. Strain the cooking liquid into a saucepan, pressing firmly on the vegetables with a ladle. Bring the cooking liquid to a gentle simmer and skim off any fat that floats to the top.

6. If you didn't flour the meat, prepare a beurre manié by working together flour and butter with the back of a fork.

7. Whisk the beurre manié into the degreased cooking liquid. Still whisking, bring to the simmer.

8. Or, purée the cooked vegetables and whisk the mixture into the degreased cooking liquid.

9. Combine the meat, the cooking liquid, glazed pearl onions, sautéed mushrooms, and lardons. Cover the pot and heat just long enough to heat through.

10. Serve on individual plates or, as shown on page 208, in a serving dish.

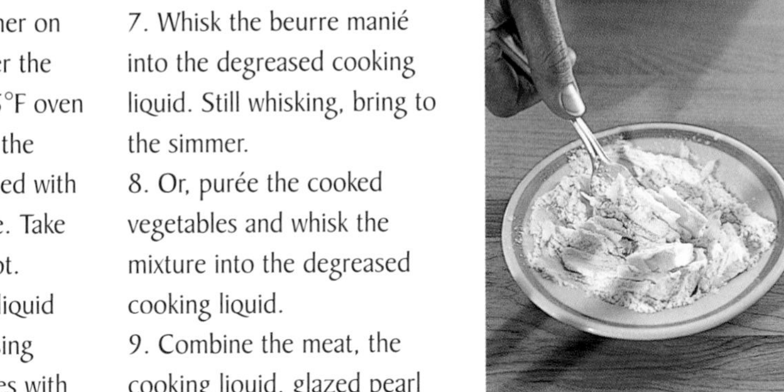

See Also

To make a stew without browning, page 210
To make a brown chicken broth, page 30
To lard individual pieces of meat, page 210
To glaze pearl onions, page 76
To make bacon lardons, page 155
To sauté mushrooms, page 91
To braise veal shanks, page 209
To make a pot roast, page 203
To cut up a breast of veal for stew, page 241
To make a veal stew, page 212

Related Glossary Entries

Degrease
Fricassée
Garniture
Lard
Marinate
Thickener

Kitchen Notes and Tips

- Use beef chuck, short ribs, or shanks for beef stews; lamb shoulder for lamb stew; and veal shoulder, veal breast, or shanks (osso bucco) for veal stews.
- Moisten the stew with wine, water or broth, or a combination of broth and wine. (Water, not surprisingly, makes the least flavorful sauce.)
- Cook the stew at a bare simmer, so that a bubble breaks the surface about every 3 seconds.
- Thicken stews with one of the three methods shown in the recipes: sprinkle flour over the meat during browning; thicken the stewing liquid with a paste of flour and butter, called a beurre manié; or strain and purée the cooked marinade vegetables and whisk into the cooking liquid. Or work cornstarch or arrowroot and water into a thin paste, sometimes called a slurry, to thicken the stew.
- Cook the garnishes separately and add them near the end of cooking, to better control their cooking time, or cook them along with the meat, estimating their cooking times and adding them to the pot accordingly (for example, add carrot sections about 30 minutes before the stew is done, baby peas only during the last few minutes of cooking, and so forth).
- Use this model for veal and lamb stews. Traditionally veal stews (called fricassées or blanquettes) are made by poaching the veal without browning or by searing the veal only lightly to keep the sauce light colored. But in practice, you can cook the veal or lamb until golden brown, particularly if the sauce is darker colored with an ingredient such as tomato.

HOW TO

Cook Veal, Beef, and Lamb Shanks

Veal, beef, and lamb shanks are great cuts for stews. Shanks are full of connective tissue that softens with long braising, making the meat meltingly soft and giving the sauce a rich, silky feel in the mouth. Braise shanks just as you would make a traditional stew, browning the meat and then simmering it very gently in liquid flavored with aromatic vegetables and herbs. Usually, the aromatic vegetables are strained out and discarded after the meat is cooked and are replaced by new vegetables and other ingredients such as bacon. But in the recipe below, the aromatic julienned vegetables are cooked with the veal shanks, and served in a kind of melting tangle over the meat. Because the gelatin released by the meat naturally adds body to the sauce, the braising liquid doesn't need to be thickened. It is simply reduced to give it a lightly syrupy consistency.

Braised Veal Shanks

1. In a pan just large enough to hold them in a single layer, brown the veal shanks on both sides in oil over high heat. Remove the shanks, discard the oil, and return the shanks to the pan.
2. Pour over enough white wine to come a quarter of the way up the sides of the shanks. Simmer over medium heat until only a couple of tablespoons of liquid remain in the bottom of the pan.
3. Add julienned carrots, leeks, and turnips to the pan and pour over enough veal or chicken broth or water to come about halfway up the sides of the shanks. Bring to a gentle simmer on the stove.
4. Cover the pan and bake at 325°F for 2 hours, or until the shanks offer no resistance when poked with a skewer; the julienned vegetables will be meltingly tender. Check periodically to make sure the liquid isn't boiling; a bubble should rise to the surface only every 2 or 3 seconds.
5. Carefully transfer the shanks to individual soup plates, place a mound of the julienned vegetables on each shank, and ladle over the hot braising liquid. (If the braising liquid seems too thin, reduce it slightly; if it seems greasy, transfer it to a saucepan and remove the fat with a spoon or small ladle or with a degreasing cup.)

See Also

To make a beef stew, page 206 (all Kitchen Notes and Tips hold true for stewing shanks)
To cut vegetables into julienne, page 13
To make a chicken broth, page 30

Related Glossary Entries

Degrease
Reduction

HOW TO

Make a Stew Without Browning

Stew recipes generally insist that we brown the meat and, sometimes, the vegetables. In fact, this step isn't essential: *Daubes* are stews in which neither the meat nor the vegetables is browned. Without the caramelization provided by browning, the stew won't have quite the same concentrated color and savor, but the difference is slight enough that, to my mind, the browning isn't always worth the extra work. *Beurre manié* is the traditional thickener for a red-wine beef stew, but you can use cornstarch, as shown in the recipe, or just reduce the braising liquid until it becomes slightly syrupy from the natural gelatin it contains.

Provençal Daube

Larding the cubed meat with fatback is optional, but it will help keep the meat moist.

1. Marinate cubes of beef in wine (here, red wine) with carrots, onions, and garlic, and a bouquet garni for 3 to 4 hours, or overnight, in the refrigerator.
2. If desired, lard each piece of beef with a strip of fatback.
3. Pour the meat and its marinade into a heavy-bottomed pot. Add additional wine or broth as necessary to cover the meat—here, I finish by adding a small amount of sherry vinegar, but this is optional. Bring the daube to a gentle simmer on the stove, cover the pot, and simmer slowly in a 325°F oven until the meat is easily penetrated with a knife, about 3 hours.
4. Strain the stew, reserving the meat and vegetables, and transfer the liquid to a saucepan.
5. Sort through the meat and vegetables, reserving the meat and discarding the vegetables.
6. Gently reduce the braising liquid. Skim off any fat and froth that floats to the top or remove the fat using a degreasing cup. Now, you can continue to reduce the braising liquid to a light syrupy consistency or you can thicken it with cornstarch as follows.
7. Combine cornstarch with an equal amount of cold water and stir until smooth.
8. Whisk the cornstarch/water mixture (sometimes called a slurry) into the simmering braising liquid. Bring back to the simmer and whisk until thickened, about 10 seconds.
9. Gently reheat the meat in the braising liquid and serve.

See Also

To make a beef stew, page 206 (except for the step of browning the meat, all Kitchen Notes and Tips for making a beef stew apply)

To make a bouquet garni, page 31

To make a beurre manié, page 206

To use a degreasing cup, page 268

Related Glossary Entries

Braise

Degrease

Lard

Marinate

Reduction

Thickener

HOW TO

Make a Veal Stew

A *blanquette de veau* is a luscious and delicate creamy veal stew in which, in the style of a daube, the meat is not browned. The braising liquid is thickened with a roux and given a satiny consistency with cream and egg yolks.

Traditionally, a blanquette is garnished with mushrooms, which are cooked separately in some of the braising liquid, which is then returned to the stew, and white-glazed onions. However, you can replace this traditional garniture with other cooked vegetables, such as baby glazed carrots, wild mushrooms sautéed or cooked separately in braising liquid, baby artichokes (or artichoke bottoms cut into wedges) cooked in water with a little oil, braised fennel wedges, glazed turnips, or glazed cucumbers—either alone or in combination. Or, simply use the recipe here as a model, adding additional ingredients such as tomato or sorrel purée, garlic, saffron, or curry to the cooking liquid to give the stew your own stamp. As is true for all stews, blanquettes can be cooked on top of the stove or in the oven; in this recipe, I gently simmer the stew on top of the stove.

Kitchen Notes and Tips

- Blanching the veal removes proteins that would make the sauce murky. Surprisingly, this preliminary blanching doesn't rob the sauce of flavor but instead gives the stew a cleaner, meatier flavor.
- For the roux, measure the amount of broth and calculate 1½ tablespoons butter plus 1½ tablespoons flour to bind 1 cup broth. These proportions will give you a light sauce. If you want a thicker sauce, either reduce the sauce once it has been bound or increase the amount of roux.
- The egg yolks are optional in a blanquette—they can be tricky, because they'll curdle if allowed to boil—but they give the stew a special velvety texture.

Creamed Veal Stew

Buy veal stew meat or cut a trimmed breast into 1- by 2-inch pieces of veal.

1. Blanch the cubes of veal stew meat: Put them in a pot with enough cold water to cover and bring quickly to the boil.
2. Immediately drain the veal in a colander and rinse with cold water. Put the veal in a heavy-bottomed pot, surround it with aromatic vegetables (here, carrots and onions) and a bouquet garni, and cover the meat with broth or water.
3. Simmer the veal gently on the stove or in the oven for about 2½ hours, until a piece is easily penetrated with a small knife. Drain and reserve the meat and broth separately. Discard the vegetables.
4. Thicken the broth by whisking it into a white roux and bringing the mixture (now a velouté sauce) to a gentle simmer.
5. Skim off any fat and scum that floats to the top of the sauce with a spoon or ladle. Simmer, skimming now and then, for about 30 minutes.
6. Prepare the cream and egg yolk liaison by whisking the yolks with cold cream.
7. Combine the cooked veal with cooked pearl onions and mushrooms and the velouté sauce in the pot used for cooking the veal or another large pot. Pour over the cream and egg yolk mixture (or use just cream if you don't care to deal with the egg yolks).
8. Heat the veal stew over low to medium heat, moving it quickly back and forth over the heat to blend in the egg yolk mixture, until the sauce takes on a silky consistency. Don't stir the veal, or it will break apart. Don't let the sauce boil, or the egg yolks will curdle. (If you've omitted the yolks, a short boil will do no harm.) Serve with fluffy rice.

See Also
To prepare artichokes, page 92
To glaze roasted vegetables, page 70
To bone, trim, and cut up breast of veal, page 241
To make fluffy rice, page 63
To make a daube, page 210
To make a stew, page 206
To make a bouquet garni, page 31
To make a white roux for velouté sauce, page 179

Related Glossary Entries
Blanch
Braise
Degrease
Garniture
Thickener

HOW TO

Prepare Sweetbreads

Veal sweetbreads—the thymus glands of young calves—are usually short-braised or sautéed, or occasionally fried. Because sweetbreads have a somewhat loose and amorphous texture, they are usually blanched and weighted before cooking to firm and compress them so they hold their shape and look more presentable when sliced. While it's not essential, it's preferable to soak sweetbreads overnight in the refrigerator in salted water before blanching to draw out any traces of blood, which would turn gray when the sweetbreads were cooked.

Braising is an excellent method for preparing sweetbreads. The sweetbreads release their juices into the surrounding liquid so that, once they are cooked, the braising liquid can be turned into a sauce simply by straining, reducing if necessary, and seasoning. Cream can be added, as shown below, to add body and richness.

Because of their delicacy, sweetbreads take very well to light breading. The breading allows you to sauté them at a lower temperature and still get them to brown without overcooking them. Sweetbreads can be breaded with flour, egg, and bread crumbs, like boneless, skinless chicken breasts. The recipe here shows how ingredients other than bread crumbs can be used for breading.

Keep in mind that sweetbreads must be cooked just right—just until they feel firm to the touch. Undercooked, they have an unpleasant rubbery texture; overcooked, they become tough and dry.

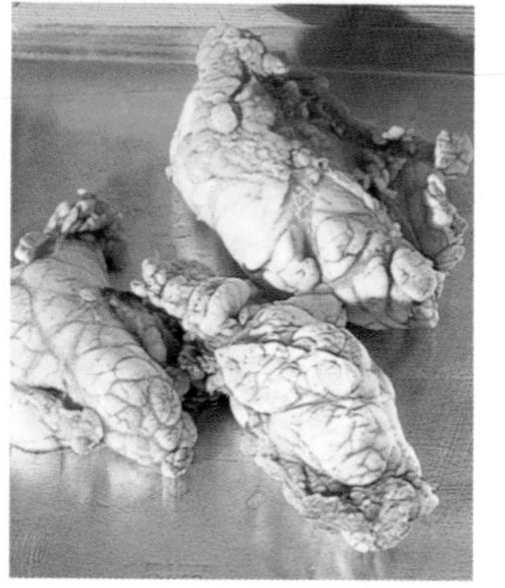

To Prepare Sweetbreads for Cooking

1. Soak the sweetbreads overnight in the refrigerator, in cold salted water to cover (optional).
2. To blanch the sweetbreads, put them in a pot with enough cold water to cover and set over high heat. As soon as the water comes to a simmer, scoop out the sweetbreads.
3. Place the blanched sweetbreads on a sheet pan or in a shallow baking pan. Place a clean cutting board or another sheet pan on top.
4. Weight the sweetbreads with a pot or other moderately heavy object. Refrigerate for at least 4 and up to 24 hours.
5. Trim off strips of membrane and clumps of fat with a paring knife. Don't overdo it, however, or the sweetbreads will come apart.

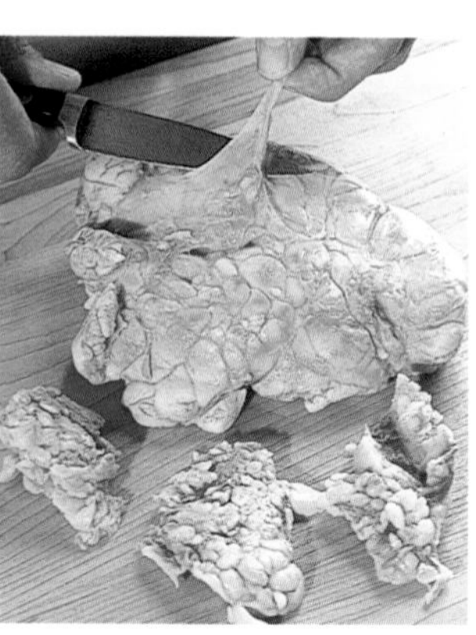

Short-Braised Sweetbreads

1. Gently sweat a fine mirepoix in a small amount of butter in a heavy pot until the vegetables soften. Add white wine.
2. Place blanched and weighted sweetbreads on top of the mirepoix. Add a bouquet garni and enough chicken or veal broth to come about one third of the way up the sides of the sweetbreads.
3. Place a parchment paper or aluminum round on top of the sweetbreads. Heat over medium heat until the liquid comes to a gentle simmer. Transfer to a 350°F oven and braise until the sweetbreads are firm to the touch, about 25 minutes.
4. Transfer the sweetbreads to a plate. Add cream to the pot and simmer gently on the stovetop until the sauce thickens to the consistency you like.
5. Strain the sauce, pushing hard against the vegetables with the back of a ladle to extract as much liquid as possible. Reduce the liquid slightly, if necessary, to thicken it.
6. Slice the sweetbreads and arrange them in a serving dish or on plates. Ladle over the sauce, or pass it in a sauceboat.

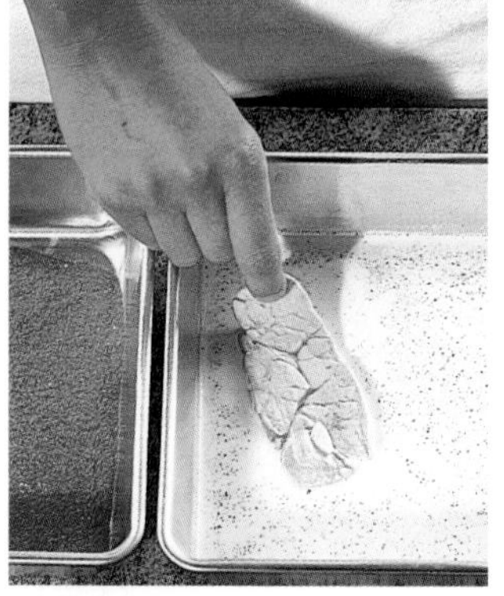

Sautéed Sweetbreads Breaded with Porcini Dust or Chopped Truffles

To Bread Sweetbreads with Porcini Dust

Here, sweetbreads are first coated with flour and beaten egg before being coated with porcini dust. For a lighter coating, coat sweetbreads directly with the porcini dust and skip the flour and egg.

1. Cut blanched and weighted sweetbreads into slices.
2. Dip the slices in seasoned flour and pat off the excess. Dip in beaten egg that has been well seasoned with salt and pepper. Remove excess egg by holding each slice between 2 fingers and sliding 2 fingers of your other hand along its sides.
3. Place each slice in a pan or shallow bowl of porcini dust and turn to coat both sides.
4. Pat the slices to remove excess porcini dust.

To Bread Sweetbreads with Chopped Truffles

1. Finely chop black truffles.
2. Coat sweetbread slices with flour and egg as described on page 216. Then coat on one or both sides with the chopped truffles.

To Sauté Breaded Sweetbreads

1. Sauté breaded sweetbreads in clarified butter in a heavy-bottomed pan over medium heat for about 5 minutes on each side, or until they feel firm to the touch.
2. Transfer the sweetbreads to a platter or to individual plates.

See Also

To bread boneless chicken breasts, page 162
To make a chicken broth, page 30
To make a bouquet garni, page 31
To make porcini dust, page 164
To clarify butter, page 46

Related Glossary Entries

Blanch
Braise
Bread
Deep-fry
Mirepoix
Parchment Paper Round
Reduction
Sauté

Working from Scratch

HOW TO

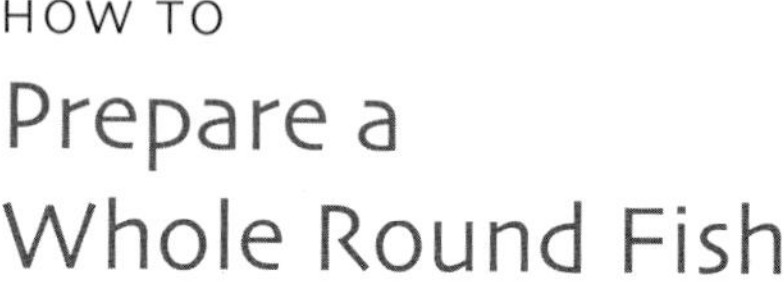

Prepare a Whole Round Fish

Most fish fall into one of two categories: flatfish, which include sole, flounders, and halibut and which are, in fact, relatively flat and as adults swim on one side with both eyes facing up, and round fish, which include most other fish, and which have a more rounded shape and swim with one eye on each side. The round fish shown here is an Atlantic sea bass.

To Remove the Fins of the Fish

Cut off the fins where they join the body, using a pair of heavy-duty scissors. Do one side first, turn the fish over, and repeat on the other side.

1. Cut off the first pectoral fin.
2. Cut off the ventral fin at the bottom front of the fish.
3. Cut off the dorsal fin that runs along the fish's back.
4. Cut off the anal fin.
5. Cut off the tail (also called the caudal fin).

To Scale the Fish

Run a fish scaler or the back of a chef's knife over the fish to detach the scales. Do this outdoors so the scales don't mess up the kitchen, or scale the fish inside a clean and clear garbage bag or while holding the fish inside a garbage can lined with a clean bag.

Be sure to remove the scales at the base of the head and the area along the stomach between the ventral and anal fins—these spots are often missed on fish at the fish store.

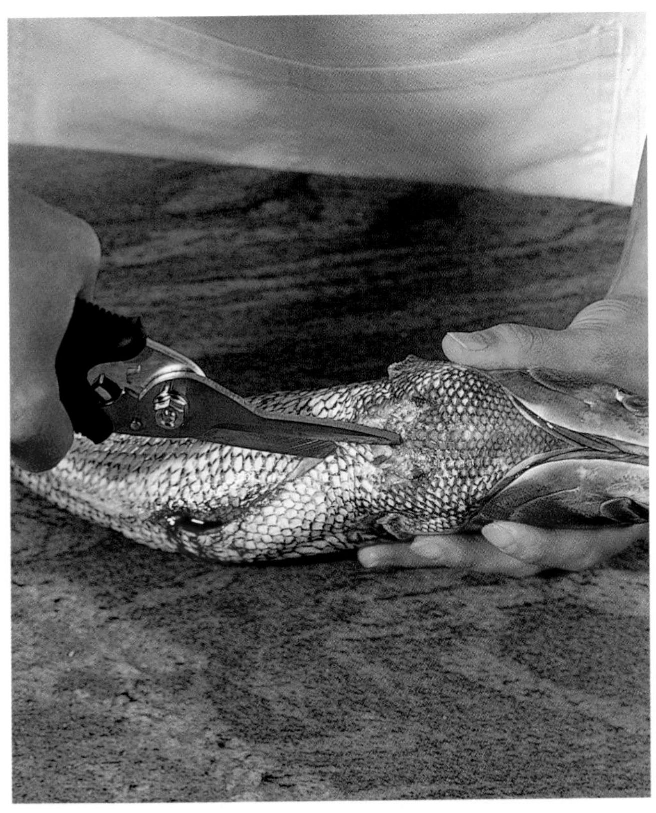

To Gut the Fish and Remove the Gills

If you're cooking whole fish, it's *essential* to gut the fish and remove the gills, but if you're using just the fillets and aren't using the fish bones for broth, there's no need to gut or remove the gills. To use the fish bones for broth, it's easiest to take out the guts and gills after filleting (see page 32).

1. Insert a pair of scissors into the anus and cut through the skin up to the base of the head. Don't insert the scissors too deep into the fish, or you may cut into some of the viscera.
2. Cut the gills away on both sides.
3. Detach the viscera where they are connected at the base of the head and pull them out. Rinse the inside of the fish and scrape a small knife against the inside of the backbone to eliminate any traces of blood.

To Fillet a Striped Bass

Scale the fish if you're cooking the fillets with the skin on, but don't bother if you are taking the skin off anyway. If you're using the head and bones for making fish broth, you can clean the fish before filleting as shown on page 221, but it's easier to clean a fish after it's filleted, as shown on page 32. If you're discarding the heads and bones, don't bother with cleaning.

1. Make a cut at the base of the head, angling the knife under the head so any flesh under the base of the head is left attached to the fillet.
2. Cut through the skin down the length of the back above the backbone, keeping the knife pressed against the bones. (If the fish has scales, use a sturdy knife; if not, a flexible filleting knife will also work.) Cut through the flesh until you come to the backbone.
3. Fold back the fillet and cut over and around the backbone. Slide the knife over the ribs, detaching the front part of the fillet. (Or cut through the ribs and remove them from the fillets later.)

4. Continue cutting and completely detach the fillet, working toward the tail.
5. Turn the fish over and around so the tail is facing away from you. Cut through the skin and flesh on the tail down to the bone. (Don't cut through the bone.) Slide the knife along the edge of the fillet, just along the top of the bones, cutting through the skin.
6. Continue cutting, working toward the fish's head, until you reach the backbone.
7. Cut the flesh away from the backbone, peel back the fillet, and detach it at the base of the head.

Once you have separated the fillets, you'll need to remove the pin bones (the small bones embedded in the upper two thirds of most fish fillets) with tweezers or needle-nose pliers as for salmon (page 225) or just cut the bones out in one strip as for red snapper (page 125). If the small rib bones are left attached to the fillets, remove them with a small paring knife.

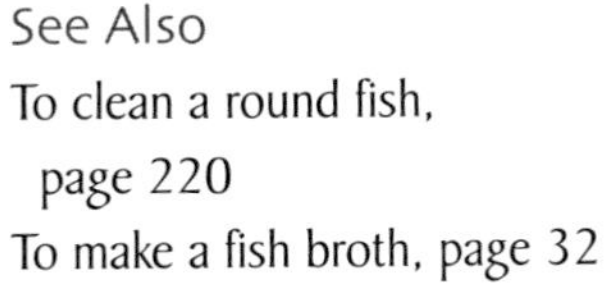

See Also
To clean a round fish, page 220
To make a fish broth, page 32

HOW TO

Fillet a Salmon

You can fillet salmon as you would any other round fish, working from the top of the back down toward the belly, but salmon are trickier than other round fish because the little bones running along the back don't touch the central backbone, making it easy to get lost while filleting and accidentally cut into the flesh. It's safer to fillet salmon through the belly opening. The salmon here has already been gutted and scaled.

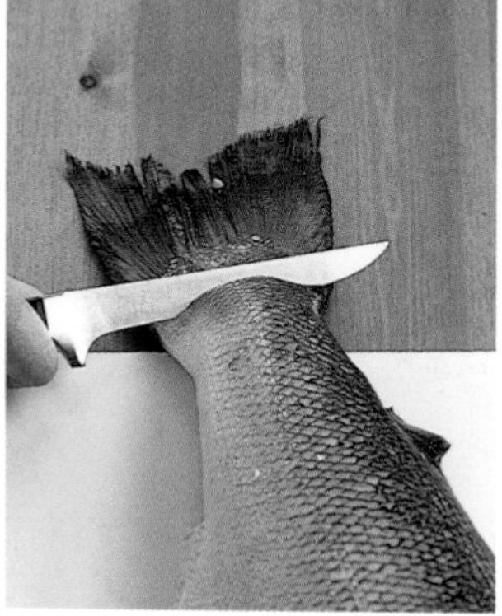

To Fillet the Fish

1. Cut away all of the fins as shown on page 220.
2. With a boning knife or other sturdy knife, make a diagonal slice under the gills at the back of the head.
3. Make a slit just above the tail, cutting down to the backbone. Don't cut through the bone.
4. Starting at the slit you've just made, slide the knife in and along the backbone, from the bottom of the fish, starting just in front of the tail, peeling back the fillet as you go, until you get to the belly opening.
5. Fold the top fillet back and pull the knife along the top side of the backbone, cutting through the rib bones that run out from the backbone along the surface of the fillet. You may need to use a rapid jerking motion to cut through the bones. Keep the knife parallel to the rib bones on the top of the fillet and don't let it penetrate too deep, or you'll cut into the flesh.
6. With a flexible knife, keeping the knife pressed flat against the bones, slide the knife along the length of the fillet, separating the backbone from the flesh as you go.
7. Fold back the top fillet and cut it away from the fillet with the bones still attached.

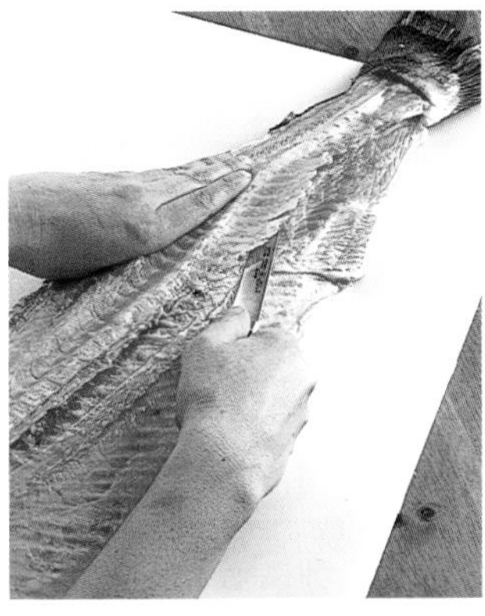

8. Cut through all of the rib bones on the bottom fillet where they join the backbone. (This is the same process as Step 5, except that you're working on the other fillet.)

9. Slide the knife under the backbone at the tail end to cut the backbone away from the flesh. Keep the knife flat, pressing up against the underside of the backbone so you don't cut into the flesh. Slide the knife toward the head.

10. Continue sliding the knife along the underside of the backbone all the way to the base of the head until you've completely detached it from the fillet. Cut the head away from the fillet.

11. Trim off the small strip of fat and bones that runs along the top of each fillet.

12. Slide a flexible knife under the rib bones on one fillet, pressing down on the ribs with one hand and up against the underside of the bones with the knife so no flesh is left attached to the bones. Repeat with the remaining fillet.

13. Run your hand against the front two thirds of each fillet to detect the tiny pin bones. Pull them out with needle-nose pliers, tweezers, or your forefinger and thumb.

See Also
To clean a whole round fish, page 220
To fillet a striped bass, page 222
To make a fish broth, page 32

HOW TO

Bone a Whole Round Fish

There are two ways to bone a round fish and leave it in one piece. If the fish hasn't already been gutted, it's easier to bone it through the back and then pull the guts out after removing the backbone. If the fish has already been gutted, it must be boned through the stomach. Boning makes the fish easier to eat and to serve and creates a pocket that is perfect for delicate stuffings.

To Bone a Whole Trout Through the Stomach

1. Cut off the fins with scissors as shown here and on page 220. (For some fish, you'll need a pair of heavy shears.)
2. Make a cut with a thin flexible knife from the end of the belly opening to the tail, keeping the knife against the backbone to expose it. Don't cut the end of the fillet away from the tail.

3. Slide the knife under the ribs on the bottom fillet and slide it toward the head to separate the ribs from the fillet. Keep the knife flush against the ribs (press on the ribs with the fingers of your other hand) so you don't cut into the fillet.
4. Cut along the ribs, going in the other direction, from head to tail, all the way down to the backbone. You'll feel the knife cutting through the pin bones, but be careful not to cut through the back of the fish.
5. Turn the fish around and cut along the underside of the ribs down to the backbone, going in the opposite direction, from the head toward the tail.
6. Pull the backbone away from the trout, cut it where it joins the head and tail, and remove it.
7. Use a pair of shears to cut away the small bones that run along the back of the trout.
8. Trim away any remaining pieces of bone or cartilage.
9. Use needle-nose pliers or tweezers to pull the tiny pin bones out of the fillets.

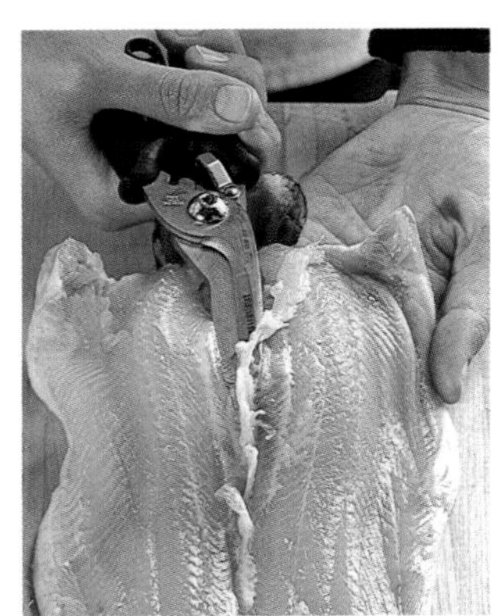

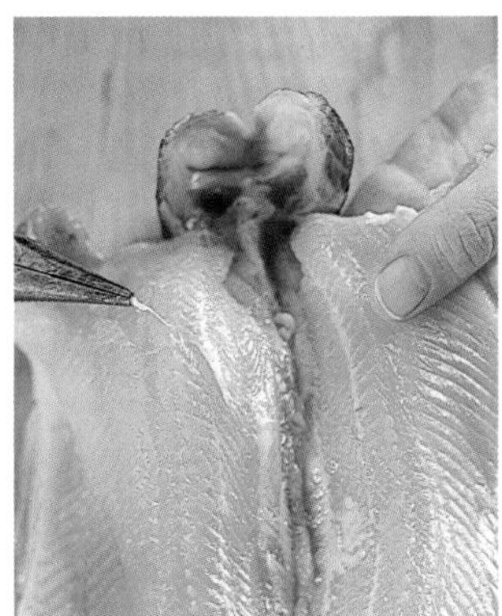

To Bone an Atlantic Sea Bass Through the Back

1. Scale the fish (if you didn't buy it scaled) and cut off the fins as shown on page 220, but don't gut it. Slide a flexible knife along the top side of the backbone.
2. Peel back the top fillet so you can see what you're doing, and to make sure you don't leave any flesh attached to the bone. As the knife hits the ribs, make rapid motions with the knife to cut through them. Don't cut in too deep, or you'll cut into the viscera or even through the skin covering the belly.
3. Turn the fish over so it's facing the other direction and repeat on the other side, starting at the tail end.
4. With a pair of heavy-duty kitchen shears, cut through the backbone where it joins the tail.
5. Cut through the backbone where it joins the head and remove the backbone.

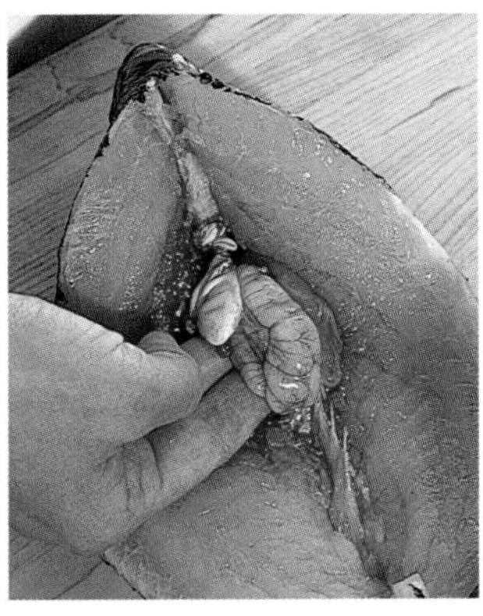

6. Pull out the viscera with your fingers.
7. Carefully slide a flexible knife under the ribs where they attach to each fillet. Pull away the ribs.
8. Remove any stubborn bones with shears.

To Stuff a Boned Whole Fish

Fish that have been boned, either through the stomach or back, are easy to stuff with very simple ingredients such as mushroom duxelles, as shown above, or chopped herbs, as shown at right. Season the cavity and spoon in the stuffing. Don't overfill the cavity, because the fish shrinks during cooking and the stuffing tends to expand.

See Also
To make duxelles, page 111
To poach a small fish, page 110

HOW TO

Prepare a Whole Flatfish

When flatfish are cooked whole, the bottom white skin is usually scaled but left attached. Some cooks remove the top dark skin, while other cooks simply scale it and leave it on. European cooks always remove the top skin of Dover sole. Dover sole is very firm fleshed, so the skin can be yanked off in one piece; don't try this with flounder or American sole, however, because the flesh is soft and will tear. Instead, cut the skin off in strips with a flexible knife. If you're filleting whole fish, leave the skin on while preparing the fish; it's easier to remove the skin from the fillets than from the whole fish.

The Fringe

When the fins are trimmed off a flatfish, a thin strip of flesh containing small bones—called the fringe—is left attached to the fish. When the fish is carved, this strip is removed from both sides of the fish. In Europe, where flatfish are usually served whole, the fringe is sometimes cut off the uncooked fish, making carving easier. To do this, clean the fish as described here, but instead of cutting off the fins where they join the body, cut farther into the fish so that you cut away these small bones. Keep in mind, when serving, that the bottom fillets of a flatfish are smaller than the top fillets, so you may want to put one of each on each plate.

Preparing a Flounder

To Remove the Fins from Flounder

1. Cut off the tail (caudal fin).
2. Cut off the dorsal and ventral fins at the top and bottom of the fish.
3. Cut off the pectoral fins near the base of the head.

To Fillet the Flounder

If you're serving the fillets without the skin, there's no need to scale the fish. Nor is there any need to clean the fish unless you're saving the bones for fish broth. If you do clean the fish, it will be easier after you've removed the fillets.

1. With a flexible filleting knife held at an angle so as not to lose any flesh, cut around the base of the head from the top to the center of the fish. Cut a slit lengthwise down the center of the fish from the head to the tail, making sure you cut all the way down to the bone. (Most fish have a line running down the middle of the lateral line to guide you.)
2. Slide the knife under the top half of the fish. Pressing firmly against the knife so it stays flat against the bones and doesn't leave any flesh attached, slide it down the length of the fillet.
3. Turn the fish around and again slide the knife under the fillet, starting at the tail this time, until you completely detach it from the bones.
4. Peel back the fillet and detach it by cutting through the skin at the edge of the fish.

Two Types of Fillets

When you fillet a flatfish as shown here, you'll end up with four long fillets, two from each side of the fish. Professionals call these quarter-cut fillets. When you go to the fish market, you may see fillets that are joined together, with a thin strip running down the middle. These are called crosscut fillets. To obtain crosscut fillets from a whole flatfish, start sliding the fillet knife in from one side of the fish instead of starting in the middle along the lateral line. Continue sliding along the bones until you hit the spinal column. Carefully follow the contours of the spinal column, crossing over it to the other side of the fish. Remove this crosscut fillet in one piece.

5. Turn the fish around and repeat the operation to detach the second fillet.
6. Turn the fish over, so the white side is facing up, and remove the two bottom fillets. (If you're using the fish bones for broth, page 32, cut out the gills and pull out any remaining viscera.)

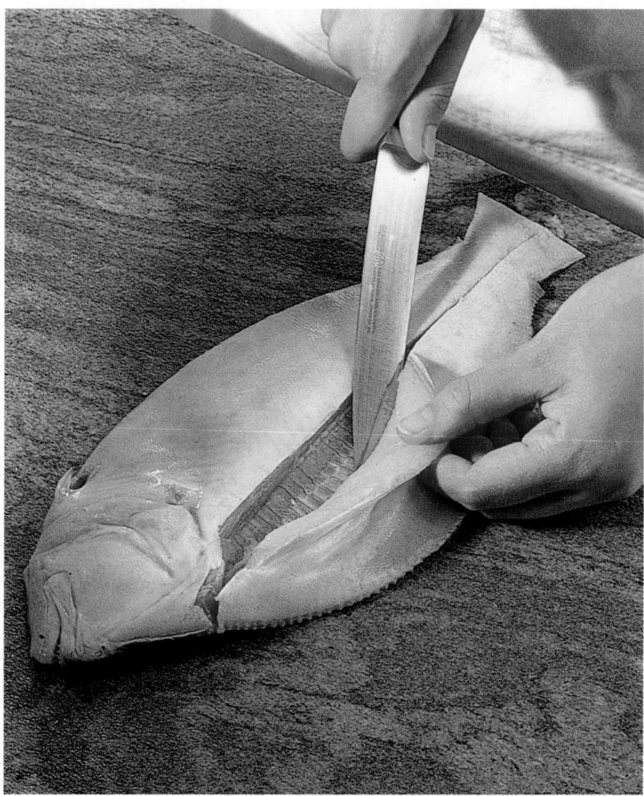

To Skin the Whole Flounder

1. Remove the dark top skin in strips with a long flexible knife. Always cut away from you.
2. Turn the fish around as necessary and work from another direction.
3. If you like, cut off the head before cooking. It's sometimes necessary to remove the head so the fish will fit into the pan.

To Skin Flounder Fillets

1. Place the fillet, skin side down, on the cutting board. Slide a flexible knife between the skin and fillet and hold the knife pressed flat against the skin. Hold the skin firmly in one hand and move it from side to side while pulling and moving the knife very slightly from side to side. Don't move the knife too much, or you'll cut through the skin.
2. Pull away the thin strip of fringe that runs down the side of each fillet. While the fringe is perfectly edible, it can look messy on the plate.

To Skin Dover Sole

1. Remove the fins as for a flounder. Make a shallow cut into the skin just above the tail.
2. Gently peel the skin back away from the cut. If you have trouble gripping the skin, grasp it with a kitchen towel.
3. Holding the tail down with a kitchen towel, pull the skin off in one rapid movement and discard it.

To Clean and Scale Dover Sole

1. Cut away the frilly edges along the sides of the fish.
2. Make a shallow slit along the stomach side of the fish, revealing the viscera. Don't cut too deep, or you'll damage the viscera and make the fish harder to clean.
3. Pull out any visible viscera—here, roe is being removed.
4. With a pair of sturdy scissors, cut out the gills at the base of the head.
5. Scale the white bottom side.
6. Press any remaining viscera out of the fish by running the back of a knife up along the side of the fish toward the opening. Rinse.

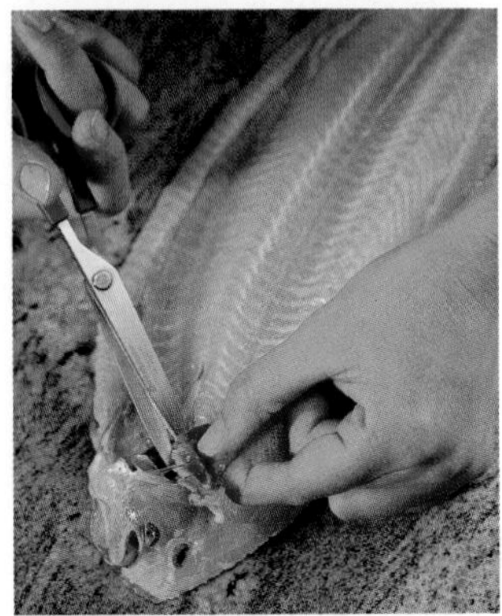

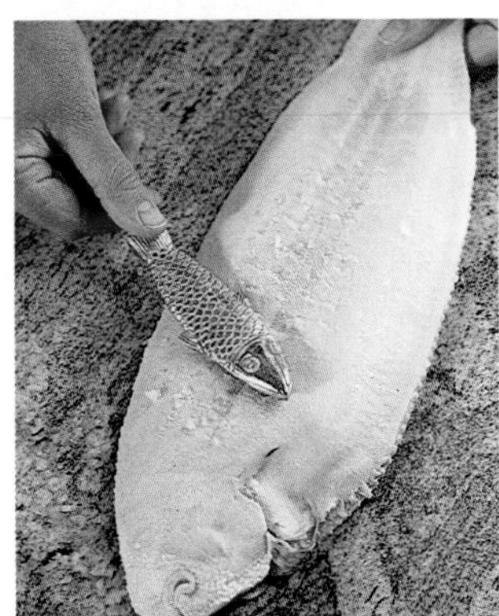

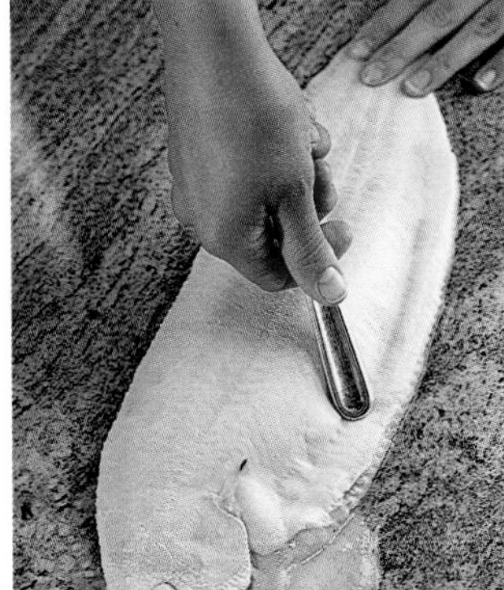

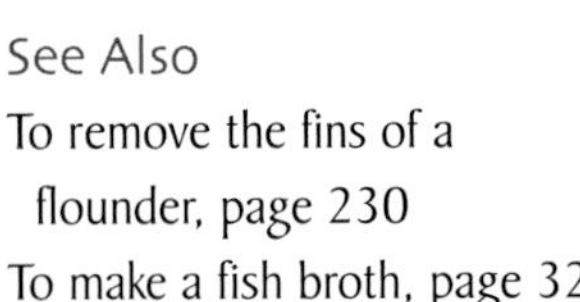

See Also

To remove the fins of a flounder, page 230
To make a fish broth, page 32

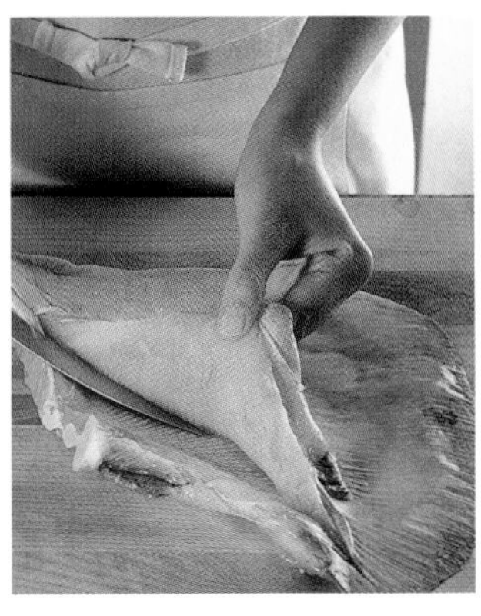

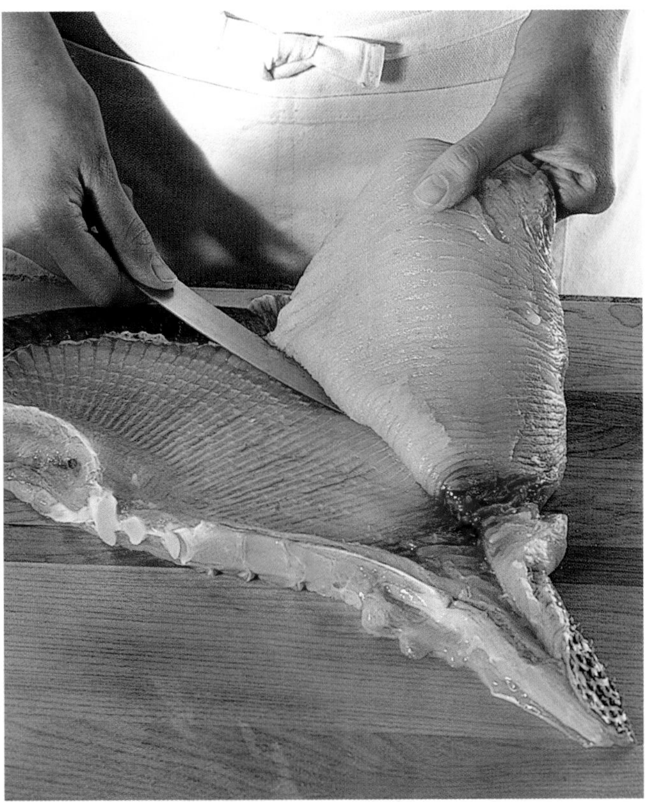

5. Holding the knife firmly, with the side of the blade pressed against the skin, move the skin (rather than the knife blade) rapidly from side to side while pulling it against the knife blade.

To Fillet and Skin Skate Wings

Nowadays, skate often comes already filleted, but if you do your shopping in an ethnic market, you may be confronted with the whole wings.

1. Place the skate wing white skin down on a cutting board. Slide a long flexible knife along the top of the bones that run along the inside of the skate wing.
2. Continue sliding the knife, pressing firmly so the blade rests against the flat cartilaginous bones and peeling back the fillet as you go, all the way to the outside rim of the wing.

3. Cut through the skin and detach the fillet. Turn the skate wing over and repeat on the other side.
4. To remove the skin, place the wing skin side down on the cutting board. Use a flexible knife to make a thin slice between the flesh and skin.

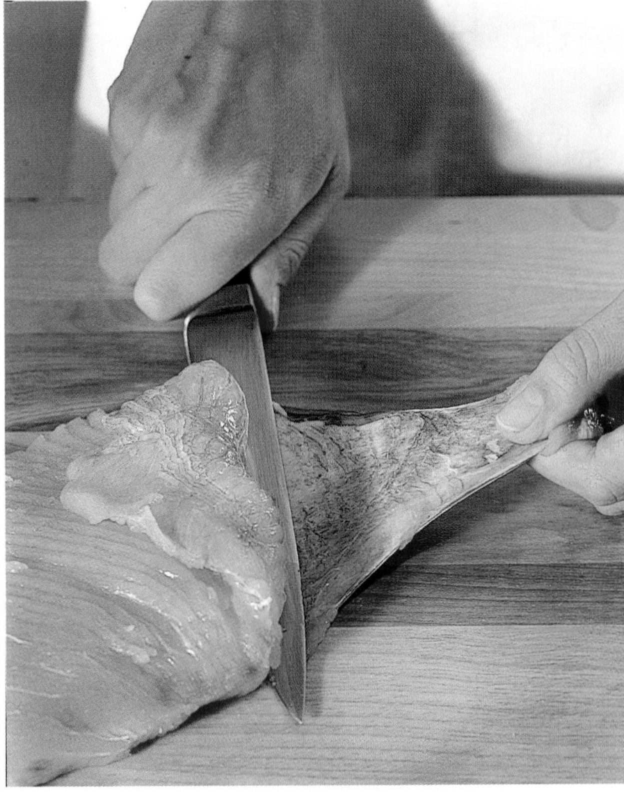

HOW TO

Scale, Clean, and Bone Whole Small Fish

Some very small oily fish such as fresh sardines and anchovies can be scaled, cleaned, and completely boned without a knife.

1. Rub the scales off each whole sardine (or other similar fish) with your fingers. It's easiest to work under cold running water.
2. Snap the head back, away from the body. The viscera should stay attached to the head.
3. Tug on the head and pull out as much of the viscera as you can. Discard the head and viscera.
4. Run your finger along the cavity, gently opening it as you go, to eliminate any remaining viscera. Rinse thoroughly under cold running water, making sure water gets into the cavity.
5. Bone the sardine by gently pulling the 2 fillets away from the backbone. Be careful—the little bones may poke you. If you like, leave the fillets attached to each other where they join at the back.

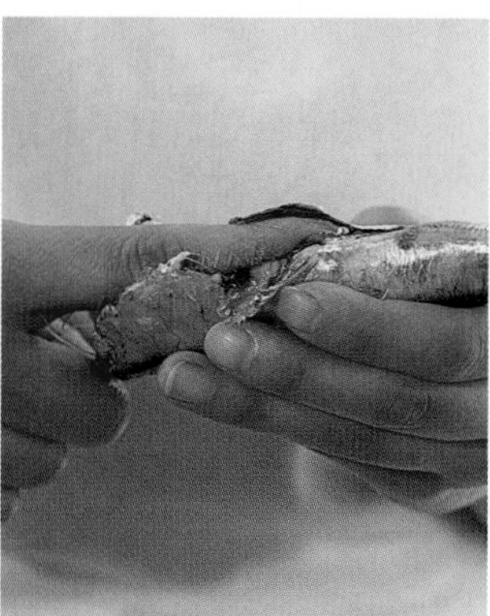

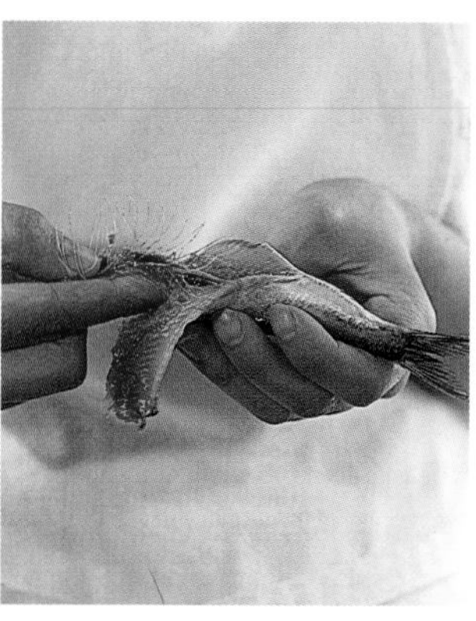

Related Glossary Entry

Marinate

HOW TO

Hot-Smoke Fish Fillets

Fillets from full-flavored and fatty fish such as the bluefish fillets shown here take very well to slow, gentle hot-smoking. Here, a small home smoker—essentially a metal box with a hotplate at the bottom—is used to smoke the fillets. Hot-smoked fillets are much tastier if they are first cured in brine.

Many cooks assume that smoked fish is so thoroughly cured that it will never go bad. This may almost be true if the fish has been heavily cured and then smoked for a prolonged period at high temperatures. But the best smoked fish is only lightly cured and lightly smoked, so it is still perishable, if not as perishable as fresh fish. Keep smoked fish in the refrigerator and eat it within a week. If you find yourself stuck with too much smoked fish (easy if you've smoked two large salmon fillets), wrap the fish tightly in plastic wrap and again in aluminum foil and freeze it.

The Best Woods for Smoking

Experienced smokers have not only their favorite cures but also their favorite woods. No one agrees on the very best wood, but everyone who smokes foods is emphatic that pine, eucalyptus, or other resiny woods give a strong unpleasant flavor to smoked foods. Fruitwoods, such as pear or apple, maple, hickory, and mesquite are the most popular in the United States.

Hot-Smoked Bluefish Fillets

1. Place sawdust (see Box) in a metal pan and place on the hotplate in the smoker. Adjust the hotplate so the sawdust smokes without flaming.
2. Arrange the fillets on the rack above the hotplate. Close the smoker. Smoke at 140° to 160°F for about 2 hours, until the fillets feel firm to the touch.
3. Present the bluefish on a platter with sour cream or crème fraîche on the side.
4. Or cut it into small pieces and present it Japanese style.

See Also

To fillet a bluefish, page 222

To brine fish fillets, page 240

Related Glossary Entries

Cure

Smoke

HOW TO

Cold-Smoke Fish Fillets

Cold smoking requires a smoker that allows the smoke to cool before the smoke comes in contact with the fish. Commercial cold smokers are expensive, but it's possible to improvise a cold smoker by buying some stovepipe and piping the smoke from a hot smoker into another container—here, the cardboard box the smoker was shipped in.

When the salmon comes out of the smoker, wrap it tightly in plastic wrap and aluminum foil (if it's not tightly wrapped, your whole house will smell of smoke) and refrigerate for at least twenty-four hours before serving. If the surface of the salmon seems wet when you take it out of the smoker, set it skin side down on a rack in the oven (with the oven turned off). Set a fan on the opened oven door and "blow-dry" the salmon for about four hours. Open all the windows, or the house will smell smoky for days.

Cold-Smoked Salmon

1. Set an oven rack or a large cake rack inside a large cardboard box on top of something that smoke can circulate around; here, I used folded cardboard, but you could also insert metal skewers through the sides of the box and place the rack on top. Place the cured fillets on the rack.

2. Insert one end of the stovepipe into the top of the hot smoker and the other end through a hole cut in the top of the cardboard box. (The hot smoker shown here came with an easy-to-remove chimney. I took out the chimney and inserted the stovepipe in the opening to connect the hot smoker and the cardboard box.) Tape the box shut. Cut a flap like a cat door, about 8 inches on each side, in the side of the cardboard box at the bottom to allow smoke to escape.
3. Place a pan of hardwood sawdust, such as maple or hickory, on the hotplate in the hot smoker as shown on page 237. Close the front of the hot smoker.

Smoke for about 4 hours, replacing the sawdust as it stops producing smoke, about every 30 minutes. Feel the pipe near where it enters the cardboard box—it should feel warm but not hot. If it feels hot, turn down the hotplate, or you may cook the fish.

To Slice and Serve Smoked Salmon

1. Slice off and discard the hard skin that has formed on the fillet. Thinly slice the salmon, starting about one third of the way up from the tail. Press a flexible knife firmly against the fillet and slice all the way to the tail. Start about ½ inch closer to the head end for each subsequent slice.
2. Serve, as shown here, with blini and crème fraîche.

See Also

To fillet a salmon, page 224
To hot-smoke fish fillets, page 237
To make blini, page 61
To dry-cure salmon fillets for cold smoking, page 239

Related Glossary Entries

Cure
Smoke

HOW TO

Cure Seafood (Brining and Salting)

Strong-flavored fish fillets, such as bluefish, benefit greatly from a short soaking—two or three hours—in brine before they are cooked. The brine draws out some of the blood remaining in the fish and helps make the fish's flavor milder. Brines often contain sugar as well as salt; the sugar softens the flavor of the fish but leaves the fish less salty than when salt is used alone. Once brined, the fish is usually smoked, but it may also be cooked by other methods, such as grilling.

Seafood, especially salmon, can also be dry-cured with salt, or, when making the Scandinavian specialty gravlax, with a mixture of salt, sugar, and dill. Gravlax is ready to eat directly after curing, but fish that is cured without herbs is often cold-smoked too, as for cold-smoked salmon. Gravlax is cured for forty eight hours in the refrigerator—and turned every twelve hours as it is cured—then is rinsed off.

To Dry-Cure Salmon Fillets for Cold Smoking

Follow the directions for making gravlax, at right, but leave out the herbs and, for fillets from an 8- to 10-pound salmon, use 2 cups salt and 2 cups sugar, kept separate. Layer and wrap the salmon fillets as described for gravlax, but start out using only the salt. Turn the salmon after 10 hours. After 10 hours more, rinse off the salt and repeat the cure for 9 hours, this time using only sugar. Turn after 9 hours, so you've cured with salt for 20 hours, with sugar for 18 hours, a total of 38 hours.

To Wet-Cure (Brine) Fish Fillets

Simmer salt, sugar, and water (use 2 cups salt and 1 cup sugar to each 4 cups water) until the sugar and salt dissolve. Let cool, then stir in ice to further cool the mixture. Soak the fish in the brine for 2 to 3 hours in the refrigerator.

To Dry-Cure Salmon Fillets for Gravlax

Dill is traditionally used for gravlax, but chefs from Sweden, where gravlax originated, and chefs from other countries have adapted the recipe to their own favorite ingredients, sometimes using different herbs, such as the tarragon shown here. When making gravlax, combine 1 cup sugar and 1 cup coarse salt for the fillets from an 8- to 10-pound salmon.

1. Spread a triple layer of aluminum foil large enough to wrap the whole fish with a quarter of the salt and sugar mixture. Place 1 salmon fillet skin side down on it. Sprinkle over another quarter of the salt and sugar mixture.

2. Cover the fillet with sprigs of tarragon and sprinkle with another quarter of the salt and sugar mixture.
3. Place the second fillet skin side up over the first and sprinkle with the rest of the salt and sugar mixture.
4. Wrap the fillets tightly in the foil.
5. Place a cutting board or a small baking sheet on the fillets and weight with something moderately heavy, such as 2 or 3 small pots. Refrigerate for 48 hours, turning every 12 hours.
6. When the cure is complete, remove and discard the tarragon. Quickly rinse the fillets and pat dry with towels.
7. Spread fresh chopped tarragon over the fillets. Serve the same way as you would smoked salmon.

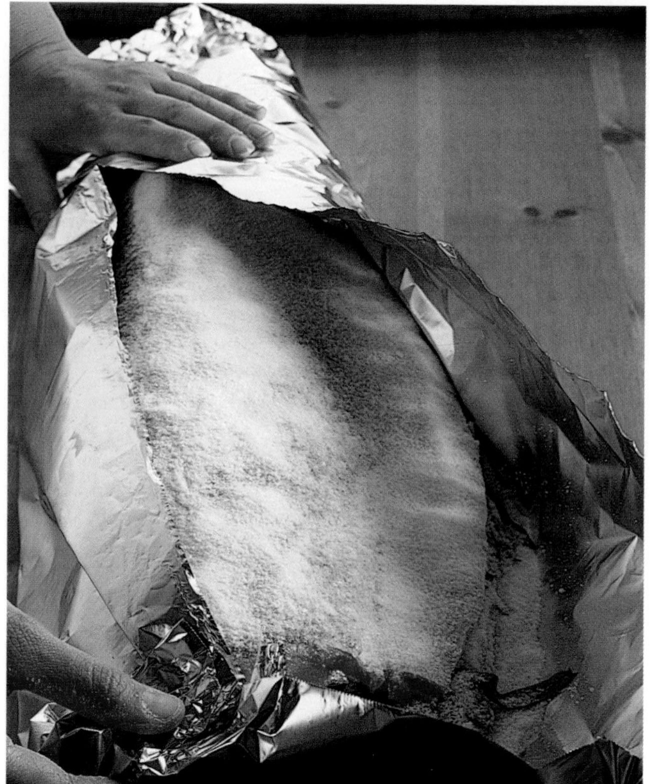

See Also

To fillet a salmon, page 224
To hot-smoke fish fillets, page 237
To cold-smoke fish fillets, page 238
To slice and serve smoked salmon, page 238

Related Glossary Entries

Cure
Smoke

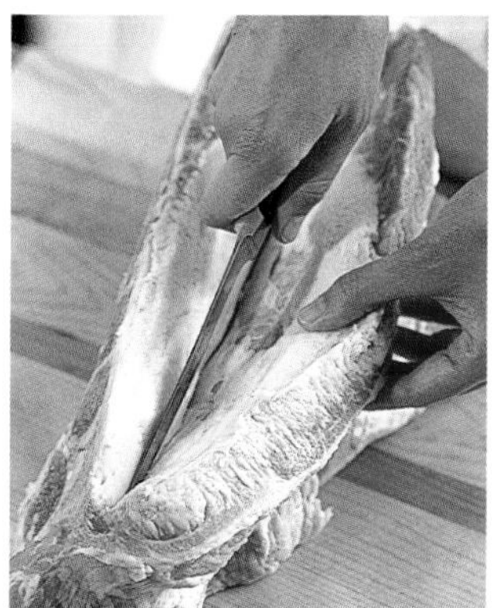

6. Once you've removed all the bones, turn the breast over, cut off the thick layer of fat that runs along one side of the breast, and trim off the layer of fat that covers the breast.
7. Cut the meat into 1- by 2-inch pieces.

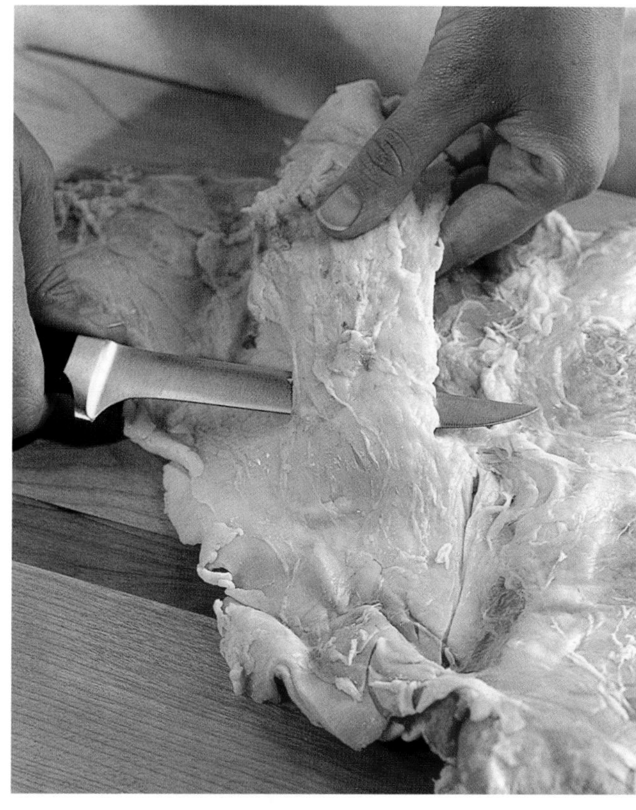

HOW TO

Trim and Cut Up a Breast of Veal for Stew

A veal breast is the least expensive cut of veal you can buy and, once boned, will make a delicious stew. The bones can be cooked along with the meat—they will add both flavor and an unctuous gelatinousness—or used for veal stock.

1. Trim off any excess fat from the outside and the edges of the veal breast.
2. Turn the breast over and cut along both sides of each rib, separating the meat from the bone as you go.
3. Slide the knife behind each rib, separating the meat from the bone.
4. Pull back the ribs, twisting and cutting until they pull away from the breast. Continue separating meat from those bones that remain along one side of the breast.
5. Cut between the cartilaginous bones that run along the center of the breast (the sternum) and the meat.

See Also

To make a veal stew, page 212

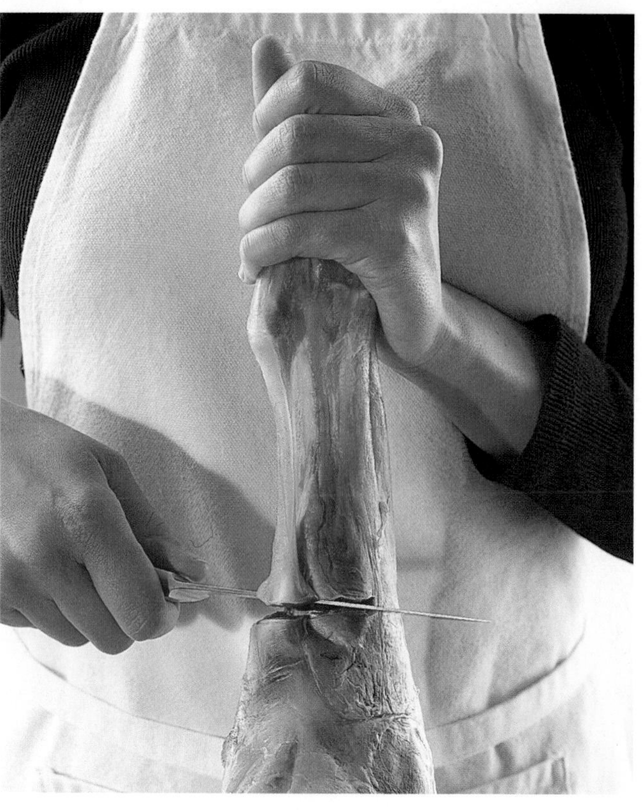

To Cut Off the Shank of a Leg of Lamb

1. Make a cut around the base of the shank (the lower part of the leg), going all the way down to the bone.
2. Trim off any meat left attached to the shank and save it for the roasting pan.
3. Cut off the shank with a hacksaw, leaving about 2 inches of bone protruding from the leg. (This makes a convenient handle when it comes time to carve.)

HOW TO

Trim and Partially Bone a Leg of Lamb

If you buy a leg of lamb from a butcher, he or she will remove the large piece of hipbone for you, but if you buy from a supermarket, you're likely to have to do this yourself. You'll rarely need to cut off the shank, but I show it here anyway, just in case.

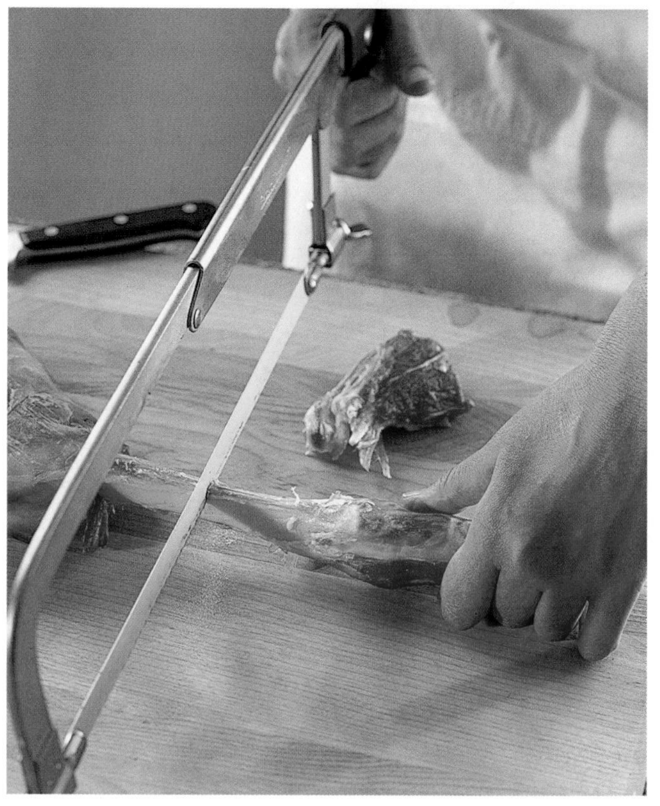

To Trim a Leg of Lamb

1. Work around the outside of the leg with a boning knife, cutting off the membrane and fat in strips, but leaving a thin layer of fat covering most of the leg to keep it moist. It's helpful when cutting off the membrane in strips to hold the strips taut while sliding the boning knife under the rest of the strip.
2. Cut along the inside of the hipbone, cutting around the bone and pushing the meat to one side as you go.
3. Continue cutting, separating the meat from the bone, following the contours of the bone and always keeping the knife against the bone.
4. Cut into the joint between the ball and socket that connects the hipbone to the end of the femur. Twist and pull out the hipbone.
5. Trim off any chunks of fat exposed by the boning.

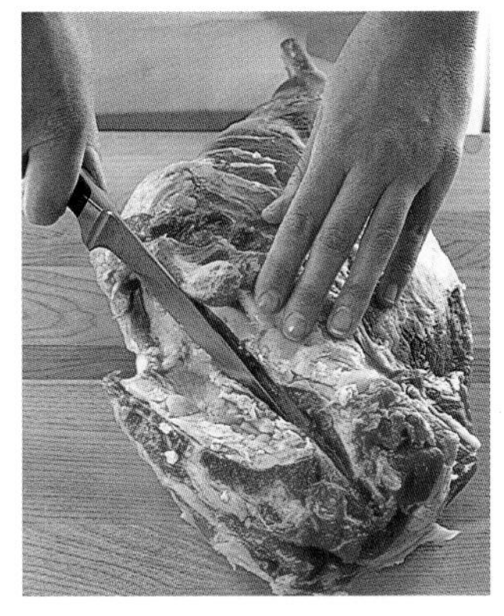

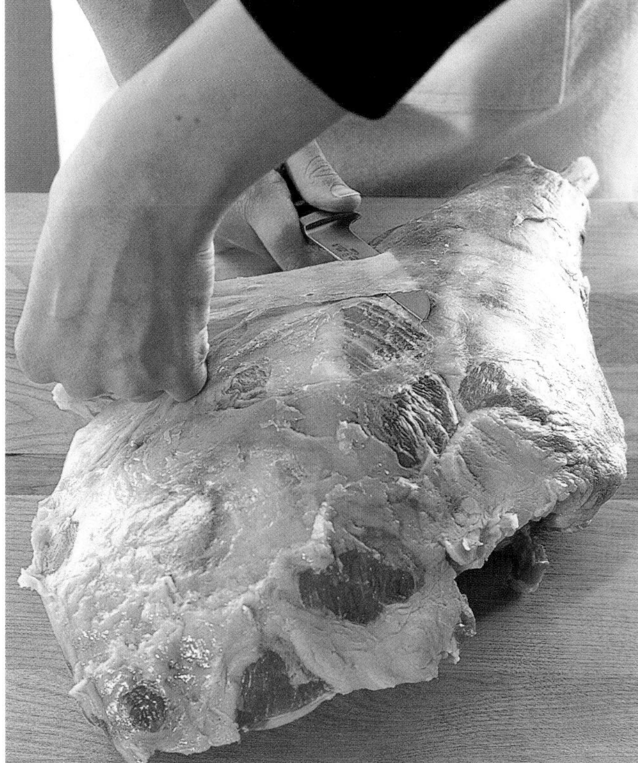

See Also

To tie up the leg of lamb and roast, page 184

Related Glossary Entry

Jus
Roasting

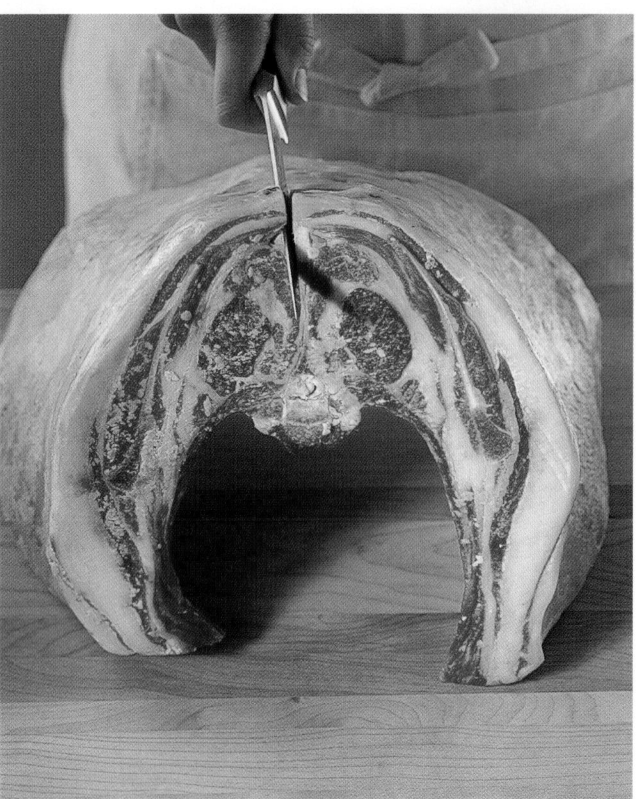

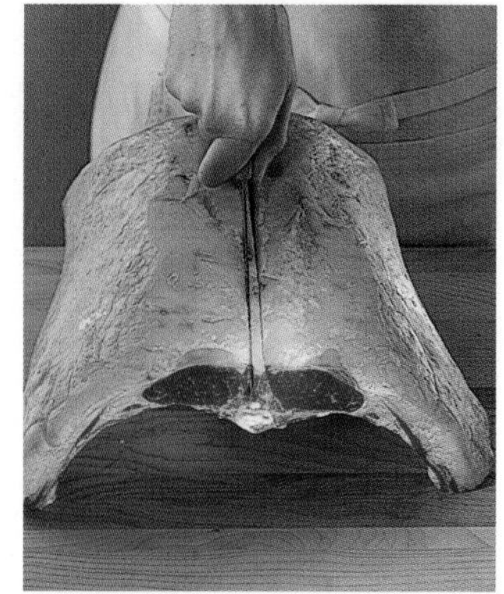

1. Feel the bones running along the back with your fingers and carefully slide a boning knife along one side of the bones, following the contours.
2. Turn the rack around and repeat on the other side of the bones that run up along the center.
3. Starting from the loin end, cut along each side of the center bones.
4. Continue cutting along each side of the center bones and around the backbone until you reach the base of the ribs.

HOW TO

Butcher a Double Rack of Lamb

The rack is the rib cage of the lamb. A rack of lamb is made up of either eight or nine ribs. The animal's hindmost rib or two are usually left attached to the saddle and three ribs are left attached to the shoulder on each side. Because lamb is sectioned crosswise (unlike pork, for instance, which is halved lengthwise), rack of lamb is sold to butchers and restaurants as a "double" rack, which is both sides of the rib cage attached to the backbone. When you buy a rack of lamb at the butcher or at a fancy supermarket, you're actually getting half of a double rack. Economical and/or ambitious cooks may want to buy a double rack of lamb and split, trim, and French it themselves. Although professional butchers cut a double rack in half with a saw, a better method, which detaches the backbone (which butchers call the chine bone) at the same time and leaves no bone dust, is to use a cleaver, as shown here.

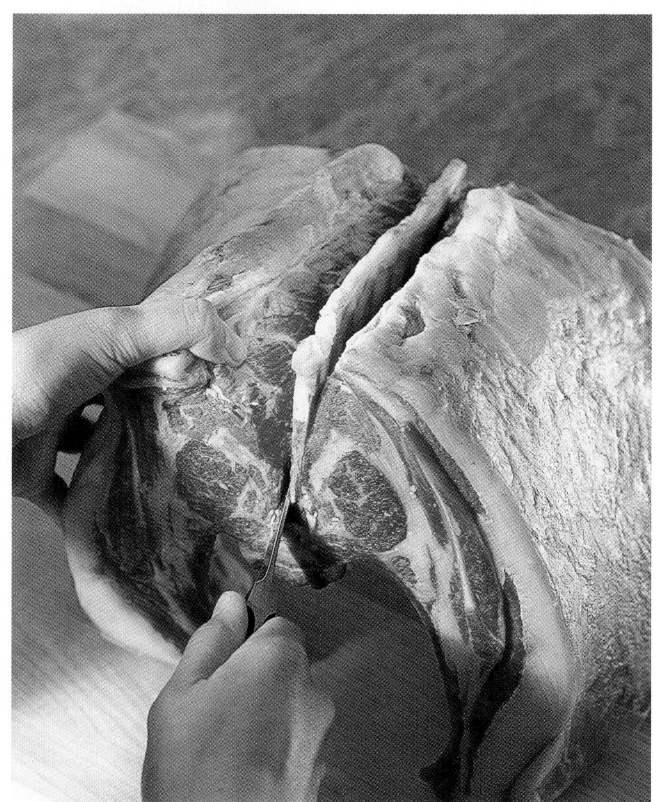

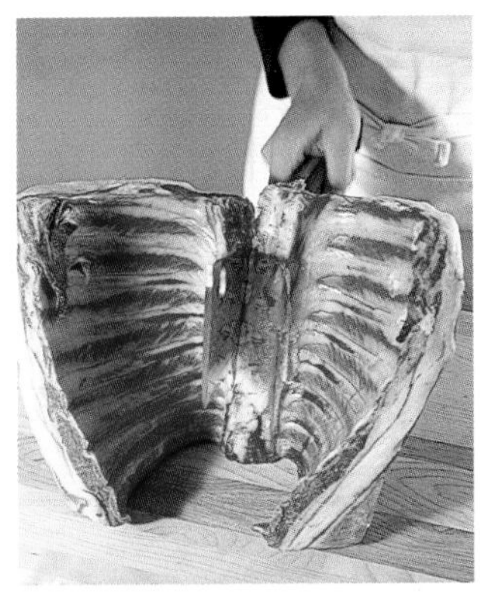

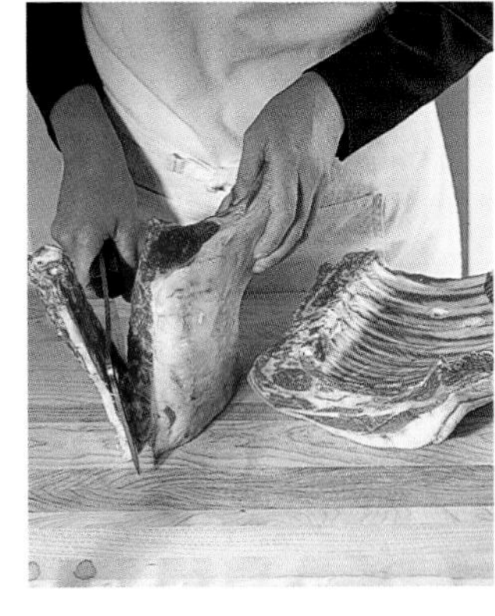

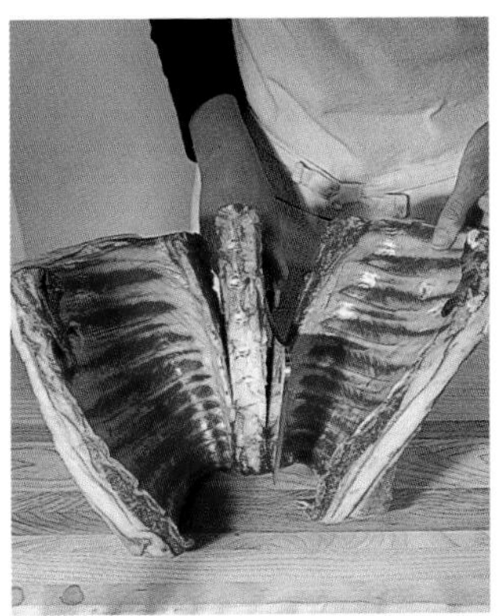

8. Go back to the first rack and use the cleaver to chop away the backbone. Chop up the backbone and save it for the roasting pan.

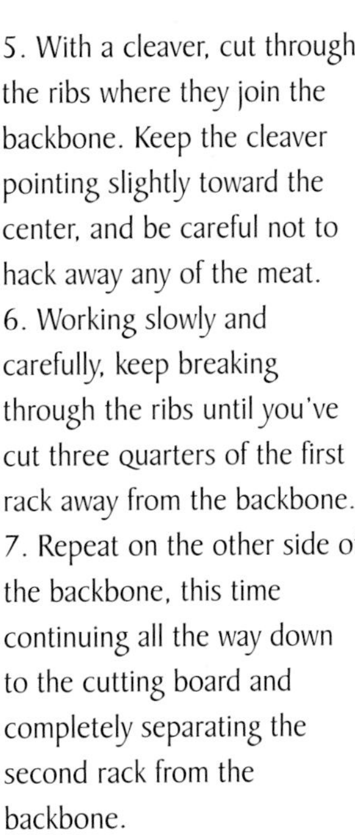

5. With a cleaver, cut through the ribs where they join the backbone. Keep the cleaver pointing slightly toward the center, and be careful not to hack away any of the meat.
6. Working slowly and carefully, keep breaking through the ribs until you've cut three quarters of the first rack away from the backbone.
7. Repeat on the other side of the backbone, this time continuing all the way down to the cutting board and completely separating the second rack from the backbone.

See Also

To trim and French a rack of lamb, page 246

To roast a rack of lamb, page 184

HOW TO

Trim and French a Rack of Lamb

Although many supermarkets and butchers sell racks already trimmed and Frenched—a decorative technique that exposes the tops of the rib bones—you may want to know how to do it on your own. When Frenching a rack, remove all the membrane and any trace of meat adhering to the ends of the ribs—any meat or membrane left on the bones will burn in the oven and look unattractive in the dining room. The technique shown here involves peeling off the meat covering the ends of the ribs in one clean piece, but you can also just scrape the meat and membrane off the rib ends. Whether you French the rack or not is purely an aesthetic decision; many cooks don't bother.

To Trim a Rack of Lamb

1. Lay the rack on the cutting board and make a cut through the fat down to the ribs on both ends of the rack. The cuts should be about 3 inches from the loin muscle, which is the largest section of meat that runs nearest where the backbone was. Slide the knife along and through the layer of fat, cutting down to the ribs and joining the two cuts on the ends.
2. Slide the knife along the ribs and detach the fat covering the ends of the ribs. Save it so you can trim off the meat and add it to the roasting pan to give extra flavor to the jus.

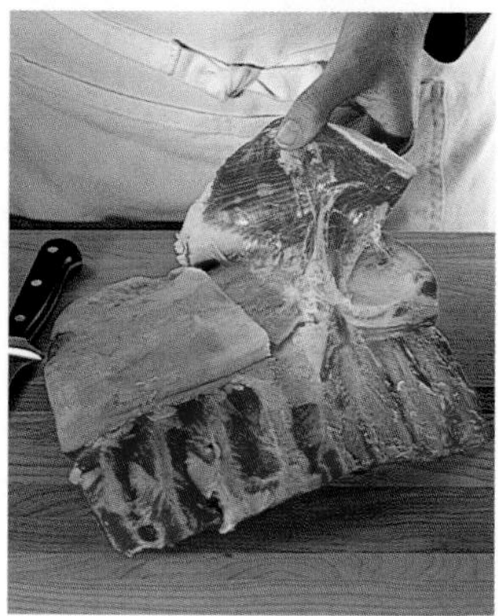

3. Cut crosswise through the layer of fat covering the loin. Be very careful not to cut into the meat. Peel off the thick layer of fat covering the shoulder end (the end shown in the photograph at left) and reserve. (This fat is removed so both ends of the rack cook evenly.)

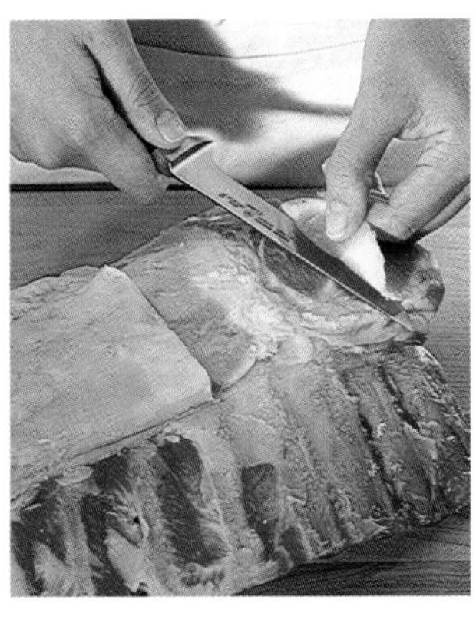

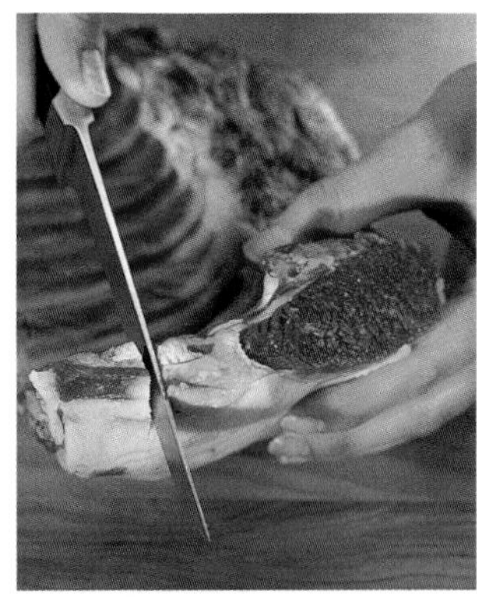

4. Slide the knife under the piece of shoulder blade cartilage left attached to the rack. Remove it and save for the roasting pan.

5. Trim off all but a ⅛-inch-thick layer of fat from the other side—the loin side—of the rack; discard. Be careful not to cut all the way down to the meat.

6. Cut out the yellow tendon that runs along the base of the rack.

7. Hold the rack flat against the cutting board and, with a cleaver, cut off the ribs at the line where you removed the first section of fat. Cut off one rib at a time, or the ribs may splinter.

To French a Trimmed Rack of Lamb

1. Make a notch in the fat lining the ribs, about an inch from the loin muscle, on both sides of the rack. The loin end is shown here.

2. Make a straight cut along the layer of fat, connecting the two notches. As you cut through the fat, cut all the way down to the bone and poke the knife between the ribs and out the back.

3. Turn the rack over and, using the holes that you've poked between the ribs as a guide, cut a line across bones and meat, cutting completely through the membrane that covers each rib and scraping the membrane from the bone thoroughly at that point.

4. Cut through the membrane that lines the inside of each rib and push it to either side of the rib.

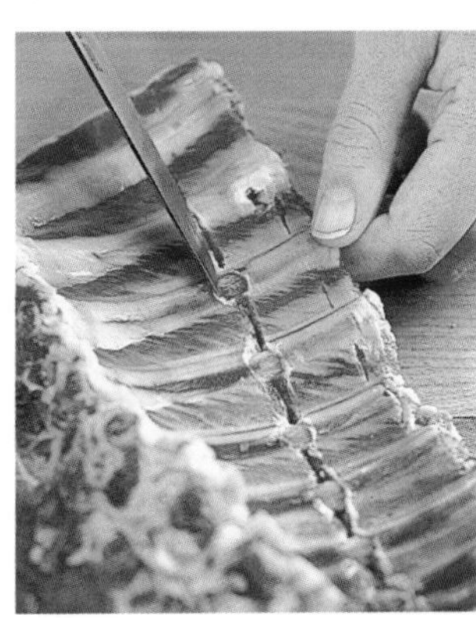

5. With the back of the knife, push the membrane farther, and even slightly around, each side of the rib. Don't cut through the membrane where it attaches to the side of the rib—just peel it back as far as possible.

6. Holding the rack up on end, continue to separate the top strip of meat and fat from the eye of the meat by scraping against the ribs and pushing the strip away from the eye.

7. Grip the strip firmly (a kitchen towel can be helpful here) and peel it away from the rib ends.

8. Trim off any thick layers of fat still left attached to the rack.

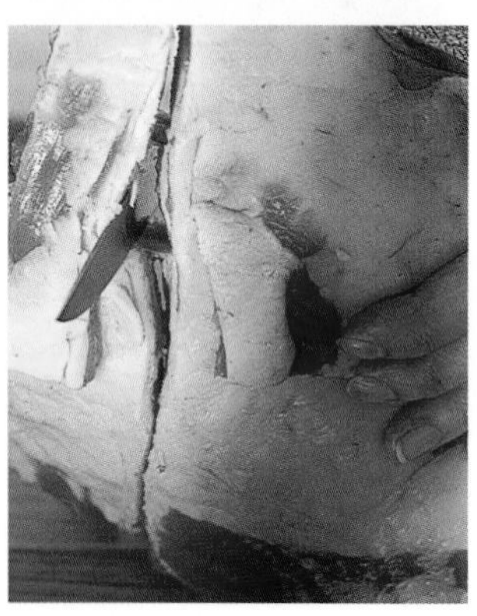

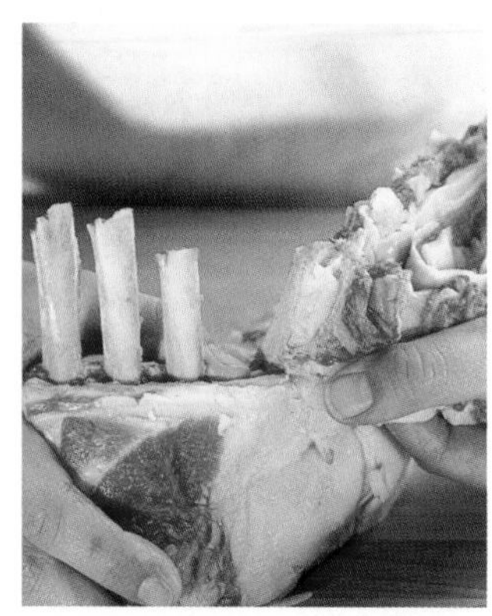

To French a Rack of Pork

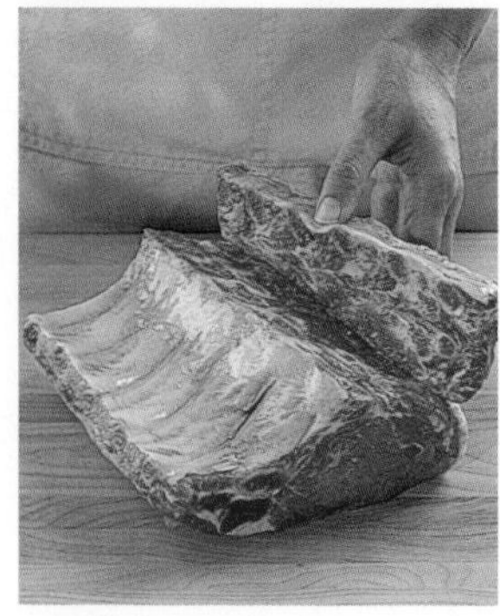

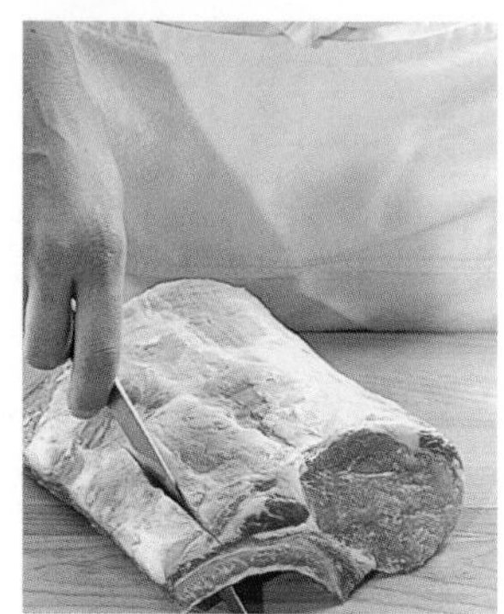

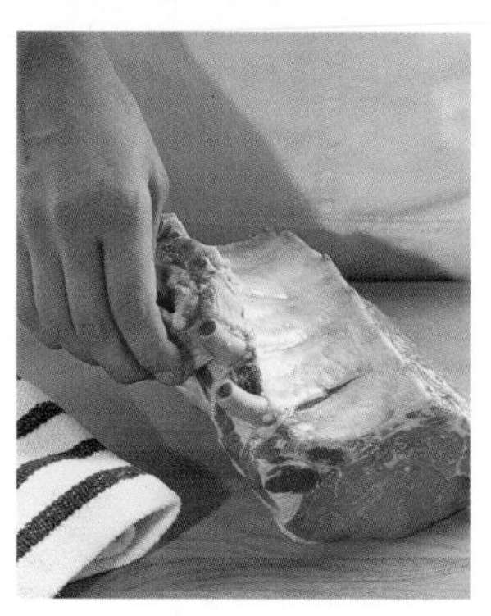

A rack of pork is Frenched in the same way as a rack of lamb except that the chine, which has usually been left attached, must be removed.

1. Have the butcher saw off the chine bone (the spinal column left attached to the ribs when the animal was butchered) so that you'll be able to slice the roast. Here, it was cut off, but it is being held to show what it is and where it was attached.
2. Cut through the meat between the ribs, about an inch in from the ends.
3. Peel the meat and fat away from the rib ends, scraping the bones with a knife to remove the meat and membranes.

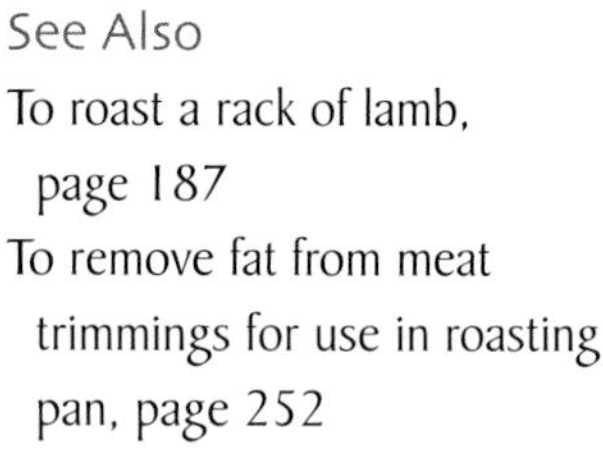

See Also

To roast a rack of lamb, page 187

To remove fat from meat trimmings for use in roasting pan, page 252

To Cut a Rack of Lamb into Chops

If you want to grill or sauté chops from a rack of lamb, trim the rack as described on pages 246 and 247. For a dramatic effect, you can also French the rack. (The rack shown here has not been Frenched.) Instead of roasting the rack, slice between the ribs to make chops or slice between every other chop to make double chops.

1. For single chops, cut between each rib.
2. Trim any excess fat off the outside of the chops with a paring knife or boning knife.
3. To make double chops, cut between every other chop.
4. If you wish, cut one of the bones out of each double chop.

See Also

To grill lamb chops, page 193
To sauté lamb chops, page 195
To roast a rack of pork, page 189
To roast a rack of lamb, page 187

HOW TO

Trim and Roast a Saddle of Lamb

The saddle is the section of lamb just behind the rack. To visualize it, put your hand on the small of your own back and work up to where your ribs start—that whole lower section, including the two bottom ribs, is equivalent to the saddle on a lamb. When a saddle is halved lengthwise and then each half is cut crosswise into chops, the chops are called loin lamb chops. Loin lamb chops look like miniature T-bone steaks (T-bones are, in fact, the same cut) and contain two main muscles, the outside muscle—or loin—and a smaller muscle that runs along the underside of the saddle—the fillet, or tenderloin. A saddle is one of the most luxurious cuts of lamb, rivaling even the better known rack.

Here are instructions for trimming a saddle of lamb. Some butchers roll up the flaps on either side of the saddle, leaving them attached (on a steer, they would be the flank steaks), but here, I remove and trim them to use them to contribute additional pan drippings.

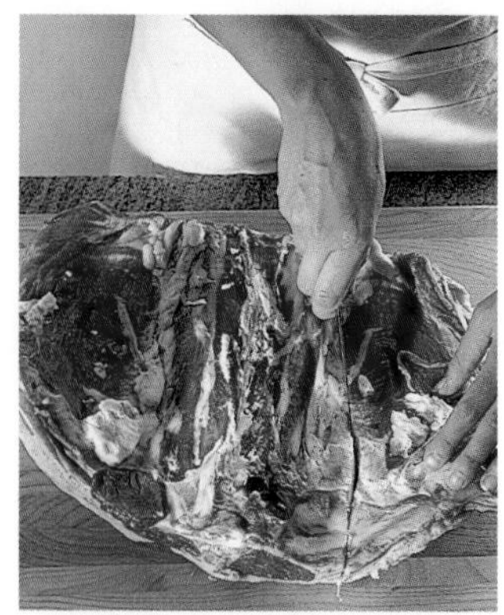

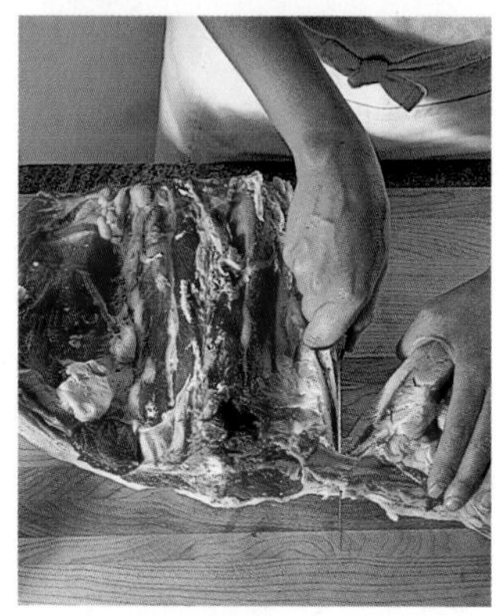

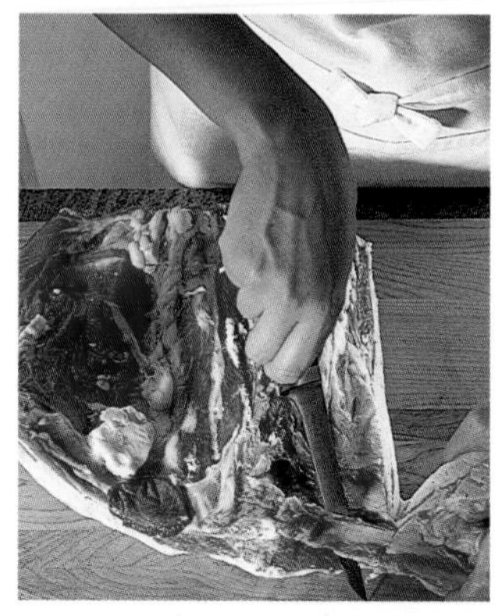

To Prepare a Saddle of Lamb

1. Place the saddle on the cutting board so that the underside faces up. Pull away and cut off any obvious chunks of fat.
2. Make a small cut at one end of the saddle flaps about ½ inch from the loin muscle. (The muscle is exposed at either end of the saddle.) Be careful not to cut into the loin. Make another cut in the same flap at the other end of the saddle, again about ½ inch from the loin.
3. Join the 2 cuts to free most of the flap. Cut around the rib (or ribs) at the top of the saddle.
4. Carefully cut away any meat attached to the rib(s). Slide the knife under the rib(s) and twist it (them) off. Save for the roasting pan.

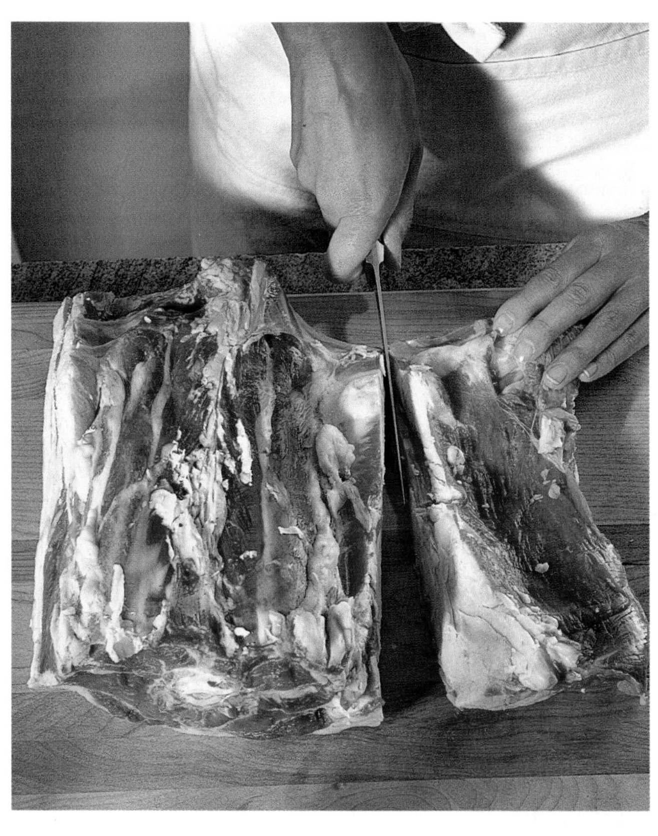

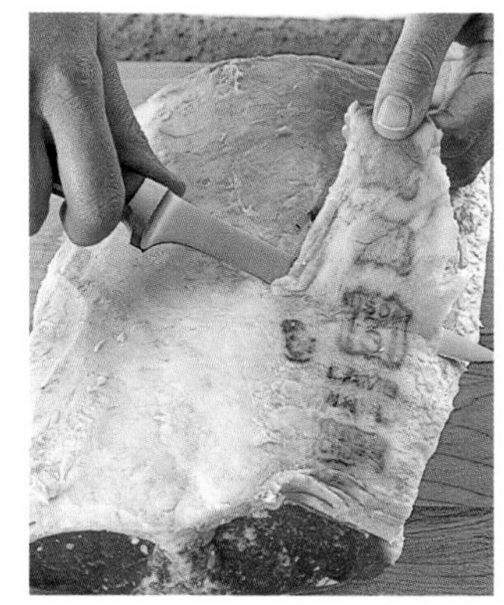

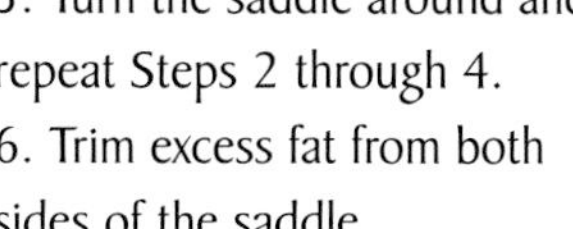

5. Turn the saddle around and repeat Steps 2 through 4.
6. Trim excess fat from both sides of the saddle.
7. Trim the membrane that covers the fat on the rounded, outer side of the saddle: Cut a small strip of membrane and hold it taut. With the blade angled up toward the membrane and away from the meat, slide the knife under the membrane, cutting it off in long strips.
8. Trim the fat to a thin layer. Don't cut all the way down to the meat or through the thin silver membrane that covers it.

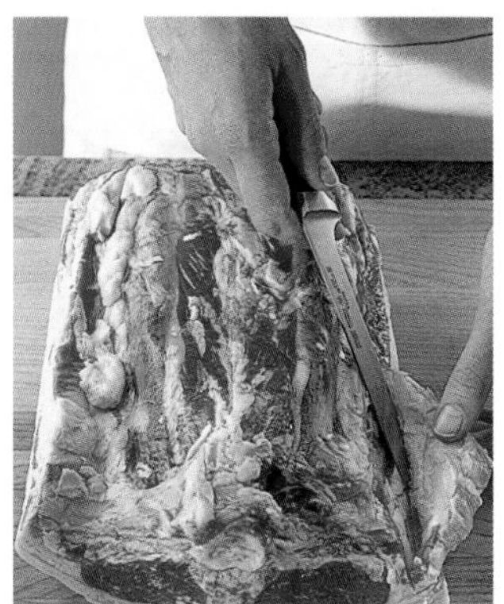

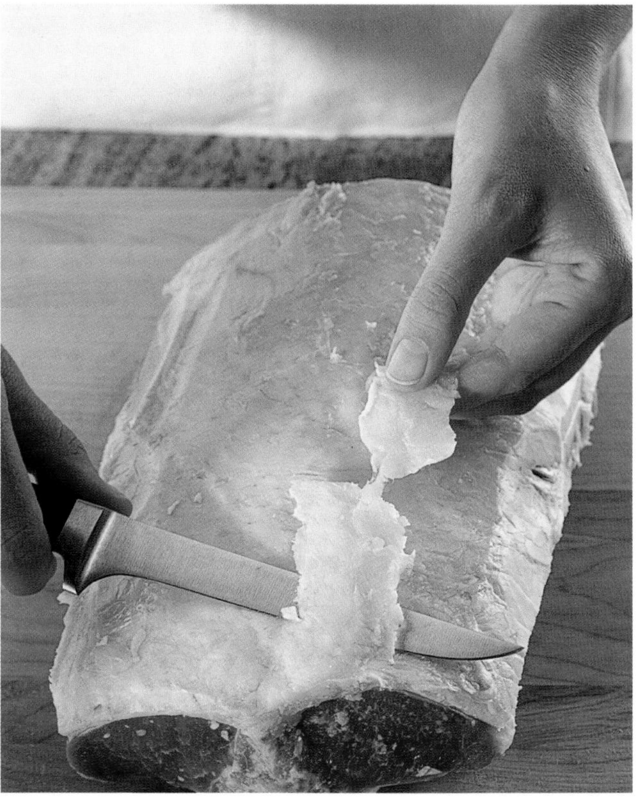

To Roast a Saddle of Lamb

The flaps that were trimmed off (see page 250) give extra flavor to the roasting juices.

1. Place the flaps fat side down on the cutting board and separate as much meat as possible from the fat; discard the fat.
2. Slice the meat into small strips.
3. Tie the trimmed saddle with string to help it hold its shape.
4. Spread the strips of flap meat, the reserved ribs, and a few peeled garlic cloves over the bottom of a roasting pan. Season the saddle with salt and pepper and set it on top of the trimmings and garlic. Roast for 25 minutes in a 425°F oven, or until a thermometer stuck into one of the loins reads 125°F (between rare and medium-rare). Take the saddle out of the roasting pan and keep warm while you prepare a jus, then serve.

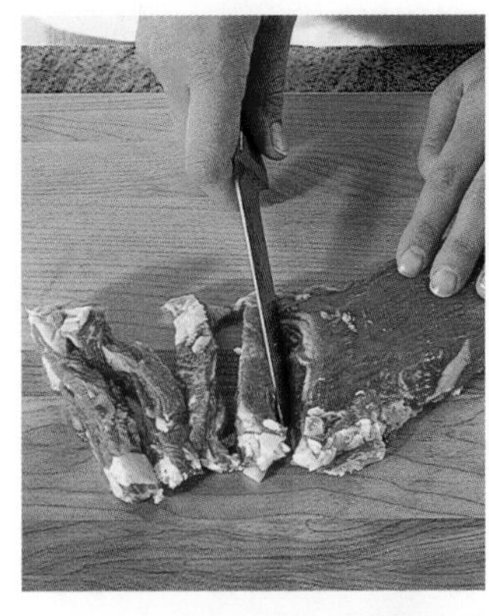

See Also

To roast a rack of lamb and make jus, page 187

To Carve a Roast Saddle of Lamb

A roast saddle of lamb can be carved in one of two ways. The first method, and perhaps the most elegant, is to slice the loin and tenderloin lengthwise into strips. The other method is to carve out the loin and tenderloin and then cut the loin into round slices called noisettes, and the tenderloin into thin strips.

To carve a lamb saddle into strips

1. Hold the saddle with a fork and slide a carving knife along the right side of the center strip of bones, keeping the knife against the bone. Cut around the small ridge at the base of the bones.
2. Cut the first loin crosswise in half. (If you want to serve the meat in very long strips, skip this step.)
3. Trim off the top layer of fat and slice the loin into strips.
4. Continue slicing off strips, as shown here, until you run into bone.

To carve a lamb saddle into rounds (noisettes)

1. Slice along both sides of the center bone. Remove both loins, each in one piece.
2. Slice the loins into small rounds.

To carve lamb tenderloins

1. After carving off both loins, turn the saddle over and cut the small tenderloin crosswise in half. Slide the knife under the tenderloin halves and cut them away from the bones. Repeat on the other side to remove the second tenderloin.
2. Because the tenderloins are so small, cut them lengthwise into strips rather than in rounds.

HOW TO

Cut Up a Rabbit

A rabbit is usually cut up into two thighs, the saddle, and the forelegs and rib cage. If the rabbit is large, the saddle can be cut crosswise in half so the rabbit will feed four. If the rabbit is small, or your guests are hungry, a thigh and half a saddle can be served to each person. The forelegs and rib cage can be cooked along with the rest of the rabbit—they'll enrich the braising liquid—and they too can be served at a family meal (they also make great left-overs), but they're usually not served at more formal dinners. Because most people aren't familiar with the anatomy of a rabbit, it's often confusing to be confronted with a piece of rabbit saddle with bones seemingly going in all directions. For this reason, it helps to bone the saddle before you cook it.

The rabbit shown here is an older rabbit, suitable for braising. Smaller rabbits are cut up in the same way but cooked for less time, in the same way as chicken—sautéed or like a stew.

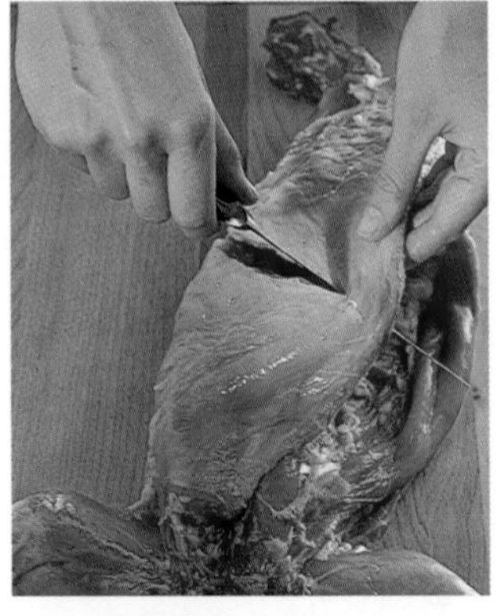

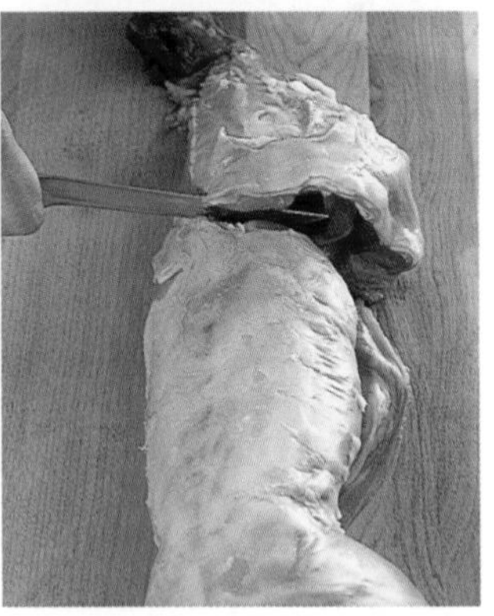

To Cut Up a Rabbit

1. Pull any clumps of fat out of the inside of the rabbit.
2. Cut through the skin that attaches one of the forelegs to the rabbit. Remove the foreleg. Repeat to cut off the other foreleg.
3. Feel along the ends of the ribs on the sides of the rabbit. Cut between the second and third ribs (counting from the hind end of the rabbit) on one side.
4. Cut all the way down to the backbone. Repeat on the other side.
5. Cut off the whole rib cage and neck section where you've cut down to the backbone between the ribs.
6. Cut the rib cage into chunks with a cleaver so that it will render its flavor in the rabbit stew or sauté, or in a broth.

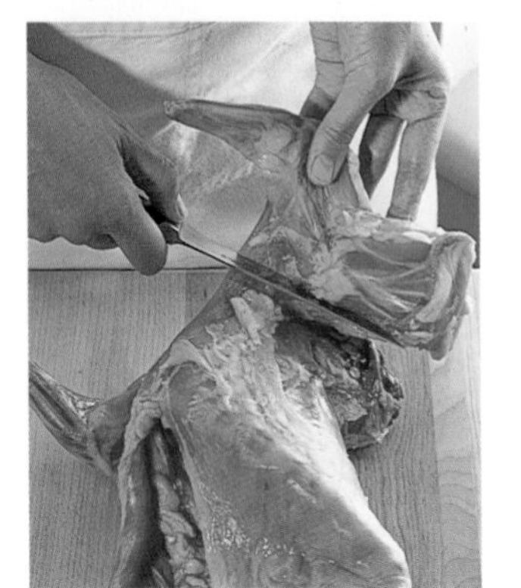

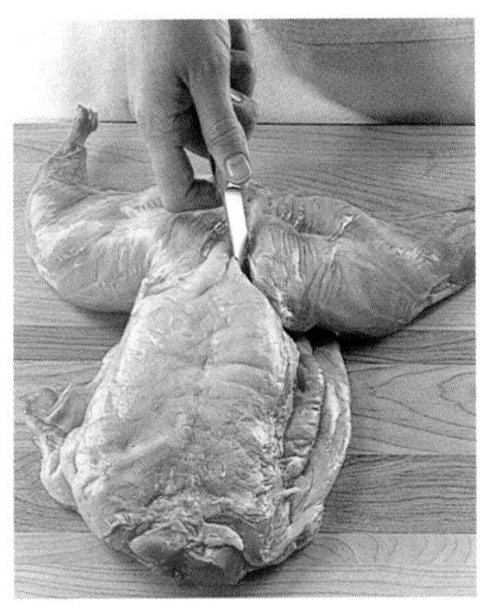

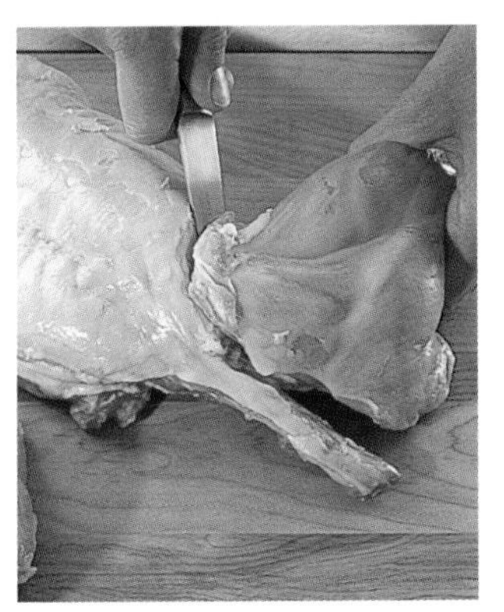

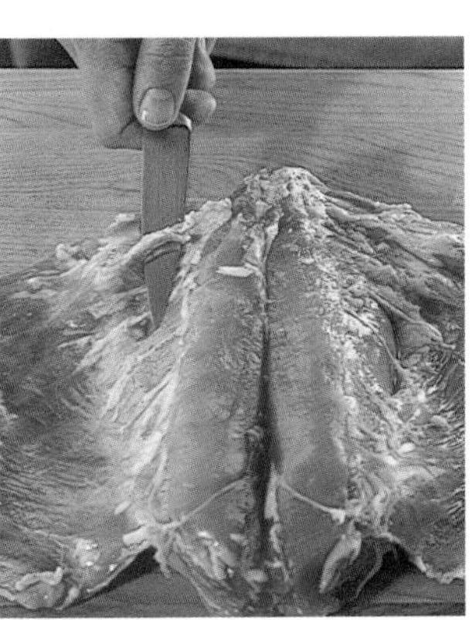

7. Place the rabbit, back up, on the cutting board. Cut along the tailbone, keeping the knife against the bone, and detach the thigh.
8. Repeat to cut off the second thigh, starting this time at the end of the tailbone.
9. Cut the tailbone away from the saddle with a cleaver.
10. Turn the saddle over, spread out the flaps on its sides, and slide a small knife under the 2 ribs left attached to the meat to free them from the flesh. Snap the ribs off with your fingers.
11. Season the inside of the saddle with salt and pepper. Herbs or other stuffings could also be added at this point.
12. Fold the flaps over the inside of the saddle.
13. Tie up the saddle with string, then cut it in two with a large heavy chef's knife. You may need a cleaver to cut through the backbone.
14. Slide a small knife against the underside of the small pelvic bones left attached to the thighs.
15. Remove the bones. (Save for adding to the rabbit as it is cooking or for broth.)

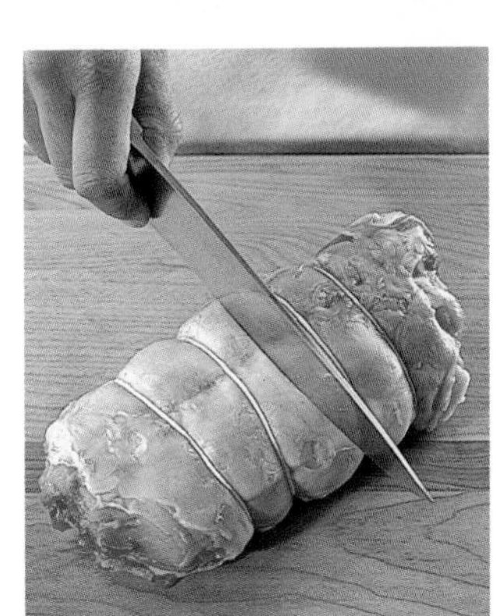

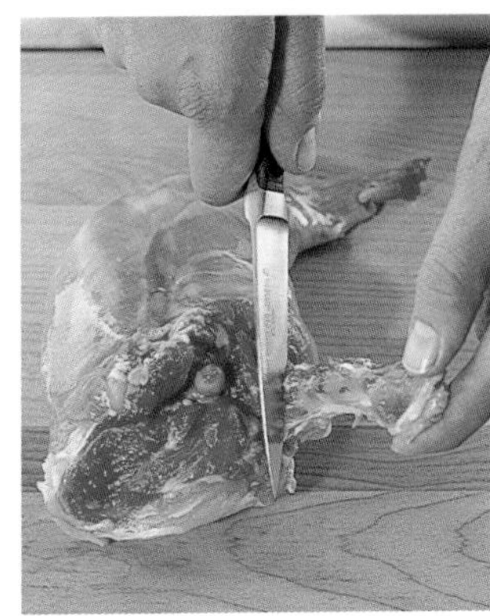

To Bone a Saddle of Rabbit

1. With the back of the saddle on the cutting board, unfold the flaps and, with a small paring knife, starting from the center, cut under the small muscles—the tenderloins—that run the length of the saddle.
2. Scrape against the small bones that stick out from the backbone while pushing the tenderloins to the ends of the bones. (There's no need to detach the tenderloins.)
3. Slide the knife under the bones protruding from the backbone on each side so the bones are detached from the larger loin muscles.

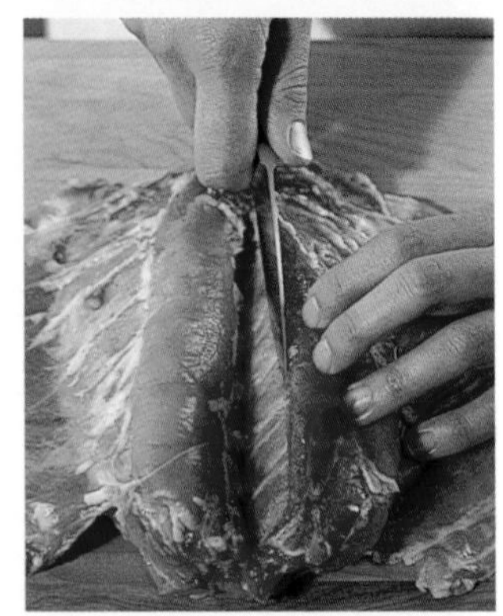

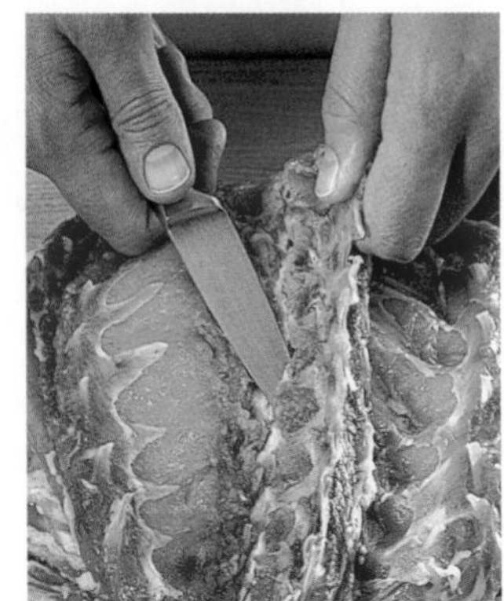

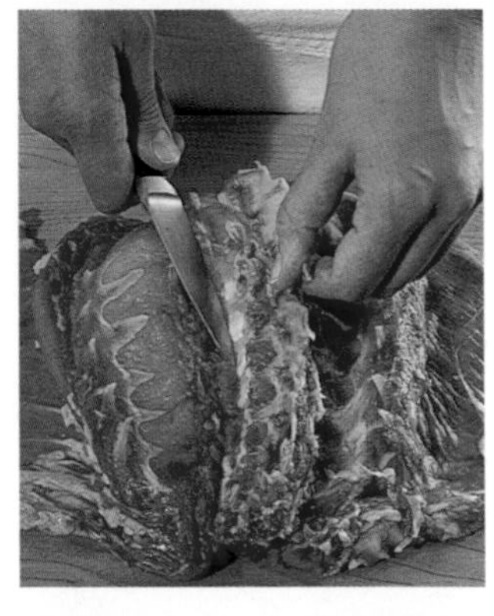

4. Work the knife around the backbone. You'll find another ridge of bones that you'll need to cut around and under. Keep the knife against the bone so you don't cut through the skin.
5. Continue cutting around the backbone until you see the white underside of the skin lying under the bone. Avoid cutting through the skin (a small hole or two is not serious).
6. Lift up the backbone and cut it away from the skin. To do this, you'll need to cut through the cartilaginous tips of the bones, leaving them embedded in the skin.
7. Work along the backbone, cutting through the bones one by one until you detach the entire backbone. The saddle is now ready to be stuffed and tied.

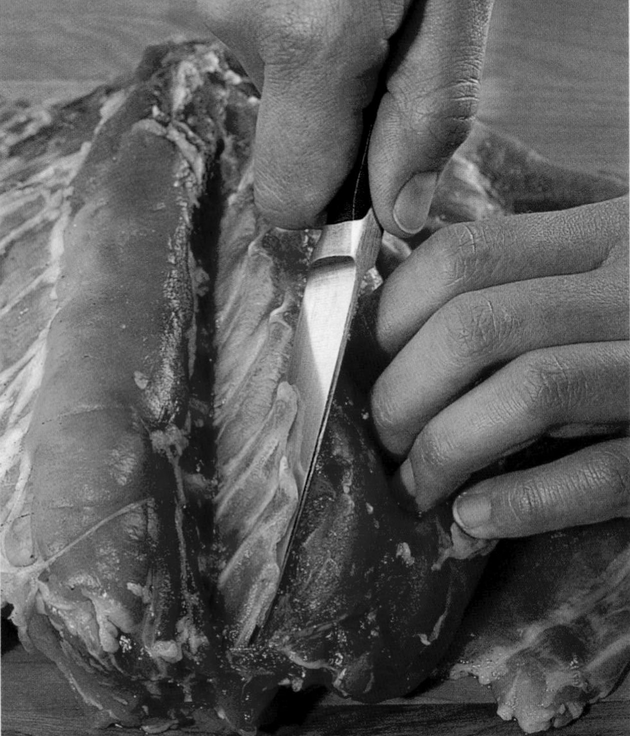

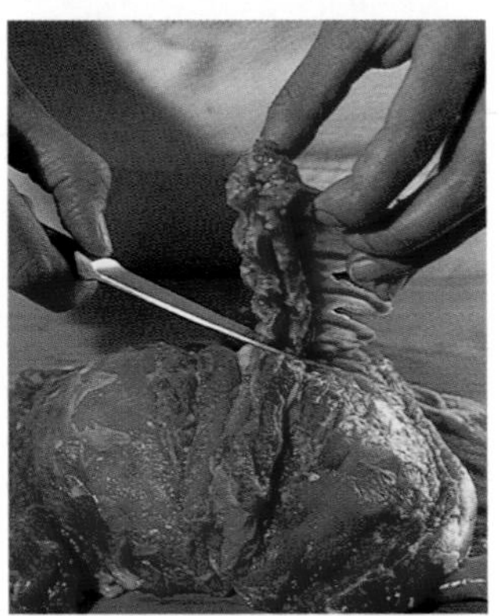

See Also
To braise a rabbit, page 257
To stuff and tie a rabbit saddle, page 257
To make a chicken sauté, page 157
To make a chicken stew, page 154

HOW TO

Prepare and Braise a Large Rabbit

Small young rabbits, the kind most often available at butchers and in supermarkets, can be cooked in the same way as chicken—simply sautéed or short-braised until cooked through. Large rabbits, however, need a much longer cooking time to become tender. The flavor of a long-braised rabbit is incomparable.

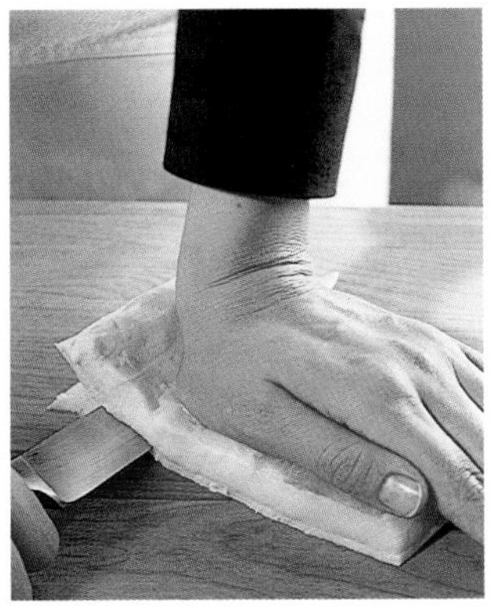

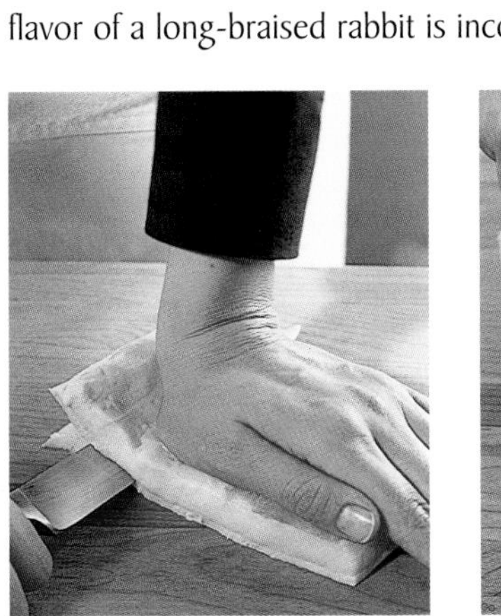

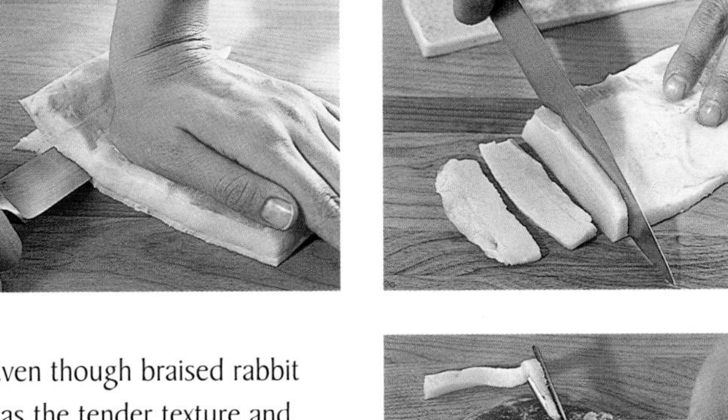

Even though braised rabbit has the tender texture and depth of flavor of the best stews, larding, while optional, will keep it especially moist and will contribute to its melting texture.

1. Prepare "lardons" by cutting the rind off a piece of fatback. (Some fatback is sold with the rind already trimmed off.)
2. Cut the fatback into slices about ¼ inch thick, then cut each slice into ¼-inch-wide strips.
3. To interlard the rabbit thighs, clamp a lardon in an interlarding needle and pull it firmly through the flesh.

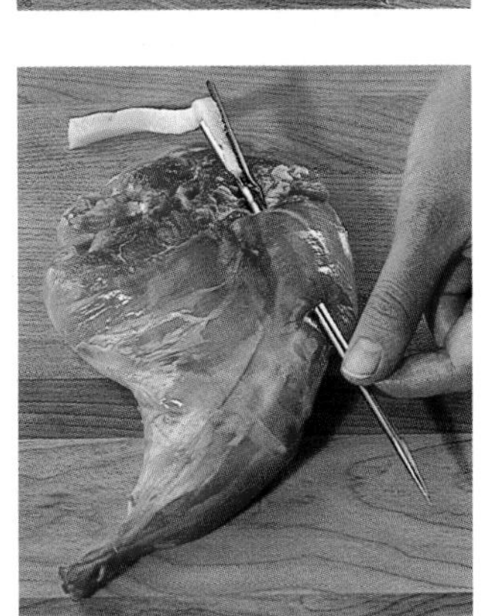

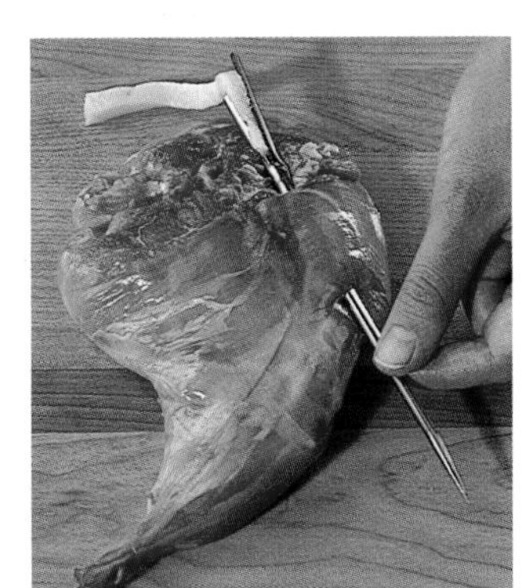

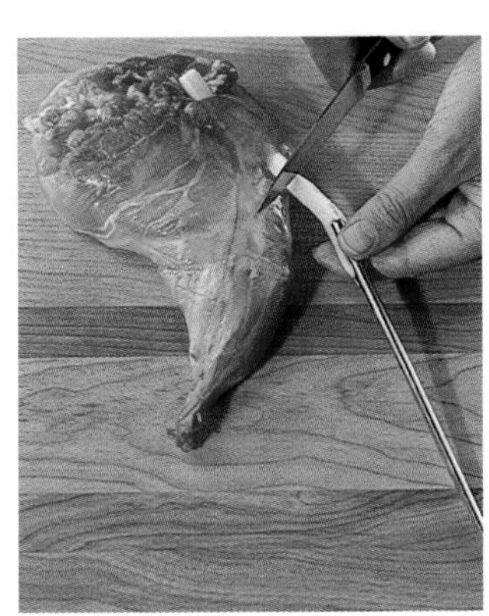

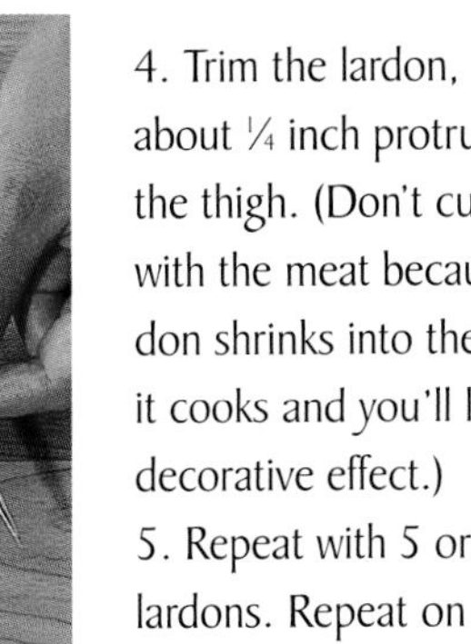

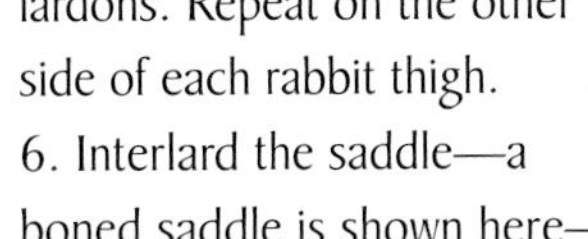

4. Trim the lardon, leaving about ¼ inch protruding from the thigh. (Don't cut it off flush with the meat because the lardon shrinks into the meat as it cooks and you'll lose the decorative effect.)
5. Repeat with 5 or 6 more lardons. Repeat on the other side of each rabbit thigh.
6. Interlard the saddle—a boned saddle is shown here—starting on the inside.
7. Place 2 sage leaves along the center of the saddle (or sprinkle the saddle with your favorite chopped herbs, if you like). Season the inside with salt and pepper.

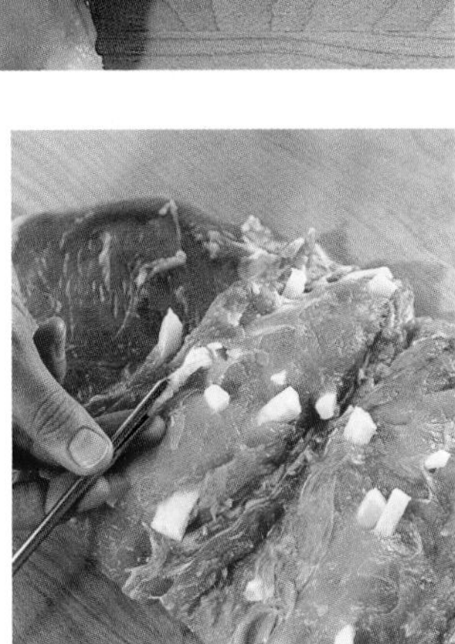

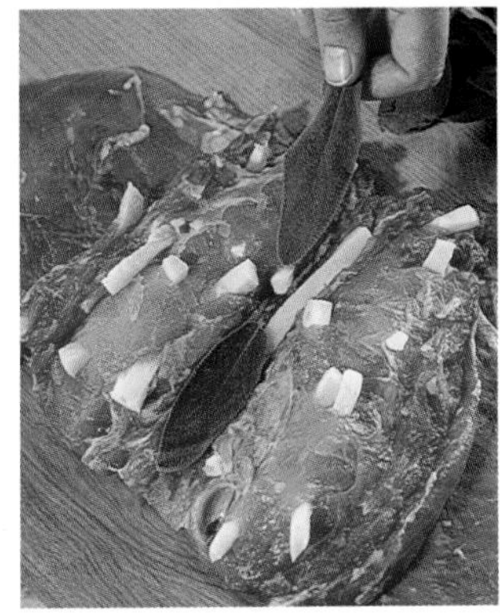

8. Fold the flaps inside the saddle and form the saddle into a roll. Lard the outside and tie up with string.
9. Coarsely chop the forelegs and any bones left from boning and sectioning the rabbit. Combine the bones in a heavy-bottomed pot with coarsely chopped aromatic vegetables (*mirepoix*).
10. Place the thighs and the saddle on top of the vegetables.
11. Roast in a 375°F oven until the top of the rabbit is well browned. Turn the rabbit pieces over and continue roasting until the other side is well browned.
12. Check the bottom of the pot during roasting to make sure the juices don't burn. If the juices look too brown, as though they're on the verge of burning but the rabbit hasn't finished browning, add a little broth or water to the pan. Continue cooking until the rabbit is well browned and the juices in the pan have caramelized.
13. Nestle the browned rabbit pieces in the bones and vegetables. Add a bouquet garni and pour over enough chicken or beef broth to come halfway up the rabbit.

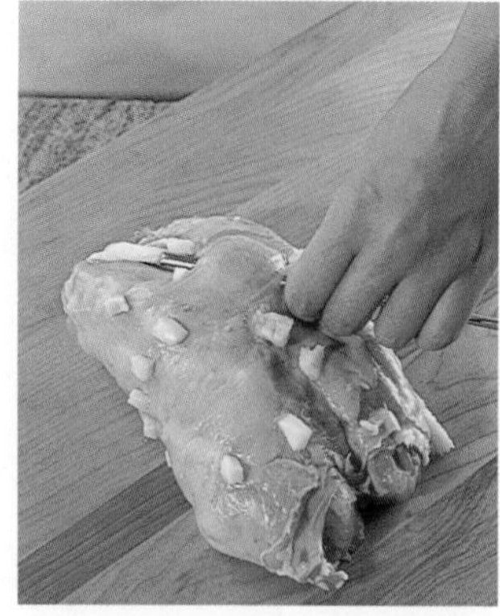

14. Bring the broth to a gentle simmer on the stove top, cover the pot, and braise in a 325°F oven for about 2 hours, until the meat is easily penetrated with a skewer. Check periodically to make sure the liquid stays at a bare simmer; a bubble should rise to the surface every 2 or 3 seconds. Transfer the rabbit to a plate and strain the braising juices. Press firmly on the vegetables with the back of a ladle to extract as much liquid as possible. Discard the bones and vegetables.

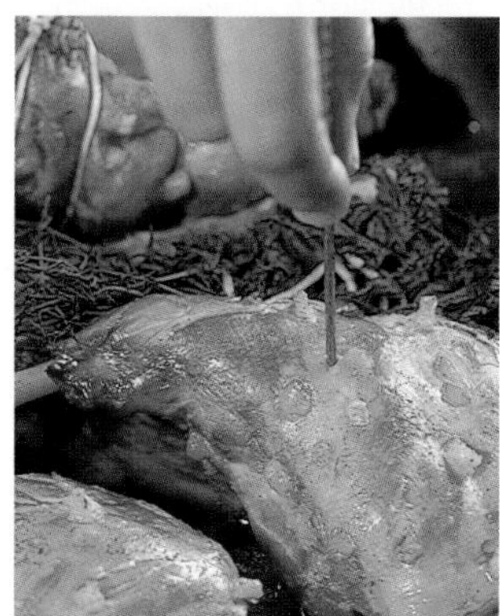

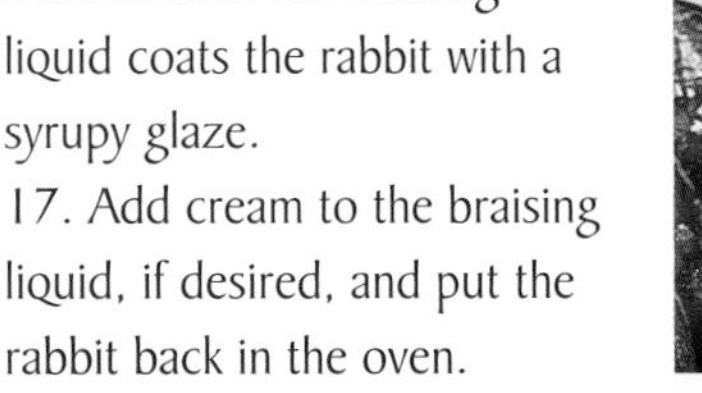

15. Degrease the braising liquid with a degreasing cup. Transfer the rabbit to a clean pot (or clean out the one used for braising) and pour over the degreased braising liquid.
16. Put the rabbit back in the oven and continue cooking, basting it every 10 minutes until the braising liquid coats the rabbit with a syrupy glaze.
17. Add cream to the braising liquid, if desired, and put the rabbit back in the oven.

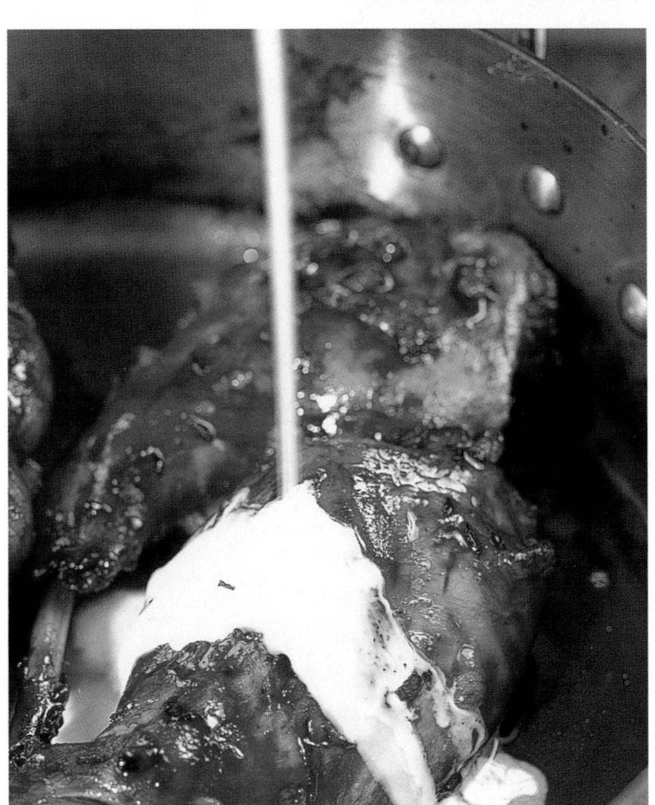

18. Continue basting until the sauce thickens to the consistency you like, about 5 minutes. Transfer to a serving dish.
19. Slice the saddle into rounds. Slice the thighs. Serve each guest slices of both saddle and thigh.

See Also

To make a chicken broth, page 30
To make a bouquet garni, page 31
To use a degreasing cup, page 268
To make a chicken sauté, page 157
To make a chicken stew, page 154

Related Glossary Entries

Braise
Deglaze
Degrease
Glaze
Lard
Mirepoix

Glossary

À la Nage

Cooking *à la nage* means poaching food, usually seafood, in a court bouillon and serving the court bouillon and the court bouillon vegetables around the food as part of the garniture. When making a court bouillon to use for cooking *à la nage*, cut the vegetables in a decorative way, such as the julienne shown on page 13.

Aromatic Garniture

See Garniture.

Aromatic Vegetables

Vegetables that lend a distinct flavor and aroma to stocks, broths, soups, sauces, and braised dishes are sometimes called aromatic vegetables. In French cooking, carrots, onions, and celery—often in a combination called mirepoix—are used to contribute flavor. In other cuisines, aromatic vegetables might include garlic, ginger, or lemon grass. (See also Garniture, Mirepoix.)

Bain-marie

A *bain-marie* is a pan of water that is used to help mixtures such as custards bake evenly and to protect them from the direct heat of the oven or, in some cases, the stove. *Bains-marie* are usually used for dishes that are baked in small containers—ramekins or casseroles—because the constant temperature of the water helps them all cook at the same rate regardless of the evenness of the oven. The water for a *bain-marie* is usually brought to a boil on top of the stove—cold water would cause the food to cook too slowly—and poured around the containers in a pan just large enough to hold them. Usually the *bain-marie* is placed on the stove for a few seconds to bring the water, cooled by the ramekins, back to the simmer. A triple layer of parchment paper or newspaper or a kitchen towel on the bottom of the *bain-marie* protects the foods from the direct heat of the stove.

Bake

To cook in the oven. The terms *baking* and *roasting* are often used interchangeably, but roasting usually implies cooking at a higher temperature—at least at the beginning—to get the surface of foods to brown. (Roasting also implies a number of secondary techniques, such as deglazing the roasting pan and making a jus or gravy.) Foods are usually baked in a moderate oven so there's plenty of time for the heat to penetrate and for the cooking process to occur. Baking is an excellent technique for ingredients that contain a lot of water, such as tomatoes and mushrooms, because the gentle heat of the oven concentrates their flavors by causing the natural moisture to evaporate slowly. (See also Roast.)

Bavarian

A kind of mousse (most of us are familiar with the sweet version, Bavarian cream) made by folding together whipped cream and a flavorful liquid mixture, usually a crème anglaise flavored with vanilla, coffee, chocolate, or a fruit purée. More contemporary fruit Bavarians are sometimes made without crème anglaise. Savory Bavarians made by folding whipped cream with various savory purées, of course, never contain crème anglaise. Gelatin is added to the liquid mixture to cause the Bavarian to set once it has chilled. (See also Mousse.)

Beurre Blanc

A rich butter sauce made by whisking butter into a reduction of white wine, white wine vinegar, and shallots.

Blanch

Blanching is a method of cooking in boiling water, with the implication that the food will be further cooked after blanching.

For instance, root vegetables or tubers such as potatoes or turnips may be blanched in boiling water until barely cooked through before being sautéed, grilled, or roasted. (Slow-cooking root vegetables would otherwise overcook on the outside before the intense heat of the sauté pan or grill penetrated the dense flesh to the interior.) Large root vegetables are blanched starting in cold water so that the heat penetrates them gradually and they cook more evenly. (If potatoes, for example, are plunged into boiling water, the outside will get mushy before the heat penetrates to the center.)

Blanching is also used to get rid of some of the strong flavor of certain ingredients. Bacon lardons, for example (see Making Bacon Lardons, page 155), are sometimes blanched to soften their strong, smoky flavor, which can overwhelm the flavor of braised dishes such as boeuf à la bourguignonne or coq au vin. Older turnips are sometimes sectioned and blanched, starting in cold water, to eliminate any bitterness. Meats and bones are sometimes blanched (see Creamed Veal Stew, page 212) to eliminate the scum that would otherwise cloud the poaching liquid or broth. Sweetbreads are blanched to firm them so they hold their shape when cooked. And tomatoes and peaches are often blanched to loosen their skins and make peeling them easy.

Sometimes people add baking soda to the water used for blanching green vegetables. Because baking soda is alkaline, it neutralizes natural acids contained in the vegetables and turns the vegetables bright green. Unfortunately, baking soda also causes vegetables to turn mushy. And there is some evidence that baking soda neutralizes some of the vegetables' nutrients.

Blanquette

A creamy veal stew made by poaching pieces of veal breast, then thickening the poaching liquid with roux and finishing this sauce with a mixture of cream and egg yolks. (See also Roux.)

Boil

To cook in water or other liquid heated until bubbling vigorously. Few techniques cause as much confusion as boiling, simmering, and poaching. Boiling is, in fact, often a technique to be avoided. Most foods—meat and seafood, for example—are poached instead (cooked in liquid held just below the boil so that it just shimmers slightly on the surface), because boiling turns them dry or stringy, and it can cause the liquid to become murky or greasy.

Some foods, however, are best cooked at a rolling boil. Rice and pasta cook more quickly and evenly in boiling water. Green vegetables are often cooked uncovered in a large amount of boiling salted water. The large quantity of water prevents the vegetables from lowering the temperature of the water, which would slow their cooking and cause them to lose their bright color. The salt also helps the vegetables retain their green color. As soon as the vegetables are done, immediately drain them in a colander and either plunge them into ice water or quickly rinse them under cold tap water until completely cool. This technique of immediately chilling the drained vegetables so they retain their flavor and color is called refreshing or, sometimes, shocking. (See also Blanch, Poach.)

Braise

To cook in a small amount of liquid (also called stewing or pot roasting). In contrast to poaching, in which the food is completely submerged in simmering liquid, braised dishes use a relatively small amount of liquid. Usually, the purpose of braising is to concentrate the food's flavors in the surrounding liquid so that it can be made into a sauce, or allowed to reduce so that it coats or is reabsorbed by the foods being braised.

Braising can be a relatively rapid process (called short-braising) by which foods are very gently simmered just until they cook through (see pages 116, 128, and 154), or it can involve long, slow cooking (long-braising), used most often but not always for tough cuts of meat that require long cooking to tenderize them (see pages 128, 203, 206, and 257). Foods may be browned or not before adding the liquid, meats may be larded with fat to keep them moist, and the cooking liquid can be varied. (Most foods are braised with enough liquid to come halfway up their sides, but some recipes call for very little; others use none at all and rely on the foods to braise in their own juices.) Usually, foods are braised in a covered pot, but some foods, such as seafood or vegetables—those that release a lot of liquid and cook relatively quickly—are braised uncovered so the braising liquid reduces and concentrates.

Short-braising vegetables, also called glazing (see page 76), is an excellent way to cook root vegetables such as carrots, onions, and turnips. Short-braising is also a flavorful alternative to steaming or boiling green vegetables. Although the vegetables may lose their crunch and bright color, slow-cooking in a covered pot often reveals a depth of flavor that quick-cooking does not.

Fish can be braised whole, in fillets, or in steaks, with just enough liquid to come halfway up its sides. Shellfish can be cooked with even less liquid, just enough to generate steam and leave enough cooking liquid for making a sauce. Most seafood braises are short-braises—the seafood is cooked only long enough for the heat to penetrate and cook the flesh. Some shellfish, however, such as squid, octopus, razor clams, conch, and whelks, require long, slow braising to tenderize the flesh and release their flavor.

Braising is the method used for most slow-cooked meat dishes, including stews and pot roasts. Traditional braising, or long-braising, involves cooking the meat slowly and gently so that the tough proteins in the meat have time to soften and the flavors of aromatic vegetables, herbs, and, sometimes, wine meld into a delicious natural sauce. Tender cuts of red meat and pieces of poultry such as chicken can be short-braised, just long enough to cook them through. If they are braised for too long, they will be tough and dry.

Meat stews—braised dishes in which the meat is cut into cubes—can be varied almost endlessly. The meat can be browned in hot fat or in the oven before the liquid is added to give the stew a deeper flavor or the meat can be braised, without browning. Aromatic vegetables such as onions, carrots, leeks, garlic, and celery are usually added to braised meat dishes at the beginning of cooking and may also be used, combined with wine, to marinate the meat before cooking. In most braised meat dishes, the aromatic vegetables are chopped, and they are discarded when the meat is finished cooking, but for more rustic stews or pot roasts, the vegetables are cut into large pieces and then served with the dish. In more refined braises (such as the Long-Braised Beef Stew, page 206), fresh vegetables or other garnitures are cooked separately and added to the dish just before serving.

Meats destined for long-braising are sometimes larded with strips of pork fat inserted into the meat with a larding needle (see page 273). While many of us don't like the idea of adding extra fat to a dish, no other technique is as effective in ensuring that braised meats will remain moist and have a perfect, melting texture.

Braise meat and poultry in liquid held at the barest simmer, with a single bubble or two coming to the surface every few seconds. If you allow the liquid to boil, the meat will end up stringy and dry and the braising liquid will be greasy. If the liquid isn't hot enough, the meat will take too long to cook. The easiest way to check the temperature of the braising is to just lift the lid and look at the liquid, but this can be inconvenient (if you're dealing with a large pot) and may dissipate some of the flavors of the herbs, wine, and aromatic vegetables. (Older French recipes for braised meats often recommended sealing the lid on the pot with a flour-and-water paste.) Instead, bring a small ovenproof saucepan of water to the boil, cover it with a lid, and put it in the oven next to the braise. Then you can check the water in the saucepan instead of the liquid in the pot.

(See also Étuver, Glaze, Lard, Poach, Reduction.)

Bread

To coat quick-cooking foods to be sautéed or deep-fried with flour or a bread crumb mixture to create a crust. To make truly delicious breaded foods, always use fresh bread crumbs (page 164). (Stale bread crumbs are dry and will absorb too much fat.) For very fine, delicate bread crumbs that will absorb a minimum of fat, work the bread crumbs through a strainer or drum sieve. When sautéing breaded foods, use clarified butter (page 46) or extra virgin olive oil for the best flavor. (If you use whole butter,

you risk having the milk solids burn and stick to the breading, leaving black dots. This isn't a big deal unless you want a perfect golden crust.) Because breading browns at a relatively low temperature, sauté breaded foods over gentler heat than you would unbreaded foods. You can also replace the bread crumbs with other ingredients, such as powdered dried porcini mushrooms (page 164), chopped truffles (page 217), chopped nuts, and grated Parmesan cheese. Plain flour and simple batters are also sometimes used to coat foods, especially for sautéing. Fried tomatoes (page 79), sautéed eggplant (page 91), shrimp tempura (page 122), fried goujonettes (page 121), and fried chicken (page 160) are some examples.

Broil

To cook with a direct heat source—usually a gas flame or an electric coil—above the food. Broiling is sometimes called grilling, but here I use the term *grilling* to mean cooking with the food above the heat source.

Professional broilers, which have an adjustable broiler at eye level that makes it easy to control the cooking, are far more practical than home broilers, but home broilers can be effective if you use them properly.

Always preheat your broiler for at least 5 minutes before sliding in any food so the heating element has time to get hot. Some cooks like to line the broiler rack with aluminum foil to make it easier to clean. I don't recommend this, because the foil can collect the liquid released by the meat or seafood, which, in turn, will cause the food to steam. To prevent the surface of foods from drying out under the broiler, rub the foods with a little oil before cooking.

The only way to regulate the heat of a home broiler is to adjust the height of the rack that holds the food. Thin pieces of meat or seafood should be placed closer to the heat source so they brown quickly without overcooking. Red meat being served rare also should be broiled very close to the source so it browns quickly before it overcooks. Slower-cooking foods, such as chicken, which must be cooked completely through, should be broiled farther away from the heat source so they don't brown too much before they are cooked. If you're unsure, keep a close eye on the food and adjust the broiler rack height accordingly.

At times, the broiler is used just to brown the top of cooked dishes, such as gratins, that don't brown enough in the oven. To brown these foods, just slide the dish under the preheated broiler. Move the dish around as necessary so the surface browns evenly, and watch it like a hawk—a broiler can char the surface very quickly.

You can also use a broiler to cook very quick-cooking dishes, such as thinly sliced seafood, directly on the serving plate. To prepare such dishes, each portion of the thinly sliced seafood is carefully spread over a sheet of buttered aluminum foil. Just before serving, the dinner plate is heated in the oven. The foil is inverted over the plate, the foil is peeled away, and the plate slid under the broiler. The plate is rotated (so the seafood cooks evenly) under the broiler for 10 to 20 seconds, usually brushed with a light sauce, and served immediately. (See also Grill.)

Broth

I use the terms *broth* and *stock* interchangeably to mean a flavorful liquid made by gently cooking meat, seafood, or vegetables (and/or their by-products such as bones and trimmings), often with herbs, in liquid, usually water. Sometimes the ingredients are cooked in broth, creating what is sometimes called a double broth. The word *stock* is more likely to be used in professional settings—perhaps because it's kept "in stock" for use in soups, sauces, and braised dishes. Occasionally you'll see a recipe that makes a stock without the usual bouquet garni and aromatic vegetables, the assumption being that these flavoring ingredients will be added later, when the stock is incorporated into a soup or sauce. In French, a stock is a *fond,* which means "base." A broth, on the other hand, should be self-sufficient, flavorful enough to stand on its own.

Brown Sauce

Traditional brown sauces are based on concentrated beef or veal stock that has been thickened with a brown roux into what is called a *sauce espagnole,* which is then concentrated by slow, careful reduction into *demi-glace.* By adding various flavorful ingredients, such as aromatic vegetables, herbs, wines, truffles, mushrooms, and/or green peppercorns, to demi-glace, French chefs developed a large family of classic brown sauces. Nowadays, however, most brown sauces are made without roux, but instead are based on a highly reduced veal or beef stock, called *glace de viande* ("meat glaze"). Typically, a small amount of *glace de viande* is combined with flavorful ingredients in the same way as demi-glace was once combined with these ingredients. The sauce is then finished with butter or cream to thicken it slightly and give it a silky texture. (See also Glace de Viande, Monter au Beurre, Roux.)

Brunoise

Tiny dice, usually slightly less than ⅛ inch.

Caramelize

The flavor of many foods, including vegetables, meats, and seafood, is often enhanced by a gentle browning that caramelizes natural sugars and other compounds and intensifies their flavor. Meats for stews, for example, are usually browned to caramelize juices that if not caramelized are much less flavorful. Chopped vegetables, especially aromatic vegetables such as carrots and onions, are often caramelized—sometimes with cubes of meat such as prosciutto—in a small amount of fat before liquid is added to enhance the flavor of soups, stews, and sauces. Braised dishes such as pot roasts (page 203) and stews such as rabbit (page 257) are sometimes caramelized in several stages: Aromatic vegetables and meat trimmings are caramelized in the pan before the pieces of meat are added; a small amount of broth is added along with the meat and reduced in the pan so that it caramelizes before the actual braising liquid is added; and the braising liquid is then caramelized on the surface of the meat during the final glazing process. Vegetables, especially baby onions and root vegetables, are also sometimes caramelized after first being glazed. The braising liquid evaporates to almost nothing so that it caramelizes on the bottom of the pan before being deglazed with water, broth, or cream, creating a saucelike glaze that then coats the vegetables. (See also Aromatic Vegetables, Braise, Garniture, Glaze, Mirepoix.)

Casserole

See Gratin.

Chiffonade

To finely shred leafy vegetables or herbs (see page 20).

Chop

To cut into irregular pieces. Foods can be chopped from very fine (minced) to coarse. (See also Dice.)

Concassée

In French, *concassée* means, literally, "broken apart." In cooking, *concassée* refers to coarsely chopped vegetables, usually tomatoes. A tomato concassée is a chunky, rough mixture that can be used as a sauce. Tomatoes for a tomato concassée must be peeled and seeded because, unlike a coulis, a concassée isn't strained. (See also Coulis.)

Confit

Traditionally, confit is made by slowly cooking pieces of duck, goose, or pork in their own gently rendered fat. The meats are then stored, covered with the rendered fat, in jars. Before refrigeration, the method was used as a way to preserve meats, because covering completely with fat prevents the development of bacteria. Nowadays, confit is usually made for the simple reason that it's delicious and, in fact, relatively fat-free because most of the fat has been rendered and is no longer attached to the meat. In modern French cooking, the term is sometimes used more loosely to describe anything that has been gently cooked, submerged in fat, to concentrate its flavor. Confit differs from deep-frying because it uses very slow and gentle heat, whereas deep-frying uses very high heat.

Coulis

In contemporary cooking, a coulis is a mixture—often a fruit purée—that has been strained of tiny seeds or pieces of peel so it is perfectly smooth. A tomato coulis is similar to a concassée except that a coulis is strained. Tomatoes destined for a coulis don't need to be peeled or seeded, because the seeds and pieces of peel will be strained out. (See also Concassée.)

Court Bouillon

A vegetable broth made by simmering onions (or leeks), carrots, celery, and, sometimes, other vegetables, such as fennel, with a bouquet garni in water and, often, white wine. Court bouillon is especially useful for poaching seafood. (See also À la Nage.)

Cure

To treat with an ingredient, usually salt and/or sugar, originally (before the advent of refrigeration) for the purpose of preserving foods by protecting them from bacteria, molds, and parasites. Nowadays, curing is more often used to enhance flavor and texture. Many foods, such as pickles and some seafood, are cured in brine (saltwater) that has been flavored with herbs and/or spices. Meats and seafood are also sometimes cured by rubbing them thoroughly with salt, sometimes mixed with sugar. Salt and sugar draw moisture out of foods, while enhancing their flavor. Some cured foods, such as gravlax (page 240) and prosciutto, are ready to serve as soon as the curing is complete. Salmon and other seafoods may be further cooked or smoked after curing. (See also Smoke.)

Custard

A liquid mixture that is combined with whole eggs, egg whites, or egg yolks, or a combination, and gently baked until set. A quiche filling is an example of a custard, as are crème caramel and crème brûlée.

Deep-fry

To cook completely submerged in hot oil. Deep-frying is the quickest way to cook some foods and, as a result, often seems to seal in the flavors of food better than any other technique. Deep-fried at the proper temperature, foods absorb little oil and are surprising light. (A coating of flour or a light breading also helps prevent foods from absorbing oil.) But if the oil is too hot, foods will brown too quickly and stay raw in the middle. If the oil isn't hot enough, the foods will sit in the oil too long and absorb too much oil. Foods cut into larger pieces should be fried at a lower temperature so the heat has time to penetrate all the way through.

A deep-frying thermometer is the easiest way to make sure your oil is at the right temperature, but if you're in a pinch, you can judge the oil by how certain foods behave. When the oil is too cool for frying, foods sink to the bottom and stay there. In somewhat hotter oil (but still not hot enough to fry in), foods sink to the bottom and then slowly rise to the top. The oil is at the right temperature when the food doesn't drop all the way to the bottom when it is added and then bobs back to the surface within a second or two. When the oil is too hot, foods immediately float, remaining on the surface, surrounded with bubbles. Of course, these aren't hard-and-fast rules. The final stage of frying French fries, for instance, requires oil that's hot enough to immediately surround the potatoes with bubbles. Frying a whole fish may require oil that's cooler than for most other purposes.

Coatings also affect the texture of deep-fried food. French fries require no coating at all to brown, but other foods, especially fish and shellfish, benefit from a light coating of flour, to give them an almost imperceptible crunch. Cooks debate endlessly over how fried chicken should be coated, some championing flour alone, while others swear by a batter. My own preference is for flour, which makes the chicken crispy but not oily. Vegetables often benefit from a very light batter of flour and water or flour and club soda (page 78). Very moist vegetables, such as tomatoes, are best when coated with egg and bread crumbs (see page 79). Breaded veal and chicken cutlets are sometimes deep-fried, but they have much better flavor when sautéed in butter or olive oil (see page 162).

Safety tips: Remember that frying oil is extremely hot and can cause painful burns.

- Use a deep-fryer, electric frying pan, or heavy pot for deep-frying.
- Never fill a deep-fryer or other pot for frying more than two thirds full with oil. When you add foods, the oil may boil over.
- Make sure that foods are dry (except for batter, of course), before plunging them into the hot oil. Wet foods may cause the oil to spatter or boil over.
- Don't put foods in the oil with your hands, because the oil may splash up and burn you. Use a spoon, "spider," fry basket, or, for large items, tongs. (If you must use your hands, hold the food close to the surface of the oil and let it slide gently into the oil so it doesn't splash you.)
- Keep the hot frying oil on the back of the stove or somewhere else out of harm's way. Don't let any long handles reach out where you can bump into them.
- Keep a box of baking soda handy to extinguish any fire.

(See also Shallow-fry, Spider.)

Deglaze

To add liquid to a pan in which foods have been sautéed or roasted in order to dissolve the caramelized juices stuck to the bottom of the pan. The purpose of deglazing is to make a quick sauce (or jus or gravy) for a roast, steak, chop, or a piece of seafood fillet or steak. To make a pan-deglazed sauce, first pour out any fat left in the sauté or roasting pan, and make sure that the juices clinging to the bottom of the pan haven't blackened and burned. (If you can't tell, swirl a tablespoon of water in the hot pan and taste the juices—if they're bitter, you're out of luck.) Add a few tablespoons of flavorful liquid, such as wine, broth, or, in a pinch, water, to the pan. Gently scrape the bottom of the pan with a wooden spoon to loosen the caramelized juices. You can use such a sauce as is, or you can turn it into something richer and more elaborate by adding reduced broth, swirling in a few little pieces of butter, adding a little heavy cream, or thickening it with a vegetable purée, such as garlic or tomato, and then reducing the sauce to the consistency you like. You can add nuance and flavor to the sauce by adding chopped herbs or ingredients such as green peppercorns (see Sautéed Beef Tenderloin Steaks with Green Peppercorn Sauce, page 197). (See also Gravy, Jus, Monter au Beurre, Sauce, Thickener.)

Degrease

To remove the fat that forms on the tops of simmering broths, sauces, jus, and braising liquids. (Fat is lighter than water, so it floats to the top.) There are several reliable methods for degreasing broth. The first, which requires a little practice, is to use a ladle or spoon to skim around the edges of the simmering broth to catch and remove just the surface fat and scum. (Move the saucepan to one side of the burner so that the scum and fat are pushed to one side, where they will be easier to skim off.)

Skimming with a ladle

Removing fat from cold broth

Spooning fat off roasting juices

Degreasing cup

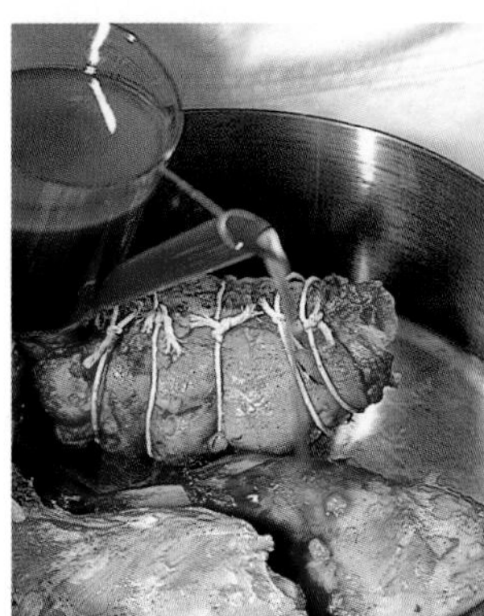

Leaving fat behind

An easier method, if you have the time, is to chill the broth overnight in the refrigerator and then remove the fat that has congealed on the surface. Degrease the small amounts of juices from roast meats by tilting the roasting pan and skimming off the fat with a spoon. Larger quantities of meat drippings are easily degreased by pouring both juices and fat into a degreasing cup and then pouring out the liquid, leaving the fat behind.

Demi-glace

In classic French cooking, *demi-glace* (literally, "half-glaze") was the basis for most brown sauces. Demi-glace is made by reducing a *sauce espagnole* until it becomes very concentrated and lightly syrupy. *Sauce espagnole* is itself made by thickening brown veal stock with a roux and then reducing the sauce slowly while skimming. Today most chefs use *glace de viande* (meat glaze) instead of *demi-glace* for making brown sauces. (See also Brown Sauce, Glace de Viande, Roux.)

Dice

To cut into cubes (unlike chopping, which cuts foods into irregular pieces). (See also Brunoise, Chop, Macedoine.)

Emulsion

An emulsion is a smooth mixture of two liquids, such as oil and water, that normally do not mix. On a microscopic level, an emulsion consists of tiny particles of one liquid (or, occasionally, a solid) suspended in another. These tiny particles are kept separate from one another by an extremely fine coating of an emulsifier that surrounds each particle, keeping them from touching one another and from clumping into larger globules, which would float or sink. Mayonnaise is an example of an emulsion in which microscopic globules of oil are suspended in a relatively small amount of water-based liquid. The suspension is held in place by the emulsifier, which, in this case, is egg yolk. Other familiar emulsions are beurre blanc (globules of butter fat suspended in a medium of white wine and vinegar, emulsified by the milk solids in the butter), hollandaise (emulsified with egg yolks, like mayonnaise), cream sauces (milk solids in the cream keep the butterfat and liquid in it in a stable emulsion), vinaigrettes (mustard holds the oil and water in an emulsion), and béchamel sauce (the flour in the roux stabilizes the milk into an emulsion that can withstand heat).

Cooks rely on various emulsions to make sauces, custards, soufflés, and cakes and pastries. But some emulsions are undesirable. If a meat broth or jus is allowed to boil, the fat that is slowly being released by the meat is churned back into the liquid and will eventually become emulsified, resulting in a cloudy, greasy, muddy-tasting broth. (Simmering allows the fat to float to the surface, where it can be skimmed off.) For the same reason, the first step in making gravy from pan juices is to skim off the fat floating in the roasting pan. Otherwise, the thickener in the gravy—usually flour—will emulsify the fat into the gravy. An exception is the sauce for the roast pears on page 101. In that recipe, I want the juices released by the pears to combine with the melted butter. To achieve this, I stir in heavy cream, which emulsifies the two components into a buttery sauce. (See also Degrease, Gravy, Jus, Roux.)

Étuver

A method of braising with very little or no liquid, usually used for seafood or delicate meats, such as veal. Foods cooked *à l'étuvée* capture the pure essence of the foods being braised because the foods braise in their own juices instead of in other liquids.

Flambé

To ignite a sauce or other liquid so that it flames. Dishes that contain spirits can be flambéed either in the kitchen or in the dining room. Most of the time flambéing has no real function other than to delight your guests. In professional kitchens, sauces or other liquids containing boiling spirits are ignited—usually by just tilting the pan over the stove's gas flame—as a safety precaution, so the mixture doesn't ignite unexpectedly and burn someone. Here are a few tricks for flambéing dishes in your dining room.

- Make Sure Everything Is Hot: It's impossible to flambé a cold dish by sprinkling it with spirits and trying to light it—the spirits only release their flammable fumes (the alcohol) when hot. For this reason, cook foods that you intend to flambé in heavy pots or baking dishes that will retain their heat when you take them into the dining room.
- Ignite the Spirits in the Kitchen: Unless you're used to flambéing, igniting hot alcohol in the dining room can be a little scary. Instead, set the hot pot or baking dish on a trivet in the dining room and bring the alcohol—the brandy or rum, or spirit-laced sauce—to a boil in a heavy-bottomed saucepan in the kitchen. When the alcohol starts to boil, carefully tilt the pan toward the flame while it ignites (if you have an electric stove, use a long match), then dim the lights and march proudly into the dining room. Use a long spoon to spoon the flaming alcohol over the food.
- Don't Pour Flaming Spirits: With a long spoon, gently spoon the flaming spirits over the hot food. Don't ever pour the flaming liquid straight out of the pan—you'll get too many flames.
- Shake the Dish Slightly to Get More Flame: Once you've spooned the flaming spirits over the hot food, you may notice the flames dying down very quickly. Holding the serving dish with a kitchen towel—be careful not to let the towel get into the flames—give the dish a quick shake so the flames rise up again. You can repeat this several times.

Flan

A liquid or semiliquid mixture, held together with whole eggs, egg whites, or egg yolks, that is gently baked in a mold or pastry shell. Quiches, crème caramel, crème brûlée, and the carrot flan on page 97 are all familiar examples of sweet and savory flans. Any purée, or even a puréed soup, can be converted to a flan with the addition of egg. One whole egg, 2 egg whites, or 2 egg yolks will bind ¾ cup of liquid.

Fricassée

Although French cooks have long used this term more or less loosely to refer to various types of stew, nowadays, a fricassée is almost always a stew in which the meat, usually poultry, is cut up, lightly cooked in butter, and then simmered in liquid until done. A fricassée is different from a blanquette because the meat in a blanquette (page 212) is cooked directly in liquid without the preliminary gentle sautéing in butter. A fricassée differs from a sauté because the meat or poultry in a fricassée is finished by being simmered in liquid, whereas the meat in a sauté is cooked completely in fat—usually butter—and a sauce is made by deglazing the pan with flavorful liquids and usually thickeners. (See also Blanquette, Sauté.)

Fruit Brandy

Fruit brandy—sometimes called *eau-de-vie*—is made by fermenting fruit into fruit wine and then distilling the wine. The best-known fruit brandy is kirsch, made from cherries, but almost any fruit can be used. Framboise (raspberry), mirabelle (yellow plum), and quetsch (dark plum) are also popular. A pure fruit brandy that hasn't been aged (many of the best fruit brandies don't benefit from aging) is perfectly clear and dry on the palate. When shopping for a fruit brandy to use for cooking, keep in mind that there is a difference between fruit brandy and "fruit-flavored" brandy. "Fruit-flavored" brandies are made by flavoring grape brandy with a fruit syrup. They are usually excessively sweet and have a cloying "cough medicine" quality that makes them almost useless in the kitchen. Because authentic fruit brandies are expensive, they should be used sparingly and should be added to mixtures near the end of cooking or after the mixtures have cooled; if the brandies are heated, they lose their lovely pure-fruit aroma.

Garniture

To most of us, a garniture, or garnish, means a sprig of parsley added to the plate at the last minute, almost as an afterthought, to provide a little color. In French cooking, and in many professional kitchens, however, a garniture is an important and integral part of the dish: It is the vegetables or other ingredients added to a stew, braised dish, roast, or sautéed piece of meat or fish that give the dish its specific character and name. (For example, pearl onions, bacon, and mushrooms are the classic garniture for boeuf à la bourguignonne and coq au vin.) When the garniture is changed—even if the basic technique of cooking the meat, and the meat itself, remains the same—the character and name of the dish change.

Understanding how to work with different garnitures allows the creative cook to make endless variations on a basic dish. Cooked vegetables such as carrots, turnips, fennel, wild mushrooms, cucumbers, spinach leaves, and others can all be used, alone or in combination, to give fresh color and flavor to a traditional dish. In addition, your choice of when to add the vegetable creates a particular effect and defines just how the garniture is associated with the meat, poultry, or seafood. For example, if you add vegetables early on, they'll absorb the flavor of the broth and meat and echo the taste of the meat and sauce, whereas if you add the garnish at the end, it will provide its own fresh and flavorful contrast to the main ingredients.

In classic French cooking, a related term—*aromatic garniture*—refers to those ingredients added to a stew or braised dish at the beginning to contribute the flavors that are basic and integral to the dish. The most common aromatic garniture, called a *mirepoix*, is chopped carrots, onions, and celery—but other ingredients such as garlic, fennel, and tomatoes are also common. In more refined recipes, the aromatic garniture is removed from the dish before serving and replaced by fresh vegetables and other ingredients—the final garniture. In more rustic dishes, the aromatic garniture is left in the dish and served with it. In some stews and braised dishes, the cooked aromatic garniture is puréed and used as a thickener for the braising liquid. (See also Mirepoix, Thickener.)

Glace de Viande

Glace de viande, or meat glaze, is made by reducing stock, usually made from browned veal or beef bones, to a thick syrup that's so concentrated it has the consistency of hard rubber when cold. Glace de viande is used to give body to pan sauces, to build classic French brown sauces, and to add body to soups and meat juices (jus). Unlike demi-glace, which is thickened with flour, meat glaze contains no starch. It has largely replaced demi-glace in contemporary professional kitchens. (See also Brown Sauce, Demi-glace, Jus.)

Glaze

Meats and root vegetables are sometimes glazed by allowing braising liquid to reduce into a concentrated liquid that coats the foods and gives them an appetizing sheen and flavor. Root vegetables (page 76) are usually glazed with a little water or broth, a pinch of sugar, and butter. Braised meats, such as rabbit (page 257) and pot roast (page 203), are glazed by baking in the oven, uncovered, and basting so the braising liquid concentrates on the surface of the meat.

Gluten

When water is added to flour, two proteins, glutenin and gliadin, combine to form gluten, which is elastic and sticky. When doughs or batters are kneaded or beaten, the elasticity of the gluten increases. Sometimes this is desirable, as when making bread, because the gluten strands trap carbon dioxide, which is what causes the bread to rise. At other times, such as when making batters for deep-frying, crêpes, or pie dough, it is best to avoid the activation of gluten because gluten contracts—leaving deep-fried foods exposed—and becomes tough when it cooks. The best way to avoid the formation of gluten is not to work or beat dough or batter and to give these mixtures a rest in the refrigerator before they are used. (The combining of glutenin and gliadin to form gluten reverses itself as doughs and batters rest.)

Goujonette

A thin strip of fish cut from a larger fillet, intended to look like a tiny fish, that is most often floured and deep-fried (see Fried Flounder Goujonette, page 121).

Gratin

A way of binding together, or combining, cooked or raw foods (usually vegetables or pasta—baked macaroni and cheese is a gratin) with a liquid such as cream, milk, béchamel sauce, or tomato sauce, in a shallow dish and baking until cooked and set. Typically, the gratin is sprinkled with cheese or bread crumbs so a crunchy, savory crust forms on top. A gratin is really the same thing as a casserole, except that a gratin is usually baked in a special oval, relatively shallow dish, so there's a higher proportion of crust to the ingredients it tops.

Cassoulet is one of the world's most famous gratins, and one of the richest. It is made by layering beans and meats in an earthenware pot, sprinkling the mixture with bread crumbs, and slowly baking until a savory crust forms on top. But there's also a special trick to making a cassoulet: Once a crusty layer has formed on top, the layer is carefully spooned back into the mixture, more bread crumbs are sprinkled over, and the cassoulet is baked until a second crust forms. This careful folding back in of the crusty layers is repeated until several layers of crunchy and savory crust have been worked into the cassoulet.

Gravy

A gravy is an American-style jus that has been thickened with a roux. The roux can be made using butter and flour or by cooking flour into some of the fat skimmed off the jus (see page 169). Cornstarch mixed with a little water (see page 210) can also be whisked into the jus and the jus brought to a simmer to get the cornstarch to thicken. (French cooks call gravy a *jus lié,* literally, a "bound juice.") Once the gravy is thickened, other ingredients, such as herbs or chopped giblets (see page 162), can be added to it to give it extra flavor. Vegetable purées can also be used to thicken a natural jus and turn it into a flourless gravy (see page 286). Garlic, roasted along with meats and poultry, or separately, is excellent puréed and whisked into the jus to thicken it (see page 184). (See also Jus, Roux, Thickener.)

Grill

To cook above the heat source (traditionally over wood coals) in the open air. Grilling differs from spit-roasting because roasts are traditionally cooked on a spit in front of the heat source. Some people also call broiling grilling, but I use *broiling* to mean cooking the food below the heat source.

Some cooks cover the grill during cooking, a method that causes the food to take on a very smoky flavor; if not done right, it can also coat the food with a layer of soot and grease. Traditional grilling is done in the open air and every effort is made to keep the amount of smoke to a minimum. (Some professional European grills, in fact, have small ventilators behind the grill to whisk away any smoke and soot.) If you decide to cover the grill—a good method for cooking turkey, large fish, and large pieces of meat such as leg of lamb—move the coals to one side of the grill and put the food on the other side so the food is not directly over the coals, where the rendering fat would drip down and produce soot.

Many of us use the words *barbecue* and *grill* interchangeably, but in some parts of the country, barbecuing is its own special technique of slow cooking, in a covered grill, often with a basting sauce or marinade. Barbecued foods are usually very smoky and may be cooked until they are falling off the bone, much like braised foods.

Grilling has traditionally meant cooking on an outdoor grill over a bed of charcoal. Gas-fired grills are more convenient than charcoal, but they don't impart the same delicate scent as good-quality hardwood charcoal or wood chips or chunks.

• Using Marinades and Herbs: Because grilling naturally imparts so much flavor, you don't need to do much else to the food. But grilled foods also hold up well to the assertive flavor of ingredients such as garlic and dried herbs. The easiest marinades are simple drizzles of olive oil with a sprinkle of chopped fresh or dried herbs, such as thyme, oregano, rosemary (be careful—rosemary is very strong), or marjoram. More elaborate marinades are similar to those used for stews (see Chicken with Red Wine, page 156) and braised meat dishes and may contain wine and chopped aromatic vegetables. One of the simplest and tastiest ways to marinate grilled meats is to sprinkle over a little soy sauce and rub the meat with chopped garlic. Seafood marinades should be kept very simple and delicate—a drizzle of olive oil is usually all that's needed—or they'll overwhelm the seafood's delicate flavor. Do not add lemon juice or vinegar to a seafood marinade—the acid will cook the surface of the seafood and may cause it to stick to the grill.

• Starting the Fire: There are dozens of contraptions on the market for starting a charcoal fire, but by far the easiest and least expensive is what is called a chimney. Pile charcoal in the top of the chimney and stuff two crumpled-up sheets of newspaper in the bottom. Set the chimney in the bottom of the grill, light the newspaper, and wait for about 30 minutes for the heat to work up the chimney and ignite the coals, then dump them out into the grill.

• Getting a Crosshatch Pattern: To give your grilled foods that lovely crisscross pattern you see in magazines and on TV, you need a grill grate with heavy cast-iron bars. The grates on most home grills are made of thick wire that isn't wide enough and doesn't retain enough heat to mark the food. (Surprisingly, inexpensive hibachis often have just the right kind of grill grates.) To make the crosshatch pattern, grill on one side for a few minutes and then give the food a 90-degree turn on the grill so that marks from the grill grate burn into the food at a right angle to the first marks. You only need to mark the foods on the first—the "presentation," or best—side. If you're really out to impress, brush grilled foods with a little melted butter or olive oil just before serving to give them a nice sheen.

• Using a Grill Pan: Most grill pans are made of heavy cast iron (occasionally with a nonstick coating) and have a raised, ribbed surface that leaves foods with characteristic grill marks and a lightly smoky flavor. Though it won't replicate the flavor of foods grilled over wood coals, a grill pan is handy when you're in a hurry or it's suddenly started to rain. Get the grill pan very hot on the stove, then quickly wipe the ribbed surface with a paper towel dipped in a little olive oil and place lightly oiled meats, seafood, or vegetables in the pan.

• Cleaning the Grill or Grill Pan: To clean a black and soot-encrusted grill, spray it with a heavy-duty oven cleaner such as Easy-Off. Remember, however, that these cleaners contain lye (sodium hydroxide), so be very careful to avoid contact with skin or eyes. A stiff wire brush is also useful for cleaning a grill with encrusted charring. After brushing, be sure to wipe the grill with a lightly oiled rag or paper towel to remove soot loosened by the brush. (See also Broil, Marinate.)

Interlard

See Lard.

Julienne

To cut into long thin strips (see page 13).

Jus

Ideally, the natural juices released by roasting meats and poultry. A jus differs from a gravy in that a jus is transparent and only lightly thickened, if thickened at all, while a gravy is opaque because it has been thickened with flour.

Preparing a jus can be a simple matter of skimming the fat out of the roasting pan, leaving the jus behind. The problem, however, is that there's rarely enough jus to go around, because most roasts, especially those that are cooked rare, don't release enough of their own juices. The natural juices must therefore be augmented in some way. A common solution is to add liquid, such as broth or water, to the pan to stretch the juices, but since these liquids don't have as intense a flavor as the juices from the roast, they tend to dilute the juices' flavor. This dilution in flavor can be compensated for somewhat by cooking the roast over a layer of coarsely chopped bones (usually from the roast), meat trimmings (also from the roast), and aromatic vegetables—usually onions, carrots, a little celery, and occasionally garlic—spread over the bottom of the roasting pan. This layer browns along with the roast and, when extra liquid is added to deglaze the roasting pan, releases its flavor into the liquid.

Sometimes a roast releases so few juices that it's almost impossible to separate the fat from the small amount of juices. At other times, the juices are pale and lack flavor. To solve either problem, place the roasting pan on top of the stove and boil down the juices until they caramelize on the bottom of the pan; the caramelization will intensify their flavor. As the juices caramelize, the fat will separate and float to the top, making it easy to pour or skim it off. Once the fat is removed, deglaze the pan with a little broth or water and simmer for a couple of minutes while scraping the caramelized juices on the bottom of the pan with a wooden spoon. (See also Deglaze, Degrease, Gravy, Thickener.)

Skimming the fat off the jus

Deglazing the roasting pan

Scraping to dissolve caramelized juices

Lard

To insert strips of fat into pieces of meat to ensure that the braised meat stays moist and juicy. It's a common misconception that liquids such as wine, water, or broth keep meats moist. In fact, it is fats and certain kinds of tissues in the muscles that keep meats moist and give them a melting texture in the mouth. Larding may seem an unlikely technique in an era of low-fat foods, but today's leaner meat benefits more than ever from larding.

Larding

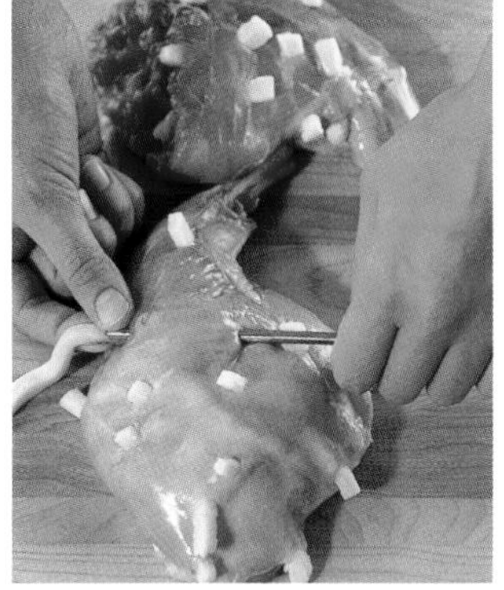
Interlarding

Larding consists of inserting a strip of fatback (pork breast that has no lean and isn't smoked or salted) into the long, hollow tube of a larding needle and then sliding the larding needle into a large chunk of meat. When the needle is withdrawn, the strip of fatback remains in the meat. Meat should be larded perpendicular to the direction the meat will be sliced so that the strips of larding make a decorative cross section in each slice.

Interlarding differs slightly from larding in that the strips of fatback are usually cut thinner than for larding and are hooked to the end of an interlarding needle and "sewn" into the outer surface of the meat. Interlarding is used for smaller pieces of meat such as rabbit or smaller pieces of game.

Macedoine

Small cubes of vegetables, or sometimes meat or fish, slightly smaller than ¼ inch. (See also Brunoise, Dice.)

Mandoline

See Slicer.

Marinate

To combine foods—usually meat or seafood, and occasionally vegetables—with aromatic ingredients in order to flavor the food. Most marinades are based on flavorful liquids such as wine, soy sauce, or lemon juice and flavored with herbs such as thyme or rosemary and aromatic vegetables such as onions and garlic. Foods are usually allowed to stand in the marinade for a period of time before cooking so that the flavors can penetrate the food (see Chicken with Red Wine, page 156).

Marinades are often used in the preparation of meat or poultry stews. For some stews, the marinade is strained before cooking, the aromatic vegetables browned like the meat, and the marinade liquid, usually wine, is used as all or part of the stewing liquid. For other stews, the marinade, vegetables and all, is simply added to the meat, without browning the vegetables (see page 206). Some marinades, especially those for quick-cooking meat, poultry, or seafood stews, are cooked and allowed to cool before they are used. This allows the aromatic vegetables to release their flavor into the wine, and also cooks off some of the aggressive raw acidity of the wine. Marinades for seafood often contain lemon juice, but I avoid this because it can cause the food to stick to the grill or pan. Delicate seafood rarely requires a marinade, which could interfere with its flavor, but for grilling, a simple mixture of extra virgin olive oil and a chopped fresh herb, tossed with the seafood or brushed on before grilling, is best. Dry marinades, called rubs, are also sometimes used for meat, seafood, and vegetables. Rubs can be made with finely chopped dried or fresh herbs, ground spices, or ground dried mushrooms (page 164). Rubs are usually left on the meat or seafood during cooking.

Occasionally marinades are added to foods after the foods are cooked, as is the case in the Mediterranean or Latin American seafood preparation referred to as *en escabeche.* Escabeche was most likely invented as a way of preserving seafood. The marinade is made by cooking aromatic vegetables—the vegetables vary, but most recipes include at least garlic and onions—in olive oil, then adding wine vinegar. The marinade is cooled and poured over the sautéed seafood.

To make sardines en escabeche: Most recipes for escabeche call for sardines, but the method works well for any small, relatively oily, full-flavored fish, such as red mullet, mackerel, trout, or small Spanish mackerel. Traditional recipes leave the fish whole, but in the recipe here, the fresh sardines are boned and the heads removed (see page 236). Start by patting the sardines with flour. Sauté, turning once, in a frying pan until cooked through. Transfer the sardines to a serving dish and wipe out the pan. Gently cook onions, garlic, and herbs in a small

Sautéing floured sardines

Marinating cooked fish

Cooking the marinade

Serving escabeche

amount of olive oil until softened. Add more olive oil and good wine vinegar and remove from the heat. Let the marinade cool and spoon over the fish. Cover and refrigerate for at least 2 hours and up to 3 days.

Marrow

The insides of some bones are filled with marrow, a fatty substance that produces red blood cells and that also happens to be very good to eat. In cooking, marrow is sometimes used to give a luxurious melting texture to stuffings and pâtés. It is also used, cut into disks or cubes, as part of a bordelaise sauce, usually served on top of sautéed steaks. The best marrow bones are long leg bones, sawed by the butcher into 2-inch cylindrical sections from which it is relatively easy to extract the marrow. Don't confuse marrow bones with knuckle bones—cartilaginous bones that are simmered to produce gelatinous stocks.

Recipes that call for marrow rarely explain how to get it out of the bone. Some bones are easy—just press against the marrow from one side with your thumb and the marrow will slide out the other end. More stubborn bones need to be cracked on two sides with a cleaver until the bone splits open and you can pull out the marrow in one piece. Once the marrow has been removed, refrigerate it overnight in a bowl of salt water. The salt water draws the blood out of the marrow so it won't turn gray when cooked.

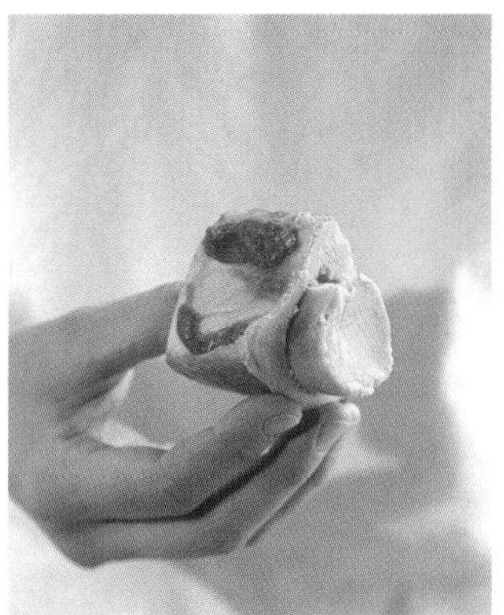

Pressing with the thumb

Using a cleaver

Meat Glaze

See Glace de Viande.

Mince

To chop very fine. (See also Chop.)

Mirepoix

Many cooking preparations, particularly braises, stews, roasts, and soups, call for sweating various mixtures of chopped aromatic vegetables before liquid is added. These mixtures are designed to add freshness and flavor to meats and seafood. The best-known mixture is the French *mirepoix*, a mixture of 2 parts onion, 2 parts carrot, and 1 part celery, but other countries and regions have their own variations. Italy has its *soffritto* (onion, carrot, celery, and, usually, garlic), Spain has its *sofregit* (Catalonia) and *sofrito* (onion, carrot, celery, ham, and sometimes tomato), Indonesia its spice-based *bumbu* (recipes vary, but most mixtures contain garlic, shallots, spices, and shrimp paste), and Portugal its *refogado* (onion, carrot, celery, and a little saffron). The ingredients in these mixtures can be chopped larger or smaller, depending on how long the mixture will cook. For a long-simmering broth, the vegetables can practically be left whole. For a quick last-minute sauce, the vegetables must be chopped very fine. (See also Garniture, Sweat.)

Monter au Beurre

Monter au beurre, or "to mount with butter," means to whisk cold butter into a hot liquid to give the liquid a silky consistency and depth of flavor, essentially turning it into a sauce. The technique is used to finish pan sauces and to finish modern versions of classic brown sauces usually made today with *glace de viande* instead of *demi-glace*. Beurre blanc is an example of a sauce made by using this technique. Keep in mind, however, that beurre blanc uses an unusually high proportion of butter to liquid. Most sauces that have been mounted with butter contain considerably less butter. (See also Beurre Blanc, Demi-glace, Glace de Viande.)

Mousse

A general term that can describe any mixture lightened with something airy, usually beaten egg whites or whipped cream. (In French, *mousse* means "foam"; shaving cream is *mousse à rasoir*, and the foam of a breaking wave is also *mousse*.) Some mousses are based on a purée of cooked seafood, vegetables, or meat, into which lightly beaten cream is folded. For these kinds of mousses, butter is usually mixed into the purée base to give it a smooth texture and to help the mousse hold its shape when chilled. Chicken liver mousse (page 165) is a familiar example of this type of mousse, but the same method can be used with mushrooms and tomatoes.

Bavarians are a kind of mousse based on a savory liquid such as tomato or sorrel purée, an intensely flavored broth, crème anglaise, or a fruit purée, into which whipped cream is folded. Gelatin is added to the liquid base of Bavarians to ensure that the mixture sets when chilled. Dessert mousses are based on fruit and chocolate mixtures. A soufflé is technically a mousse, built on a thickened sauce base (page 177). Mousses may be served hot or cold. (See also Bavarian, Mousseline, Soufflé.)

Mousseline

A purée of raw meat or seafood blended with a large amount of heavy cream or crème fraîche, and often egg whites—older recipes are also bound with a velouté sauce—and then baked in individual molds or poached. The term can also be used more loosely to refer to individual savory mousses baked in molds. Mousseline mixtures range in texture from relatively stiff—if they are to be shaped and poached as quenelles (see page 280)—to runny—if the mixture is to be cooked in a mold (see page 277). The principle behind these mixtures is that the protein in the flesh (and egg white, if there is any) firms during cooking so that the mousseline can be very airy but still hold its shape.

The trick to making a truly superlative mousseline mixture is to work as much cream as possible into the puréed raw meat or seafood to make it light and airy. If the mixture is destined for quenelles, the amount of cream you can add is limited by the fact that the uncooked mixture must be stiff enough hold to its shape in the poaching liquid. If, on the other hand, the mixture is to be baked in individual molds, the mixture can be completely liquid, like a flan mixture. Egg white is often added to molded mousseline mixtures to compensate for the high proportion of cream (just as egg is used to set a liquid flan mixture). The amount of cream you can add to a mousseline mixture also depends on how much the particular protein (meat or seafood) you're working with firms during cooking.

To get the most cream possible into the mixture and still have it set, the puréed base mixture must be ice-cold and the cream worked in in stages—every few hours or so—with the mixture refrigerated between additions. Once it's made, you'll need to test the mixture to judge the finished texture.

To make salmon mousseline: A basic salmon mousseline mixture can be shaped into quenelles and poached (see page 280) or baked in individual molds (see page 277). To make salmon mousseline, remove any bones and dark patches from the salmon fillet (the dark patches taste fine but might discolor the mixture) and cut the fillet into 1-inch cubes. Purée the cubes in a food processor and then work the purée through a drum sieve, forcing it through with the back of a small mixing bowl or large spoon. Put the puréed salmon in a bowl set in another bowl filled with ice and work in the egg whites, a bit at a time. When the mixture is perfectly smooth, cover and place in the refrigerator for 1 to 2 hours. When the mixture is well chilled, work in a third of the cream with a wooden spoon, cover the mixture with wax paper or plastic wrap, and chill again for 2 to 12 hours. Work in the rest of the cream, chill again, and season to taste with salt and pepper. (If tasting the raw mixture bothers you, taste it after poaching a little piece.) Test the consistency and flavor: If the mixture is to be used for quenelles, poach a dollop in simmering water; if it is to be used to make molded mousselines, fill a small mold half full with the mixture and bake it in a small pan of simmering water. (Don't put too much water in the pan or the mold will bob up and capsize.) If the mixture doesn't hold its shape, work in another egg white or two and test it again. If the mixture sets but seems dry, work in more cream. Adjust the seasoning as necessary.

Working through the drum sieve

Adding heavy cream

Testing the mousseline for texture

To bake salmon mousselines in individual molds:

Butter individual molds with softened butter. Chill the molds so the butter hardens and forms a firm "nonstick" layer. Fill the chilled molds with the mousseline mixture. To protect the mousselines from the direct heat of the stove, line the bottom of a pan just large enough to hold the molds with a triple layer of parchment paper or newspaper. Place a round of buttered parchment paper on top of each mousseline to prevent the top from browning or drying out.

Pour enough boiling water into the pan to come halfway up the sides of the molds. (This is easier if you take one of the mousselines out while pouring.) Place the pan over medium heat and heat until the water comes to a simmer. Bake in a 350°F oven for about 45 minutes, until set. (Jiggle one of the mousses to see if the top stays still.) Unmold onto individual plates. Sauce with the lightly creamed tomato sauce (page 50) shown here, or a crayfish sauce (page 141).

When mousses and other mixtures are baked in molds, they release a small amount of liquid. If you just flip the cooked molds onto serving dishes, you'll end up with a puddle on the dish around the unmolded mousse. To prevent this, place a kitchen towel over the mold and turn the mold over for a few seconds so the water runs out into the towel. Turn the mold back over and place a serving plate face down on top of the mold. Grip the mold and the plate in a towel, turn the whole thing over, and give the whole assembly a quick up-and-down jerk to release the mousse onto the plate. (See also Bain-marie, Flan, Quenelle, White Sauce.)

Buttering molds

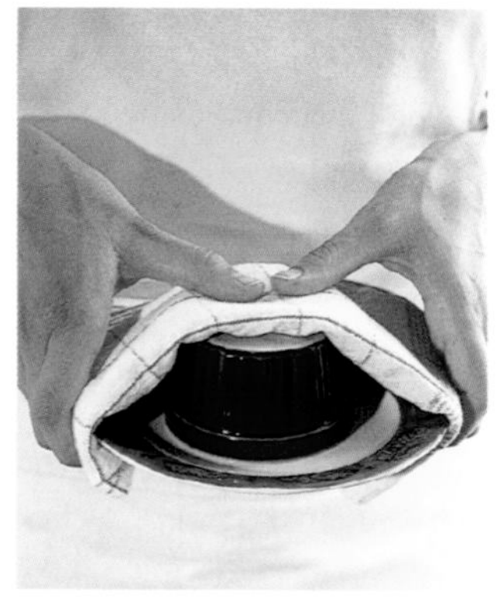

Unmolding mousselines

Covering with parchment rounds

Serving with creamy tomato sauce

Noisette

Very small medallions of meat are sometimes called *noisettes*, which translates literally as "hazelnuts." Pork tenderloins, veal tenderloins, the narrow end of a beef tenderloin, and lamb loins can all be used to make noisettes. Noisettes are best sautéed.

Panfry

Most cooks use the terms *panfry* and *sauté* interchangeably, but strictly speaking, there is, in fact, a difference. Although both terms refer to cooking in a small amount of hot oil, butter, or other fat, *sautéing* in the strictest sense means to toss foods over high heat—the French word *sauter* means to jump—while *panfrying*, technically, describes cooking pieces of meat, seafood, or large pieces of vegetables like eggplant in a hot pan, turning with tongs, a spatula, or a fork only once or twice. (See also Sauté.)

Parchment Paper or Aluminum Foil Round

Some braised foods, because they are cooked only partially submerged in liquid, are cooked covered so that the heat stays in the pot and the top of the food cooks at the same time as the parts that are submerged. With other foods, such as sweetbreads (See Short-Braised Sweetbreads, page 214) and glazed onions (See Brown-Glazed Pearl Onions, page 76), the foods should be covered in such a way that the braising liquid reduces during cooking, concentrating and reducing at the same time. This can be accomplished by partially covering the pot so that heat is held in, allowing some of the moisture to escape or, more efficiently, by covering the foods with a round of parchment paper or aluminum foil, which holds in heat but allows moisture to evaporate and the braising liquid to reduce and concentrate into

The folded parchment

Cutting the round

a flavorful sauce or glaze. To do this, cut out a round of parchment paper or aluminum foil just large enough to fit in the pan and cover the food. Fold in half a square of parchment paper or aluminum foil large enough to cover the top of the pan. Fold it in half again in the opposite direction. Using the center corner, as though it were the tip of a paper airplane, make several diagonal folds. The paper will, in fact, end up looking like a paper airplane. Hold the tip of the folded paper in the middle of the pan and cut the paper where it meets the rim of the pan. Unfold the paper and place the round on top of the food. (See also Braising, Glazing, Reduction.)

Persillade

A mixture of garlic, crushed to a paste, finely chopped parsley, a little olive oil, and, sometimes, bread crumbs. Other herbs such as thyme, marjoram, lavender, and oregano can be added or used instead of the parsley. Add persillades to hot sautéed vegetables a minute or two before the end of cooking and toss or stir so that the persillade comes in contact with the heat of the pan and releases its flavor (page 90). Use persillade to coat the surface of roasts, especially rack of lamb, to create a crust, and to flavor baked tomatoes (page 72).

Poach

To cook completely submerged in barely simmering liquid. Don't confuse poaching with boiling, which causes most meats to become dry and tough and delicate fish fillets and eggs to break apart.

Almost any liquid can be used for poaching, but water and broth are the most common. One familiar poaching liquid is the vegetable broth called court bouillon, made by simmering aromatic vegetables such as carrots, onions, leeks, and fennel with a bouquet garni in water with some white wine (page 113). Other poaching liquids include meat or fish broth, light sugar syrup (for fruit), and, simplest of all, water flavored with herbs and a little white wine or wine vinegar.

Sometimes the poaching liquid is served around the poached foods in wide soup bowls so that the liquid serves as a delicate broth-like sauce. When the aromatic vegetables are served with the poaching liquid, the dish is referred to as *à la nage*. For some poached foods, especially poached meats, such as French *pot-au-feu* (page 201) or Italian *bollito misto*, the poaching liquid is served separately as a first-course bouillon. The poaching liquid can also be saved and used for making soups or sauces.

For even cooking, start large whole fish and larger pieces of meat in cold liquid and smaller, quicker-cooking foods, such as small whole fish and fish steaks, in hot liquid. There are several reasons for this: If a large fish is started in simmering liquid, the outside of the fish will cook before the heat has a chance to penetrate to the inside, so that the outside will overcook before the center is cooked. If, on the other hand, a small fish is started in cold water and the water slowly heated, the fish can overcook before the liquid even reaches the simmer. Starting in cold liquid encourages slow-cooking meats to throw off scum that can be carefully skimmed to keep the broth clear. But quick-cooking tender meat cuts are best started in simmering liquid so that the outside cooks quickly, leaving the inside rare to medium-rare. (See also À la Nage, Blanch, Boil, Court Bouillon.)

Purée

To work or strain foods until they are completely smooth. Purées may be served on their own—mashed potatoes (page 94) and applesauce (page 95) are probably the most familiar purées in the American kitchen—or used as the base for more elaborate dishes, such as mousses (page 165), quenelles and mousseline mixtures (page 276), flans (page 97), soups (page 100), and pasta stuffings (page 57). There are a variety of techniques and gadgets available for puréeing. Choose the one best suited to the food you are puréeing.

• Blender: Blenders are best for puréeing thin mixtures and liquids such as soups. Don't try to purée stiff mixtures in a blender—they won't move around the blade.

• Drum Sieve: A drum sieve, which does look, in fact, a little like a drum, consists of a screen held in place by a sturdy outer ring, usually wood or metal. Drum sieves, which are available with both coarse- and fine-mesh screens, make the absolutely finest purées. For some difficult to purée mixtures, such as raw seafood, it's best to purée the mixture in a food processor before working it through the drum sieve. Work mixtures through a drum sieve with the back of a spoon, a plastic pastry scraper, or the bottom of a small metal bowl. Scrape off any mixture clinging to the underside of the sieve. Wooden drum sieves do not usually have interchangeable screens—when the screen wears out, you have to buy a new sieve. Metal drum sieves, while more expensive, allow you to use different screens and to replace the screens when they wear out.

• Food Mill: A food mill is a strainer with a hand crank and a series of propeller-like blades that work mixtures through a perforated metal plate. Some food mills have several interchangeable plates so they can purée mixtures to different degrees of fineness. Food mills are wonderful for semi-liquid mixtures with peels, seeds, or fibers, because they strain at the same time they purée. A food mill is the best possible gadget for straining cooked tomatoes.

Inserting perforated disk

Assembled food mill

To use a food mill to purée sweet potatoes: Insert the finest-mesh grid in the food mill, with the top of the center facing up, as shown here. Set the food mill over a bowl. Scoop the pulp out of roasted sweet potatoes into the food mill. Crank, holding firmly onto the handle, until all the pulp is worked through.

• Food Processor: A food processor works well for stiff mixtures such as raw fish or meats that would be very difficult to purée using any other method. Don't use a food processor to purée potatoes, however, because the processor will overwork the starch in the potatoes and make them gluey. Potatoes are better puréed with a ricer. Don't use a food processor to purée liquid mixtures—the liquids will run out the bottom of the bowl. Food processors can also be used to grind dry ingredients such as nuts and dried mushrooms.

• Immersion Blender: An immersion blender has a blade at the end of a long handle that you immerse into pots or bowls of liquid. The advantage is that you don't have to transfer hot liquid to a blender container—you just stick the end of the immersion blender into the pot or bowl of whatever you want to purée. Use an immersion blender to purée soups and sauces.

Immersion blender

• Ricer: A ricer is excellent for making mashed potatoes and other vegetable purées, because the purée is forced through tiny holes. A ricer makes very smooth purées—only fine-mesh drum sieves result in a finer texture.

• Strainer: Almost every kitchen has a strainer, so it's good to know how to use one for puréeing. Strainers are best for relatively fine or liquid purées that won't be too hard to work through the strainer. Work liquid and semiliquid mixtures through a strainer by moving a ladle back and forth, with the rim of the ladle bowl facing down into the mixture (see page 96). Strainers come with fine-, medium-, and coarse-mesh screens. For a very smooth purée, it is sometimes useful to strain first through a medium-or coarse-mesh strainer and then again through a fine-mesh strainer. (See also Quenelle.)

Quenelle

Classically, a raw purée of seafood (pike is most traditional) or veal, lightened with cream—which turns it into a mixture called a mousseline—and then formed into an elongated egg shape and poached. (Lyons is famous for its classic pike quenelles, poached in fish broth and served with a crayfish sauce, or baked in a gratin.) *Quenelle* can also refer to the shape alone; ice cream, sorbets, and mousses are often shaped into quenelles. Quenelles are usually served as a first course. Here, cooked quenelles are coated with a saffron hollandaise sauce and baked as a gratin.

To shape quenelles: Here, cooked chicken liver mousse (page 165) is shaped into quenelles. To do this, dip 2 spoons of the same size in cold water. Scoop up a rounded spoonful of the mixture in 1 spoon. Then, smooth the top of the mixture with the other spoon, facing in the opposite direction. Slide the top spoon partway under the mixture in the bottom spoon. Gently slide quenelle-shaped mounds of mousse onto a plate or into a baking dish.

Forming quenelles with 2 spoons

Spooning quenelles onto a plate

To poach salmon quenelles: Cook quenelles at a bare simmer so that they don't fall apart. Make a salmon mousseline mixture just stiff enough to poach in quenelle shapes (page 276). Shape the mixture into quenelles and place them in rows in a buttered cake pan or other flameproof baking dish deep enough so they can be submerged in liquid. Gently ladle over simmering fish broth or saltwater to cover the quenelles. Place the pan over a low to medium heat and cook the quenelles at a bare simmer. When the quenelles have all floated to the top,

Placing quenelles in cake pan

Draining on a towel

Ladling in simmering broth

Quenelles baked in a gratin

gently roll them over so the half that was above the surface of the liquid is now submerged. Poach for about 3 minutes more, until done. (If you are cooking quenelles larger or smaller than those shown here, you can cut into 1 to see if it's done—when undercooked, the center will still look moister than the rest of the quenelle.) Remove with a slotted spoon and drain on a towel. Sauce and serve immediately or, if necessary, reheat before serving. Here, the quenelles have been coated with saffron hollandaise and baked. (See also Mousse, Mousseline.)

Reduction

The technique of cooking liquids down so that some of the water they contain evaporates. Reduction is used to concentrate the flavor of a broth or sauce and, at times, to help thicken the sauce by concentrating ingredients such as natural gelatin.

Resting

See Roast.

Roast

In the oldest and strictest sense, to cook on a spit in front of a fire in the open air. Now, most of us roast in the oven, but we try to get as close to the effect of open-air spit-roasting as possible. The purpose of roasting is to create a golden brown crust on whatever it is we are roasting and, at the same time, make sure the meat, fish, or vegetable properly cooks in the center. When roasting, no liquid such as broth, wine, or water comes in contact with the food—only hot air, or, if the roast is being basted, hot fat. Roasting is both simple and complex—simple, because there's very little to do except slide the food into the oven; complex, because if the temperature isn't right, the food may never brown or cook properly.

Roasting is the best method for cooking relatively large—at least larger than a single serving—tender cuts of meat and young tender birds. Such tender and relatively lean cuts don't benefit from long, slow cooking in liquid (braising), which would cause them to dry out. Because lean and tender meats and poultry dry out if even slightly overcooked, judging doneness is an essential part of good roasting.

Some cooks roast on a roasting rack, but I don't recommend it. With the roast suspended over the roasting pan, the juices drip down from the roast, hit the hot roasting pan, and burn. Setting the roast over a layer of coarsely chopped bones (usually from the roast), meat trimmings (also from the roast) and aromatic vegetables (usually onions, carrots, and a little celery) spread over the bottom of the roasting pan will keep the roast from sticking to the bottom of the pan and help distribute the heat evenly so the juices don't burn. This layer also adds flavor to the jus.

• Determining Oven Temperature: Because home ovens can be up to 100 degrees off, there's no point relying blindly on oven temperature until you learn how accurate your own oven is. The easiest way to approach roasting meats and poultry is to start at a fairly high temperature, so you're reasonably guaranteed that the roast will brown before it overcooks. If, once it's browned, you then find that it's not cooked through, lower the oven temperature and keep roasting until done. Usually, the larger the roast, the lower the roasting temperature, because a large roast takes a relatively long time to cook and will have plenty of time to brown. Small roasts, like rack of lamb, need a high temperature—425°F. For a roast above 5 pounds, 400°F is a good place to start. A heavier roast, or a turkey, which may be in the oven for 3 or more hours, will have plenty of time to brown even at the relatively low temperature of 350°F.

If the roast is approaching doneness but still hasn't browned properly, turn the oven up to brown the meat quickly. If, conversely, the meat is well browned but raw inside, turn the oven down to let the meat finish cooking without continuing to brown. For some very small roasts—for instance, quail, squab, or Cornish hens—the oven may not be hot enough to brown the bird without overcooking it. Brown these small birds before roasting in a frying pan with a little oil.

• Determining Doneness: The easiest and most reliable way of determining the doneness of a roast is to stick an instant-read thermometer, or skewer, into the center of the roast, or between the breast and thigh of a bird. White-fleshed birds, such as chickens, turkeys, and Cornish hens, should read 145°F in the coolest part, the area between the breast and the thigh right near the joint. Birds with red flesh, such as duck, should be cooked to about 125°F. The same methods work for pork and veal, which should always be cooked to 140°F. Red meats such as beef, lamb, venison, and rabbit are roasted to taste, with rare meat registering about 120°F; medium-rare between 125° and 130°F; medium between 130° and 135°F; and medium-well between 135° and 140°F. (Remember that the internal temperature will rise while the roast rests.)

• Resting: Roasted meats should not be served straight out of the oven, but should be allowed to rest in a warm place for 20 to 30 minutes, loosely covered with aluminum foil. (The foil keeps the meat warm; loose wrapping ensures that the outside of the meat doesn't steam and lose its crispness.) Resting allows the muscle (meat is muscle) to relax so the juices become redistributed in the meat and aren't squeezed out onto the platter during carving.

Resting also allows the heat in the outer part of the roast to penetrate to the middle so the roast ends up more evenly cooked. The internal temperature of a roast increases by about 5 degrees during the resting. For this reason, a rare roast may be cooked to 120°F or even less because the temperature increases—and the roast continues to cook—as it sits.

Most roasts are sauced with a simple gravy or jus. (See also Jus.)

Roux

A mixture of flour and butter used to thicken sauces, soups, and gravies. Usually the butter is cooked with the flour in a heavy-bottomed pan over a medium heat, although some recipes suggest toasting the flour in the oven before combining it with the butter. Most roux are white roux, made by cooking the flour for only a minute or two. In older recipes, brown roux—made by cooking the flour until pale brown—is also used. Cajun cooks often use a very dark, long-cooked roux. (See also Thickener.)

Sabayon

A light, frothy mixture made by beating egg yolks with water or other liquid over gentle heat. The frothy egg yolk base used for making hollandaise sauce and its derivatives (page 44) is sometimes called a sabayon. In contemporary sauce making, flavorful liquids such as seafood braising liquids are sometimes beaten with egg yolks to form light and savory sabayons—much like hollandaise without the butter. A sabayon may also be a dessert sauce made by beating egg yolks with white wine and sugar until frothy and thickened. The Italian version, zabaglione, is made in the same way except that sweet Marsala wine replaces the dry white wine used in the French version.

Sauce

Some sauces are designed to reinforce the innate flavor of the foods—for example, a spoonful of jus or gravy on a slice of roast beef—while others, such as hollandaise sauce or mayonnaise, are designed to enhance flavors and provide contrast and excitement. Some sauces, such as mustard, are more usually thought of as condiments, but they too provide contrast and give dishes just the right amount of extra zip.

In classic French cooking, there are "integral" and "nonintegral" sauces. Sauces such as gravy, the liquid in a stew or braised dish, and the sauce made from a deglazed sauté pan are the natural result of cooking—they are derived from the food itself—and are called integral sauces. Nonintegral sauces are made separately from what they will accompany. Nonintegral sauces are divided into seven major types: hollandaise, mayonnaise, vinaigrette, butter sauce or compound butter, white sauce, brown sauce, and tomato sauce. All the hundreds of classic and modern sauces are derivatives of one or more of these basic types. Therefore, once you know how to make the basic sauces, it's easy to make derivatives by plugging in different ingredients. (See also Deglaze, White Sauce.)

Sauté

To cook over a high heat in a small amount of fat in a sauté pan or skillet. The purpose of sautéing is to brown foods to intensify their flavor. An advantage of sautéing is that most sautéed foods leave flavorful caramelized juices on the bottom of the sauté pan. These juices can be dissolved—deglazed—with a small amount of liquid such as water, wine, or broth to make an instant and delicious sauce.

As a general rule when sautéing, the pan must be heated to very hot before adding the food. The liquid in the juices must be able to evaporate immediately so that proteins caramelize and form a crisp, savory crust. If the heat is too low, the food will sweat rather than sauté, or the juices may pool in the bottom of the pan and steam the food. Foods that release a lot of water, such as mushrooms, cubes of stew meat, and scallops, may need to be added to the pan a few pieces at a time so that the temperature of the pan doesn't drop too much. Breaded and floured foods are sautéed over a moderate heat because the coating browns at a lower temperature than the food itself would; very thick pieces of meat or fish are sautéed over a moderate heat because there's plenty of time for browning without any risk of overcooking. Breaded and floured foods can be cooked in whole butter—which burns at high temperatures—because they're cooked over moderate instead of high heat.

Unlike deep-frying, which requires a lot of hot oil, sautéing uses only enough fat to keep the food from sticking to the pan. Since most sautéing happens over very high heat, it's important to use a fat that can be heated to a high temperature. Whole butter burns at a low temperature, so it's often clarified for sautéing. Vegetable and olive oils are excellent for sautéing because they tolerate very high temperatures. Use regular olive oil, usually labeled "pure," instead of extra virgin olive oil for sautéing. The "pure" oil has good flavor, and the delicate flavor of the more expensive extra virgin oil would be destroyed by the high heat anyway.

Usually the terms are used interchangeably, but strictly speaking there is a distinction between sautéing and panfrying. Both mean cooking over high heat, but sautéing means to cook smaller foods by tossing in the pan, while panfrying means to cook larger foods by laying them in the pan and turning only once or twice with tongs or a spatula.

To choose a sauté pan: Beginning cooks often spend a lot of energy and money trying to find just the right sauté pan. In fact, it's possible to make perfect sautéed dishes in any old pan—it's just easier if the pan is of better quality. Whenever possible, sauté in a pan just large enough to hold the food in a single layer, but not so large that it's difficult to handle. If the pan is too large, the juices released by the sautéing foods may run out to the edges of the pan and burn; if the pan is too small, the foods will be crowded and will steam in their juices instead of brown.

- The most important quality to look for in a pan is that it be heavy-bottomed, so that the heat will be evenly distributed over its surface. If the pan is thin, the patch directly over the heat will get much hotter than the rest of the pan, and foods in that spot will burn while foods in the rest of the pan cook too slowly.
- Use a pan with sloping sides to toss foods such as sliced vegetables, scallops, or small pieces of meat; the sloped sides help toss the food back onto itself.
- Use a pan with straight sides for sautéing larger pieces of seafood, poultry, meat, and vegetables that are turned with tongs rather than tossed. A straight-sided pan is also best when you'll be deglazing the pan for a sauce; otherwise, the sauce might stick to the sloping sides of the pan and burn as it reduces. If you're making a deglazed sauce, it is best to choose a pan with a light rather than dark surface—such as aluminum, tin, or stainless steel—so you can see if the juices have burned before you deglaze. Straight-sided pans with lids are also perfect for dishes such as fricassées, when sautéing is only the first step in a two-stage process and liquid will be added after the food is sautéed.
- High-quality nonstick pans make the easiest work of sautéing, but well-made, heavy-bottomed nonstick pans are expensive. A well-seasoned cast-iron skillet makes a good substitute, but some cooks find them too heavy, especially for foods that need to be tossed. The French iron skillets called *poêles* are somewhat lighter and have sloping sides for tossing.

Sauté is also a noun that refers to a dish in which meat or poultry is sautéed and a sauce is made in the pan used for the sautéing (see pages 157 and 195). The meat or poultry is then heated in the sauce at the last minute. A sauté is different from a fricassée because in a fricassée, pieces of poultry or sometimes meat are lightly cooked in fat and then finish cooking in liquid. Both are different from stews because the meat or poultry is cooked only long enough for the flesh to cook through, whereas stews are cooked over several hours. (See also Braise, Deep-fry, Deglaze, Fricassée, Panfry, Shallow-fry, Sweat.)

Shallow-fry

To fry in only enough oil to come halfway up the sides of the food (see page 160). This is the method most cooks use for making fried chicken. Shallow-frying uses less oil than deep-frying, but it does make it necessary to turn the food over halfway through cooking. (See also Deep-fry.)

Shred

To cut into fine strips. Shredding is similar to cutting into chiffonade but less precise. A slicer or mandoline makes easy work of shredding vegetables such as cabbage or fennel. (See also Chiffonade, Slicer.)

Slicer

A useful piece of equipment for slicing vegetables into a variety of different thicknesses. The most common kinds of slicers are the relatively small plastic slicers, sometimes called Benriner cutters, that you hold up with one hand while moving whatever it is you're slicing across the blade. The most useful of these has two small nuts on the back for adjusting the blade for the

Shredding cabbage with plastic slicer, using guard

exact thickness desired. The other type offers only two or three thicknesses, none of which ever seems to be exactly right. A third type of slicer, called a mandoline, is usually made of stainless steel and stands up on its own. A mandoline is best for slicing potatoes—it has blades for French fries and for making ruffled and waffled potato chips (page 80). I find a Benriner slicer to be sharper than a mandoline and substantially cheaper. Both are available at kitchenware stores.

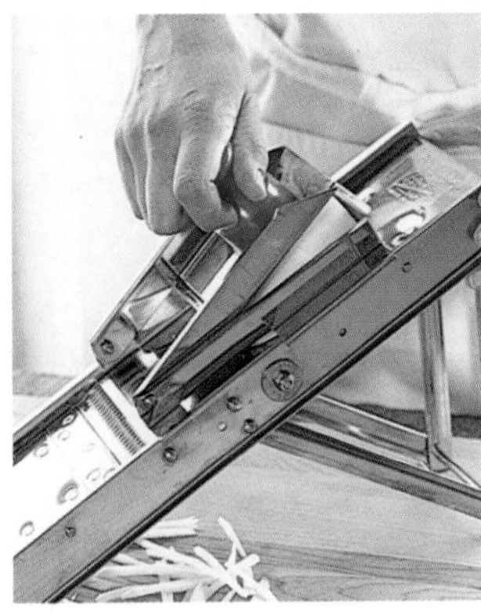

Making French fries with French mandoline, using guard

Slurry

A mixture of equal parts by volume cornstarch and water, used to thicken sauces. (See also Thickener.)

Smoke

To expose foods to wood smoke to enhance their flavor and, in some cases, to help preserve or even cook them. Foods may be hot- or cold-smoked. Hot-smoking cooks foods and flavors them with smoke, while cold-smoking flavors foods with smoke but doesn't cook them. Hot-smoking is the more common of the two methods and can even be accomplished in a covered barbecue by placing hardwood charcoal to one side of the grill and the foods on the other. Chips of wood or sawdust are usually sprinkled over the coals to generate more smoke. Any fat released from the foods as they cook will land in the empty side of the grill bottom instead of on the coals, where it would generate soot and the wrong kind of smoke.

Experienced smokers not only have their favorite cures but also have their favorite woods. No one agrees on the very best wood, but everyone who smokes foods agrees that pine, eucalyptus, and other resiny woods give a strong unpleasant flavor to smoked foods. In the United States, fruitwoods such as pear or apple, maple, hickory, and mesquite are the most popular woods for smoking.

Soufflé

A mixture, usually a thickened sauce (béchamel for savory soufflés, pastry cream or sabayon for dessert soufflés) that is folded together with beaten egg whites and baked in a mold (see page 177). Frozen soufflés aren't really soufflés—they're never baked; they are actually a type of mousse that is frozen in a soufflé mold.

Spider

A gadget that looks like a metal spider web with a long metal handle attached (see page 77). A spider is used for adding and retrieving deep-frying foods to or from the hot oil. It is better for this than a slotted spoon because it catches very little oil and can be used quickly.

Steam

To cook in steam by suspending foods over (not in) boiling water, in a covered pot or steamer. The method is simple: A small amount of water (sometimes scented with fresh herbs or aromatic vegetables) is brought to a rapid boil in the bottom of the steamer over a high heat. The food to be steamed is placed inside the perforated steamer compartment, the steamer is covered, and the food is cooked by the heat of the steam. Steaming is a popular method for vegetables (see page 86) and seafood because it cooks rapidly, allowing foods to retain color and nutrients. When cooking with steam, be sure to let the steam dissipate before you reach into the steamer.

There are several different types of steamers on the market.

- The smallest and least expensive is the collapsible metal steamer that folds out, fanlike, in the bottom of a pot (see page 86). These folding steamers are convenient for small amounts of vegetables (they're awkward with fish), because they adjust to the size of the pot.
- A second type of steamer is a perforated metal insert shaped like a pot, with little feet and a handle. The steamer is placed inside a larger pot (see page 86).
- Chinese bamboo steamers fit on top of a pot or in a wok above boiling water or other liquid (see page 86). Because they are usually fairly big and because they can be stacked, Chinese steamers are convenient for steaming large amounts of foods and for steaming different foods at once.
- A *couscousière,* designed for steaming couscous, can be used to steam other foods as well. Couscousières have a bottom pot that is partially filled with boiling water and a second top pot, with a perforated bottom, that is set on the pot of boiling water

and holds the food. Couscousières can be very inexpensive and, because they can also be quite large, they are convenient for steaming seafood.

Lastly, you can improvise your own steamer with a circular cake rack and three empty tuna cans with both ends removed. Set the cans in the bottom of a pot with a lid, add the water, and set the rack on top.

To use a Chinese steamer to steam root vegetables and green vegetables at the same time:

A Chinese steamer can be used to cook different foods, some with different cooking times, at the same time. The slower-cooking foods are added first, followed by the foods that cook more quickly.

Arrange the root vegetables in the steamer. Bring a small amount of water to a rapid boil in the bottom of a wok or in a pot with the same diameter as the steamer. Place the steamer of root vegetables over the boiling water and cover.

When the root vegetables are about 5 minutes from being done (poke one and judge by the texture), place another steamer rack with the green vegetables over it and cover again. Steam until all the vegetables are done, about 5 minutes more.

To use a collapsible steamer to steam leafy greens:

Collapsible steamers are convenient for small amounts of leafy green vegetables (for example, spinach). Place the steamer in a pot with about an inch of water. Be sure the water doesn't come up into the bottom of the steamer.

Bring the water to a boil over a high heat and add the greens. Cover the pot and steam for 5 minutes. (More tender greens such as spinach or sorrel will cook in a minute or two.) Remove the lid, turn off the heat, and allow about 30 seconds for the steam to dissipate, then take the greens out of the steamer.

Stir-fry

Stir-frying is almost identical to sautéing, except that the food is quickly stirred over the heat instead of being tossed or turned with tongs or spatula (see page 130). A wok is often used in Asia instead of a sauté pan or skillet. Although we usually associate stir-frying with Asian, especially Chinese, dishes, there is no reason why Asian foods can't be sautéed in a skillet and Western dishes stirred in a wok. (See also Sauté.)

Stock

See Broth.

Sweat

To cook foods over gentle heat, usually covered or partly covered, until they release their moisture. Vegetables, meats, and seafood are often sweated when making soups, stews, and sauces so that the foods release their juices into the pan and surrounding liquid. Sweating is the opposite of sautéing, in which food is cooked over high heat so a savory brown crust forms, giving a rich caramelized flavor to foods and sealing in their flavor. Here, julienned leeks are sweated in a covered pan over gentle heat until they soften and become tender. (See also Sauté.)

Thickener

An ingredient used to thicken and give body to flavorful liquids to give them a traditional sauce-like consistency. These flavorful liquids can be the juices from a roast or a deglazed sauté pan, reduced and concentrated broths, acidic reductions of vinegar or wine with shallots and herbs (as for a béarnaise sauce or a beurre blanc), braising liquids from stews or pot roasts, or simple condiments such as mustard.

- Butter: Small amounts of whole butter are often whisked into flavorful liquids, such as the juices in a deglazed sauté pan or concentrated braising juices (the technique is called *monter au beurre*), to give them a silky texture, a sauce-like consistency, and a delicate, suave flavor. Larger amounts of butter are used to make butter sauces such as beurre blanc (page 48) or emulsified egg yolk sauces such as hollandaise sauce (page 41).

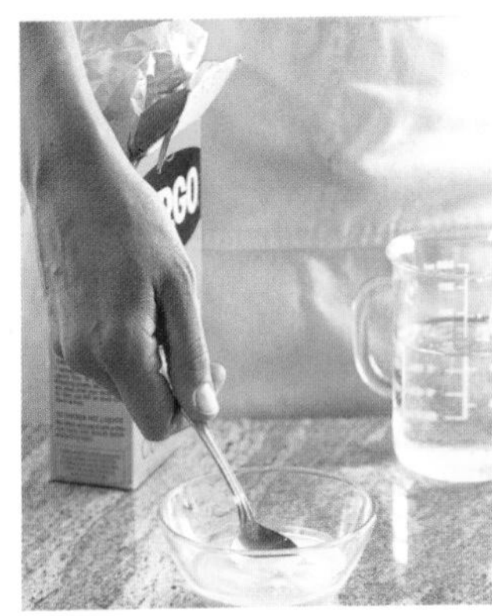

Making cornstarch slurry

Cream-and-egg-yolk liaison for blanquette

• Cornstarch: Cornstarch can be stirred into an equal amount of cold liquid—this mixture is sometimes called a slurry (see page 210)—and then stirred into hot liquids shortly before serving, to give them sheen and to thicken them. Cornstarch is used often in Chinese cooking as a thickener. In classic French cooking, it's used to thicken roasting juices.

• Egg Yolks: Egg yolks are used in several ways to thicken sauces. Traditionally they were combined with cream and added to roux-thickened mixtures to give them sheen and a silky consistency (page 191). They are also whisked up into what is called a *sabayon* to form the base of hollandaise sauce and its derivatives.

• Flour: Flour can be used as a thickener in several ways. It is sometimes turned into a roux by combining it with butter and cooking it gently in a heavy-bottomed saucepan until it smells toasty. White roux is cooked only for a few minutes; brown roux, used in traditional brown sauces, is cooked gently until the flour turns pale brown. Liquids such as milk (for béchamel sauce) and stock (for velouté sauce) are whisked into hot roux and the sauces gently cooked and often skimmed. Flour is also sometimes sprinkled on meat and vegetables as they are browned for stews; in this way, the flour cooks onto the surface of the meat and helps thicken the braising liquid. Flour is also sometimes worked with an equal amount of butter into a paste called *beurre manié*. It is whisked into red-wine stews and sauces as a last-minute thickener.

• Heavy Cream: Heavy cream can be combined with flavorful mixtures such as concentrated stock and then reduced until the sauce reaches the desired consistency.

• Puréed Vegetables: Cooked vegetable purées are sometimes whisked into flavorful liquids to add texture and flavor. Sometimes the vegetables are part of the cooking process, as, for example, when the aromatic vegetables cooked in a stew are puréed and whisked back into the stewing liquid, or when vegetables are cooked around a roast and then puréed to thicken the jus. Vegetable purées can also be made ahead of time and

Combining flour and butter for roux

Cooking the roux

Making beurre manié

Whisking in beurre manié

Flouring to brown and thicken

Making a garlic purée

then used as last-minute thickeners and flavorings for deglazed pan juices, stews, pot roasts, and roasting juices. Garlic purée, onion purée, and sorrel purée are some of my favorites. (See also Beurre Blanc, Monter au Beurre, Roux, Sabayon, Slurry, White Sauce.)

Timbale

A mixture, usually based on puréed vegetables, that is gently baked in a large mold or in individual molds, usually in a *bain-marie*. A timbale is similar to a flan but often contains bread crumbs to add substance. (See also Bain-marie, Custard.)

White Sauce

Traditional white sauces are divided into two types: those based on béchamel sauce and those based on velouté sauce. A basic béchamel sauce is made by adding hot milk to a white roux, and a basic velouté sauce is made by adding hot broth to a white roux. In classical French cooking, innumerable variations are made by adding various ingredients to these two sauces. For example, if cheese is added to a béchamel sauce, the sauce becomes a Mornay sauce; when cream is added to béchamel, it becomes a cream sauce. When tomato purée is added to a velouté sauce, the sauce becomes a *sauce aurore*; when cream and mushroom cooking liquid is added to a velouté sauce, it becomes a *sauce suprême*. Many chefs have eliminated the flour from white sauces and prepare "modern" versions using other thickeners, such as reduced cream, butter, vegetable purées, and egg yolks.

The consistency of a béchamel or velouté sauce can be adjusted by varying the proportion of liquid to roux. The thickness desired depends on what the sauce will be used for. Thick béchamel sauces are used for soufflés; medium béchamel sauces are used for gratinéing foods; and thin béchamel sauces are used as a base for soups.

Traditional recipes for roux call for equal parts by weight of flour and butter, but since most of us use measuring spoons, here are some volume measurements for different thicknesses of béchamel sauce and velouté sauces.

Amounts for 2 Cups Sauce

	FLOUR	BUTTER	MILK / BROTH
Thin, Soupy Sauce	3 tablespoons	3 tablespoons	2 cups
Medium Sauce	4 tablespoons	4 tablespoons	2 cups
Thick Sauce (for gratins)	5 tablespoons	5 tablespoons	2 cups
Soufflé Base	6 tablespoons	6 tablespoons	2 cups

Index

Acorn squash:
- purée, 94, 95
- in soup, 98

aïoli, 41, 42, 43
- for artichokes, 92
- and fried chicken, 160
- for squid stewed with red wine, 128

à la ficelle, 202
à la meunière, 125
à la nage, 112, 113, 262
Algérienne, sautéed chicken, 159
aluminum foil, 146, 148, 166, 177, 265, 277–78
- for braising fish, 116
- collar, 181
- for pot roast, 205
- for salmon *en papillote,* 115

anchovies, 142
- fillets, braised broccoli with grilled bell pepper and, 75
- preparing, 236

apples, 23
- roasting, 101
- in *sauce suédoise,* 42
- in sautéed chicken à la Normande, 159

applesauce, 94, 95, 278
appliances:
- blenders, 100, 279
- electric frying pans, 160
- electric mixers, 179, 181
- food processors, 34, 53, 94, 141, 279
- home smokers, 237
- pasta machines, 54–55, 56
- *see also* utensils

apricots, 25
- poached strawberries and, 104

arborio rice, 63
Archiduc, sautéed chicken, 159
Arctic char:
- poaching and serving, 108
- roasting, 118

Arlésienne, sautéed chicken, 159
aromatic vegetables, 262, 264, 275
- caramelizing, 266
- in court bouillon, 278
- in *demi-glace,* 265
- roasting and, 281
- *see also bumbu*; mirepoix; *refogado*; *soffritto*; *sofregit*; *sofrito*

arrowroot, for thickening stews, 208
artichokes, 92–93
- aïoli for, 43
- baby, 92
- in boeuf à la bourguignonne, 206–7
- in creamed veal stew, 212
- mayonnaise for, 41
- in sautéed chicken Bordelaise, 159

Artois, sautéed chicken, 159
arugula, in salad, 35
asparagus, 2
- in creamy vegetable soup, 100

Atlantic sea bass:
- boning, 228–29
- preparing to cook, 220–21

Bacon:
- bitter-flavored greens and, 35
- with braised green vegetables, 75
- as garnish, 270
- in sautéed broccoli rabe with garlic, 90
- in stews, 206, 209

bacon lardons, 155, 263
bain-marie, 97, 175
baked, baking:
- bananas with rum, 103
- eggs, 175
- fish, 116, 117
- roasting vs., 262
- salmon mousseline, 277
- soufflé, 180
- tomatoes with garlic and fresh basil, 72

baking dishes, 146
baking soda, 263
balloon whisks, 179, 181
balsamic vinegar, in vinaigrette, 37
bamboo steamers, 86
bananas:
- baked, with rum, 103
- roasting, 101

barbecue, 272
basil, 10, 13, 20, 35
- baked tomato with garlic and, 72
- for grilling vegetables, 84
- oil infused with, 39
- in pesto sauce, 99

basmati rice, 63, 64
bâtonnets of vegetables, 18
batters:
- flour and club soda, 77, 78, 267
- light frying, 78
- tempura, 77, 121, 122

Bavarians, 262, 276
bay leaves, in bouquet garni, 31
beans:
- in cassoulet, 271
- dried, in chunky vegetable soup, 98

béarnaise sauce, 44, 45
béchamel sauce, 177, 180, 181, 269, 284, 286
- for cheese soufflé, 179
- for gratin, 271
- white sauce variations with, 287

beef:
- boeuf à la bourguignonne, 206–7
- broth, 30
- in Provençal daube, 210–11
- rib roast, 191–92
- shanks for stews, 208, 209
- *see also* beef chuck; beef tenderloin

beef chuck, 200
- for pot roast, 203
- for stews, 206, 208

beef tenderloin, 191
- (fillet) steaks with green peppercorn sauce, 197
- poaching, 202
- in pot-au-feu, 200

beets:
- juice of, 42, 52
- julienne of, 18
- peeling, 71
- roasting, 70, 71, 72
- vinaigrette for, 37

bell peppers:
- braised broccoli with anchovy fillets and grilled, 75
- coring and seeding after roasting, 9
- julienne of roasted, 19
- peeling, 2, 5
- roasting, 5
- in *sauce andalouse,* 42
- in stir-fried shrimp with cashews, 130

Belon oysters, 134
Benriner cutter, 283–84
béarnaise sauce, grilled steaks with, 193
Bercy, sautéed chicken, 159
beurre blanc, 47, 48, 49, 262, 269, 275, 285
beurre manié:
- for boeuf à la bourguignonne, 207
- in daubes, 210–11
- in sauces for baked fish, 117
- for thickening stews, 208, 286

beurre noisette, 46
- for *à la meunière,* 125
- in hollandaise sauce, 45
- in sautéing chicken breasts, 162
- *see also* clarified butter

Bibb lettuce, in salad, 35
bisques, 139
- shrimp broth in, 34

blackfish, sautéed, 125
black pasta, 52
black sea bass, 109
blanching, 262–63
- bacon, 155, 263
- potatoes for sautéing, 91

blanquette de veau, 30, 208, 212–13, 263, 270
blenders, 100, 279
blini, 61, 62
- cold-smoked salmon and, 238

bluefish:
- brining, 239
- hot-smoked, fillets, 237

blue point oysters, 134
boeuf à la bourguignonne, 155, 206–7, 263, 270
boeuf à la ficelle, 66, 67, 200, 201
boeuf à la mode, 203
boiling, 263
- artichokes, 92
- carrots, 70
- crayfish, 139
- eggs, 172–73
- green vegetables, 88
- pot-au-feu, 200–201
- vegetables, 86

bollito misto, 200, 278
bolognese sauce, 50
bones:
- for fish broth, 231
- for veal broth, 241

boning:
- Atlantic sea bass, 228–29
- chicken breasts, 163
- rabbit, 256
- round fish, 226–29
- salmon for medallions, 112
- small fish, 236
- snapper, 223

bonito, dried, in miso soup, 143
Bordelaise, sautéed chicken, 159
Boston lettuce, in salad, 35
bouillabaisse, brown fish broth in, 32
bouquet garni, 14, 31
Bourguignonne, sautéed chicken à la, 159

Index

braised, braising, x, 263–64, 277–78
beef stew, *see* boeuf à la bourguignonne
broccoli with anchovy fillets and grilled bell pepper on toast, 75
duck thighs, 170
fish, 114, 116
green vegetables, 75
meats, 67
pot roast and, 203
rabbit, 254, 257–59
shanks for, 209
short-, sweetbreads, 214, 215
veal shanks, 209
vegetable garnish for, 10
whole fish, 117
see also stews
brandy, fruit, 270
bread crumb coating, 264
for deep-frying fish, 121, 267
for frying, 77
on roasted vegetables, 70
for sautéing chicken breasts, 162
for sweetbreads, 214
for tomatoes, 77, 79
bread crumbs, 164, 264
in bisque, 139
in timbale, 287
breading, 264, 266
for *à la meunière,* 125
for sautéed sweetbreads, 216–17
for sautéing chicken breasts, 160, 162
for sautéing fish, 126, 282
brining:
bluefish, 239
fish fillets, 239
broccoli:
braising, 75
in creamy vegetable soup, 100
broccoli rabe, sautéed, with garlic, 90
broiled, broiling, 265
chops, 194
fish and shellfish, 265
mixed grill, 193, 194
broth, 30–34, 265
aromatic vegetables, 262
beef tenderloin and, 202
from boiled meats, 200
in braised broccoli, 75
chicken, 30–31, 70
chicken wings for, 153
crustacean, 34, 139
for deglazing, 157, 195, 266, 268
duck, 31, 171
fish, 32–33
in mayonnaise, 42
for miso soup, 143
parsley stems for, 14
poached chicken and, 149
in red wine pot roast, 203–5
in root vegetable gratin, 74
shrimp, 34, 64, 65
shrimp heads for, 131
soup from, 30
for steaming shellfish, 132
veal, 241
brown chicken fricassée, 30, 154
see also coq au vin
brown fish broth, 32
brown glazing, 76, 277
brown roux, 265, 282
brown sauce, 265–66, 268, 275
brunoise, 10, 266
Brussels sprouts, 7
bumbu, 275
butter, 38, 46–49
clarified, 46
compound, 47, 282
crustacean, 139
in hollandaise sauce, 44–46
monter au beurre, 275
in roux, 180, 181, 282
for sautéing, 91, 125, 159
tarragon, 47
as thickener, 285
see also beurre blanc; beurre manié; beurre noisette

Cabbage, 10, 18
braising, 75
vinaigrette for, 37
Calvados, in sautéed chicken à la Normande, 159
canola oil:
in mayonnaise, 41
in vinaigrette, 37
capers:
in gribiche, 42, 43
in *sauce rémoulade,* 42
caramelizing, 266, 273
carnaroli rice, 63
carrots:
braising, 264
in broth, 31, 32, 33, 139
caramelizing, 266
in court bouillon, 113, 266, 278
cutting, 13, 14, 15, 19, 21
flan, 97, 270
for garnish, 208, 270
peeling, 2
puréed in soup, 100
roasting vs. boiling, 70
vinaigrette for, 37
carving, xi
chicken, 146, 149
fish, 118–19
lamb, saddle of, 253
pork, rack of, 189, 190
rib roast, 191, 192
turkey, xi, 168
cashews, stir-fried shrimp with, 130
cassoulet, 271
Catalonian cooking, *sofregit* in, 275
cauliflower, 8
caviar, for blini, 61
celeriac, 2, 3
cutting, 18
in mashed potatoes, 94
celery, 2, 14
braising, 264
in broth, 31
in court bouillon, 266, 278
for sautéing meat, 195
see also mirepoix
celery root, 2
cèpes, sautéed chicken with, 159
cephalopods, 128–29
see also cuttlefish; octopus; squid
chard, *see* Swiss chard
château potatoes, 89
cheese:
baked eggs with, 175
in omelets, 176
in potato gratin, 73
soufflé, 177–80, 181
see also Parmesan cheese
cheesecloth, 109, 110, 141
cherries, pitting, 25
chestnuts, 2, 4
purée, 96
chicken, 145–63, 165
in a pot, 150
broiling, 265
broth, 30–31, 70
carving, 146, 149
cutting up raw, 151–53
fricassée, 30
frying, 160, 265, 267
grilling, 161
in paella, 63, 64
with red wine, *see* coq au vin
with roasted vegetables, 70, 147
roasting, 146–49
sautéed, breasts and thighs with mushroom sauce, 158
sautéed boneless, breasts, 162–63
sautéing, 157–59
short-braising, 154, 264
stews, 154–56
trussing, x, 146–47, 148, 150
see also chicken liver
chicken broth, 30–31
for roasting vegetables, 70
chicken liver:
mousse, 165, 275
in port-wine-and-shallot pan sauce, 165
chiffonade, 10, 266
basil, 10, 20
of leafy greens, 8, 19, 266
chiles:
in beurre blanc, 48
with braised green vegetables, 75
roasting and peeling, 5
in sautéed broccoli rabe with garlic, 90
in stir-frying seafood, 130
chine bone, 248
of rack of pork, 189–90
Chinese cooking, stir-frying in, 130
Chinese steamer, 284–85
chips:
potato, 80
root vegetable, 81
chives:
for grilling vegetables, 84
in sautéed chicken with fines herbes, 159
chlorophyll:
extracting, 52
in green mayonnaise, 42, 43
in green pasta, 52, 53
chopping, 10, 266, 269
herbs, 14
vegetables, 12, 14
chops, 195
grilling, 193
sautéing, 195
chopsticks, 25, 124, 130
chorizos, in paella, 63, 64
chuck roast, in pot-au-feu, 201
cilantro, stemming for salad, 36
cinnamon, for poaching fruit, 104, 105
citrus fruits, 24
see also lemons; oranges
clams:
razor, long-braising, 264
steaming, 132, 133

clarified butter, 46, 264
in chicken liver mousse, 165
for hollandaise sauce, 44, 45
for sautéing, 91, 125–26, 162, 282
cleaning:
Dover sole, 234
leeks, 9
mussels, 133
small fish, 236
squid, 129
cloves, for poaching fruit, 104–5
club soda and flour batter, 77, 78, 267
coatings:
for deep frying, 77–79, 121, 267
for sautéing tomato, 89
see also bread crumb coating; breading
cockles, steaming, 132, 133
coconut, 29
milk, 29, 130
cod, for goujonettes, 122
cold-smoked salmon, 238
collar:
of aluminum foil, 181
for soufflé, 177, 180
compound butters, 47, 282
grilled steaks with, 193
concassée, 266
tomato, 6, 50
conch, long-braising, 264
confit, 266
of duck thighs, 170
cookie cutters, 57
copper bowls, 179, 181
coq au vin, 156, 270, 272
bacon lardons in, 155, 263
brown chicken broth in, 30
coring:
apples, 23
cabbage, 18
pears, 101
roasted bell peppers, 9
whole pears, 105
corn, shucking and kernel removal of, 7
cornichons, in gribiche, 42, 43
Cornish hen:
grilling, 161
roasting, 147, 281
cornstarch:
in Chinese cooking, 130
in gravies, 271
for pot roast braising liquid, 205
in Provençal daube, 210–11
in slurry, 284
for thickening stews, 208, 286
coulis, 266
tomato, 50
court bouillon, 108–9, 113, 266, 278
for boiled crayfish, 139
for poaching fish, 110, 266
for seafood *à la nage,* 112, 113, 262, 278
for steaming vegetables, 86
see also vegetable broth
couscousière, 284–85
crab:
with baked eggs, 175
in crustacean broth, 34, 139
crayfish, 139–41
in crustacean broth, 34, 139
heads and tails for sauces, 139, 141
poaching, 112
sauce, with salmon mousseline, 141, 277
in sautéed chicken dishes, 159
sautéing, 139
stir-frying, 130
cream:
in beurre blanc, 49
in braised rabbit, 257–59
in crustacean broth, 34
for deglazing after chicken sauté, 157, 266, 268
in mousseline, 276
in potato gratin, 73
roasted pear halves with, 101–2
in root vegetable gratin, 74
sauces, 269
in sauces for baked fish, 117
in sautéed chicken dishes, 159
see also heavy cream
creamed, creamy:
onions, 76
soups, 98
spinach, 88
veal stew, 30, 208, 212–13, 263
vegetable soup, 100
cream of tartar, for egg whites, 179, 181
crème anglaise, 262, 276
crème brûlée, 267, 270
crème caramel, 267, 270
crème fraîche:
for blini, 61
in mousseline, 276
cremini mushrooms, for sautéing, 91
crêpes, 61, 62
croutons, in sautéed chicken Marengo, 159
crustacean:
broth, 34, 139
butter, 139
cucumbers, 14, 15, 16
as garnish, 270
seeding, 8
curing, 266–67
fish fillets, 237
seafood, 239–40
curry:
in beurre blanc, 48
in creamed veal stew, 212
custards, 267, 269
bain-marie for, 262
doneness of, 67
cutting:
beef tenderloin (fillet), 197
chicken, 151–53
herbs, 10
pasta dough, 54, 56, 59
potatoes for frying, 80, 81, 82
rabbit, 254–55
raw lobster, 135–36
veal breast for stew, 241
vegetables, 10, 266
cuttlefish:
ink, in black pasta, 52
stew, 128

Dandelion, in salad, 35
dashi, 143
in dipping sauce for shrimp tempura, 122
daubes, 206, 210–11
brown chicken broth in, 30
meats for, 200, 203
Provençal, 210–11
deboning, *see* boning; filleting
deep-frying, 121–22, 267, 284
confit vs., 266
fish and shellfish, 121–22
fried flounder goujonettes, 121, 265
potatoes, 80
squid, 128
vegetables, 77, 78, 160
see also tempura
deglazing, 266, 267–68, 270, 282
chicken, 157, 159
pan for sautéed skin-on red snapper fillets, 125
roast rack of lamb, 187, 188
steaks, 195
degreasing, 268
broth, 31
demi-glace, 265–66, 268, 275
desalting anchovies, 142
deveining shrimp, 131
dicing, 10, 266, 269
turnips, 17
vegetables, 13
dill, in gravlax, 239
doneness, 66–67
of chicken liver, 165
of chicken sauté, 157
of fish *en papillote,* 114
of poached fish, 109, 110
of poached fish steaks, 112
of poached meat tenderloin, 202
of red wine pot roast, 204
of roasted fish, 120
of roasted meats, 189, 191, 281
of soufflé, 180
of sweetbreads, 214
Doria, sautéed chicken, 159
dough:
egg pasta, 51
for gnocchi, 60
Dover sole:
cleaning and scaling, 234
preparing, 230
skinning, 234
whole, *à la meunière,* 125, 126
dried porcini mushroom:
dust, 164, 265
oil infused with, 40
drum sieves, 94, 95, 96, 164, 264, 279
dry-curing salmon for cold smoking, 239
duck, 31, 170–71
fat, for sautéing, 157, 195
duck breasts:
poaching, 202
sautéing, 171
dumplings, gnocchi, 60
durum flour, in egg pasta dough, 51
duxelles:
with baked eggs, 175
stuffing, 110, 111

E*au-de-vie,* 270
eggplant, 2, 3
frying, 77
gratin, 73
grilling, 84
panfrying, 277
in sautéed chicken Arlésienne, 159
sautéing, 89, 90, 91, 265
eggs:
baking, 175
boiling, 172–73

eggs (*continued*)
omelets, 176
poaching, 174
separating, 178, 181
soufflés, 177–81
see also egg whites; egg yolks
eggs Benedict, hollandaise sauce for, 44
egg whites:
beating, 181
separating, 178, 181
soufflés and, 179, 284
egg yolks, 269
in aïoli, 43
in *blanquette de veau,* 212, 263
in blini, 61, 62
for cheese soufflé, 179
in hollandaise sauce, 41, 44, 45
in mayonnaise, 41, 42
in pasta dough, 51
raw, 41
in sabayon, 44, 45, 282
separating, 178, 181
in tempura batter, 122
as thickener, 286
electric frying pan, 160
electric mixer, 179, 181
emulsion, 48, 269, 285
sabayon, 44
endive, 35
grilling, 84
vinaigrette for, 37
en escabeche, 274
en papillote, 114–15
Escoffier, 159
étuver, 269
eye of round, for poaching, 202

Fatback, *see* larding
fava beans, peeling, 4
fennel, 2, 5, 10, 16, 22
in broth, 31
in court bouillon, 266, 278
in creamed veal stew, 212
frying, 77
as garnish, 270
grilling, 84
filleting, 127
flounder, 231–32
salmon, 223, 224–25
skate wings, 235
striped bass, 222–23
fins, removal of, 220, 230
fish, small:
poaching, 109, 110, 112, 278
preparing, 236
fish, whole:
frying, 267
grilling, 123
sautéing, 125
fish and shellfish, 107–43
aïoli for, 43
à la nage, 112, 113, 262, 278
baked, 116–17
with baked eggs, 175
big, 108–9
bitter-flavored greens and, 35
braising, 114, 116–17, 264
brining, 239
broiling, 265
cephalopods, 128–29
curing, 237, 239–40
deep-frying, 121–22, 267
doneness of, 67
en escabeche, 274–75
en papillote, 114–15
filleting, 127, 222–23, 224–25, 231–32, 235
fried flounder goujonettes, 121, 265
grilling, 123–24, 272
hollandaise sauce for, 44
hot-smoked fillets, 237
in paella, 63, 64, 65
poaching, 108–11, 112, 263, 266, 278
porcini dust for sautéing, 164
preparing, 220–40
quenelles of, 280
roasting, 118–20
sautéing, 123, 125–26
short cooking, 128
steaming, 132–33
stir-frying, 130
vinaigrette as sauce for, 37
see also specific fish
fish broth, 32–33, 116
bones for, 221, 222, 231
brown, 32
classic, 32
in paellas, 32
red-wine, 32
fish poacher, 108, 109
flambé, flambéing, 101, 103, 269
flank steak, slicing, 196
flans, 97, 269–70
doneness of, 67
purée in, 279
flatfish, 220, 230–35
filleting, 232
in fish broth, 32
flounder, 220, 230–32
baking, 117
cooked, filleting of, 127
fried, goujonettes, 121–22, 265
sautéing, 125
whole, baked with white wine and shallots, 116
flour:
for *à la meunière,* 125
in béchamel sauce, 180
and club soda batter for frying, 77, 78, 121, 267
in crêpes, 62
in egg pasta dough, 51
for fried chicken, 160
for roast turkey, 167
in roux, 180, 181, 282
sautéing and, 91, 126, 138, 265
in tempura batter, 122
as thickener, 208, 286
fond, 265
food mills, 94, 100, 279
for applesauce, 95
food processor:
for crayfish sauce, 141
crustacean broth and, 34
for pasta dough, 53
purée and, 94, 279
framboise, 270
freezing:
broths, 31
herb butters, 47
mushroom stems, 111
shrimp heads, 131
French cooking, 10, 264, 265
aromatic vegetables, 262
bacon lardons in, 155
blanquette de veau, 30, 208, 212–13
boeuf à la mode, 203
boiled crayfish and, 139
broth in, 30
château potatoes, 89
chicken fricassées, 154
confit in, 266
coq au vin, 155, 156
étuver, 269
garnish in, 270
grilled steaks with béarnaise sauce, 193
jus lié, 27
pike quenelles in, 280
pot-au-feu, 200, 201, 278
sauces for sautéed chicken, 159
sauces in, 282
white sauces in, 287
see also Provençal cooking
French cut:
lamb, rack of, 187
pork, rack of, 189
French fries, 80, 82, 267
russet potatoes for, 81
Frenching:
rack of lamb, 246, 247–48, 249
rack of pork, 248
fricassées, 270
brown chicken, 30, 154
sautéing vs., 283
veal, 208
white chicken, 30, 154–55
see also stews
frisée:
in salad, 35
vinaigrette for, 37
fruit brandy, 270
fruits, 23–29
applesauce, 95, 96
cooking, 94, 95, 101–5
poaching, 104–5
puréed, 94, 96
roasting, 101–2
fruitwoods for smoking, 237, 284
frying, x
chicken, 151, 160, 265
fennel, 77
flounder goujonettes, 121, 265
shallow, 160, 283
sweetbreads, 214
tomatoes, 79
vegetables, 77–82
zucchini slices, 77
see also deep-frying

Garlic, 10, 11
in aïoli, 42, 43
as aromatic vegetable, 262
baked tomato with fresh basil and, 72
with braised green vegetables, 75
braising, 264
for grilled chicken marinade, 161
paste, 11, 43
purée, 268, 287
and sage butter sauce for gnocchi, 60
sautéed broccoli rabe with, 90
sautéed zucchini with parsley and, 91
for sautéing meat, 195
for steaming shellfish, 132
garnish, 270
for chicken fricassées, 154
for chicken sauté, 157

for miso soup, 143
for pot roast, 205
for sautéed chicken dishes, 159
for stews, 206, 208, 264
vegetable cuts for, 10
gelatin:
in Bavarian, 262, 276
in fish broth, 32
ghee, 46
giblet gravy, 166, 169, 271
gills, removal of, 221
ginger, 90, 122, 130
as aromatic vegetable, 262
gizzard, turkey, in giblet gravy, 169
glace de viande, 265–66, 268, 270–71, 275
glazing:
meat, 270–71
pot roast, 271
rabbit, 271
root vegetables, 76, 271
vegetables, 70
gluten, 271
gnocchi with garlic and sage butter sauce, 60
goujonettes, 121, 265, 271
fish used for, 122
gratin, xi, 73–74, 265, 271
potato, 73
gratin dishes, 146
gravies, 271
giblet, 166, 169, 271
gravlax, 239–40, 267
green beans:
in boeuf à la bourguignonne, 206–7
braising, 75
green mayonnaise, 43
green pasta, 52, 53
green peppercorn sauce, sautéed beef tenderloin (fillet) steaks with, 197
greens, bitter-flavored, vinaigrettes for, 35, 37
greens, leafy, 8, 10, 19, 266, 285
green vegetables:
boiling, 88, 263
braising, 75, 264
steaming, 87
gribiche sauce, 42, 43
and fried chicken, 160
for fried flounder goujonettes, 121
grill basket, 124
grilling, x, 265, 271–72
butterflied leg of lamb, 193
chicken, 151, 161
chops, 193
Cornish hen, 161
duck thighs, 170
fish and shellfish, 123–24
lamb, 249
mixed vegetable kebabs, 85
potatoes, 84, 263
scallions, 39
squab, 161
steaks, 193
turnips, 263
vegetables, 83–85
grill pan, 123, 193, 272
grouper, sautéed, 125
Guide Culinaire, Le, (Escoffier), 159
gutting, whole fish, 221

Half-rounds, for carrots, 15
halibut, 220
ham:
with baked eggs, 175
in *sofrito,* 275
heart, turkey, in giblet gravy, 169
heavy cream:
with baked eggs, 175
for chicken sauté, 157
for deglazing, 199, 268
emulsion and, 269
as thickener, 286
herb butters, 47
in beurre blanc, 49
in fish *en papillote,* 114
herbs, 10, 13, 14
for grilling vegetables, 84
stuffing for whole fish, 229
hickory, for smoking, 237, 238
hollandaise sauce, 41, 44, 45, 269, 282, 285
saffron in, 280
home smokers, 237, 238
Hongroise, sautéed chicken à la, 159
horseradish, in *sauce suédoise,* 42
hot-smoked fish fillets, 237
hot smokers, *see* home smokers

Immersion blenders, 100, 279
improvisation, x
Indonesian cooking, *bumbu* in, 275
infused oils, 39–40
basil, 39
dried porcini mushroom, 40
in hot vinaigrette, 38
in vinaigrettes, 40
Italian cooking:
bollito misto, 200, 278
minestrone col pesto, 98
zabaglione, 28

Jalapeño chiles, in stir-fried shrimp with cashews, 130
Japanese cooking:
miso soup, 143
shrimp tempura, 122
jasmine rice, 64
julienne, 10, 272
lemon zest, 25
potatoes, 80, 81
vegetables, 13, 18, 19, 20
vegetables for braised veal shanks, 209
vegetables for fish *à la nage,* 112, 113, 262
jus, 272–73
for chicken, 146, 147, 148
for lamb, leg of, 184
for lamb, rack of, 187–88
for pork, rack of, 189
for rib roast, 191
see also glace de viande
jus lié, 271

Kale, braising, 75
Kamimoto oysters, 134
kelp, in miso soup, 143
kirsh, 270
kiwis, peeling and slicing, 26
knives:
chopping and mincing with, 12
peeling with, 2, 3
stemming with, 8
konbu, 143

Lamb, 184–86
carving, 185–86
grilling, 249
for pot roast, 203
purchasing, 184
roasting vegetables and, 70
saddle of, 250–53
sautéing, 249
shoulder, 200
stews, 208, 209
tenderloins of, 253, 277
see also lamb, leg of; lamb, rack of; lamb chops
lamb, leg of, 242–43
grilling, 193, 272
poaching, 202
preparing, 242–43
purchasing, 242
roasting, 184–85
lamb, rack of, 244–49
chops, 249
Frenching, 246–48, 249
persillade on, 278
preparing, 244–49
roasting, 187–88, 281
lamb chops, 249
broiled, 194
loin, 250
larding, 263, 264, 273
for boeuf à la bourguignonne, 206
in Provençal daube, 210–11
rabbit, 257
red wine pot roast, 203–5
lavender, in persillade, 278
leeks, 9
baby, grilling, 84
braising, 264
in court bouillon, 113, 266, 278
julienne of, 20
soup, puréed potato and, 100
vinaigrette for, 37
leftovers, 97
with baked eggs, 175
mushroom stems, 111
lemon grass, 262
lemon juice:
in aïoli, 43
for *à la meunière,* 125
in hollandaise sauce, 44, 45
in mayonnaise, 41, 42
to prevent darkening, 23, 92, 95
in sautéed chicken dishes, 159
in vinaigrette, 37
lemons, 24
zest of, 25, 143
lettuces, 35
grilling, 84
lettuce spinners, 35, 36
Ligurian cooking, *minestrone col pesto,* 98, 99
liver, turkey, in giblet gravy, 169
lobster, 135–37
with baked eggs, 175
in crustacean broth, 34
killing, 132, 135
in omelets, 176
poaching, 112
removing meat from, 136–37
roe, 135, 136
steaming, 132, 133, 135
loin lamb chops, 250
London broil, sautéing, 195
long-braising, *see* boeuf à la bourguignonne; stewed, stewing

M*acedoine,* 10, 274
Madeira, 165, 197
in sautéed chicken dishes, 159
malt vinegar, 121
mandoline, 13, 80, 81, 82, 274, 283–84
mangoes, pitting and peeling, 28
maple wood, for smoking, 237, 238
Marengo, sautéed chicken, 159
marinades, 274
for boeuf à la bourguignonne, 206–7
for coq au vin, 156
for grilled chicken, 161
for grilling, 272
for pot roast, 203
for Provençal daube, 210–11
white wine, for fried chicken, 160
marjoram, 83
for grilling vegetables, 84
oil infused with, 39
in persillade, 278
marrow, removing, 275
Marsala wine, in zabaglione, 282
mayonnaise, 41–43, 193, 282
for artichokes, 92
garlic in, 11
green, 43
infused oils in, 39
sabayon in, 41, 45
see also aïoli; gribiche sauce
meat, 184–217, 241–53
bitter-flavored greens and, 35
braised, 67, 264
broiling, 265
caramelizing, 266
cuts of, 195, 200
doneness of, 66–67
glaze, 159, 270–71
in gratin, 74
grilled strip steaks, 193
poached, 67, 263, 278
pot roast, 203–5, 264
roasting vegetables and, 70, 72
vinaigrette as sauce for, 37
see also beef; lamb; pork; rabbit; veal
medallions:
of meat, 199
poached salmon, 112–13
for sautéing fish, 126
sautéing of meat, 195
medium boiled eggs, 172
mesquite wood, for smoking, 237
mincing, 10, 266
garlic, 11
vegetables, 12
minestrone col pesto, 98
mirabelle, 270
mirepoix, 116, 262, 275
in braised rabbit, 257–59
as garnish, 270
for short-braised sweetbreads, 215
mirin, in dipping sauce for shrimp tempura, 122
miso soup, 143
mixed grill, 193, 194
mollusks:
grilling, 123
steaming, 132
see also mussels; oysters
monter au beurre, 275, 285
Mornay sauce, béchamel sauce in, 287
mortar and pestle, 41, 42, 43, 99
mousse, 275–76
chicken liver, 165, 275
purée in, 279
see also Bavarians
mousseline, 276–77
purée in, 279
of veal, 280
mushrooms:
with baked eggs, 175
butters, 47
chopping, 14
duxelles stuffing for whole fish, 229
frying, 77
as garnish, 270
gratin, 73
grilling, 83, 84
roasting, 70, 72
in *sauce suprême,* 287
in sautéed chicken dishes, 158, 159
sautéing, 91, 282
stuffing, 111
tempura batter for, 77
mussels, 133
steaming, 132, 133
mustard:
in mayonnaise, 41, 42
in vinaigrette, 37

Noisettes, 195, 277
of lamb, 253
preparing pork, 198
noodles:
cutting pasta for, 56
in miso soup, 143
Normande, sautéed chicken à la, 159
nutmeg, in potato gratin, 73
nut oils, 37, 41
nuts:
as breading, 265
stir-fried shrimp with cashews, 130

Oak leaf lettuce, in salad, 35
octopus, 128
deep-frying, 121
stewing, 128, 264
oeufs en cocotte, 175
oeufs mollets, 172
oils:
for chicken stews, 155
for fried chicken, 160
for frying, 78
nut, 37, 41
for sautéing, 91, 292–93
okra, frying, 77
olive oil, 37, 43, 51, 155
for fried chicken, 160
for grilling vegetables, 83
in hot vinaigrette, 38
in mayonnaise, 41
to prevent basil from darkening, 13, 20
in salad, 35
for sautéing chicken, 157, 162, 267
for sautéing zucchini, 91
omelets, 176
onions, 2, 10
braising, 264
in broth, 31, 32
brown glazing, 76
caramelizing, 266
in court bouillon, 113, 266, 278
in mirepoix, 262, 275
in Provençal daube, 210–11
roasting, 70
in sautéed chicken dishes, 159
for sautéing meat, 195
see also pearl onions
orange pasta, 52
oranges, 24
oregano:
for grilling, 272
for grilling vegetables, 84
osso bucco, 208
oysters, 134
hollandaise sauce for, 44
sautéed chicken with, 159
Paellas, 63, 64, 65
crustacean broth in, 34
fish broth in, 32
seafood, 64, 65
pancakes, 61
pancetta:
in chunky vegetable soup, 98–99
in sautéed broccoli rabe with garlic, 90
panfry, sautéing vs., 277, 283
pan juice, *see* jus
pan sauce, 10
port-wine-and-shallot, 165
from roasted fruits, 101
paprika, in sautéed chicken à la Hongroise, 159
parchment paper, 76, 215, 277–78
for braising fish, 116
for *en papillote,* 114–15
lids made of, 64
paring knives, 2, 25
parmentier, sautéed chicken, 159
Parmesan cheese:
as breading, 265
for cheese soufflé, 179, 181
in pesto sauce, 99
for sautéing chicken breasts, 162
parsley, 14, 36
for grilling vegetables, 84
oil infused with, 39
sautéed zucchini with garlic and, 91
steamed mussels with white wine and, 132
for steaming shellfish, 132
parsnips, 14, 19
in chunky vegetable soup, 98
gratin, 73
for pot-au-feu, 200
roasting, 70
pasta, 263
ravioli, 57, 58, 59
sauce from steaming shellfish, 132
stuffings for, 279
tortelloni, 57
zucchini in, 15
see also pasta dough
pasta cutter, 59
pasta dough, 51, 53–56
coloring, 52, 53
cutting, 54, 56, 59
food processor for, 53
rolling, 54–55
pastry bags, 57, 58, 59

peaches, 263
roasting, 101–2
pearl onions, 2, 5
brown-glazed, 76, 277
as garnish, 270
in sautéed chicken Artois, 159
pears, 101, 105
poached in red wine, 105
roasted halves with cream, 101–2, 103, 269
peas:
in artichoke bottoms, 92
in creamy vegetable soup, 100
for garnishing stews, 208
for pot roast, 205
peelers, 2, 25
nonswivel (fixed blade), 2, 3, 23, 105
swivel-type, 2
peeling:
apples, 23
bell peppers, 5
celeriac, 3
chestnuts, 2, 4
citrus fruits, 24
eggplant, 3
fava beans, 4
fennel, 5
hot chiles, 5
kiwis, 26
mangoes, 28
peaches, 263
pearl onions, 2, 5
pears, 101
pineapples, 27
roasted beets, 71
shrimp, 131
tomatoes, 6, 263
turnips, 3
vegetables, 2–6
vegetables for roasting, 70
pepper, bell, *see* bell peppers
pepper, white, in hollandaise sauce, 44, 45
peppercorn sauce, green, 197
persillade, 91, 278
persimmons, 26
Peruvian purple potatoes, in château potatoes, 89
pesto sauce, 11, 99
in chunky vegetable soup, 98
in mashed potatoes, 94
Phillips head screwdrivers, 29
pickles, French sour, 42, 43
pike, quenelles of, 280
pilaf, rice, 63, 64
pineapples, peeling and sectioning, 27
pine nuts, in pesto sauce, 99
pistou, 98, 99
pitting:
fruits, 25
mangoes, 28
poaching, x, 263, 278
beef tenderloin, 202
chicken, 149
chicken in a pot, 150
eggs, 174
fish, 108–13, 262, 278
fruit, 104–5
meats, 67, 200
oysters with sautéed chicken, 159
pears in red wine, 105
salmon medallions, 108
salmon quenelles, 280
shellfish, 112
strawberries and apricots, 104
tenderloin, 66
vegetables, 86
see also boiling
pompano, grilling, 123
porcini dust, 164, 264
sautéed sweetbreads breaded with, 216–17
for sautéing chicken breasts, 162
porcini mushrooms:
dried, oil infused with, 40
sautéed chicken with cèpes, 159
see also porcini dust
pork:
chops, broiled, 194
Frenching rack of, 248
loin, 190
medallions, 199
preparing, 244
roasting rack of, 189–90
sautéing, 199
tenderloin, 195, 198, 277
see also ham; pancetta; prosciutto
port, 165
for deglazing sautéed venison loin, 199
portobello mushrooms, grilling, 84
Portugese cooking, *refogado* in, 275
potatoes:
blanching, 263
château, 89
chips, 80
French fries, 80, 82
frying, 77, 81
gnocchi, 60
gratin, 73
grilling, 84
mashed, 94, 278
roasting, 70, 72
sautéed, 89, 91
in sautéed chicken dishes, 159
soup, puréed leek and, 100
straw, 80, 81
see also russet potatoes
potato mashers, 94
pot-au-feu, 200–201, 203, 278
pot roast, 263–64
brown chicken broth in, 30
caramelizing, 266
glazing, 271
pot-au-feu vs., 203
purchasing meat for, 200
red-wine, 203–5
poule au pot, 150
poultry:
doneness of, 67
roasting with vegetables, 72
see also chicken; Cornish hen; duck; turkey
proofing yeast, 61
prosciutto, 267
with baked eggs, 175
caramelizing, 266
in chunky vegetable soup, 98–99
Provençal cooking:
daube, 210–11
soupe au pistou, 98, 99
puréed, purées, 278–79
acorn squash, 94, 95
applesauce, 94, 95, 278
bread crumbs for bisques, 139
carrot, 97
carrot soup, 100
chestnuts, 96
chicken liver, 165
for flan, 97, 270
fruits, 96
leek and potato soup, 100
mashed potatoes, 94, 278
pesto sauce, 99
root vegetables, 95
sorrel, in creamed veal stew, 212, 276, 287
sweet potatoes, 279
tomato coulis, 50
vegetables, for boeuf à la bourguignonne, 207
vegetables, for creamy soup, 100
vegetables, for pot roast braising liquid, 205
vegetables, for thickening, 208, 271, 286–87

Quail, roasting, 281
quenelles, 280
purée in, 279
of salmon mousseline, 276
quetsch, 270
quiche, 97, 267, 270

Rabbit, 254–59
boning, 256
braising, 254, 257–59, 266
cutting, 254–55
doneness of, 67
glazing, 271
larding, 257
rack of lamb, *see* lamb, rack of
radicchio:
grilling, 84
in salad, 35
ramps, grilling, 84
ravioli, 57, 58, 59
ravioli form, 58
red lettuce, in salad, 35
red pasta, 52
red snapper, *see* snapper
reductions, 262, 280
red wine:
in brown chicken fricassée, 154
pan sauce, sautéed flank steaks with, 196
poached pears in, 105
pot roast, 203–5
in Provençal daube, 210–11
in sautéed chicken à la Bourguignonne, 159
squid stewed with, 128
for stewing seafood, 128
red-wine fish broth, 32, 33
baked whole snapper with, 117
in braised fish, 116
salmon for, 32, 33
snapper baked with a, 32, 33
refogado, 275
refreshing, of boiled green vegetables, 263
resting, 291–92
rack of lamb, 187, 188
roast chicken, 148
roasts, 66, 189, 191, 291–92
rib of beef, roasting and carving, 191–92

Index

rice and rice dishes, 63–65, 263
in bisque, 34, 139
fluffy, 63, 64
paella, 63, 64, 65
see also risotto
ricers, 94, 279
risotto, 63, 64
alla Milanese, 63
crustacean broth in, 34
roast beef, roasting vegetables and, 70
roasted, roasting, x, 281–82
apples, 101
baking vs., 262
bananas, 101
beets, 70, 71, 72
bell peppers, 5
chicken, 146–49
Cornish game hens, 147
fish, 118–20
fruits, 101–2
hot chiles, 5
leg of lamb, 184–85
meats, 66
meat with vegetables, 72
pear halves with cream, 101–2, 103, 269
poultry with vegetables, 72
rack of lamb, 187–88
rack of pork, 189–90
resting meat after, 66, 291–92
root vegetables, 70, 72
saddle of lamb, 252
turkey, xi, 166–68
vegetable garnish for, 10
vegetables, 70–72
whole fish, 117
roasting racks, 167, 281
roe, lobster, 135, 136
rolling pasta dough, 54–55
rolling pins, 34, 141
romaine lettuce, in salad, 35
root vegetables:
blanching, 263
braising, 264
caramelizing, 266
in chicken in a pot, 149
for chips, 81
glazing, 76, 264, 271
gratin, 73, 74
julienne of, 10
purée of, 95
roasting, 70, 72
sautéing, 91
steaming, 285
see also carrots; potatoes; russet potatoes; turnips
rosemary:
for grilling, 272
for grilling vegetables, 84
oil infused with, 39
round fish, whole:
boning, 226–29
preparing, 220–29
rounds of vegetables, 15
roux, 180, 181, 269, 282, 287
in *blanquette de veau,* 212, 263
brown, 265
in creamy vegetable soup, 100
in gravies, 271
as thickener, 286
rubs, 274
rum, flambéed, 101, 103
russet potatoes:
for frying potatoes, 81
roasting, 70, 72
in slices, sautéed, 89

Sabayon, 282, 286
dessert soufflés and, 177, 282, 284
egg yolks in, 44, 45
for hollandaise sauce, 44, 45, 282
for mayonnaise, 41
saddle:
of lamb, 250–53
of rabbit, 254
safflower oil, in mayonnaise, 41
saffron, 42–43, 52
beurre blanc, 49
hollandaise sauce, 280
sage:
in braised rabbit, 257
butter and garlic sauce for gnocchi, 60
Saint-Lambert, sautéed chicken, 159
salad dressings, 35, 36
see also vinaigrettes
salads:
corn in, 7
green, 35
watercress in, 36
salmon:
à la nage, 113
cold-smoked, 238
dry-curing for cold smoking, 239
en papillote, 115
filleting, 223, 224–25
gravlax, 239–40, 266
mousseline, with crayfish sauce, 141, 276–77
poached medallions, 112–13
poaching, 108
quenelles, 280
in red-wine fish broth, 32, 33
roasting, 118
salting, 239
sauces for, 33
smoked, for blini, 61
steak, 112
salsas:
corn in, 7
and fried chicken, 160
grilled steaks with, 193
salt, salting:
coarse, 124
for copper bowl, 179, 181
for garlic, 43, 99
in salad, 35
salmon, 239
sardines:
en escabeche, 274–75
preparing, 236
sauce andalouse, 42
sauce aurore, 287
sauce chantilly, 42
sauce espagnole, 265–66, 268
sauce rémoulade, 42
sauces, 282
aromatic vegetables for, 262
for baked fish, 117
béchamel, 177, 180, 181
beurre blanc, 47, 48, 49, 262
bisques vs., 139
bolognese, 50
broth from, 30
brown, 265–66
butter in, 139
for chicken sauté, 157
from crustacean broth, 139
deglazing as, 267–68
dipping sauce for shrimp tempura, 122
flambéed rum and caramelized butter-sugar, 101, 103
for fried flounder goujonettes, 121
green peppercorn, 197
for grilled steaks, 193
hollandaise, 44
infused oils as, 39
mornay, 287
pan, after sautéing meat, 195
pesto, 99
for poached fish, 112
port-wine-and-shallot pan, 165
for roast chicken, 147
for salmon, 33
for sautéed chicken, 154, 159
sautéed chicken breasts and thighs with mushroom, 158
for sautéed crayfish, 139, 141
sautéed flank steaks with red-wine pan, 196
for sautéed meats, 199
for sautéed skin-on red snapper fillets, 125
shrimp broth reduced for, 34
shrimp heads for, 131
soups vs., 139
for steaming shellfish, 132
for sweetbreads, 214–15
tomato, 50
vegetables purées and, 94
velouté, 212, 287
vinaigrette as, 37
see also jus
sauce suprême, 287
sautéed, sautéing, x, 282–83
à la meunière, 125
beef tenderloin (fillet) steaks with green peppercorn sauce, 197, 268
broccoli rabe with garlic, 90
broth and, 30
Brussels sprouts, 7
chicken, 151, 154, 157–59
chicken breasts, 162–63
chicken breasts and thighs with mushroom sauce, 158
chops, 195
crayfish, 139
duck breasts, 170, 171
eggplant, 89, 90
fish, 123
flank steaks with red-wine pan sauce, 196
fricassée vs., 270
infused oils and, 39
lamb, 249
medallions of meat, 195
noisettes of meat, 277
oils for, 91
panfry vs., 277
pork, loin of, 199
potatoes, 89, 263
rabbit, 254
seafood, 125–26
skin-on red snapper fillets, 125
soft-shell crabs, 138
squid, 128
steaks, 195–97
stewing vs., 154
sweetbreads, 214
sweetbreads breaded with porcini dust or chopped truffles, 216–17
veal loin, 199

vegetables, 89–91
venison loin, 199
zucchini, 89
zucchini with parsley and garlic, 91
sauté pan, 112, 283
savory, for grilling vegetables, 84
sawdust, for hot-smoked blue fish fillets, 237
scales:
on Dover sole, 234
on roasted fish, 120
sautéing fish and, 126
small fish, 236
on whole fish, 117, 220
scallions, grilling, 84
scallopini, 195
scallops:
grilling, 123
poaching, 112
sautéed, 125, 282
stir-frying, 130
Scandinavian cooking, gravlax, 239–40
scrod, for goujonettes, 122
sea bass:
in fish broth, 32
grilling, 123
roasting, 118
seaweed, in miso soup, 143
sectioning:
citrus fruit, 24
pineapples, 27
seeding:
cucumbers, 8
pears, 101
roasted bell peppers, 9
tomatoes, 36, 50
semolina, in egg pasta dough, 51
separating eggs, 178, 181
serving:
Arctic char, 108
roasted fish, 119–20
stuffed and poached trout, 111
shallots, 10
for sautéing meat, 195
for steaming shellfish, 132
whole flounder baked with white wine and, 116
shallow frying, 160, 283
shank of lamb, 242
shaping:
potatoes for frying, 80, 81, 82
vegetables, 21
see also turning
shark, grilling, 123
shaving, fennel, 16
shell beans, for pot roast, 205
shellfish:
poaching, 112
steaming, 132–33
see also specific shellfish
shells:
crayfish, for sauce, 139, 141
for crustacean broth, 139
for crustacean butter, 139
sherry vinegar:
in Provençal daube, 210–11
in white chicken fricassée with wine vinegar, 154
shocking, of boiled green vegetables, 263
shopping:
for anchovies, 142
for beef chuck, 200
for coconut, 29
for crayfish, 139
for leg of lamb, 184, 242
for lobster, 135
for persimmons, 26
for pork tenderloin, 195
for pot roast, 200
for rack of lamb, 187–88
for rack of pork, 189–90
for rib roast, 191
for sauté pan, 283
for veal tenderloin, 195
short-braising, 263
chicken, 154
fish and shellfish, 264
squid, 128
short-cooking seafood, 128
short ribs, for stews, 208
shredding, 10, 283
cabbage, 13, 18
shrimp:
with baked eggs, 175
in crustacean broth, 34, 139
deep-frying, 121
deveining, 131
grilling, 123, 124
paste, in *bumbu,* 275
peeling, 131
poaching, 112
sautéed, 125
stir-fried, with cashews, 130
tempura, 122, 265
shrimp broth, 34
in bisque, 34
in seafood paella, 64, 65
shucking:
corn, 7
oysters, 134
simmering, 263
skate wings, filleting, 235
skewers:
for grilled mixed vegetable kebabs, 85
for grilling, 84
skinning:
baked fish, 117
chicken sauté and, 157
Dover sole, 234
flounder, 233
grilled fish, 124
poached fish, 109, 110
roasted fish, 120
sautéed fish, 125
skate wings, 235
slicers, 283–84
slicing:
apples, 23
citrus fruits, 24
cucumbers, 16
fennel for grilling, 84
flank steak, 196
kiwis, 26
potatoes for grilling, 84
red-wine pot roast, 204
truffles, 16
vegetables, 12
slow-cooking, *see* braised, braising
slurry, 284
in Provençal daube, 210–11
for thickening stews, 208
smoked:
cold-, salmon, 238
fish storage, 237
foods, 284
hot-, fish fillets, 237
smoking, wood for, 237, 284
snails, in paella, 63, 64
snapper, 109
baked whole, with red-wine fish broth, 32, 33, 117
baking, 117
boning, 223
in fish broth, 32
grilling, 123
roasting, 118
sautéed skin-on red, fillets, 125
soffritto, 275
sofregit, 275
sofreit, 65
in seafood paella, 65
sofrito, 275
soft-boiling eggs, 172
soft-shell crabs, 138
sole, 220
baking, 117
fillet, 127
for goujonettes, 122
preparing, 230
sautéing, 125
see also Dover sole
sorrel, 8
purée, 212, 276, 287
soufflés, 177–81, 269, 276, 284, 287
doneness of, 67
soupe au pistou, 98
soups:
aromatic vegetables for, 262
broth from, 30
chunky vegetable, 98–99
corn in, 7
creamy, 98
creamy vegetables, 100
garlic in, 11
miso, 143
puréed carrot, 100
puréed leek and potato, 100
purée in, 279
sauce vs., 139
shrimp heads for, 131
vegetable purée and, 94
from vegetable trimmings, 13
zucchini in, 15
Southern cooking, boiled crayfish and, 139
soy sauce, in dipping sauce for shrimp tempura, 122
Spanish cooking, *cocido,* 200
spatulas, 124, 125, 126
spiders, 80, 82, 284
spinach:
boiling, 88
chiffonade of, 10, 19
chlorophyll from, 52
creamed, 88
creamed, with baked eggs, 175
in creamy vegetable soup, 100
steaming, 87
stemming, 8
spirits:
for deglazing after chicken sauté, 157
for flambé, 269
for poaching fruit, 104, 105
spit-roasting, 271
spoons, 26
spring onions, roasting, 70
squab:
grilling, 161
roasting, 281
squid, 128–29
cleaning, 129
deep-frying, 121
long-braising, 264
preparation of, 128–29

squid (*continued*)
- short-braising, 128
- stewed with red wine, 128
- stir-frying, 130

squid ink, in black pasta, 52
standing rib roast, 191
steaks, 195
- doneness of, 66–67
- grilled strip, 193
- grilling, 193
- hollandaise sauce for, 44
- sautéed flank, with red-wine pan sauce, 196
- sautéing, 195
- T-bone, 250

steamers, 86, 284–85
steaming, x, 284–85
- Brussels sprouts, 7
- green vegetables, 87
- lobster, 132, 133, 135
- mussels with white wine and parsley, 132
- shellfish, 132–33
- spinach, 87
- vegetables, 86–87, 284

stemming:
- cilantro, 36
- leafy greens, 8
- parsley, 36
- sorrel, 8
- spinach, 8
- Swiss chard, 8
- watercress, 36

stewed, stewing, 263–64
- brown chicken broth in, 30
- cuttlefish, 128
- sautéing vs., 154
- squid, 128

stews:
- boeuf à la bourguignonne, 206–7
- braised veal shanks, 209
- caramelizing, 266
- chicken, 151, 154–56
- meat, 200, 206–13, 264
- rabbit, 254, 266
- from shanks, 209
- squid, with red wine, 128
- tough cuts of meat for, 203
- veal, 208, 209, 212–13, 241
- vegetable garnish for, 10
- white chicken fricassée with wine vinegar, 154–55
- *see also* daubes

stir-frying, 285
- shrimp with cashews, 130
- squid, 128

stocks, *see* broth
stone fruits, preparing, 25
storing:
- anchovies, 142
- broths, 31
- chlorophyll, 52
- crustacean shells, 34
- herb butters, 47
- mushroom stems, 111
- poached eggs, 174
- smoked fish, 237
- truffles, 176
- *see also* freezing

strainers, 94, 100, 279
- for purée of chestnuts, 96

strawberries:
- in crêpes, 62
- poached apricots and, 104
- trimming, 28

straw potatoes, 80, 81
string beans:
- in chunky vegetable soup, 98
- for pot roast, 205

stringing, fennel, 2, 5
striped bass, 108, 222–23
- filleting, 222–23
- in fish broth, 32
- roasting, 118

stuffing:
- artichoke stems in, 93
- for omelets, 176
- poached trout and, 110–11
- for roast turkey, 166, 167
- whole round fish, 226, 229

summer, salads during, 35
summer squash:
- gratin, 73
- grilling, 83

sweating foods, 285
sweetbreads, 214–17, 277
- doneness of, 67
- poaching, 263
- porcini dust for sautéing, 164
- sautéed, breaded with porcini dust or chopped truffles, 216–17

sweet potatoes:
- puréed, 279
- roasting, 72
- in sautéed chicken Algérienne, 159

Swiss chard:
- braising, 75
- chiffonade of, 19
- in creamy vegetable soup, 100
- stemming, 8

Swiss Gruyère, for cheese soufflé, 179
swordfish, grilling, 123

Tarragon:
- in béarnaise sauce, 44, 45
- butter, 47, 115
- for grilling vegetables, 84
- sautéed chicken, 159
- and tomato beurre blanc, 49

tartar sauce, for fried flounder goujonettes, 121
T-bone steaks, 250
tempura:
- batter, 77, 121
- shrimp, 122, 265

tenderloin:
- beef, 191, 193
- lamb, 250
- poached, 66

tentacles, of squid, 128, 129
Thai cooking, 130
thermometers, instant-read, 66, 109, 167
thickeners, 208, 271, 285–87
- *monter au beurre,* 275, 285

thyme:
- for grilled chicken marinade, 161
- on grilled summer squash or zucchini, 83
- for grilling, 272
- for grilling vegetables, 84
- oil infused with, 39
- in persillade, 278

timbale, 287
tofu, in miso soup, 143
tomalley, 135, 136
tomato coulis, 50, 266, 279
- in tomato and tarragon beurre blanc, 49
- in zucchini gratin, 73, 74

tomatoes:
- baked, with garlic and fresh basil, 72
- baking, 262, 278
- for chicken sauté, 157
- coating for frying, 77, 79
- concassée, 6, 50, 175, 266
- for deglazing, 157, 268
- fried, 79, 265
- peeling, 2, 6, 263
- roasting, 70, 72
- sauce, 50, 277
- in *sauce andalouse,* 42
- in *sauce aurore,* 287
- in sautéed chicken dishes, 159
- sautéing, 89
- seeding, 36, 50
- in *sofreit,* 65
- in *sofrito,* 275
- and tarragon beurre blanc, 49
- tempura batter for, 77
- *see also* tomato coulis

top round roast, 191
tortelloni, 57
tossing, when sautéing, 89, 125, 130, 282–83
Treviso lettuce, grilling, 84
triangular shapes:
- for vegetables, 14
- for zucchini, 15

trimming:
- brussels sprouts, 7
- cauliflower, 8
- leeks, 9
- rack of lamb, 246–47
- strawberries, 28

trout:
- sautéing, 125
- stuffed and poached, 110–11

truffles:
- butter, 47
- chopped, sautéed sweetbreads breaded with, 216–17, 265
- in *demi-glace,* 265
- in omelets, 176
- slicing, 16

trussing, chicken, x, 146–47, 148, 150
tubers, *see* potatoes; turnips
tuna:
- doneness of, 67
- grilling, 123

turkey:
- grilling, 272
- roasting, 166–68, 281

turning:
- artichokes, 92, 93
- vegetables, 10, 13, 21, 70

turnips:
- bâtonnets of, 18
- braising, 263, 264
- dicing, 17
- as garnish, 270
- julienne of, 18, 19
- peeling, 2, 3
- in potato gratin, 73
- for pot-au-feu, 200
- roasting, 70
- turning, 21
- wedges of, 10, 21, 22

United States cooking, New England boiled dinner, 200
utensils:
- aluminum foil, 114–15, 146, 148, 166, 177, 181, 205, 265, 277–78
- baking dishes, 146

balloon whisks, 179, 181
cheesecloth, 109, 141
cherry pitters, 25
chopsticks, 25, 124, 130
copper bowls, 179, 181
couscousière, 284–85
cutting instruments, 2, 3, 12, 13, 25, 57, 59, 80, 81, 82, 83, 274, 283–84
drum sieves, 94, 95, 96, 164, 264, 279
food mills, 94, 95, 100, 279
gratin dishes, 146
for grilling, 123, 124, 193
instant-read thermometer, 66, 109, 167
lettuce spinners, 35, 36
for making homemade wine vinegar, 38
mesh strainers, 94
mortar and pestle, 41, 42, 43, 99
parchment paper, 64, 76, 114–15, 116, 215, 277–78
pastry bags, 57, 58, 59
peelers, 2
Phillips head screwdrivers, 29
pins, 172
potato mashers, 94
pots and pans, 44, 45, 108, 109, 112, 130
ravioli forms, 58
ricers, 94, 279
rolling pins, 34, 141
skewers, 84, 85
spatulas, 124, 125, 126
spiders, 80, 82, 284
spoons, 26
steamers, 86, 284–85
strainers, 96, 100, 279
tongs, 124

Vanilla, for poaching fruit, 104, 105
veal:
broth, 30
étuver, 269
fricassées, 208
medallions, 199
mousseline of, 280
noisette of, 277
porcini dust for sautéing, 164
quenelles of, 280
sautéing loin of, 199
sautéing tenderloin of, 195
sweetbreads, 214
veal breast:
for *blanquette de veau,* 212
for stews, 208, 241
veal broth, 241
bones for, 241
in braised veal shanks, 209
in short-braised sweetbreads, 215
veal shanks, 200
braised, 209
for stews, 208, 209
veal shoulder:
for pot roast, 203
for stews, 208
veal stews, 209
creamed, 30, 208, 212–13
veal stock, *see* veal broth
vegetable broth:
in court bouillon, 113
see also court bouillon
vegetable purées:
in beurre blanc, 48
in sauces for baked fish, 117
for thickening stews, 208
vegetables, 70–100
aromatic, 262
in baked fish, 116
boiling, 86
braising, 264
breaded, sautéing, 91
in chicken broth, 31
chunky, soup, 98–99
creamy, soup, 100
cutting, 10
deep-frying, 77, 160, 267
dicing, 13
flans, 97
frying, 77–82
glazing, 70
gratin, xi, 73–74
grilled mixed, kebabs, 85
grilling, 83–85
julienne cut for, 13
in miso soup, 143
peeling, 2–6
poaching, 86
poaching tenderloin and, 202
for pot-au-feu, 200
purée, 94, 100, 271, 286–87
roasted with chicken, 147
roasting, 70–72
sautéing, 89–91
shaping, 21
slicing, 12
steaming, 86–87, 284, 285
"turning," 10, 13
vinaigrette as sauce for, 37
see also specific vegetables
vegetable slicers, 12, 80, 81, 83
cabbage shredding by, 13
shaving fennel with, 16
velouté sauce, 286
in creamed veal stew, 212
white sauce variations with, 287
venison:
medallions, 199
sautéed loin of, 199
vialone nano rice, 63
Vichy, sautéed chicken, 159
vinaigrettes, 37–38, 269, 282
for artichokes, 92
grilled steaks with, 193
hot, 35, 37, 38, 125
infused oils in, 39
vinegar:
in aïoli, 43
in brown chicken fricassée, 154
in chicken fricassées, 154
for copper bowl, 179, 181
in mayonnaise, 41, 42
mother, 38
for poached eggs, 174
in vinaigrette, 37
see also white wine vinegar; wine vinegar

Waffled potato chips, 80, 284
washing:
leeks, 9
salad greens, 35, 36
watercress, 35, 36
waxy potatoes, in château potatoes, 89
wedges:
fennel, 22
round vegetable, 21
turnip, 21
vegetable, for roasting, 70
whelks, long-braising, 264
whipped cream:
in chicken liver mousse, 165
in *sauce chantilly,* 42
white chicken fricassée:
in white chicken broth, 30
with wine vinegar, 154–55
white glazing, 76
white sauces, 287
white wine:
in beurre blanc, 48, 49
in braised veal shanks, 209
in court bouillon, 108, 113, 266, 278
in court bouillon for fish, 112
in fish broth, 32
for grilled chicken marinade, 161
in pot roast, 205
in salmon *en papillote,* 115
in sautéed chicken dishes, 158, 159
in short-braised sweetbreads, 215
for short-braising squid, 128
steamed mussels with parsley and, 132
for steaming lobster, 133
for steaming shellfish, 132
whole flounder baked with shallots and, 116
white wine marinade, for fried chicken, 160
white wine vinegar:
in béarnaise sauce, 44, 45
in beurre blanc, 48, 49
whole Dover sole *à la meunière,* 125, 126
whole flounder baked with white wine and shallots, 116
Windsor pan, 44, 45
wine:
in braised fish, 116
in chicken fricassées, 154
for deglazing, 157, 268
in *demi-glace,* 265
see also red wine; white wine
wine vinegar:
in green salad, 35
homemade, 38
in hot vinaigrette, 38
in pot roast, 205
in salad, 35
see also white wine vinegar
winter, salads during, 35
winter squash, peeling, 2
wishbone, 146, 150
woks, 130, 285

Yams, roasting, 72
yeast, 61
in blini, 61, 62

Zabaglione, 282
zesters, 25
zucchini, 14, 15, 21
fried, slices, 77
gratin, 73, 74
grilling, 83
sautéed, with parsley and garlic, 91
sautéing, 89, 91